ONE SIGNAL
PUBLISHERS
ATRIA

FIGHT LIKE HELL

THE UNTOLD HISTORY OF AMERICAN LABOR

KIM KELLY

ONE SIGNAL PUBLISHERS

ATRIA

New York | London | Toronto | Sydney | New Delhi

ONE SIGNAL PUBLISHERS
ATRIA

An Imprint of Simon & Schuster, Inc.
1230 Avenue of the Americas
New York, NY 10020

First One Signal Publishers/Atria Paperback edition August 2023

ONE SIGNAL PUBLISHERS / ATRIA PAPERBACK and colophon are trademarks of Simon & Schuster, Inc.

Interior design by Silverglass

Manufactured in the United States of America

3 5 7 9 10 8 6 4 2

Library of Congress Control Number: 2022931666

ISBN 978-1-9821-7105-6
ISBN 978-1-9821-7106-3 (pbk)
ISBN 978-1-9821-7107-0 (ebook)

For my grandparents, George W. Johnson and Nancy Stolz Johnson.
You were always on my side.

And for all the workers of the world.

I never thought in terms of fear. I thought in terms of justice.

—Emma Tenayuca

What labor wants is land for the landless, produce to the producer, tools to the toiler—and death to wage slavery.

—Lucy Parsons

Pray for the dead, and fight like hell for the living.

—Mary "Mother Jones" Harris

CONTENTS

FOREWORD

Sara Nelson, International President, Association of Flight Attendants-CWA

No matter what the fight, don't be ladylike! God almighty made women and the Rockefeller gang of thieves made the ladies.

—MOTHER JONES

From the moment I read Kim's work the first time, I knew Mother Jones would have loved her.

I remember clicking a link to an article "What a Labor Union Is and How It Works," only to discover that it was inside the pages of *Teen Vogue.* In between pieces about style and pop culture was a story explaining unions to teenagers.

I thought it must have been a fluke, but then Kim kept publishing stories about how workers had built—and still could build—power. Kim's stories created something I had never seen anywhere as I was coming of age in the "greed is good" years of the eighties: a sense that worker power wasn't just achievable, but cool.

By the time Kim made waves in the labor movement with her piece "Everything You Need to Know about General Strikes," I was hooked.

As a flight attendant, I've spent my career in one of the most densely organized sectors of our economy. While aviation as a whole is dominated by men, flight attendants are nearly 80 percent women. Many of the workers who join our ranks have never been union members, and many—like me when I started—know nothing about unions.

The people who founded our union were women. For decades, you could be a flight attendant only if you were an unmarried woman with no children who was younger than thirty-two. (Ironically, it was our union who fought for men to be able to hold these jobs.) Even in the mid-'90s, the Association of Flight Attendants leaders around me early in my career were nearly all women, representing an array of national origins, races, sexual orientations, and gender identities. These are the people who taught me about solidarity, power, the humility and responsibility required when representing others, and the smarts demanded for every single fight. But as I looked at our broader labor movement, I saw so few women, people of color, and LGBTQ+ workers in leadership. Even in unions where women and people of color dominated the profession, it was common to find men holding most of the senior positions.

Growing up, I never heard anyone tell me I could hold power in the workplace. So every time I saw another piece of Kim's work in *Teen Vogue*, I celebrated. Millions of young women—tweens, teens, and twentysomethings—would follow a magazine they looked to for life advice and find features about how they had the power to grab the reins of our economy in their own hands.

It's a power that took me years to really understand, and one I'm still learning about today. I was raised in a union family, but it wasn't talked about. In early-eighties America, Wall Street was king and unions were enemy number one. I didn't learn about unions around the dinner table, and I certainly didn't learn about them in school.

In my first week as a flight attendant, my flying partner pulled me aside. She said, "Listen. Management thinks of us as their wives or their mistresses. Either way, they hold us in contempt. Your only place of worth is with your flying partners. Wear your union pin and if we stick together, there's nothing we can't accomplish."

During my more than twenty-five years in this uniform, I've seen over and over the truth of those words. I've spread that message of the power in our unity whenever I could, from new-hire training to organizing drives and contract fights. And I've loved it every time I saw the light of solidarity come on in a flight attendant's eyes.

But what if workers entered the workforce knowing not just what unions were but that women, people of color, and anyone defined as "different" could and should play a leading role in our workplaces, our unions, and our democracy?

Kim's work—introducing the next generation to the labor movement and to the power we hold when we join together in unions—became a staple of my reading. In the topics she chose and how she brought them to life, I could tell she was someone special. But all the reading in the world couldn't prepare me for the force of nature I would meet and come to call my friend.

It wasn't the first time we met (she had interviewed me a few months before at a restaurant in D.C.), but I'll always remember meeting Kim for dinner in the summer of 2019. I was in Philadelphia to participate in Netroots Nation, an annual convention of organizers, activists, and all sorts of people who are fighting to make our world a better place. Kim had agreed to moderate a panel titled "Is It Time for a General Strike?" and everyone on the panel was getting together to meet beforehand.

I walked up to a Chinese restaurant, and there Kim was.

I had just finished her piece in *Allure* magazine titled "How to Keep Up Your Skin-Care and Self-Care Routines During Workplace Bargaining," a practical piece of reading for everyone involved in activism and workplace action. But where the author of a piece like that might be expected to present a more conventional figure, Kim cut against the grain.

She was wearing her trademark all black, in a leather jacket covered in buttons and patches, with piercings and visible tattoos. Her hair was immaculate in two impossibly long braids. She was like a heavy metal Princess Leia standing on a corner in the birthplace of our democracy.

In more than two years since, I've been fortunate to spend time with Kim, not just on a panel stage in hotel conference rooms, but in dive bars in different cities and on picket lines with striking workers.

In April 2021, I visited my labor family in Alabama, where mine workers had gone on strike to demand many of the same working conditions Mother Jones had helped them organize around nearly a century before, only this time not just against coal barons but also the hedge funds that dial up their greed. And, of course, Kim was there.

I've had the incredible opportunity to work closely with the United Mine Workers of America in recent years—coming out for each other's fights and learning the history of our labor movement by traveling with the union to historic places of labor struggles or labor tragedies like the Ludlow Massacre, the Farmington mine disaster, and the hollers of West Virginia like Cabin Creek, where radical labor leaders were born and raised in company housing. I've been blessed to call their president, Cecil Roberts, a dear friend, and listen to him tell firsthand stories of Mother Jones as told by his mother and grandmother. In the early days of these gatherings, rank-and-file workers sometimes looked at me funny when I showed up in their union halls and at their rallies, wondering who this blond flight attendant was and what she was doing there. In no time at all, though, we bonded in our common experience of mourning those we've lost at work and "fighting like hell" for those of us living.

I remember introducing Kim to the Warrior Met miners. She was there with a cameraperson to capture video and report on their strike. If she's an arresting figure on a bustling Philly street corner, in a park deep in the woods of rural Alabama, Kim *really* stands out.

But it took no time at all for her to be adopted. Because the thing that shines through when you spend time with her is her empathy, her genuine curiosity, and her fierce, unwavering working-class solidarity.

The most recent time I visited those same miners, still on strike months later, Kim had become their family, just as I consider her mine. Her reporting on the Warrior Met strike has been extensive and incisive. At a time when the media often loses interest soon after the picket lines go up, Kim has doggedly followed the story.

I wasn't surprised the miners took to Kim just as I had. Kim is not someone Rockefeller and his gang of thieves would ever call "ladylike," but she's someone Mother Jones would embrace as a woman and a sister in the struggle.

Kim is fierce. Kim is fearless. Kim is tough. Kim is authentic. But to me the thing that shines the brightest when I think of Kim is her blazing empathy. When Kim talks to you, she's not imposing her own judgments, she's seeking to understand who you are and what makes you do what you do. She has a writer's intellectual curiosity and a reporter's nose for the truth, and it shows in this book.

Everything that makes Kim Kim—her tenacity, her clarity of purpose, her curiosity, her generosity, her empathy—shines through in this book.

Most important, to me, this book continues the work I first read in the pages of *Teen Vogue*.

Through powerful, human writing, Kim tells the stories that are so often left out of the history of American labor. In bringing forward the stories of the rebels and rabble-rousers whom the "official" history wants us to forget, Kim doesn't just balance our history—she opens labor to the present.

When our image of a union worker is a middle-aged (usually white) man in a hard hat, millions of workers never even imagine themselves participating in workplace democracy, much less seeking to form or lead unions themselves.

In *Fight Like Hell*, Kim throws wide the doors to inspire all of us to seize power for ourselves by showing how—yesterday and today—the oppressed and overlooked, the outcasts and the misfits, shaped history.

While there are many who wish we would forget, Kim's thrilling and incisive look at our history reminds us of a fundamental truth: the labor movement belongs to all of us.

PROLOGUE

The first time I met Jennifer Bates, she was almost as nervous as I was. One of us had racked up a decent amount of on-camera experience by then, but you wouldn't have guessed who. She was dressed in a royal blue blouse and black overcoat, her hair and makeup impeccable, as I trailed behind her in my grubby Carhartt jacket and braids. It was a moody gray day in early February 2021, and I'd just arrived in Alabama for my first big reporting trip since the COVID-19 pandemic hit a year prior. I hadn't left Philadelphia for more than a year, and I was still a little rattled at the notion of getting up close and personal with anyone, but figured that holding interviews outside on a park bench was the best-case scenario given the circumstances. A digital media nonprofit called More Perfect Union had sent me down there to cover a story that was developing in an Amazon warehouse a few miles down the road, in a struggling town called Bessemer.

Once an industrial powerhouse known as the "Marvel City," Bessemer had fallen down on its luck with the decline of manufacturing in the area. Alabama's $7.25 minimum wage made it difficult for workers to turn their noses up at any kind of work that paid a little better, and Amazon's promise of $15 an hour appeared to be a step up from what was currently on offer. It wasn't until the warehouse opened in March 2020—just as the pandemic had begun its death march—that the people hired to spend their days inside the concrete behemoth began to realize what exactly it was that they had signed up for, and realized they needed to do something about it, together.

By the summer, the workers there had decided to unionize. If successful, their union would be a first for Amazon's sprawling U.S. operations and, as the labor faithful hoped, would also be a shot across the bow for the hundreds of thousands of workers toiling in the company's 110 other U.S. warehouse facilities. Past efforts to organize at Amazon had had mixed results; though Amazon CEO Jeff Bezos and his C-suite lieutenants cracked down on the mere hint of organizing wherever possible, small gains had sneaked through here and there, and the workers relished their tastes of collective power. It was a given that it would take something big and bold and visionary to finally crack Amazon's seemingly impenetrable armor, but all of a sudden it seemed as though that moment was upon us. And it was being led by a group of middle-aged Black warehouse workers in a struggling Alabama exurb whose union-town roots ran as deep as the coal mines outside its borders.

Other journalists have been adeptly covering the corporation, its myriad offenses, and its hollow ethics for years, but this time, I would be one of the first reporters on the ground digging deeper into the story. My elastic schedule as a freelancer and willingness to travel during a pandemic worked in my favor, and Amazon's infamously secretive labor practices made it all the more enticing. I had been hired to narrate and produce video coverage—a step outside my usual writing—and the added layer of complexity was irresistible. This particular story was fascinating on so many levels, too, and so potentially significant for labor's future that I couldn't turn it down, even if I was anxious. I couldn't have predicted then how huge the campaign would become, or how much of my own life would come to revolve around its ups and downs. My biggest priority that day was to find out what Jennifer Bates and her coworkers wanted the rest of us to know about their will to win.

We exchanged pleasantries in the union hall's parking lot for a moment before piling back into our respective vehicles and heading over to Birmingham's Civil Rights District to scout interview locations. Jennifer was a striking, soft-spoken woman, armed with a steely resolve that was immediately apparent through her initial shyness. I could sense that she was deeply kind, but also not inclined to suffer fools. As we walked through a park that abutted the famous Sixteenth Street Baptist Church, where four little Black girls had been murdered by the Ku Klux Klan just a few years before Jennifer was born, we passed by statues of slavering police dogs and terrified Black children. Her black coat billowed in the wind beneath the watchful eye of a statue of Dr. Martin Luther King, Jr. History was alive in that park, and in that city, and in the campaign that Bates and her coworkers had launched. The civil rights leader's final earthly action before his life was extinguished by a sniper's bullet, after all, had been in service to labor, rallying a crowd of striking unionized sanitation workers in Memphis, Tennessee.

Bates emphasized that connection once the camera started rolling, too; Dr. King was a union man, and the Amazon workers of Bessemer saw themselves as following in his footsteps on the long road toward justice. Like him, Bates was guided by her faith; as the union election edged closer, she let go of her worries, and left it up to God. "If it is meant to be, God is gonna make sure it comes to pass—and if it doesn't, then there was something in there that we should have learned," she later told me in a March interview for *Vox*. "We are supposed to learn out of it."

Bates grew up in Marion, Alabama, a small city about an hour-and-a-half drive from Bessemer. Despite its humble stature, Marion occupies an outsized role in civil rights history: in 1965, a Black man named Jimmie Lee Jackson was shot and killed by Alabama state trooper James Bonard Fowler during a civil rights protest. His killing inspired the first Selma-to-Montgomery march, and King spoke at Jackson's funeral. Bates was born eight years later. Always a hard worker, by thirteen Bates was picking okra in a neighbor's field for a few dollars a week, and her first legal job, at a Hardee's, came at sixteen. She eventually married and made her way north to South Philadelphia, but she later returned to Alabama, where she worked in restaurants, in retail, as a 911 and police dispatcher, and in factories making automobile parts. Through all those hours and all that sweat, she had never quite gotten what she deserved.

I knew I was asking a lot from her that day. She was about to go on record about the conditions that had driven her and her coworkers to go up against one of the most powerful companies in the world, whose economic might was inconceivable, whose reputation for cruelty and retaliation was legendary, and whose political power seemed absolute. I was just there to bear witness. Her story would soon become national news, her face would soon grace the pages of major publications, and her struggle would inspire millions, but right then, it was just her and me, sitting on a park bench, talking about the pain in her legs and the fire in her heart. As the old saying goes, the cause of labor is the hope of the world, and as we spoke, that hope shined hard in Bates's deep brown eyes. I could feel the heat roll off of her words as she spoke.

No great labor leader works alone, and Bates was no exception. Her coworker Darryl Richardson was there too that day, telling me in his soft drawl about the grueling conditions and pervasive feeling of unfairness that had led him to take action. Like Bates, he had had prior experience with unions, and had seen firsthand the impact they could have on righting wrongs and pushing for change in a flawed workplace. After some quick Googling, Richardson placed the fateful call that ended up drawing a small army of Retail Wholesale and Department Store Union (RWDSU) organizers down to Bessemer, and launched one of the most-watched, hardest-fought union election campaigns in recent U.S. history. A gentle man with a warm heart, he took the campaign personally, and had made the forty-odd-minute drive from his home in Tuscaloosa to the Amazon warehouse in Bessemer and then to the RWDSU union hall in downtown Birmingham more times than he could remember.

The footage from those interviews ended up in a series of videos that racked up millions of views, and drew attention from the political elite. More importantly, organizers in Bessemer sent them around to the workers themselves to help counteract Amazon's merciless anti-union propaganda. The media alone cannot win a union election, but organizers did appreciate being able to use it as a corrective or to add additional context during conversations with workers. They faced an uphill battle; by the time I arrived, Amazon had already spent months plastering anti-union banners throughout the warehouse, sending anti-union messages to workers' personal phones, and even hanging flyers in the same bathroom stalls that workers barely had time to visit during their backbreaking ten-hour shifts. Far worse, Amazon had taken to forcing workers to attend captive-audience meetings, in which their high-priced "union avoidance" consultants sang the company's praises and lectured them about the evils of organized labor. Those who challenged their talking points or spoke up in favor of the union were kicked out, or targeted with one-on-one lectures on the shop floor. Somehow, this was all perfectly legal under the United States' toothless labor laws, and as would become apparent later, it had a chilling effect on the campaign.

But as the media attention began to increase, more workers became comfortable with the idea of speaking out publicly, and momentum began to build. What began as a trickle turned into a flood, as the Bessemer union drive picked up steam and journalists from around the country and across the globe parachuted into Greater Birmingham to sniff out their slice of the story. I kept coming back, making three trips in as many months and invariably plotting ways to return as soon as I left. More workers took the microphone, like Emmit Ashford and Linda Burns; organizers like Michael "Big Mike" Foster, a veteran poultry plant worker and shop steward who became a beloved figure and was eventually hired by the union, had their moment in the sun, too.

The Amazon union drive became front-page news, and when the campaign finally came to an end and the votes began to be counted, no less than the *New York Times* even saw fit to run a vote tracker with live updates. The momentum felt unstoppable heading into the final count; the weekend before, Senator Bernie Sanders and rapper/activist Killer Mike had traveled to Alabama to whip up enthusiasm for the union, and as the deadline neared, all eyes were on Bessemer.

Despite the massive roadblocks in their way, after seeing everything that Jennifer and Darryl and everyone else had poured into this election, after witnessing firsthand the excitement and energy around it, after meeting the dozens of locals and out-of-towners alike who had dedicated months of their time to boosting the union drive, after reading the coverage around it and doing my own reporting for months, I couldn't fathom that they wouldn't win.

But then . . . they didn't. When the final tally came out, Amazon had prevailed, besting the union by a wide margin. The effort had been a moonshot at first, but Jennifer Bates and the other pro-union workers at that Bessemer warehouse had bought their tickets anyway, and taken the ride as far as they could. They fell short this time, but the fight would not stop there. RWDSU immediately filed almost two dozen objections against Amazon with the National Labor Relations Board, alleging a bevy of unfair labor practices. In 2022, a second election was run; for a second time, the effort failed, and the union again filed a raft of charges against Amazon alleging improper conduct. As I write this, the results of that second election remain tied up in court, and workers at that Bessmer warehouse have continued their organizing efforts. They haven't given up.

When I spoke to Bates the day after the vote tally came out, she made it clear that she and her coworkers weren't ready to back down. She didn't try to mask her disappointment or her suspicions of Amazon using dirty tactics to undermine the election. But most clear was her enduring hope, the same determination and faith that I'd seen when we first met. She wasn't nervous this time, either. Since those first few interviews in February, she has given hundreds more, appeared in front of dozens of cameras, spoken at countless meetings with her coworkers, met with celebrities and politicians, and testified in front of Congress. The David-and-Goliath fight that consumed her time and attention for months never consumed her spirit; that, she gave freely and abundantly to the cause, like so many other labor leaders before her. Jennifer Bates was a woman with nothing left to fear but her creator, and as far as she was concerned, Jeff Bezos was a mere speck of dust beneath her sandals.

As I write this in my little office in South Philly, a lot has changed since that first Amazon vote in Alabama. They may still be waiting for their win, but the impact of what those workers accomplished has already set an incredibly important precedent. As I wrote back in 2021, "Someone had to be the first, and now the next group of workers who decide to take a moonshot of their own and go toe-to-toe with a giant will get even closer." A few months after I turned in the manuscript for the hardcover version of this book, that prediction came true: workers at an Amazon warehouse in Staten Island, led by the charismatic, rank-and-file leadership of Christian Smalls, Derrick Palmer, Angelika Maldonado, Michelle Valentin Nieves, and all the others on their committee of worker-organizers, successfully unionized under the banner of the Amazon Labor Union. The ALU's ongoing accomplishment shows the constant work of progress and revolution. It's the unfinished business of centuries of fighters and thinkers and dreamers; each subsequent generation brings us just a little bit closer, until we can finally see liberation in the distance just ahead.

I've been lucky. I grew up in a firmly working-class, blue-collar, union household. My dad, grandpa, and uncles all worked construction. My granddad was a millwright; my grandma was a teacher. While it mostly faded into the wallpaper, the union was a constant presence in my home, as much a part of our lives as my dad's gray pickup truck or the pine trees out back. I remember the times when my dad was on strike, and how we had to tighten our belts until the dispute was resolved and he was back on his regular pay. I remember the time in 2011 when he went to our state capitol to protest Wisconsin governor Scott Walker's oppressive right-to-work law, and how, when my mom got sick and her surgery bills topped the quarter-million mark, the health insurance his union provided kept us from going bankrupt.

Of course I also remember him complaining about how so-and-so at his local was a real piece of work and long, boring union meetings, which is funny to think about now that I've been to literally hundreds of them myself. My dad's never been good at sitting still, though, so I don't blame him for that. Sure, he might not have liked the less exciting parts of union membership, but he instilled in me the unshakable idea that the union was a good thing to have—and that when your boss was doing you wrong, you could count on the union to have your back. Every worker deserves to feel that way, and yet thanks to forces beyond their control, so many continue to be denied that protection at Amazon and in countless other workplaces across the U.S.

In the following pages, I'm going to introduce you to many more versions of Jennifer Bates, who have made waves across class and gender and race and time. Not all of them have made it into the history books; in fact, most of them were left out entirely, through no fault of their own. There are precious few easily accessible, mainstream history books that focus on labor at all. The same cannot be said for academic publishing, which is awash in brilliant labor books, but those specialized tomes are seldom given the opportunity to reach the wide audiences they deserve. And the stories of poor and working-class women, Black people, Latino people, Indigenous people, Asian and Pacific Islander people, immigrants of all backgrounds, religious minorities, queer and trans people, disabled people, the sex workers and undocumented people whose work is criminalized, and people who are incarcerated seldom get top billing when it's time to publish in the trade presses. It's a damned shame, too, because those are the very people who had the most to lose, yet have found it within themselves to give more and fight harder than anyone else.

I also want to be clear about the "untold" aspect: I am certainly not claiming that I personally discovered each of the individuals or moments in this book—far from it! I'm a journalist, a storyteller, a curator, and a fan; I'm not an academic or trained historian. That's why I'm so grateful to those who are. This book is deeply indebted to the scholarship of the academics, historians, researchers, and archivists who first chronicled this history, who did the hard work of digging through the past to find the truth, and who wrote important books about it that ensured that these stories were preserved. You'll see their work all over this book, like in chapter 1, where Dr. Tara W. Hunter's groundbreaking research forms the foundation for sections on the Black washerwomen of Mississippi and Atlanta; in chapter 4, where Dr. Peter Cole's tireless work piecing together the life of Ben Fletcher shines; in chapter 7, where Dr. Ann Balay documents the experiences of queer and trans truckers and steelworkers with love and respect; and throughout the book, where you'll meet many others and find even more in the bibliography. The worlds of academia and trade publishing are very different, but we have much to offer one another, and I'm eager to bridge that gap.

Every story is a labor story, and every labor story invariably builds on years—if not centuries—of previous organizing victories and failures.

The book jumps around among different eras and industries. You'll probably notice some pretty big omissions, too, and while I would have liked to include every single industry and profession possible, I had only so much time and so many words. For example, the history of labor struggles in health care, education, media, sports, and nonprofit work have shaped our world in incalculably imporant ways, and have been brilliantly covered by labor-focused authors like Sarah Jaffe, Maximillian Alvarez, Gabriel Winant, Micah Uetricht, Frankie de la Cretaz, Elizabeth Catte, Steven Greenhouse, and many others. There has also been a ton of incredible reporting done around organizing efforts in the tech industry and by app-based workers in the so-called gig economy, as well as high-profile and much-deserved wins in the digital media world, where I first got involved in labor (Vice Union forever!). With this book, I sought to make space for stories that don't always get as much coverage, and for people whose incredible contributions to the cause have largely been forgotten by history.

These workers have always been essential, but this country has often failed to recognize the value in their lives as well as their labor. In 2020 and 2021, when the COVID-19 pandemic pushed workers onto the front lines and pushed the economy—and the social fabric of the United States in general—to a breaking point, sick-outs, public calls for support, wildcat strikes, and militant action dominated the labor landscape. Millions were either left jobless or thrust into contact with a deadly disease without adequate protection. Workers whose labor keeps society running—the janitors and cleaning staff, the farmworkers and meatpackers, the grocery store workers and public transit operators, the delivery drivers and Postal Service workers—were given no choice but to work through a plague. They deserved every iota of praise they received, but it shouldn't have taken a global health crisis for the government to start taking their needs seriously.

So many of these workers newly recognized as "essential" toiled in industries that lack labor protections, were not and still have not been paid a livable wage, still cannot access affordable health care, and are still disenfranchised by a deeply flawed system that places people of color and undocumented workers at increased risk, whether there's a pandemic raging or not. People incarcerated in jails and prisons were forced to manufacture masks, gowns, and hand sanitizer for use outside the walls, even as the virus turned these grim facilities into death traps, and many there have had to dig graves for those who were lost to its grip. Those in the medical field—doctors, nurses, hospital technicians, hospital janitors and laundry workers, funeral home owners and morticians—were placed in extreme danger by personal protective equipment shortages. The entire affair exposed the rotten, hazardous conditions that have been allowed to fester thanks to capitalist cruelty and federal malfeasance, and by hitting the streets and raising the alarm, workers are now fighting back.

Now it seems workers are imagining a better way and looking to the past for inspiration. Pro-union sentiment rose to 71 percent in 2022, the highest since 1965. The United States' labor laws are outdated, the National Labor Relations Board is still a husk of itself, understaffed and weakened after decades of neglect—and yet, there is a great and mighty wave of organizing happening regardless. From fast food to academia to museums to mines to digital media to tech, workers in industry after industry are taking control, forcing bosses to the table, and fighting for their piece of the pie. There is a vibrant, vital sense of urgency, exacerbated by mounting crises and underpinned by historic levels of economic inequality. Something's got to give.

One of my favorite historical labor figures, Elizabeth Gurley Flynn, the famed rebel girl whom Joe Hill sang about and a formidable union organizer in her own right, hit the nail on the head way back in the nineteenth century while discussing the need to keep political and social justice demands on the same level as so-called bread-and-butter economic issues. In her words: "What is a labour victory? I maintain that it is a twofold thing. Workers must gain economic advantage, but they must also gain revolutionary spirit, in order to achieve a complete victory. For workers to gain a few cents more a day, a few minutes less a day, and go back to work with the same psychology, the same attitude toward society, is to achieve a temporary gain and not a lasting victory."

Every worker today stands on the shoulders of giants, people you will meet here like Lucy Parsons, Cesar Chavez, Bayard Rustin, Eugene V. Debs, and Walter Reuther. But others remain unfamiliar to the average working person, and could have never envisioned the world we're in now. Some things haven't changed; bad bosses and capitalist bloodsuckers continue to do their best to keep boots on our necks and their hands in our wallets. But imagine trying to explain Silicon Valley to Big Bill Haywood, or getting A. Philip

Randolph to understand how algorithms and robots are running Amazon warehouse workers ragged. Most people won't even recognize their names in the first place, which is exactly why we need to get that radical history into people's hands now.

Even if some of these labor leaders and rank-and-file firebrands have been forgotten or written out of history, the work they did, the battles they fought, and the fires they lit mattered. They deserve to be recognized just as much as we recognize the work of our current generation of labor icons-to-be. The indomitable Ms. Bates may be one of a kind, but she is also part of a long lineage of working-class heroes who, when faced with injustice and oppression, stood up, looked their bosses dead in the eye, and said, *enough*. It's on each and every one of us to carry the torch forward. As she would tell you herself, "Burn, let it burn."

I

THE TRAILBLAZERS

We must have money; a father's debts are to be paid, an aged mother to be supported, a brother's ambition to be aided and so the factories are supplied. Is this to act from free will? Is this freedom? To my mind it is slavery.

—Sarah Bagley, nineteenth-century labor leader

There is no one location or event that can lay a definitive claim to the founding of the American labor movement, but what is certain is the enormous debt it owes to women. Many of the crucial early battles between labor and capital have been swept aside or lost to history for lack of documentation—or, perhaps, a lack of interest in the many instances in which men did not play a lead role. In the late nineteenth century, early labor organizations like the Knights of Labor and the Industrial Workers of the World welcomed women workers into their ranks, but their relatively inclusive outlook made them outliers in the broader labor landscape. For centuries, the idea of women performing waged labor was restricted to the poor and working classes, and was a downright radical notion for those higher up the social ladder. At the turn of the century, "ladies" were still expected to stay home, marry as soon as possible, tend to the household, raise children, and be a helpmeet to their husbands. Coventry Patmore's immensely popular poem, "The Angel in the House," outlined this ideal in lines of clunky, purpled verse that idolized the sacrifice and utter devotion of his dear little wife (who, like so many others, probably had few other options available to her than to fawn over a self-important man in exchange for financial and social stability):

> ***Man must be pleased; but him to please***
> ***Is woman's pleasure; down the gulf***
> ***Of his condoled necessities***
> ***She casts her best, she flings herself.***

During the Victorian era, in the words of Bowling Green University's Dr. Susan M. Cruea, "Upper- and middle-class women's choices were limited to marriage and motherhood, or spinsterhood." For middle- or upper-class women, nearly any deviation from this norm was viewed as socially suspect unless the woman became a governess for a wealthier family (and even then, people would talk). For those who could afford it, domestic work like cooking, cleaning, child-rearing, and the endless drudgery of laundry was outsourced to hired help. The poor and working-class women they hired also shouldered the burden of those tasks for their own households, their unpaid labor dismissed as essential but valueless "women's work" (which, of course, remains an endemic issue a century later). Waged labor was seen as the exclusive realm of men, and for most middle- and upper-class women, the thought of earning money for their toil was wholly foreign; they had been raised to depend on their fathers, then their husbands, or whichever male family member was available (their own opinions on the matter notwithstanding). Self-determination and even basic education beyond appropriately ladylike pursuits like sewing and dancing were frowned upon by the upper crust. No *proper lady* would be caught dead asking to be paid for an honest day's work. (Sex workers were a different story altogether, but given their low social standing and the criminalization of their labor, they could scarcely lay claim to being involved in "respectable" society).

Of course, these standards were applied specifically to native-born *white* women, whose status as a protected class separated their experiences from those of working-class women of color in the U.S.—particularly Black women, whose relationship with work in this country began with enslavement, violence, and forced labor. Following Emancipation, their lives were still often defined by exploitation, abuse, and wage theft. Whether held in bondage or living freely, Black women were expected to work from the moment they were old enough to hold a broom; white society could hardly be coaxed to recognize their basic humanity, let alone to shield them from harm in the workplace.

But these women were hardly alone. By the 1830s, the American genocide against Indigenous people had been well underway for decades, and the few Indigenous women allowed into the workforce were treated abominably. As immigration ramped up during the middle of the nineteenth century, women workers from other ethnic groups—including, but not limited to, Irish immigrants fleeing a colonial famine and Russian Jews seeking to escape brutal repression—were also targeted by the ruling class's white supremacist paternalism, attuned to uphold the privilege of its housebound Victorian angels. But that restrictive social fabric quickly began to fray as the Industrial Revolution took flight. Middle-class white women, seeking autonomy and a stronger hand in the economic outcomes of their lives, began to seek work outside the home. And that demand for autonomy, as radical as it was back then, required radical action.

On a balmy spring 1824 day in Pawtucket, Rhode Island, 102 young women launched the country's very first factory strike, and brought the city's humming textile industry to a standstill. The day prior, eight local textile mills had jointly announced plans to extend their employees' already grueling twelve-hour workday to fourteen, and to slash wages for weavers, the workers who operated the power looms upon which the mills' cloth production depended. The factory's owners targeted the weavers, all between the ages of fifteen and thirty, specifically because of a belief that they were naturally docile, and would accept this latest affront to their dignity without question.

They could not have been less correct in their assumption. Not only did those same disenfranchised, overworked young women orchestrate the strike, but similar bands of workers would go on to do the same in other mill towns across New England and the Northeast throughout the nineteenth century.

Joined by several hundred of their male coworkers as well as sympathetic members of the public, the women blockaded the mills' entrances and loudly declared their intention to stay out of work until the new orders were rescinded. Back then the word "strike" was still alien in this context, so these women instead described their actions—walking off the job to protest management decisions—as a "turnout." That Pawtucket turnout lasted for a week, during which the strikers blocked mill entrances, threw rocks at mill bosses' mansions, and protested in the streets. The *Pawtucket Journal* breathlessly reported that a "tumultuous crowd" visited the "houses of the manufacturers, shouting, exclaiming and using every imaginable term of abuse and insult"; at one point, an unidentified party set fire to one of the mills. The fire rushed anxious mill owners to the negotiation table, and their offers of compromise officially ended the strike on June 3 of that year. The women of Pawtucket and their allies had won this first battle, but their "turnout" was just the opening salvo in a much longer war for textile workers' rights.

One of those striking Pawtucket mills, Slater Mill, holds the distinction of being the country's first cotton-spinning operation.

Its England-born owner, Samuel Slater, had spent his early years working in a cotton mill, learning how its machinery operated and absorbing the cruel management tactics that underpinned Britain's industrial boom. When he decamped to the U.S. in 1789, he arrived with a memorized cache of designs swiped from British industrialists like his mentor, Jedediah Strutt (an underhanded feat that earned him the nickname "Slater the Traitor" back home); he then sold them to Rhode Island industrialist Moses Brown, and began his own prodigious career in textiles. By 1793, Slater Mill was in full operation, staffed in part by local children aged between seven and thirteen years old. As the business expanded, Slater devised "the Rhode Island System," hiring entire families en masse. His "system" proved both effective and influential. By 1860, more than half of the mill workers in all of Rhode Island were children. He initially sought out the children of unhoused or incarcerated people to build up his workforce, but finding them too costly to house and feed, he began to encourage local working-class families to quite literally bring their children to work with them instead.

Slater's child laborers were paid between 40 and 60 cents (roughly $13 now) per week, and were expected to work up to sixteen hours per day. Lured by the promise of industrialization, thousands of families left their farms and flooded into mill towns across New England. Mill owners welcomed the influx of cheap labor, but as the machinery itself became larger and more complex, child labor became less viable. Instead, factory bosses turned to another pool of cheap, exploitable labor: young women.

By the time of the Pawtucket mill strike, their sisters of the loom had already been sweating away in mills across New England for more than a decade. Boston businessman Francis Cabot Lowell opened his first cotton mill in Waltham, Massachusetts, in 1814, and revolutionized the industry with a fully in-house production process that turned raw cotton bales into finished cloth ready to ship down South or overseas. He, like Samuel Slater, also toured England to learn the tricks of the trade. He was especially impressed by Edmund Cartwright's power loom, a device that mechanized the textile-making process and allowed factories to vastly reduce their labor needs.

Lowell also recognized the terrible human cost of Britain's industrial leap forward. He resolved that his facilities would operate differently than the "dark Satanic mills" William Blake described in one of his epic poems at the dawn of the Industrial Revolution, and that his workers would be treated morally. Compared with the way his peers operated, Lowell's paternalistic goal was a fairly noble one, but of course the road to hell is paved with good intentions. In this instance, Lowell's road led straight into the cacophonous purgatory of a nineteenth-century cotton mill.

THE MILL GIRLS OF LOWELL, MASSACHUSETTS

The appeal of young women to the factory owner was not limited solely to their low wages and supposed docility. Industrialists saw them as a transient or temporary workforce that would stick around for only a few years before leaving to get married, preventing the formation of a potentially problematic permanent working class in the mill cities. The first wave of "mill girls" were of hardy Yankee farm stock, the daughters and granddaughters of the American Revolution. Some were driven by the economic necessity of supporting family back home, saving up for a wedding, or funding their brothers' educations; others went for the sake of adventure, or at least in hopes of finding a new kind of life outside of the kitchen or the fields. It also offered the chance to be paid for their labor for the first time in their lives—and in cash, to boot.

These women workers were expected to follow a strict moral conduct code in and outside of work, to attend church regularly, and to room in company-controlled boardinghouses, where they shared rooms with up to seven other women at a time and lived beneath the watchful eye of a house matron. Workdays were long, dusty, and loud, with twelve to fourteen hours hours spent standing before a screaming spinning machine or power loom, breathing in cotton fibers and the stench of oil lamps. Accidents were common, and workers often lost fingers or other limbs; others were scalped, their long tresses yanked into a machine's gaping metal maw. Brown lung disease, the raw cotton equivalent of asbestosis, ran rampant in poorly ventilated mills. Managers nailed the windows of boiling hot factory floors shut, seeking to keep thread at maximum pliability while ignoring the well-being of those working it.

In spite of the strict rules that dictated much of their day-today existence, many women found that life as a mill girl did allow for a great deal more personal freedom than life on the farm. They enriched themselves in worker-organized "Self Improvement Circles," places where former farm girls could discuss literature, art, and philosophy after attending lectures from the likes of Ralph Waldo Emerson and Henry David Thoreau. It wasn't freedom, but for that first wave of women, who would have otherwise languished in isolation on faltering family farms or been consigned to lives of domestic drudgery, it was at least something new.

Mill operators also oversaw the *Lowell Offering*, a literary magazine written by and for the workers themselves. The publication started off as a collection of lighthearted poems and essays, but as time went on and conditions inside the mills deteriorated, notes of dissatisfaction and even rebellion crept into its pages. This shift in tone was thanks in no small part to Sarah Bagley, a talented weaver turned firebrand labor activist. Born in rural Candia, New Hampshire, in 1806, Bagley came to Lowell at the age of thirty-one to work at the Hamilton Manufacturing Company. She was initially won over by the promise of the mills, writing cheerful essays like "The Pleasures of Factory Work" for the *Offering*, but as the harsh realities of the workplace became apparent, her attitude changed. She witnessed her first labor action—a walkout over a proposed wage cut—in 1842, and by 1844, the Lowell Female Labor Reform Association (LFLRA) had been founded, with Bagley serving as its first president and one of its loudest voices. As an activist, Bagley's main focus was the growing demand for a ten-hour workday. Federal workers had won it in 1840, and skilled workers in various industries had done the same years earlier, but the mill girls were still working up to sixteen hours a day for paltry wages, and they were sick of it.

Textiles were booming, but New England as a whole struggled through economic depressions throughout the 1830s and 1840s. Mill owners constantly sought to cut costs—usually by docking workers' pay, or closing up shop unexpectedly. Dissatisfaction and anger began to spread throughout the ranks of mill workers, and labor unrest became much more common, building off that first strike in 1824. In 1834, mill managers in Lowell cut worker pay by 12.5 percent and ordered boardinghouses to begin packing eight women into each room; hundreds of women workers walked out, but the owners were able to quickly crush the strike. However, it soon spread to nearby Dover, where eight hundred others walked out over a similar pay cut: they formed strike committees, held mass rallies, and placed an ad in the local newspaper castigating the Cocheco Mill owners for treating their workers like "slaves." These strikes were unsuccessful, but the women pressed on with an ongoing wave of labor actions that culminated in the formation of the Factory Girls Association, which soon boasted twenty-five hundred members across New England. Though the bosses crushed their efforts once again and the FGA fell apart after the strike, these women had made an important contribution to the growing class consciousness among women workers.

Between 1842 and 1844, public opinion of the mills—once heralded as a utopia for godly young women—curdled as more reports on their actual working conditions surfaced. Mill bosses reacted with alarm, and sent their agents farther and farther afield to lure impoverished young women into their employ. "There are hundreds of young females shipped from this State every year to the factory prison-houses, like cattle, sheep, and pigs sent to slaughter," one Portland, Maine, newspaper lamented, as they were sent to labor "in the polluted and polluting manufacturing towns where they are prepared for a miserable life and a horrible death in the abodes of infamy."

Mill owners next turned to hiring immigrants, taking advantage of their marginalized social status to exploit and mistreat them as they saw fit. The first group of immigrant workers to enter New England's mills were the Irish. They were routinely paid less than their Yankee counterparts, and suffered virulent discrimination, prejudice, and anti-Catholic violence from their new neighbors. Hundreds of thousands of Irish emigrated during the 1840s and 1850s as potatoes rotted in the fields and the Great Famine starved their homeland. These workers arrived malnourished, penniless, haunted by British colonial terror, and desperate for work; mill owners welcomed them with open arms and turned-up noses. Tensions sometimes arose between the Irish workers and the remaining Yankee women, who had been engaged in protests and strikes over the same conditions the Irish accepted out of intense need and a profound lack of options. It was an early foreshadowing of conflicts that would be seen time and time again in the American labor struggle—different groups of marginalized workers were pitted against one other as profit-obsessed business interests scrambled to hire the most vulnerable people they could get their hands on. The

Irish would be followed into the mills by workers from Quebec, from Greece and Germany, from Russia and Poland and Italy and the Netherlands and Croatia and many others. Each new group of immigrants arrived eager to work, unaware that they'd soon be ground up by the mills.

"THE BLOOD OF SOULS IN BONDAGE"

Sarah Bagley and her LFLRA continued to advocate for the cause at conferences and women's conventions across New England, with a focus on bringing over male counterparts to join in pressuring legislators on issues of workers' concern. White men, unlike women of the time, held the threat of their *votes* as well as their labor to stir up trouble for those in power. In an early victory, anti-labor Lowell legislator William Schouler was targeted as punishment for his failure to support the LFLRA's goal of shortening the workday to ten hours. An LFLRA resolution snarled in advance of his next election: "As he is merely a corporation machine, or tool, we will use our best endeavors to keep him in the 'city of spindles,' where he belongs, and not to trouble Boston folks with him." They kept their promise, and Schouler was defeated—after which the LFLRA congratulated voters for "consigning William Schouler to the obscurity he so justly deserves."

Bagley traveled throughout the Northeast setting up new chapters of the LFLRA and its partner labor organization the New England Workingmen's Association (NEWA). As writer and editor of LFLRA's newspaper, the *Voice of Industry*, Bagley could express her more militant views without fear of censorship. There, she exposed the "slow and legal assassination" of the mill system, blasting mill owners for their hypocrisy and cruelty and illuminating the dire medical problems that afflicted many of the mill girls, from tuberculosis and lung disease to miscarriages. The publication also ran poetry from the women, one of whom, under the pseudonym "Pheney," painted a grim picture of her own daily grind: "And amidst the clashing noise and din / Of the ever beating loom / Stood a fair young girl with throbbing brow / Working her way to the tomb."

"Whenever I raise the point that it is immoral to shut us up in a room twelve hours a day in the most monotonous and tedious employment I am told that we have come to the mills voluntarily and we can leave when we will. Voluntarily!" Bagley raged in print. "The whip which brings us to Lowell is necessity. We must have money; a father's debts are to be paid, an aged mother to be supported, a brother's ambition to be aided and so the factories are supplied. Is this to act from free will? Is this freedom? To my mind it is slavery."

After a frenetic three years in the trenches and growing disputes with other editors over her feminist politics, Bagley lost her gig at the *Voice of Industry* and left the mills in 1846. Ever resourceful, she switched tack entirely to take a job as the nation's first female telegraph operator—and quickly discovered that she was paid only a quarter of what her male counterparts made. Bagley's fight for social justice continued on, from abolition and women's rights to antiwar activism and prison reform. The trail of her political involvement grows cold around this time, save for one detail: in 1850 she and her husband, James Dumo, operated a patent medicine business peddling tinctures, a nod to her memory of the Lowell mills—and her coughing, sickly coworkers with their lungs full of cotton.

Bagley and her compatriots were long gone from their posts by the time her wish for the mill girls was granted. It took until 1853 for Massachusetts mill workers to successfully force some of their employers to implement an eleven-hour day, and it took a prolonged and sometimes violent struggle to win the eight-hour day decades later with the passage of the 1938 Fair Labor Standards Act. Bagley, who died in 1889, did not live to see it.

THE FREED BLACK WASHERWOMEN OF JACKSON, MISSISSIPPI

The nineteenth-century Northern U.S. textile industry was almost entirely white. While enslaved Black workers were forced to be the backbone of the cotton industry in the South, and free Black workers and other workers of color were certainly present in New England, Black people as a whole were barred from employment in the Northern mills. However, the connection between the suffering of enslaved Black people down South and the misery in the Northern mills was clear to the mill workers themselves, many of whom held abolitionist leanings and despaired at the role they played in perpetuating enslaved people's oppression. When Alabama senator Jeremiah Clemens publicly opined that enslaved workers in the South were "better off" than Northern mill workers, Clementine Averill wrote a furious letter to the *New York Times* calling for his resignation. "Are *we* torn from our friends and kindred, sold and driven about like cattle, chained and whipped, and not allowed to speak one word in self-defence?" the mill girl asked, making clear the answer.

This tension was material as well as spiritual; one of the products made in the New England mills was a rough cotton yarn specifically intended to clothe enslaved people. Lucy Larcom, a former mill worker turned teacher and poet, reflected on that dark time in verse, writing, "When I've thought about what soil the cotton-plant / We weave is rooted in, what waters it— / The blood of souls in bondage—I have felt / That I was sinning against the light to stay / and turn the accursed fibre into cloth."

Their solidarity may have resonated throughout the abolitionist circles of the Northeast, but it is unlikely that it reached the millions of Black women laboring in the Southern heat. Denied their freedom, their autonomy, and their very humanity by the all-encompassing power of the slave economy, these workers had very few outlets to protest their mistreatment (though some tried anyway, and one could argue, as W. E. B. Du Bois did in his book *Black Reconstruction in America*, that by running away from the plantations and permanently withholding their labor from their tormentors, escapees from the slave system were, in a way, striking). It wasn't until 1866, a year after Emancipation, that formerly enslaved Black women workers were able to launch a widespread work stoppage of their own—and by doing so, jump-start a wave of Black-led labor organizing that would spread through multiple industries and set the stage for decades of labor struggles to come.

On June 16, 1866, laundry workers in Jackson, Mississippi, called for a citywide meeting. The women—for they were all women, and all were Black—were tired of being paid next to nothing to spend their days hunched over steaming tubs of other (white) people's laundry, scrubbing out stains, smoothing the wrinkles with red-hot irons, and hauling the baskets of heavy cloth through the streets. At the time, nearly all Black women workers were employed as domestics by white families, to handle the cooking, cleaning, and childcare, hauling water, emptying chamber pots, and performing various and sundry other tasks that the lady of the house preferred to avoid. Laundry, at the time a labor-intensive daylong process, topped that list in an era in which families were large, personal hygiene was negligible, and running water was scarce. The washerwomen's wages were kept so low that even poor white families could afford to send their laundry out for Black women to clean. The work itself was onerous, but the relative flexibility and independence it afforded was attractive to Black women workers: they were able to work out of their own homes, which in turn allowed them to plan around their own familial and community obligations, and it was a trade that could be passed down to their own daughters. For the newly emancipated, having the freedom to create their own work schedules and get through their daily labors without a white employer breathing down their necks was—almost—worth all the soiled diapers in the world.

In modern terms, the washerwomen were independent contractors, with lists of clients who paid a set rate for weekly service. The trouble with that system, though, was that it was easily abused by racist white clients who were still unaccustomed to having to pay Black people for their labor, and who weren't altogether thrilled with the idea. White employers were shocked and appalled whenever Black workers exercised their rights as free wage-earning people, or dared to engage in small acts of resistance against mistreatment, whether that resistance took the form of slowdowns, feigning illness, or reappropriating food and dry goods from their boss's shelves. One of their most powerful weapons was, simply, to quit, and go looking for more desirable clients as their former employers scrambled to hire replacements. This growing tension between employer and employee came to a head in 1866, when the washerwomen of Jackson presented Mayor D. N. Barrows with a petition decrying the low wages that plagued their industry and announcing their intention to "join in charging a uniform rate" for their labor. As their petition read, "Any washerwoman who charges less will be fined by our group. We do not want to charge high prices, we just want to be able to live comfortably from our work." The prices they'd agreed upon were far from exorbitant: $1.50 per day for washing, $15 a month for "family washing," and $10 a month for single people. They signed their letter "The Washerwomen of Jackson," and in doing so, gave a name to Mississippi's first trade union.

The media response to their action was withering, dismissing the women's intelligence and skills, predicting abject failure, and in a move that would become common as more Black workers' organizing efforts spread, assuming that the strike had been planned by Northern white male agitators. There is no record of the 1866 strike's outcome, but the action itself had an immediate ripple effect in Jackson and farther afield. Throughout the Reconstruction Era of 1865 to 1877, Black workers rose up and struck in Virginia, Tennessee, Alabama, Georgia, Louisiana, South Carolina, and Washington, D.C. In 1869, the Colored National Labor Union was formed to represent the unique interests of Black workers who had been shut out of the larger National Labor Union. Its first president, Isaac Myers, was cofounder of the Colored Caulkers Trade Union Society, and its second leader was the indomitable Frederick Douglass, elected in 1872.

The Great Railroad Strike of 1877, a series of often violent work stoppages in which more than one hundred thousand railroad workers struck over wages and dangerous working conditions, temporarily brought the railroad barons to their knees and unleashed a roving spirit of dissent that captured the imagination of workers across industries from coast to coast. Those winds of change arrived in Galveston, Texas, in July and August, when hundreds of workers—Black and white, men and women, dockworkers, laborers, and washerwomen—crossed the color line and struck together several times to protest their low wages. On July 30, 1877, fifty Black day laborers struck for higher wages, and their ranks grew as they paraded through the streets—recruiting others from a sawmill, a cotton farm, a construction site, and elsewhere along the way. (In August, Black dockworkers on the Morgan Wharf would launch their own fight to be paid equally to their white coworkers, who showed their solidarity by refusing to cross the Black longshoremen's picket line.)

Meanwhile, as the laborers' strike continued, their wives, daughters, sisters, and neighbors in the laundry business had been busy planning an action of their own. At first, they published an open letter demanding a wage increase to $1.50 per day. A few days later, a group of Black washerwomen gathered in front of J. N. Harding's steam laundry, where he was known to be employing white women, and forcibly prevented those employees from entering unless they agreed to abide by the $1.50 daily rate. One woman, recorded only as "Miss Murphy," refused, and rushed into the laundry to start her shift; the strikers ran after and literally carried her out of the building. With Murphy removed, the strikers next gathered tools and wood to board up the windows and doors of the business. The scene then turned ugly when the washerwomen proceeded to turn their ire to perceived rivals: Chinese immigrant-run laundries.

Anti-Chinese racism and violence on the coasts had forced many Chinese immigrants to move farther inland in search of a safe haven, and the Port of Galveston emerged as a major hub for immigration in the years prior to Ellis Island's 1892 opening. The majority of those immigrants were men working to send money back to their families in China. Many had initially found work building the Transcontinental Railroad in the American West, and as that project wound down, the U.S. government took measures to bar their employment, culminating in the 1882 Chinese Exclusion Act and the even more restrictive Scott Act several years later. Forced into the deepest margins of the workforce, Chinese workers most often took up agricultural labor, opened small restaurants, or, to the Black washerwomen's chagrin, operated their own laundry services.

The *Galveston News* painted an unfortunate picture of the ways in which xenophobia, prejudice, and perceived scarcity can turn marginalized workers against one another: "At these laundries all the women talked at once, telling Sam Lee, Slam Sing, Wau Loong and the rest that 'they must close up and leave this city within fifteen days, or they would be driven away.'" This viewpoint would prove to be a recurring theme throughout the early American labor movement, and remains a problem today, when far too many trade unionists still view immigrants as competition instead of welcoming them as fellow workers.

As with many early labor battles, the 1877 Galveston strike

came to a messy, inconclusive ending. It grew to encompass women domestic workers (a group of whom formed the Ladies of Labor in response), but also drew the ire of the respected trade unionist leader Norris Wright Cuney, a mixed-race Republican stalwart of Galveston's Black labor community, who denounced the striking workers' conduct and called for them to return to work. He would go on to play a pivotal role in building labor power on the Galveston docks, a place where Black and white workers demonstrated alongside each other. But as of 1877, Cuney was public enemy number one for the Ladies of Labor. The stage was now set for the washerwomen's biggest moment yet—this time, in Atlanta.

A SHOWDOWN IN ATLANTA

1881 Atlanta was abuzz with promise and industry. The city was amidst a campaign to position itself as an ambitious, forward-thinking powerhouse. A glittering International Cotton Exposition aimed to establish Atlanta's place as the belle of the New South and show off its purportedly pliable, happy workforce. But despite this veneer of progress, Black Atlantans were relegated to undesirable, labor-intensive jobs on society's bottom rung. Still denied the right to vote, Black women had to find other ways to build power.

Historian Dr. Tera Hunter's seminal 1993 book, *To 'Joy My Freedom: Southern Black Women's Lives and Labors after the Civil War*, documents the history of this moment. As Hunter writes, Atlanta's laundresses made up a majority of the Black female workforce in a city where 98 percent of Black women worked as domestic laborers (and washerwomen alone outnumbered male laborers).

Atlanta's laundresses made up a majority of the Black female workforce in a city where 98 percent of Black women worked as domestic laborers (and washerwomen alone outnumbered male laborers). They also made up a powerful collective organizing bloc, their greatest goals being to secure greater economic stability and to cement their own autonomy as workers. In early July, twenty of them gathered in a church in Summer Hill, one of Atlanta's first predominantly Black neighborhoods, and founded a trade association they dubbed the Washing Society. The organization's first order of business was setting a higher, standard wage rate for their labor, and they called a mass meeting to make their demands public. They told local Black clergymen to spread the word throughout their congregations, and less than a month later, on July 19, they called for a strike.

Hunter found that, over the next three weeks, the strike grew from those first twenty women to more than three thousand thanks to the organizers' brilliantly effective tactic of doing daily rounds of home visits to laundresses around the city to persuade them to join in the fight. They held daily meetings to keep up momentum, and brought in the city's white washerwomen (who made up only 2 percent of the workforce) to support their cause. Newspapers of the time declined to print the white women's names to protect their privacy (a courtesy not extended to the Black women strikers), but it is likely that they were poor Irish immigrants.

On the employers' side, the strike hit like a wrecking ball. As washerwomen began returning soiled or still-wet laundry to clients who refused to pay the higher wage, white employers scrambled to find workers to fill the laundry gap as they feared the strike would spread to other industries. And spread it did: Black waiters at the National Hotel in downtown Atlanta refused to work until their bosses raised their wages—and they won. That scene repeated itself in kitchens, nurseries, and sculleries across the city. "The Washerwomen's strike is assuming vast proportions and despite the apparent independence of the white people, is causing quite an inconvenience among our citizens," the *Atlanta Constitution* reported on July 26, a week into the strike. "There are some families in Atlanta who have been unable to have any washing done for more than two weeks. Not only the washerwomen, but the cooks, house servants and nurses are asking increases."

Ten days into the strike, police arrested six of its leaders. As Hunter writes, the women—Matilda Crawford, Sallie Bell, Carrie Jones, Dora Jones, Orphelia Turner, and Sarah A. Collier—were delicately described in the press as "ebony-hued damsels," but found themselves slapped with charges of disorderly conduct and "quarrelling" as a result of their home-visit campaign. It is true that visits were not always friendly, and some negotiations with reluctant or recalcitrant washerwomen were more aggressive, relying on threats or even engaging in street fights to hammer the message home. Five of the women were fined $5 apiece, but Collier was ordered to pay a $20 fine. She refused to pay, and as punishment, the forty-nine-year-old asthmatic mother of two was sentenced to work on a chain gang for forty days.

These workers had everything riding on this strike; the vast majority of the demonstrators were mothers who had to feed children and keep households afloat during the campaign, and couldn't count on regular relief checks or a strike fund to pay the rent. Arrest records and Hunter's work preserve the stories of several women who were targeted by police, like Jane Webb, with her six children and unemployed husband, and Sarah and Sam Gardner, a married couple who were fined for threatening a maid who'd been hired by Sarah's former employer to take her place. As the strike stretched into August, the Atlanta City Council got involved. Its solution: a $25 annual business license fee on any member of a washerwoman's association (more than $670 in 2021 dollars)—a proposition intended to economically hobble the workers at war for a mere $1 per dozen pounds of laundry.

But instead the washerwomen wrote a letter to Atlanta mayor Jim English expressing their willingness to pay the fees—so long as the city agreed to formally grant them control over the local hand-laundering industry. The strikers' letter ended with a warning: "Don't forget this. We hope to hear from your council on Tuesday morning. We mean business this week or no washing."

Atlanta's City Council backed down, and while history is murky on the resolution, it appears that the workers had successfully shifted the balance of power. Several weeks later, as the International Cotton Exposition neared, Black women workers took the opportunity to leverage their power against the ruling classes once again. The fair was intended to reassure respectable Yankee business folk that there was fun to be had and, more importantly to this contingent, money to be made in the postwar South. City boosters were well aware of the potential costs if their plan went awry—and so were the washerwomen.

As Hunter writes in *To 'Joy My Freedom*, "African-American women threatened to expose the tyranny in the New South by disrupting this celebration of new-found harmony at an early stage of its public relations campaign." As the city prepared for an influx of fashionable visitors whose arrival would require spotless hotel rooms, hearty meals, and quick laundry services, the domestic workers of Atlanta invoked labor's "nuclear option," and threatened a general strike. Hunter explains, "Ironically, it was precisely the prospect of visitors seeing them as they were that made the threat of a strike troubling" to their white employers. That threat—of the workers wielding the power they hold and realizing that the boss does have a breaking point, no matter how imbalanced the scales of power may be—has "troubled" many employers since then, and it proved to be extremely effective in this case. A cease-fire came through and the fair went on without a hitch, but Atlanta's Black women workers had prevailed in making their collective power felt. The city's white supremacist employer class had come face-to-face with the reality of Emancipation: Black workers would tolerate injustice no more.

2

THE GARMENT WORKERS

The worker must have bread, but she must have roses, too.

—Rose Schneiderman, labor activist and American Civil Liberties Union cofounder

Unless you were rich, New York City at the turn of the last century was a dreadful place to live. By the nineteenth century, its population had grown to become the nation's largest, but the city itself was hardly a gleaming metropolis. By 1910, nearly five million people called its five boroughs home, with more than two million of them squeezed onto the island of Manhattan, the heart of the nation's industry and commerce. New York City's largely immigrant workforce suffered deplorable living conditions, and workers had no safety regulations to speak of. Child labor was not only tolerated, but normalized (and even preferred in certain industries). Disease and decay were endemic in poorer neighborhoods, and workers themselves were frequently mangled or killed on the job. But the upper crust of politics and society were more than happy to leave the toiling class to their dirty, malnourished fates—as long as they didn't cause too much trouble.

Thousands of immigrant families made their home in Manhattan's Lower East Side, where creaky tenement houses teetered in the wind and open sewers clogged the streets. Charles Dickens visited the neighborhood in 1842 and recorded his impressions of Five Points, a notoriously poor, neglected slum, in the ensuing travelogue. "This is the place—these narrow ways, diverging to the right and left, and reeking everywhere with dirt and filth," he wrote. "Such lives as are led here bear the same fruits here as elsewhere. The coarse and bloated faces at the doors have counterparts at home and all the wide world over . . . see how the rotten beams are tumbling down, and how the patched and broken windows seem to scowl dimly, like eyes that have been hurt in drunken frays."

And by the 1910s, the area had only gotten more crowded, and more dangerous. Life on the Lower East Side was brutal, but still held flashes of warmth and merriment as different cultures came together to eat, drink, laugh, and argue. A sensory riot of cooking smells, colorful fabric, and languages sang through the streets, and during their scant leisure time, workers and their families could amuse themselves in public parks and beer gardens, or take in a vaudeville show. But there was also a deep political undercurrent running through the tenements, beer halls, and cafes of the Lower East Side, long known as a hotbed of radicalism. Eastern European Jewish socialists, German communists, and Italian anarchists broke bread with American trade unionists and Irish republicans, sharing ideologies and building solidarity across language and ethnic lines. Here, amid the squalor and the shared struggles, the working classes began to dream of something better than the short, cruel lives to which they'd been consigned.

While early feminist thinkers had been advocating for women's rights since the eighteenth century, in the factories, laundries, and cramped kitchens of the Lower East Side, gender equality was a dead end. Wealthy white women, of course, did not work; their job was to maintain their stately homes and keep their rich husbands happy. By the early twentieth century, women in the more genteel middle classes had gained a number of opportunities for respectable white-collar employment, from bookkeeping and secretarial work to teaching or working in the shops at the bottom of shiny new skyscrapers; despite the suffocating sexism that permeated society at the time, some were even able to pursue careers in law, medicine, higher education, journalism, and engineering.

However, working-class women remained tasked with a dual load of labor—first at home caring for their families, and then on the job, where they would be paid pennies on the dollar compared with men. Despite some significant improvements in 1911, when (white) women teachers were granted equal pay to their male counterparts, the wage gap remained shockingly wide until President John F. Kennedy signed the Equal Pay Act and made an initial dent in a problem that still persists today (when white women are making 82 cents to a white man's dollar, and women of color are paid far less). New York City's residents of color faced the added burden of racism, and were restricted to a handful of occupations, which for Black women almost always entailed domestic service. While some working-class white women also worked as domestics, they were more often employed by laundries and the garment-manufacturing industry. Those garment workers were contracted by factories to spend their days in makeshift sweatshops, or to take home piles of piecework, slowly destroying their bodies as they hunched over their tiny needles, and straining their eyes over sputtering candles long into the night.

Others worked long days in the garment factories themselves, which were still just as dark, dirty, and unsanitary as their nineteenth-century predecessors. Malnutrition, sleep deprivation, and disease were rampant. Some bosses, suspicious that their poorly paid women employees were stealing bits of fabric, liked to lock the factory doors in between shifts in order to protect their investments. Wages were as little as $6 per week, a precious little more than the New England "mill girls" had been paid a century earlier.

THE FIERY JEWISH GIRLS (*FARBRENTE YIDISHE MEYDLEKH*) OF NEW YORK CITY

In 1909, a coterie of young Jewish women workers at the Lower East Side's Triangle Shirtwaist Factory decided they'd had enough. Many had developed knowledge of labor unions and leftist political traditions through the Jewish Labor Bund, a prominent socialist Jewish group, and they also had allies to call upon. Rose Schneiderman, a queer Jewish feminist socialist, former garment worker, future secretary of the New York Department of Labor, and founding member of the American Civil Liberties Union (ACLU), was already known within their industry for her work as an organizer for the New York Women's Trade Union. History knows her best for a 1912 speech in which she proclaimed, "The worker must have bread, but she must have roses, too," but that enduring turn of phrase only scratches the surface of Schneiderman's lifelong contributions to the cause of workers' rights. Another speech she gave in 1911, as the ashes of the Triangle smoldered behind her, laid bare her mission as an organizer. "Too much blood has been spilled," she said then. "I know from experience it is up to the working people to save themselves. And the only way is through a strong working-class movement."

Rose had already become a seasoned labor activist by the time she crossed paths with Triangle worker and International Ladies' Garment Workers' Union (ILGWU) organizer Clara Lemlich. A Ukrainian immigrant and lifelong radical, Lemlich had moved to New York City in 1903 and led her coworkers at various factories out on strikes between 1906 and 1909. She, like Schneiderman and many others of her time, was one of the early U.S. labor movement's revolutionary "fiery Jewish girls" who would soon leave a mark in their new homeland's history books.

In November 1909, a twenty-three-year-old Lemlich sat in on a union meeting at Cooper Union, which is now home to a private university in Manhattan's East Village but was then a tuition-free educational meeting ground for progressive youth. The meeting droned on, dominated by discussion of the relatively high-paying jobs accessible only to men, and dealing with little of personal concern to the women present in the room. The male union contingent had long written off women workers as unmanageable and unwilling to strike, and discounted whatever organizing efforts they had undertaken as unsustainable.

Lemlich, by then the veteran of a number of bloody strikes, rose to her feet and cried out, interrupting the proceedings in her native Yiddish: "I am a working girl." Her small frame and big voice immediately commanded the room's attention. "One of those who are on strike against intolerable conditions. I am tired of listening to speakers who talk in general terms. What we are here for is to decide whether we shall strike or shall not strike. I offer a resolution that a general strike be declared now."

To the amazement of the men on stage, large swaths of the crowd roared in agreement, and raised their right arms to pledge along with her in an ancient Yiddish oath: "If I turn traitor to the cause I now pledge, may my hand wither from the arm I now raise."

Over the next few weeks, between twenty and thirty thousand young women garment workers walked off their jobs, taking Lemlich's lead. The newspapers called it "the Revolt of the Girls," but it has gone down in history as "the Uprising of the 20,000." The New York Women's Trade Union League (WTUL), a reformist organization of privileged white women suffragists who had enlisted Rose Schneiderman to help foster trust between them and the working-class women they sought to organize, took up the cause and provided financial support to the striking workers. When the action finally ended in February 1910, the WTUL had negotiated labor contracts with 339 of the Associated Waist and Dress Manufacturers' 353 firms. The deals secured stipulations over safety standards, including shorter hours, fire safety, and the proper handling of fabric scraps.

One notable holdout was the notoriously anti-union Triangle Shirtwaist Factory. The Triangle's owners, "the Shirtwaist Kings" Max Blanck and Isaac Harris, flat-out refused to agree to any of the workers' demands. Formerly garment workers themselves, they viewed the strikes as a personal attack, and saw the union as an existential threat to their high-volume business model. They initially responded to the strike by hiring police as strikebreakers to arrest and sometimes violently attack the women. While the brutality was unmistakable, this wasn't a new tactic on their part; Lemlich herself had suffered six broken ribs during earlier strikes.

Bear in mind that all this happened during a time when women were largely considered to be too fragile to live without the protection of a man, too delicate to withstand the merest hint of violence or unsavory behavior, and too empty-headed to vote or engage in politics. Yet in this case, the hired strikebreakers had no problem cracking the skulls and breaking the ribs of the working-class women on the picket lines. Local sex workers were also paid to come heckle and start physical fights with the strikers, as bosses pitted other vulnerable working-class women against one another.

Blanck and Harris never did come to the table, but the New York strikes inspired a wave of labor actions across the country, including Chicago's "Great Revolt" of sixty thousand cloak-makers in 1910, and helped lay the groundwork for industrial unionism in the garment industry. Five years after the uprising, the "needle trades" were home to some of the strongest, most militant unions in America. Back in New

York City, Lemlich and her comrades dealt with the personal frustrations of seeing their basic rights and needs ignored closest to home, but little could they have known Triangle's refusals would soon turn out to be one of the deadliest miscalculations in U.S. labor history.

"BURNING DEATH BEFORE OUR EYES"

The fire tore through the factory and its occupants swiftly, and without mercy. With the doors locked, a slow, small elevator and a narrow fire escape that clung to the side of the tall building offered the only chance to outrun the inferno. The crush of bodies trying to escape soon overwhelmed the elevator, closing off the final potential exit. There were no sprinklers, fire extinguishers, or air vents inside the factory; there were no federal safety regulations to speak of at that point, and bosses were generally left to their own devices in regards to how they treated—or mistreated—their workforces. Fabric scraps piled around the sewing machines on the factory floor provided ample fuel for the fire's ravenous hunger. It took less than thirty minutes for the building to become a roaring inferno.

No one was supposed to have been there that day. March 25, 1911, started out just like any other day inside the Triangle Shirtwaist Factory, which occupied the top three floors of the ten-story Asch Building in Manhattan's Greenwich Village. The 1909 strike had secured a fifty-two-hour workweek for most workers in these kinds of establishments, but Blanck and Harris's recalcitrance meant about five hundred people were still working there that Saturday afternoon. The workers—nearly all of them women, and overwhelmingly Eastern European Jewish and Italian immigrants—toiled away amid dusty piles of fabric scraps, churning out shirtwaist after shirtwaist as the sunlight filtered in weakly through smudged windows. As usual at the Triangle, all the doors had been locked behind the workers as they'd trickled in for their shift. Around 4:45 p.m., disaster struck.

As the fire consumed everything—and everyone—in its path, onlookers stood horrified at the sight of a dozen young women crowding onto the rickety fire escape looking desperately for an exit. The fire engines that arrived were not equipped with ladders long enough to reach the factory's windows on the ninth floor. All that could be done was to watch as the women desperately searched for a way out. And then, the bodies began to fall.

William Shepherd, a United Press reporter who had happened upon the scene, described the gruesome sight.

> Up in the [ninth] floor girls were burning to death before our very eyes. . . . Down came the bodies in a shower, burning, smoking-flaming bodies, with disheveled hair trailing upward. . . . On the sidewalk lay heaps of broken bodies. . . . I looked upon the heap of dead bodies and I remembered these girls were the shirtwaist makers. I remembered their great strike of last year in which these same girls had demanded more sanitary conditions and more safety precautions in the shops. These dead bodies were the answer.

The final toll: 146 workers dead. The panicked victims had been unable to escape the rising flames; their young bodies either lay broken on the sidewalk after they jumped to their deaths, or suffocated by the billows of smoke inside the stuffy factory. Others, some as young as fourteen, were burned alive on the factory floor. The next day, the corpses were placed in plain pine boxes and laid out in rows at the end of Manhattan's Charities Pier, colloquially known as "Misery Lane" for its enduring role as a makeshift pop-up morgue whenever a disaster struck the city. Family members and onlookers streamed past in the tens of thousands, searching for familiar faces amid the rows of burned and mangled bodies, desperately looking for their daughters, wives, sweethearts, and sisters among the victims. Some were never identified.

Photography was still in its early days at the time, and New Yorkers reacted first with abject horror and then with outrage at the photos of the fire's victims that ran in the city's many newspapers the following day. The images of dead and dying young women, their dresses gently billowing in the wind, their long hair aflame, chilled the nation and set into motion immediate efforts to reform the industry's worst aspects. In June 1911, the New York State Legislature's newly created Factory Investigating Commission sent inspectors into the city's tenements, factories, and sweatshops; horrified by their findings, the commission passed thirty-six work-safety laws in four years.

Following weeks of public outcry, Blanck and Harris were indicted on first- and second-degree manslaughter charges following the accident. But their high-powered legal defense team saw them acquitted on all charges after the jury determined that the prosecution had not proven that the owners were aware of the locked doors prior to the fire. The fact that said owners had explicitly instructed their foremen to lock the doors each day somehow did not come up during the course of the three-week trial.

Even more ghoulishly, not only did the Triangle's owners escape any measure of accountability for the lives lost due to their own paranoid greed, but they turned a profit off of the fire. Blanck and Harris collected insurance money for the burned building, and raked in $60,000 more than the fire had cost them in damages—netting them the equivalent of $400 per victim. In 1913, the pair reached a settlement with the victims' families, paying out one week's wages for each dead worker—or roughly $6 for each lost life. Later that year, Blanck was pulled up on charges for locking the doors at another one of his factories during work hours, just as he'd done two years previously. A separate, later incident saw him cited for allowing flammable materials to be left out on a factory floor.

The Triangle Shirtwaist Factory closed its doors for the final time in 1918, and its owners walked away to live out the rest of their lives in comfort. One can only hope that they saw those 146 burning bodies in their minds' eyes when they tried to go to sleep each night.

"Hundred forty-six people in a half an hour," Rose Freedman, the final remaining survivor of the fire, said in a 2000 PBS documentary, *The Living Century*. Born in Vienna, Austria, in 1893, her family emigrated to the U.S. in 1909, and after her aunt mocked her housekeeping skills, Freeman went out and got a job at the Triangle. After the fire, she went to college, got a job on a steamship line, and married. When her husband died in 1959, she lied about her age and got a job at an insurance company to support her three children, two of whom were disabled with polio. She lived a colorful, unorthodox life, and appeared at labor rallies until her death, recounting how the Triangle's factory owners had tried to bribe her to say that the doors had not been locked (she refused). She had been only seventeen when the fire broke out, and in the film she credits her survival to her decision to rush up to the executive offices on the tenth floor and follow them out onto the roof.

> I have always tears in my eyes when I think, "It should never have happened." The executives with a couple of steps could have opened the door. But they thought they were better than the working people. It's not fair because material, money, is more important here than everything. That's the biggest mistake—that a person doesn't count

> much when he hasn't got money. What good is a rich man and he hasn't got a heart?

Rose died one year after the documentary aired. She was 107.

FRANCES PERKINS: LABOR ACTIVIST TURNED ARCHITECT OF THE NEW DEAL

The fire's impact rippled out far beyond the confines of the Lower East Side, thanks in part to the presence of a young suffragist named Frances Perkins. Perkins had become invested in the fight against injustice at a young age. "I had to do something about unnecessary hazards to life, unnecessary poverty," she once wrote. "It was sort of up to me." After graduating from Mount Holyoke College, she worked as a teacher and volunteered at Hull House, a settlement house founded by Jane Addams to serve poor citizens and recently arrived European immigrants. She then moved to New York City to study political science at Columbia University; there, she became involved in the women's suffrage movement, and was appointed head of the New York Consumers League, a watchdog group advocating for the rights of workers. On that fateful day in 1911, Perkins was visiting friends in Greenwich Village when news of the fire reached their drawing room. She rushed over to investigate, becoming an eyewitness to the tragedy:

> People had just begun to jump as we got there. They had been holding on until that time, standing in the windowsills, being crowded by others behind them, the fire pressing closer and closer, the smoke closer and closer. . . . The window was too crowded and they would jump and they hit the sidewalk. Every one of them was killed, everybody who jumped was killed. It was a horrifying spectacle.

Perkins later said that the fire was a "never-to-be-forgotten reminder of why I had to spend my life fighting conditions that could permit such a tragedy." She made good on her promise in more ways than one. Perkins played an instrumental role in seeking justice for the victims and enacting workplace safety reforms, first as the chief investigator of the Factory Investigating Commission, and later as an advisor to Governor Al Smith as he signed an example-setting slate of workplace safety standards into law.

Perkins quickly earned the trust of Smith's successor, Franklin Delano Roosevelt, who promoted her to become New York State's industrial commissioner in 1929. And when Roosevelt departed office upon his election to U.S. President in 1932, he appointed Perkins to his presidential cabinet, making her the first woman to hold such a post. She had already made history the moment she walked into her first cabinet meeting, but Perkins was no ceremonial figurehead. Her work in the Roosevelt administration coincided with one of the most ambitiously pro-labor legislative efforts in the country's history: the New Deal.

Perkins was later quoted as saying that the New Deal began on March 25, 1911, the day she smelled the smoke and saw the bodies of those young women workers burn. She proved tireless in her drive to fight for workers' safety, was deeply involved in efforts to combat unemployment during the Great Depression, and spearheaded the creation of an ambitious social safety net program we now know as Social Security. Her fingerprints were also left on pro-worker New Deal initiatives like the 1935 National Labor Relations Act (which made it easier for many workers to join and organize unions) and the Fair Labor Standards Act of 1938 (which established a minimum wage and prohibited child labor in many workplaces). None of these pieces of legislation were as inclusive as they should have been or went far enough to protect those who needed it most, but they did provide crucial new protections to millions of workers where before there had been none.

Perkins's central focus was on labor, but her impact did not end there. As Adolf Hitler rose to power in late-1930s Germany, Perkins ordered her Department of Labor to aid European Jewish refugees who sought safety in the U.S. At the time, the Immigration Service was within the Department of Labor, and Perkins refused to stand down despite FDR's hesitance to relax the country's strict immigration limits. She found various legal means to bypass the challenges she encountered, and was often the lone voice standing against her colleagues' antisemitic and xenophobic attitudes. By 1937, she had arranged for the safe passage of nearly three hundred thousand temporary and permanent refugees to the United States. She was attuned to injustice at home, as well; in 1933, her first act as labor secretary was to desegregate the Department of Labor's cafeteria.

As Perkins herself once said, "Most of man's problems upon this planet, in the long history of the race, have been met and solved either partially or as a whole by experiment based on common sense and carried out with courage." The courage she exhibited undoubtedly saved countless workers' lives, and the reforms she helped carry out set the stage for another century of hard-fought battles, and hard-won progress. Perkins helped ensure that those who perished in the "horrifying spectacle" of the Triangle Shirtwaist Factory fire would not be forgotten, and while her name is nowhere near as well known as that of the president she served alongside, the progress she made on behalf of the country's working class has changed millions of lives for the better. The woman behind the New Deal was a queer feminist, a self-proclaimed "revolutionist" who fought for what was right even when it was unpopular, and refused to back down even after her bitter male colleagues in Congress tried to impeach her in 1939 over her support for radical union leader Harry Bridges. "I came to Washington to work for God, FDR, and the millions of forgotten, plain common workingmen," she said of her time in government. And that is exactly what she did.

"A TURNING POINT IN MY LIFE": SUE KO LEE AND THE NATIONAL DOLLAR STORES FACTORY STRIKE

Even with an ally in the White House, a garment worker's life was far from easy, and those who were immigrant women of color shouldered the heaviest burdens of all. In San Francisco, where a large community of Chinese immigrants had made their homes, the ILGWU reached out to Chinese-owned garment factories in hopes of raising industry standards (and by extension preventing them from "undercutting" their white-owned competitors, who remained the union's primary targets). "The white shops were already organized and they were clamoring that the contractors were sending work out to the Chinese workers," Chinese labor leader Sue Ko Lee later explained. "So they had to organize the Chinese." Despite its intentions, the union made little progress until it brought in organizer Jennie Maytas in 1938. As an immigrant (Maytas was born in Hungary) and a former child garment worker, she was able to connect and build trust with the Chinese women who labored in the cramped garment factories, and the workers—already fed up with their deplorable working conditions and paltry wages—voted to form the Chinese Ladies' Garment Workers' Union, Local 341.

Sue Ko Lee, a Hawai'ian-born Chinese American garment worker, became a leader in the new union, and an even more powerful force when they voted to go on strike against National Dollar Stores later that year. The chain of factories was regarded as the best employer of its kind, yet still paid its workers only $13.30 per week. The workers demanded more, but their entreaties fell on unlistening ears. "We have tried repeatedly to negotiate in good faith with our employer, but he has consistently used the oppressive tactics of the capitalist to delay us," a Chinese ILGWU flyer explained. The resulting strike lasted three months, during which 108 workers struck and American-born Chinese and Chinese immigrant women walked the picket line together. At the time, the 105-day strike was the longest in San Francisco Chinatown's history. The workers ultimately won a new contract that included a forty-hour workweek—and a guaranteed pay raise. Not all the members were happy with it, but as Sue told them, "You have to start someplace."

The win was short-lived, as National Dollar Stores shut down the following year. But with the union's backing, Chinese workers were empowered to venture outside Chinatown's borders and break through racial barriers to find jobs in white-owned factories. Among those propelled to new opportunities? Sue Ko Lee, who later joined the ILGWU as a staff member in Local 101. "In my opinion, the strike was the best thing that ever happened," Lee told historian Judy Yung. "It changed our lives. . . . I know it was a turning point in my life."

VIVA LA HUELGA: ROSA FLORES AND THE SAN ANTONIO FARAH STRIKE

Rosa Flores never set out to become an icon. On a balmy September day in 1970, the young Chicana was just another face in a sea of workers streaming out of the Farah Manufacturing Company factory in San Antonio, Texas. But hers was the one that the news cameras happened to capture as she raised her fist and cried out, "*Viva la huelga!*"—"Long live the strike!" In the heat of the day's pro-union protest, Flores unwittingly became the face of a movement, as well as a literal poster girl. Her eye-catching image was printed on thousands of flyers and distributed around the county to rally consumers around the message "*Viva la Huelga*—Don't Buy Farah Pants!"

The boycott was launched in the midst of a contentious two-year strike that saw three thousand garment workers, 85 percent of whom were Chicanas, take on one of the largest clothing manufacturers in the U.S.—and win. Sylvia M. Trevino, the first woman to walk out that day, and Flores, who had been one of the first workers to sign a union card and display a pro-union button on the factory floor a year prior, were part of a group of tireless women workers dead set on organizing their workplace. Even though they voted overwhelmingly to unionize with the Amalgamated Clothing Workers of America (ACWA) in 1970, management refused to recognize the effort and asked the National Labor Relations Board (NLRB) to intervene. The resulting commotion put Flores in front of the cameras, and launched the factory into the public eye.

The NLRB finally ruled in the employer's favor nearly two years later, but by then, pro-union workers' organizing efforts had taken root throughout the factory. "I believe in fighting for our rights, and for women's rights," said one striker quoted in Philip S. Foner's *Women and the American Labor Movement.* "I began to realize, 'Why did I put up with it all these years? Why didn't I try for something else?'"

At the beginning, many of the Farah workers were unfamiliar with unions, or worried about retaliation from the company; most of the organizing took place clandestinely, in one-on-one conversations during breaks and in the cafeteria. The concern was justified—when word leaked, management wasted no time in cracking down on workers they suspected of supporting the union, and used intimidation, threats, and retaliation as well as heavy-handed anti-union messaging to try to bust the union drive. "When we began organizing," one woman recounted, "[the company] put even harsher supervisors who tried to humiliate people more. If there was a shortage of work on a line, they made me sweep," she said. "They did it to humiliate us and to assure that no organization would succeed."

Six workers at the San Antonio factory were illegally fired for union activity on May 3, 1972, almost immediately leading five hundred of their coworkers to walk out in protest. As news spread, Farah workers in El Paso and Victoria, Texas, and Juárez, Mexico, joined as well. These workers' days had been defined by low wages, nonexistent job security, substandard medical care, and blatant sexual harassment and racism on the job. Workers who approached retirement age were fired or forced out; those who became pregnant had no hope of maternity leave. The factory environment itself was a health hazard; workers developed respiratory illnesses from the lack of ventilation, ever-increasing quotas restricted access to the bathrooms, burdening workers with kidney and bladder infections. Still others lost fingers—or eyes—to the needles on their whirring sewing machines. As one young striker said in Manuel Castaneda's 1973 film *The People vs. Willie Farah*, "They just want to work you like dogs."

During the first week of the strike, Farah management came out swinging, hiring private guards to harass the women on the picket line and menace them with unmuzzled dogs. After the company obtained an injunction to curtail picketing, 1,008 workers were cited for violations, and many were slapped with exorbitant $400 bonds (about $2,500 in today's cash), and thrown in jail overnight. Company-side violence quickly escalated. Several strikers were hit by Farah trucks, and Willie Farah's own mother ran down a striking woman with her car. As tensions flared, the ACWA filed an unfair labor practices complaint with the NLRB, and threw its institutional weight behind the strike, as well as its financial support. Weekly $30 checks from the union's coffers didn't stretch very far in a strike composed primarily of working parents, but it was better than nothing. Before long, outside donations began to pour in from the rest of the labor movement.

The idea for a nationwide boycott came soon after. It was supported by a number of major labor unions, including the Teamsters, the United Auto Workers, and the United Farm Workers (whose own 1965–1970 boycott of Delano Grapes surely provided inspiration for the tactic) as well as the American Federation of Labor and Congress of Industrial Organizations (AFL-CIO), which had merged in 1955 and whose president, George Meany, encouraged affiliates to "Adopt a Farah Striker's Family" to gin up contributions for the cause. Meanwhile, Farah boosted its ranks with replacements and brought in Mexican workers from just across the border. Juárez, Mexico, then had a 40 percent unemployment rate that left job opportunities scarce, pushing even sympathetic workers across the picket line to join other Farah workers who had felt squeezed by intimidation and financial pressure. As one young man told the *New York Times*, "I'm working because I need the money. I have a family to support. I'm for the union and all but the way things are now with prices and everything, I've got to keep working."

The outside support was appreciated, but it was the Chicanas at the heart of the strike who kept it beating. For many of these women, the strike expanded their social and political horizons and challenged the traditional gender roles they'd long accepted as immutable; for some, those organizing meetings and pickets were the first independent activities they'd ever participated in outside of their homes and their roles as wives, daughters, and mothers. As Laurie Coyle, Gail Hershatter, and Emily Honig's pioneering *Women at Farah: An Unfinished Story* documented: "For years I wouldn't do anything without asking my husband's permission," said one Chicana striker. "I see myself now and I think, good grief, having to ask to buy a pair of underwear! Of course, I don't do this anymore. [The time of the strike was] when it started changing. All of it. I was able to begin to stand up for myself, and I began to feel that I should be accepted for the person that I am."

As the strike stretched into its second year, that initial taste of independence became a full-fledged revolution. By 1974, even with their armies of scabs to keep the factories running, Farah began to feel the pinch. The boycott hurt sales, slashing yearly revenue by $20 million; the company's stock was dropping; bad press over Willie Farah's incendiary racist statements about the strikers—he once dismissed them as alcoholic "Latin kids"—damaged the company's image; and by the end of 1973, four Farah locations had been closed down. Twenty-two months in, Willie Farah finally broke after the NLRB castigated his company for repeatedly violating federal labor law and abusing its workers. The resultant contract recognized the strikers' union, increased wages, offered a health and dental plan, and affirmed job security and seniority rights.

La huelga was over for now, but Farah's strikers were far from finished with fighting for *la causa*—the cause. Farah would spend the next few years trying to break the newly established union down again. "I felt that I was inferior to my supervisors, who were at the time only Anglo," one striker explained in *Women at Farah*. "None of this affects me anymore. I have learned that I am an equal. I have all the rights they have. I may not have the education they have, and I may not earn the money they earn. But I am their equal regardless."

Half a century later, as the coronavirus pandemic swept the globe and demand for personal protective equipment like masks and gloves skyrocketed, some retailers took advantage of the moment to score some good PR—and rake in a few extra bucks. Opportunistic designers and Etsy hobbyists alike took advantage of mask mandates to profit off the sale of cloth masks, but as local governments started handing out contracts to factories to speed up production of masks for medical personnel and other essential workers, it was garment workers who shouldered the burden. A 2016 Department of Labor survey found that 85 percent of garment shops in Southern California that were randomly selected in the investigation failed to pay the minimum wage, and relied heavily on the practice of subcontracting.

With many of those workers living in the U.S. without documents or being paid under the table, they were left unprotected by existing labor laws. When bad bosses are given the opportunity to exploit these vulnerable populations at will, it's a recipe for disaster.

The lessons of the Triangle Shirtwaist Factory fire should still serve as a dire warning for those who care about the well-being—as well as the survival—of the workers engaged in the garment industry. And yet in too many cases, that memory has been allowed to fade. In 2016, the UCLA Center for Labor Research and Education produced a shocking study of the industry called *Dirty Threads, Dangerous Factories: Health and Safety in Los Angeles' Fashion Industry*. Sixty percent of garment workers surveyed reported that poor ventilation, excessive heat, and dust accumulation in the factories made it difficult for them to work, and even to breathe. Rats, mice, and other vermin were common, bathrooms and common areas were kept filthy, and 82 percent of the workers reported having never received any kind of safety training. The most chilling part of the report—a revelation that comes straight out of 1911—showed that 42 percent of those surveyed reported seeing exits and doors in their shops regularly blocked.

The report also emphasizes how the industry runs on the exploitation of immigrant workers from Latin America and Asia. "This workforce, despite being vital to the fast fashion industry, is frequently subject to exploitative, unhealthy, and dangerous workplace conditions," it explains. "To fill the stores with a constant trendy clothing supply, manufacturers must contract low-wage labor not only in Asia but also in L.A."

During the pandemic, Los Angeles mayor Eric Garcetti looked to the city's bustling garment industry as a way to keep its manufacturing sector afloat, pressuring factories and sweatshops to remain open even as the virus decimated communities across L.A. This low-paid workforce, largely made up of immigrant Asian and Latina women (many of whom were also undocumented, barring them from receiving federal relief benefits), was ushered into crowded, windowless sweatshops to manufacture clothes and masks day after day for upward of sixty hours a week. They put their own health on the line to help protect others', but few of them were given a choice either way. They, like many other low-wage workers in this country, had few if any other options. To borrow a phrase from Mark Twain, history does not repeat itself, but it does rhyme.

Today, workers like Virginia Vasquez find themselves working under conditions that would be all too familiar to those turn-of-the-century seamstresses who lost their lives to the Triangle-era garment industry. Vasquez moved to California from Guatemala in 2009 and now works as a trimmer in a Los Angeles garment factory. Like the factory girls of old, she is paid by the piece—between 10 to 12 cents per garment—and currently takes home between $250 and $280 per week for her labor. Her counterparts on the Lower East Side in the early 1900s would have recognized the conditions Vasquez and her coworkers face as they sweat in a windowless room, where rats and roaches crawl over piles of merchandise and the women are consumed with worry for their health and well-being. As Vasquez explained to me how "the heat got trapped down there," it was hard not to think of that horrible day in 1911, and about how little has really changed.

Today's garment workers are also laboring under yet another system of financial oppression: wage theft. Wage theft, a situation in which an employer refuses to pay a worker some or all of their earnings, impacts millions of workers across multiple industries. It is especially prevalent in this one, where a 2016 analysis by the U.S. Department of Labor found wage violations in 85 percent of the 77 Los Angeles garment factories it investigated. This finding directly reinforces the Garment Worker Center's 2021 claim that

85 percent of L.A.'s garment workers experience wage theft. Workers interviewed by the *Guardian* in 2021 spoke about drawing wages as low as $6 per hour—well under the prevailing minimum wage in Los Angeles, which is the center of the country's garment production industry (California also employs the most garment workers of any state, with forty thousand in Los Angeles alone).

In 2021, the Garment Worker Protection Act (SB 62) sought to rectify the rampant wage theft in the garment industry and properly protect and compensate the workers who keep the industry running. Business interests opposed it, of course, but the workers aren't ready to give up. "With this law I will have a salary that I have never had for twenty years and I would not have to worry about wage theft," Santa Puac, a worker-organizer at the Garment Worker Center, said.

So much has changed since 1911, and yet the working class continues to be left behind, its most vulnerable communities left overworked, underpaid, and unprotected. Immigrant women of color make up the bulk of the garment industry's workforce, both in the U.S. and globally, and are forced to bear the brunt of its dangerous conditions, low pay, and high-volume output. Through decades of organizing, strikes, and knock-down, drag-out fights, they have worked to change that status quo and push back against an industry that devalues their humanity and their labor in equal measure. The century and scenes and actors may change, but the struggle remains the same: for dignity, for a living wage, for a safe workplace, for bread, and for roses, too.

As Puac said, "Every garment worker is an expert in her or his profession, and it may seem simple, but each of us has certain skills that must be respected as in all other professions. We want to be respected equally."

3

THE MILL WORKERS

They'll have to kill me to make me give up the union.

—Ella Mae Wiggins, North Carolina worker, protest singer, and labor activist

Matilda Rabinowitz was fed up. It was 1912, and the textile workers' strike she had been tasked with leading was dragging on into a cold and unforgiving upstate New York winter. The diminutive twenty-five-year-old had been called up from her home in Bridgeport, Connecticut, to help organize the strike, and found herself thrust into the midst of a bitter struggle between more than five hundred workers at a knitting mill and their unyielding bosses. The strike's original organizers, Filippo Bocchini and Rabinowitz's on-and-off romantic partner, Ben Legere, were already in jail by the time she arrived, and it fell to her to lead the strikers to victory. She was lonely and cold and tired. Her needy, incarcerated boyfriend was wearing her down, and an unfriendly local paper had recently attempted to embarrass her and discredit the strike by publishing a series of the couple's love letters. Rabinowitz, all of five feet tall and left on her own, proved that she was more than up to the challenge.

Though she was new to labor organizing, Rabinowitz was no stranger to the inside of a textile mill. She'd begun working in garment factories at the age of thirteen, as soon as she and her family first arrived from Ukraine. She took leadership in New York already well versed in the movement through her involvement in the Industrial Workers of the World (the IWW, or more commonly "the Wobblies"), a radical Chicago-based industrial union aligned with the anti-capitalist politics of the early twentieth century.

Rabinowitz now found herself on the way to an IWW meeting in upstate Little Falls, New York, greeted by corporate agents sniffing around the platform as her train pulled up. Mill bosses used surveillance and intimidation as a matter of course, and they had been alerted to the pint-sized rabble-rouser who'd already been nicknamed "the Russian beauty."

As Matilda entered the conference and was brought up to speed on what had happened thus far, she must have looked around and seen many faces like her own: immigrants from Italy, Poland, and Bohemia. Rabinowitz, who was fluent in English, Russian, and Polish, fit right in. The scene must have brought her straight back to Lawrence, Massachusetts, where she'd first gotten her feet wet volunteering for a diverse, twenty-five-thousand-worker-strong 1912 strike that stretched for more than two months in the city's booming mills—the "Bread and Roses Strike."

Inspired by a proposal from Italian workers who had seen the tactic used successfully in their native land, IWW organizers Elizabeth Gurley Flynn and Big Bill Haywood had organized a campaign to send 150 of the town's children out to stay with sympathetic IWW families in New York City, and relieve some pressure off their cash-strapped striker parents. This "Children's Crusade" would call attention to Lawrence's shockingly high child mortality rate, and the painfully low life expectancy for those sent to work there. Unexpectedly, the conflict ramped up higher when frustrated Massachusetts police blocked and viciously beat a train full of arriving strikers.

The gruesome episode drew national headlines, and goaded political leaders to intervene on the workers' behalf. In Flynn's words, it was "a day without parallel in American labor history . . . a reign of terror prevailed in Lawrence which literally shook America."

The Lawrence strike also played up the tensions between a growing, diverse, and more radically anti-capitalist element in the union movement and its conservative counterpart. The IWW's more straightlaced rival, the American Federation of Labor (AFL), maintained a contractual right to organize the mill, but had assumed that its "unskilled" immigrant laborers weren't worth their time or energy. The UTW's vehemently anti-immigrant president, John Golden, even tried to directly undermine the strike by encouraging workers to cross the picket lines, but stood down when skilled German workers joined in solidarity with the other laborers.

INNOVATION AND BLOODSHED ON THE PICKET LINE

It would be far from the first (or last) case of conflict between established labor organizations and those in need of radical solutions to address systemic inequities—in fact, it will be an obvious theme throughout this book. But the Lawrence strike's most enduring legacy was its picket lines. Pickets were not necessarily a new concept in 1912, but the way they were organized in Lawrence was revelatory; daily lines of strikers wound their way in front of the mills, skirting illegality by virtue of constant motion. In addition, it was an early attempt to directly engage the families of workers in the demonstrations, as both women strikers and the wives of the men on strike joined the picket lines, some with babes in arms. The move was not without its opponents, but as Elizabeth Gurley Flynn explained, "We resolutely set out to combat these notions. The women wanted to picket. They were strikers as well as wives, and were valiant fighters."

Those valiant women became famous for their ferocious resolve on the line. "One policeman can handle 10 men," Lawrence's district attorney griped, "while it takes 10 policemen to handle one woman." Journalist Mary Spicuzza reported much the same at the time:

> A group of enraged Italian women happened upon a lone police officer on an icy bridge. After stripping him of his gun, club and badge, they sliced the officer's suspenders and took off his pants—a humiliation technique popular with the disorderly women of Lawrence—and dangled the officer over the freezing river.

In addition to their being present on the picket lines, holding meetings, and furnishing victuals to the strikers, women also held a strong presence on the strike committee. One of them, Annie Welzenbach, who started her career in the mills at age fourteen, became known as a firebrand who confidently led parades of strikers through the streets of Lawrence each day. When she was arrested for a picketing violation, she'd go straight to another strike rally to speak, and her words held power. As one journalist who observed Welzenbach in action observed, "They say that she could tie up three of the largest mills in Lawrence by a word."

But it took more bloodshed and more suffering to get to the finish line: John Ramey, a young Syrian musician, was bayoneted by National Guardsmen during a rally. A pregnant Bertha Crouse was beaten unconscious by police on her way home from a meeting, and later miscarried. (Six months after the strike's end, Jonas Smolskas, a Lithuanian immigrant, would be murdered by a gang of men who saw his union pin.) The Lawrence strike was finally won after a grueling January-to-March stretch, and forever proved that "nontraditional" workers—women, immigrants from disparate cultural backgrounds, and non-English-speakers—could not only pull together a successful work stoppage, they could win the whole damn thing. When it came time to negotiate the final agreement, Annie Welzenbach, the terror of the bosses, was there at the table hammering out the terms.

Rabinowitz had played a bit part in the Lawrence strike, but truly came into her own at Little Falls. That strike ended on January 13, 1913, with an agreement between the town's workers and mill owners that protected returning strikers from retaliation and compelled bosses to furnish sixty hours of pay for fifty-four hours of work. It was a win, and must have been exhilarating for Rabinowitz, who immediately took her talents as a labor organizer and militant socialist back on the road, joining Elizabeth Gurley Flynn on the books as the IWW's only other paid female organizer. She spent the next three years traveling from strike to strike, from the South to the Midwest to California and back again, rallying workers at textile mills, automobile factories, steel mills, and cigar factories. Back in Lawrence, when the city's mill workers struck again in 1919 for similar reasons, they carried the lessons they'd learned years earlier through a veil of blood, sweat, and tears. The workers won again, and Rabinowitz must have smiled at the news from wherever she was by then.

While she didn't receive the kind of publicity that trailed some of her contemporaries in the IWW, Rabinowitz took a practical approach to her work, and played a pivotal role in many lesser-known strikes, like the 1913–1914 strike in Connecticut where she became known as the "Joan of Arc of Shelton" for her work organizing one thousand weavers and mill workers at the Sidney Blumenthal & Company mills. She was so effective that the company actually hired a private detective to kidnap her (luckily, he failed in his mission). As she later wrote of the Little Falls strike, "What an example it was that men and women of different backgrounds, and speaking different languages, could strive together against great odds in unbroken solidarity for three months, determined to wrest a little more life for themselves and their children."

Rabinowitz continued working as a union organizer and remained a proud Wobbly until her death in 1963. In 2017, she was inducted into Labor's International Hall of Fame as a "feminist, fighter, writer, and organizer."

OLA DELIGHT SMITH AND THE BATTLE TO ORGANIZE THE SOUTH

"This woman's personality is disgusting."

Ola Delight Smith did not make a very good impression on the Fulton Bag and Cotton Mill Company operative being paid to surveil the July 14, 1914, union meeting at which she was speaking. Smith was a railroad telegrapher by trade who had spent her childhood bouncing around the South before settling in Atlanta as an adult; she was no stranger to labor unrest, and was certainly no shrinking violet. A feminist and advocate for working-class women, Smith had made her name as a labor columnist for the *Journal of Labor* and joined her first union, the Commercial Telegraphers Union of America (CTUA), in 1904. Three years later, after she moved to Atlanta, she became involved in the 1907 Western Union telegraphers' strike—earning her a blacklisting from the company until the practice was banned almost thirty years later. Unable to depend on her sporadically employed husband, Smith worked odd jobs in secretarial work and real estate to make ends meet. And she threw herself into organizing, crusading against Georgia's child labor laws and championing economic independence for (white) women.

Smith's writing was ahead of its time for a turn-of-the-century white Progressive organizer, but like many labor leaders of her era,

Smith's version of labor solidarity was myopic, and far from inclusive or intersectional. Her approach included typical Progressive Era handwringing over "moral depravity" and sex work, and was tainted with racism, nativism, bigotry, and ambivalence toward the plight of Black workers and immigrant workers. Her focus was on white workers, and more specifically white women; that focus, coupled with her Southern location, helps explain how this middle-class railroad telegrapher ended up involved in a cotton mill strike in Georgia.

By 1914, the city of Atlanta had undergone a significant demographic shakeup. White agricultural workers poured in from surrounding rural areas, displacing Black laborers, stoking racial tension, and forcing the two groups to compete against one another for industrial jobs. The Fulton Bag and Cotton Mill had seen its first strike in 1885 over wages; then, in 1897, two hundred white women and girls at the mill struck to protest the hiring of twenty-five Black women. By the time a third strike unfolded, the mill's workforce was still primarily white, and the situation had become far more dire. These mill workers faced the same wretched conditions that plagued their Northern counterparts in Lowell and New York City, with the addition of Southern heat, an especially nasty boss, and an even nastier strain of racism underpinning life in the factory. In addition to the usual indignities of low wages and poor working conditions, mill owner Oscar Elsas was also a big fan of surveillance. He hired private spies to keep watch over his employees on the clock and off. He was also a slumlord; the workers were paid pennies, but often refused to take advantage of the shoddy company housing that was offered due to its "unspeakable" conditions. He would intentionally stoke racial tensions by forcing Black workers to evict white families from company housing, amplifying resentments and neutering any nascent workplace solidarity. For the poor white and Black workers employed there, men, women, and children included, escape must have felt impossible.

So when the AFL-affiliated United Textile Workers (UTW) came calling, the workers at Fulton Bag welcomed them with open arms. It would be the first real attempt of the twentieth century to unionize a workplace in the South—and, unsurprisingly, management was not on board. Pro-union workers were fired, and the conflict spilled over into the streets on May 14, 1914, when more than nine hundred workers—two-thirds of them women, and one hundred and thirty of them children as young as sixteen—walked off the job. Elsas, a staunchly anti-union dandy (a contemporary report described him as "assuming an air of dignity that would put a turkey gobbler to shame"), evicted eighty-five striking families as punishment, but the workers refused to waver.

As the strike picked up steam, the UTW hired Ola Delight Smith as a paid organizer. The gig meant that she could support herself financially and devote herself fully to the work of labor organizing, an almost unheard-of luxury for a woman in her position. Smith was new to the textile industry, but her enthusiasm helped fill in the gaps, and her years in the media had taught her how to harness the power of publicity. She surreptitiously photographed striking workers (including child laborers), their struggling families, and the heartless company men skulking at the margins, and hung up their photos in storefronts around town. By embracing this new technology, she was able to put a human face on the workers' struggle and drum up public sympathy as the strike dragged on (and by extension create a robust historical record for future historians and labor nerds to ponder).

Smith knew she was onto something with her media strategy, and didn't stop there. She organized a motion picture crew to film the picket lines and held screenings in a local theater to boost morale. She pitched her images to tug at the public's heartstrings: one photo, of an emaciated ten-year-old mill boy named Milton Nunnally, was made into postcards and sent around the country. Once it caught wind of it, the company fired Milton—who apparently had a hard time focusing on his work, perhaps because he was a malnourished ten-year-old boy who had earned a grand total of 24 cents for two weeks of work—for "mischief."

Smith also made a habit of documenting the undercover agents and spies who'd been brought in to weaken the strike and report on union meetings, and saw several of her cameras smashed as a result. "Thugs and spotters were ever around me," she wrote, but she took heart in her success stirring up public support. As the weeks went on, Fulton Bag trained its sights on Smith and made her the target of a virulent smear campaign. The company's men used surveillance, blackmail, intimidation, and entrapment to sully her character by insinuating that Smith was promiscuous—at the time, a catastrophic accusation to throw at a married woman—and cast the strike in a negative light. It got so bad that her absentee husband, Edgar, reappeared and, after a little monetary persuasion, sided with the company; a Fulton Mills lawyer even filed his petition for divorce. Smith countersued for cruelty and neglect, but the judge ultimately sided with her husband. The UTW buckled under the assault and, seeking to cut its losses, fired her on November 18, 1914. Workers stood up for Smith, knowing Fulton Mills' tactics all too well, but their protestations were to no avail.

With one of its lead organizers gone, the strike faltered, and by May 1915 it was over. The union had made other glaring missteps beyond firing Smith, including engaging in divisive racist rhetoric of its own, fracturing support and ceding to the will of its hungry strikers. However, the strike marked a significant moment in Southern industrial labor history, and planted seeds for rebellions to come. As for Smith, following her expulsion, she decamped to Texas, then Oregon, where she remarried, got more telegrapher jobs, and took up the pro-union cause wherever she laid her head. Despite her shoddy treatment back in Atlanta, she never lost faith, even becoming known as "the first lady of Oregon labor" by the time she passed away in 1958. "I have 'cast my bread on the waters' all through my half-century in the labor movement," she wrote before her death. "It has returned to me tenfold."

MILITANCY IN THE SOUTHERN MILLS: THE 1934 TEXTILE STRIKE

By 1934, the Great Depression had cast a pall over the entire country, but the workers of Birmingham, Alabama, were having a particularly tough go of it. During this period of economic collapse, Birmingham—which the Roosevelt administration deemed to be "the worst hit town in the country"—saw its massive steel mills close down and its coal mines left idle. The journalist Alexander Kendrick now saw fit to call the town, once a manufacturing powerhouse, a "paralyzed giant." Its cotton mills fared little better; the national textile industry had begun its decline even before the Depression really got going in 1929, and by the time Roosevelt's National Recovery Administration (NRA) was established in 1933, textile workers were champing at the bit for change. When the NRA finally bowed to popular pressure and loosened restrictions on worker organizing, union membership exploded across the country. In Birmingham alone, fifty thousand workers, the majority of them Black, rushed to join unions like the United Mine Workers of America and the International Union of Mine, Mill, and Smelter Workers (both of which were already racially integrated), and a rash of strikes blossomed across the area.

But union membership didn't magick away the crushing reality of work in the mills, and the NRA's cotton textile production apparatus showed a disappointing lack of commitment to winning material improvements for its members. In some ways, its recommendations, like cutting back hours, and its refusal to demand sufficient factory staffing levels, made things even worse. Members of the newly minted United Textile Workers Union were incensed at this state of affairs, and a strike threat got the NRA to offer the textile unions a seat on its adjudicatory board. Union leadership may have been placated by this administrative concession, but the workers weren't having it. In their eyes, the NRA had betrayed them, and they weren't going to let a bunch of red tape slow them down.

On July 16, 1934, twenty thousand textile workers at forty different cotton mills in Alabama staged a walkout. The Roosevelt administration had left it up to the National Labor Relations Board to broker a meeting between mill owners and the union, but the bosses refused to meet. On August 1, the UTW called an emergency convention to address the situation, and the membership voted to compel its leaders to declare an industry-wide general strike. The call went out, and hundreds of thousands listened.

Sixty-five thousand workers in the heart of North Carolina's Cotton Belt were the first to hit the bricks on Labor Day, September 3, 1934. For some, it wasn't their first rodeo. Just five years before, the Loray Mill in Gastonia, North Carolina, had walked out over a forty-hour workweek, a $20 minimum weekly wage, union recognition, and the abolition of staffing minimums.

As tensions rose, police began attacking the Loray strikers outright, and when the Communist-led National Textile Workers Union (NTWU) called for a mass rally on September 14, a mishmash of company agents, upset townspeople, and law enforcement officers mobilized against it. But tragedy struck before the first speaker even reached the podium. On her way to the rally, a union organizer named Ella May Wiggins was pulled out of a car full of strikers and murdered by the angry mob. At the time, she was pregnant with her tenth child.

Wiggins, whom Woody Guthrie later dubbed "the pioneer of

the protest ballad," played an integral role in the strike, and her song, "A Mill Mother's Lament," later covered by Pete Seeger, brought comfort to the strikers themselves whenever she sang it for them on the picket lines. She was no stranger to political struggle, either; despite the textile industry's endemic racism, Wiggins made a point of opposing segregation and including Black workers in her organizing efforts, and she raised her family in a Black neighborhood. Her commitment to multiracial working-class solidarity placed a target on her back, but she stood unafraid; as she once said, "They'll have to kill me to make me give up the union."

Her murder sent shock waves through the movement, and had a chilling effect on the strikers. The strike itself collapsed, but the national attention that her death brought to the workers and their cause had an important impact on future organizing efforts. So when the call came down from the United Textile Workers in 1934, the workers in North Carolina looked around at their deplorable working conditions, remembered her sacrifice, and held the line.

The 1934 textile strike spread quickly throughout the Carolinas, Alabama, Georgia, and Mississippi, and traveled north to New England, Pennsylvania, and New Jersey. Organizers employed the use of newly accessible technology—the automobile—to assemble "flying squadrons" of workers who had successfully closed down their mills and send them out to spread the strike. By utilizing novel, unpredictable tactics, the strikers were able to ambush mill owners across the South, and recruit thousands of workers to the cause.

The strike lasted just over three weeks, during which four hundred thousand workers took part. At the time, that number made it the largest strike in U.S. history, and seeing an exhibition of working-class power on that massive scale made employers and the government mighty nervous. The flying squadrons in particular set them on edge, and had mill owners crying that their workers were being "coerced" into striking. While the federal government remained hands-off, in several states the National Guard was called in to break the strike. The bloodshed and body count continued to rise, as strikers were murdered by police and National Guardsmen in places like Trion and Augusta, Georgia, and Honea Path, South Carolina. Rhode Island's governor declared martial law following a thirty-six-hour shoot-out between strikers and police in Saylesville, as did Georgia's. The latter went so far as to direct the Guard to arrest and imprison every striker in the state of Georgia in Fort McPherson, a Civil War–era army base used in World War I as a prisoner-of-war camp; while only about one hundred strikers ended up there, the draconian measure effectively ended picketing activity in the state.

Though the union itself was beginning to crumple under the pressure of organizing and attempting to feed nearly half a million workers and their families (as the strikers were denied any sort of relief from the government), it ultimately took President Roosevelt's intervention to break the strike. Upon release of a report recommending further study of the workers' plight and the creation of a Textile Labor Relations Board, FDR personally encouraged mill owners not to penalize strikers—effectively calling on the workers to end the strike. The general strike of 1934 had thrown the hellish conditions textile workers labored under into sharp relief, stirred up public sympathy for their struggle, and set a powerful precedent for organizing in the South, but those lofty effects weren't felt by the average striking worker. Few real concessions were extracted on behalf of the workers, and for many the results were even worse than the conditions that had precipitated the strike in the first place. Many never returned to work in the mills and had to find other ways to earn their daily bread.

And radicals, stirred up by the pro-labor fervor and coaxed from cities across the nation to dedicate their time—and some, their lives—to the work of organizing, had seen another effort not come to fruition. The stuff of Southern gentility-class nightmares, so called "Yankee Communist agitators," never quite materialized on the ground of North Carolina, but that's not to say that they didn't exist at all . . . or that they weren't already scattered across the country, working on an industrial scale to build one big union. The Wobblies had been busy, and more were on their way.

4

THE REVOLUTIONARIES

The time will come when our silence will be more powerful than the voices you strangle today.

—August Spies, Haymarket martyr, November 11, 1887

What is the point of a union? The answers may come easy for some—with a good contract can come guaranteed pay raises, health-care benefits, better working conditions, protection from discrimination, a voice at the table, and if you're really lucky, a pension. Those are all obvious and important perks of organizing one's workplace, but for some unionists, there's also a political, ideological, and maybe even metaphysical component at play. See, some workers expect their union to not only stick up for them on the job, but also to fight side by side with them in the class war—or, at the very least, to share their critique of capitalism and actively advocate for its downfall. For at least one union, those kinds of big, pie-in-the-sky notions are not only welcome, they're the very foundation on which it stands. The Industrial Workers of the World (IWW), more than any other union in U.S. history, has sought to exercise the power of a union not merely to serve its own members, but to shatter the exploitative systems on which this country was constructed. It is certainly the only one that managed to strike such enduring fear into the heart of the U.S. government, and to so doggedly imperil the capitalist status quo.

The IWW's mission has been simple: to organize all workers into one big union, regardless of trade, in order to build a better world. What that has often meant in practice is working to organize those whom other unions dismissed as "impossible," like women, recent immigrants, and migrant workers, and leaning on direct workplace action like strikes and protests instead of bargaining contracts with the boss. At the time of the IWW's founding in 1905, they were outliers within an organized labor movement that had only begun to pick up steam a few decades prior. Unlike most comparable unions throughout history, the IWW has always seen the working class as operating in direct opposition to the employer class. And it has set itself apart by welcoming workers of all genders, races, and creeds from the onset (later updating its constitution to add more inclusivity and to explicitly bar police, prison guards, and landlords). While the IWW welcomes all workers, it has not always been a union for the faint of heart. As its long list of working-class heroes—and martyrs—makes clear, revolutionary change can also call for revolutionary actions, and sacrifice.

During the Gilded Age, with its brutal robber barons and extravagant excesses, the IWW's radical message of equality resonated with a new generation of workers who were desperate for change. By advocating for workplace democracy, cross-industry solidarity, and welcoming all comers with open arms, the IWW offered something exciting and different. Workers were ready to listen, and opposing forces within the government and capital were listening, too. But the latter's response was all too often marked with disproportionate displays of violence and blood, now nearly unthinkable crackdowns that still echo through the labor movement today.

The IWW's founding convention in 1905 featured a marquee lineup of the twentieth century's most famed—and in some cases, notorious—leftist labor luminaries. People whose words and faces were known far and wide (and in one case, seen on the covers of magazines) during their respective eras, from the Western Federation of Miners' Big Bill Haywood and Vincent Saint John, to American Railway Union president Eugene V. Debs and United Mine Workers organizer Mary Harris "Mother" Jones. Some of those early boosters became die-hard Wobbly organizers and dedicated their political lives to the union, risking jail time, deportation, and even death as the state increased its program of surveillance and repression against the IWW. Others maintained more tenuous ties to the organization, and would find themselves pulled in different directions amid the tumultuous political landscape of nineteenth- and early-twentieth-century America.

LUCY PARSONS AND THE HAYMARKET EIGHT

The nineteenth century allowed little room for women of color to find their voices—let alone share them with the masses—and the few who did manage to break their silence often became figures of mixed curiosity and revulsion. There are few greater examples of that than Lucy Parsons. Throughout her career as a political activist and notorious public figure, Parsons would assume many roles and identities to best survive whatever circumstances she encountered. She took advantage of the ethnic ambiguity that her dark eyes, glossy black hair, and coppery complexion conferred upon her to "pass" in the predominantly white radical spaces where she made her greatest impact. As an orator, writer, and organizer, Parsons's fiery devotion to the working class endeared her to countless fed-up American workers, but little did her followers—mostly white men as racially aware as could be expected of any turn-of-the-century middle-class laborer—know that she began her story as Lucia Carter, born enslaved to mother Charlotte on Thomas J. Taliaferro's Virginia plantation. Her light skin would give her access to spaces that her darker-skinned mother and siblings would never see. Her marriage to Albert Parsons, a former Confederate soldier turned anarchist firebrand, took her from small-town Waco, Texas, to the revolutionary hub of Chicago, where the couple immersed themselves in a heady brew of radical political thought imported straight from the old country. They found a permanent political home in the burgeoning anarchist movement, and became heavily involved in the fight for an eight-hour workday.

In 1878, Lucy joined the Chicago Working Women's Union and began to find her voice as a writer, contributing anti-capitalist fiction and journalism, and ferocious opinion essays that became her calling card and would make her infamous. Her enthralling demeanor, sophisticated oratory skills, and blistering anti-capitalist rhetoric also made her a star to live crowds, defying the nineteenth-century social convention against women addressing mixed crowds. It was nothing less than extraordinary to see Lucy confidently preach fire, brimstone, and anarchy to halls full of rowdy white male factory workers.

While she was involved with multiple labor groups and was a constant fixture at union meetings and gatherings of workers throughout the city, Lucy was happy to leave the nitty-gritty shop-by-shop organizing work to more methodical compatriots like her best friend, Lizzy Swank Holmes, a fellow anarchist activist, writer, and dressmaker. Parsons had realized that harnessing her power as a public figure was her most effective means to advance the causes of labor and anarchy. All the world was a stage for the "Goddess of Anarchy," as the newspapers had dubbed her, and she intended to take it.

Lucy and Albert were also both involved with the Chicago chapters of the Knights of Labor, the first national labor organization to accept women and Black members. The Knights made strides in organizing across hierarchical and religious grounds, rejecting notions that "skilled" and "unskilled" workers could not negotiate terms as a singular force and successfully bringing together groups of Catholic and Protestant Irish workers. Unfortunately, their interpretation of multiracial class solidarity went only so far. The Knights allowed its Southern branches to hold racially segregated meetings and excluded Asian and Asian American workers; in 1882, they supported and lobbied alongside the AFL for the racist Chinese Exclusion Act. Despite their glaring flaws, the Knights of Labor did lay important groundwork for the struggles to come. At the height of their influence, the Knights boasted nearly a million members, but by the end of the nineteenth century, the organization had crumbled under the pressures of state violence, anti-leftist repression, and competition from other unions. Class conflict was reaching a historic peak in the United States, and the rise, or collapse, of insurgent groups like the Knights stood at a precipice like few others in their history. An inflection point, tinged with death, chaos, and Red Scare–style propaganda was right around the corner.

On May 4,1886, a mass meeting of workers gathered in Chicago's Haymarket Square to listen to a handful of local anarchists and labor organizers speak in support of workers at the nearby McCormick Reaper Works, who were on strike for an eight-hour workday and had been viciously attacked by police the day before. Among the speakers were Lucy's husband, Albert, August Spies, and Samuel Fielden, three anarchists who were steadfast advocates for the eight-hour workday movement that had been gathering momentum among the city's laboring classes. Albert Parsons in particular favored grandiose, often violent rhetoric in his speeches and editorials; he developed a habit of calling for workers to embrace "the dear stuff," dynamite, to make the bosses pay, but even his political opponents later admitted that his remarks on May 4 were rather tame.

Fielden was up next, and as he was finishing his speech, police arrived to break up the rally. A bomb was thrown into the path of the advancing phalanx, and the cops began firing wildly into the crowd. In less than five minutes the square was emptied, eleven people were dead, and more than seventy had been injured. Despite the fog of chaos making it nearly impossible to tell who had done what exactly in the melee, Parsons, Spies, Fielden, and fellow anarchists Adolph Fischer, George Engel, Michael Schwab, Oscar Neebe, and Louis Lingg were arrested and tried for conspiracy and murder. There was no firm evidence connecting any of the men to the bombing itself, and as one policeman who'd been present told a reporter, "A very large number of the police were wounded by each other's revolvers."

An openly hostile judge and jury, along with the public's distrust of the defendants' anarchist politics, sealed their fates. All were declared guilty, with Parsons and Spies among the four sentenced to the gallows. In the moment before he was killed, Spies let out a prophetic cry, "The time will come when our silence will be more powerful than the voices you strangle today." In death, the Haymarket Martyrs achieved a kind of secular sainthood among labor's revolutionaries, their sacrifice reverberating throughout history and their story a chilling footnote in the state's long war on dissent. Today a National Historic Landmark, the Haymarket Martyrs' Monument, stands in their honor in Forest Park, Illinois.

Lucy Parsons vowed to avenge her husband's death, and she devoted the rest of her life to keeping the memory of Albert and the Haymarket Martyrs alive and advancing their shared cause of working-class revolution. Police and politicians feared her and her militant message, which only intensified following Albert's execution. Her impassioned entreaties on behalf of suffering laborers earned her both awe and scorn from the press, which would call her a "red-mouthed anarchist" in one line and then breathlessly wax on about her beauty and fashionable dresses in the next. She had found her calling, but it came at an immense cost. While Lucy's star burned bright in the press and in the minds of sympathetic activists, the post-Haymarket crackdown decimated Chicago's anarchist community.

In 1905, when she was invited to appear at the founding convention of a new radical industrial union christened the Industrial Workers of the World, Lucy thought she'd found her niche once again. Unfortunately, she realized that the other founders saw her as more of a mascot than a comrade. Undeterred, the Widow Parsons joined anyway, and stridently pushed the IWW to ramp up its efforts for working women and children. She also founded and edited the *Liberator*, an IWW-affiliated magazine that railed against capitalist exploitation and advanced the union's cause of free speech.

Lucy Parsons was a study in contradictions, many of them of her own devising. She strove to project the image of the perfect Victorian wife and mother, even while writing columns encouraging workers to dynamite the homes of the rich. She feuded with fellow anarchist Emma Goldman over the idea of "free love," wearing her public persona of pious chastity like a mourning veil while taking on new lovers in private. Her identity as one of the best-known anarchists in America clashed with her later involvement in the Communist Party, and the harsh criticism she reserved for generations of younger anarchist activists. Her horrific treatment of her son, Albert, Jr., whom she had confined in a psychiatric institution after he expressed his desire to join the military, remains difficult to fathom.

There's no telling how much of her shape-shifting was tied to her fear of what might happen if she cast aside her protective layer of propriety and notoriety, a suit of armor for a woman of color allowed to "pass" in an overtly racist world. Albert could gamely repeat her cover story whenever he was asked about her ancestry; after he was gone, she carried the secret on her own. In one of her few instances of accurate official recordkeeping, Lucy's children with Albert—Albert, Jr., and Lulu—were marked Black on their birth certificates, yet the most famous Black woman of her time refused to tell the world who she really was. As she told a nosy reporter in 1887, "The public have no right to my past. I amount to nothing to the world and people care nothing for me. I am simply battling for a principle."

Her lifelong refusal to acknowledge her Blackness may have made it easier for her to find success within predominantly white spaces, but it also separated her from her roots, her painful memories of slavery, and what could have been an expansion of her community. It clouded her perception of the working class, which at that time included millions of formerly enslaved Black Americans who had begun to reshape the urban proletariat right in Parson's backyard. The white European Marxist analysis popular in her circles disregarded race in favor of a wholly class-based perspective, and Parsons was no exception. She focused her energies solely on agitating on behalf of white factory workers, dismissing or outright ignoring the labor struggles of Black workers in the South and in her own adopted home of Chicago. They certainly could have benefited from her talents for provocation and publicity, rendering her blind spots all the more regrettable.

Parsons took her secret to the grave. Even as her name and legend have faded out of mainstream history, America still feels her outsized impact on the campaign for the eight-hour workday, important contributions to a number of labor organizations (including the IWW and the International Ladies' Garment Workers Union), and her eloquent, unreserved rage against capitalism, workers' exploitation, and child labor. The latter point is especially poignant, because unlike so many of her contemporaries on the labor left—the bulk of whom still struggled to fully embrace their racially diverse working-class brethren—Parsons alone had begun her life working in a white man's house as a slave.

BEN FLETCHER AND THE RISE OF RACIAL CAPITALISM

Born the free son of formerly enslaved parents, Ben Fletcher was never given the option to "pass" as Parsons had, nor would he have taken it; he took pride in his Blackness. His parents had moved north following Emancipation, and Philadelphia was a logical choice for a destination. The city offered a booming maritime industry, as well as relatively progressive racial politics thanks to the influence of local abolitionist Quaker communities and its status as an important stop on the Underground Railroad. As Professor Peter Cole notes in *Ben Fletcher: The Life and Times of a Black Wobbly*, Philadelphia boasted the largest Black community in any Northern U.S. city at the time of Fletcher's 1890 birth and had become a multiracial hub for all kinds of migrant workers. Young Ben would have grown up with immigrants from Ireland, Italy, and Eastern Europe along with his Black community. That familiarity and ability to move among worlds would come in handy later as he got involved in organizing at his workplaces.

Assuming he could convince any of the city's litany of racist employers to hire him at all, Fletcher would have found few who took advantage of his education or skills. Black workers were finally able to demand payment for their toil, but those opportunities came almost solely in manual labor and domestic service. Even nominally liberal Philadelphia, with its proud abolitionist history, remained mired in systemic racism, and segregation along racial, ethnic, and gendered lines further divided the economic, social, and civic lives of its denizens. Its employer class accepted Black employees only grudgingly, assigning them the most difficult, dirty, and dangerous occupations. In Fletcher's case, that meant becoming one of at least a thousand other Black men working on Philadelphia's docks. Black workers had labored in the city's maritime industry since its colonial days, loading and unloading the same cargo ships that had traversed the Atlantic Ocean to bring them and their relatives to this country as captives, ships that then helped to propel the United States' rise as a major player in the global economy.

Fletcher was also a card-carrying member of both the IWW and the Socialist Party of America alongside a number of his Wobbly comrades, like Big Bill Haywood, Eugene V. Debs, and Hubert Harrison. Harrison, a West Indian immigrant, was known for his writing on socialism and Black liberation as well as his involvement in the 1913 Paterson Silk Strike, and was dubbed "the father of Harlem radicalism" by labor and civil rights leader A. Philip Randolph. As a fellow Black Wobbly, Fletcher's involvement with Harrison in both entities spoke volumes about his personal and political commitment to working-class liberation, but it was his work with the IWW that would come to define his weighty contributions to American labor in general, and to Black workers in particular.

By 1912, Fletcher had already become a well-respected figure among the thousands of dockworkers who kept Philadelphia moving. His coworkers on the docks, a full half of which were Black, reflected the racially diverse neighborhood that had raised him. Fletcher spoke directly to their struggle in his speeches at local IWW meetings and in the union's newspaper, *Solidarity*, drawing direct lines between the subjugation of the Black worker, the racist, capitalist exploitation that defined their working lives, and the promise of uniting workers along industrial lines. His speeches deftly illustrated the concept of "racial capitalism" nearly a century before Cedric Robinson defined the term in his 1983 book, *Black Marxism: The Making of the Black Radical Tradition*.

Fletcher also pulled no punches when addressing racism and discrimination within the labor movement itself. In 1913, during a grueling strike that called out four thousand workers and paralyzed the docks, both the IWW and the AFL-affiliated International Longshoremen's Association headed to Philadelphia to solicit the striking workers to join their respective unions. The Wobblies won out, and Ben Fletcher emerged as a leader of the newly christened Local 8 branch of the IWW's Marine Transport Workers Industrial Union. Local 8 was immediately home to the IWW's largest contingent of Black members, which made up a third of the chapter. Fletcher's vision for the advancement of his community through labor action was coming together. "[Industrial unionism] is the abolition movement of the 20th century," he wrote in a letter to the *Baltimore Afro-American* in 1920. "And if sufficient number of workers rally to its standard, complete industrial emancipation will be the heritage of all us workers and we will become disenthralled from the thralldom of the rich."

The race to organize the docks had been contentious, but the continued tolerance of bigotry within the local branches of the AFL and labor at large proved to be a decisive factor. A 1923 essay Fletcher wrote for A. Philip Randolph's labor periodical the *Messenger* characterized the mainstream U.S. labor movement's attitude toward Black workers as "replete with gross indifference and, excepting a few components . . . a record of complete surrender before the color line," continuing, "organized Labor for the most part, be it radical or conservative, thinks and acts in the terms of the White Race." He went on to laud the efforts of interracial industrial unions like the IWW, the United Mine Workers of America, and the Amalgamated Textile Workers for organizing across racial lines, while also calling for a "nation-wide movement" of Black workers to harness the power of their labor on their own terms. Fletcher's thinking had less in common with Lucy Parson's class reductionist analysis than fellow Wobbly Hubert Harrison's pre-Garveyite "New Negro Movement," a militant class-conscious precursor to the Harlem Renaissance.

Local 8 would control Philadelphia's waterfront for the next decade as one of the IWW's strongest and most effective locals. Fletcher himself became a bit of a celebrity, well known up and down the East Coast as a traveling organizer and speaker, and spent time organizing Black dockworkers in Boston, Baltimore, and Norfolk, Virginia. He traveled to IWW conventions in Chicago, befriending Elizabeth Gurley Flynn and writing approvingly of Matilda Rabinowitz's work on the Little Falls textile mill strike. In 1916, a crowd of racist white men in Norfolk instigated a fight with Fletcher during one of his speeches by pressing him for his opinion on miscegenation, a then-controversial issue. Fletcher shut down the mob with a characteristically witty response, but had to leave town under the cover of darkness for fear of being lynched. A year later he and his first wife, Carrie Danno Bartlett, a white woman, married in a time when about half of the U.S. states still had anti-miscegenation laws on the books.

THE UNITED STATES OF AMERICA VS. THE WOBBLIES

Fletcher's work went swimmingly up until 1917, when the U.S. plunged into World War I. The conflict stirred up a frenetic outpouring of patriotism that spelled doom for political dissidents and labor agitators. The IWW itself was riven by disagreements over whether the union should come out in opposition, but the union ultimately decided to leave the question up to its individual members. Nonetheless, dark clouds of suspicion were cast on anyone who seemed less than thrilled about sending working-class youth to die in an imperialist war overseas.

In Philadelphia, Local 8 pledged not to strike while the war was on (save for the annual one-day strike honoring the union's anniversary); hundreds of its members joined the military and bought "liberty bonds" to fund the war effort. Fletcher himself had a brother on the front lines, and he was among those leaders who urged the membership to support the war effort (or at least, not to actively oppose it). Yet he was among the 166 Wobblies snatched up by the Department of Justice in a massive sweep on September 5, 1917.

The nation's entry into World War I had been accompanied by the passage of a portentous series of bills: the 1917 and 1919 Espionage Acts and the 1918 Sedition Act. Together they essentially made it illegal to publicly criticize the government, the military, the draft, or the flag itself, and law enforcement took the opportunity to ramp up its long-running war on anti-capitalist, pro-worker organizing. Philadelphia's district attorney made the government's intentions clear when he described the September 1917 raids as having been launched "very largely to put the IWW out of business." Its members were slapped with a litany of draconian charges like conspiring to strike, interfering with the draft, mail fraud, and, of course, violating the broadly written Espionage Act. The trial dragged on for four months, and its result was devastating. Despite Local 8's peaceful reputation and support for the war, as well as Fletcher's own role in orchestrating that support, the twenty-seven-year-old was sentenced to ten years in federal prison and fined $30,000 (roughly $541,356 in 2021 currency). As the sentencing was read, Fletcher quipped wryly to his friend and fellow defendant Big Bill Haywood, "The judge has been using ungrammatical language. . . . His sentences are much too long!"

Gallows humor aside, the situation was dire. Fletcher and ninety-three other Wobblies were shipped off on a special "convict train" to the United States Penitentiary in Leavenworth, Kansas. Nicknamed "Hell's Forty Acres," Leavenworth has long held a fearsome reputation in the popular imagination as a storehouse for the worst of the worst, and during Fletcher's time there, he and his fellow Wobblies were subjected to all manner of abuse, neglect, and torture amid the prison's squalid conditions. The FBI surveilled all of the political prisoners and monitored Fletcher's correspondence for "Negro agitation," though Ben's frequent contributions to the *Messenger* during this time indicate the efforts were unsuccessful. While he and the others were stuck in a living hell in Kansas, their IWW comrades outside raised money and launched appeals for their release. With the end of World War I, the public skepticism toward the hundreds of wartime arrests led to a flood of releases between 1920 and 1921—among them Fletcher, who immediately dove back into his work with Local 8.

A few years later, he and his second wife, a Black nurse named Clara, moved to New York City, where Fletcher set up an IWW recruiting office and spoke out in support of striking coal miners in Harlan County, Kentucky. It seemed as though his time in prison had not dampened Fletcher's revolutionary zeal, or his core belief that the capitalist system as it existed could not stand for long—if only he and his fellow workers fought hard enough to seize it.

Fletcher remained active until 1933, when a serious stroke sent his health into a sharp decline. That same year, President Franklin Delano Roosevelt finally pardoned him and many of his fellow Wobblies who had been sent to prison more than a decade earlier. Fletcher died in 1949, having devoted his life to the cause of the multiracial working class and laid the groundwork for the next decades of struggle. As he wrote in the *Messenger* in 1923, "It is to be hoped that in the near future, all labor will be united for one common cause. It is an undeniable fact that all labor has something in common: a desire for a higher standard of living. This can only be attained through interracial solidarity in the mixed union."

DR. MARIE EQUI, PORTLAND'S "QUEEN OF THE BOLSHEVIKS"

Ben Fletcher was not the only Wobbly to suffer a long prison stint as punishment for service in the class war. Oregon's Dr. Marie Equi was a former teen textile worker who became a highly respected doctor, known for assisting the poor and unemployed, administering abortions to those who needed them, and throwing herself wholeheartedly into the struggle for women's suffrage. Much of what we know about her now is thanks to Nancy Krieger's in-depth biographical profile, "Queen of the Bolsheviks," in a 1983 issue of the journal *Radical America*. Equi was also one of the Pacific Northwest's most prominent lesbians, and held true to her principles even when it seemed like the entire world—or at least, the entirety of the U.S. government—was against her. One of her first appearances in the *Oregonian* concerned her horsewhipping a boss who'd stolen wages from a romantic partner—one of countless moments that earned her "Queen" moniker.

Equi took special care to ensure that the most economically disadvantaged women could access her services, pioneering a sliding scale model in which rich patients were charged more to subsidize the cost of treating poorer ones. A lifelong outsider, she was unbothered by the social stigma and potential legal implications surrounding her work. Her friend Lew Levy once explained, "She did most of it for nothing, because working-class women needed it. If they could, they paid, if not, not."

Her abortion work placed Equi at odds with many of her cohort in the Progressive movement, and she gradually found herself drifting into more radical waters. When women workers at a fruit cannery on Portland's east side walked out, she was called to one of the workers' homes to render medical attention. It was the height of cherry season, in which women were expected to work for 5 to 8 cents an hour in filthy conditions; when two hundred of them walked out in protest, the ensuing battle became one of the Pacific Northwest's first strikes led by women workers. As Equi passed by the picket line en route to a house call, she recognized several of her former patients among the strikers. When they invited her to join, she hopped up on a barrel and began to exhort the workers still inside the plant to come out and join the strike. The initial protest turned into a full-fledged labor battle, and Equi's commanding presence became a fixture on the increasingly volatile picket lines. Local police grew more emboldened as it went on, charging the strikers on horseback as the women faced off against them in the streets. Equi herself got wrapped up in the violence, once nabbed for stabbing a policeman with a steel hatpin, and found herself radicalized by the walls the cherry workers found themselves pushed up against. The final vestiges of her faith in liberal government reform fell away, and she was reborn a revolutionary. "I started in this fight a socialist but I am now an anarchist," she proclaimed. "I'm going to speak where and when I wish. No man will stop me."

That commitment to free speech was a defining aspect of the IWW's activism in the twentieth century. Unlike modern interpretations that have been twisted by subsequent generations of bad-faith right-wing reactionaries, the Wobblies' definition of free speech was simple, and served as a defining plank in their organizing strategy. They fought for the basic right to speak in public, to stand on their soapboxes and spread their message of industrial unionism, anticapitalism, and the One Big Union to whoever wished to listen. Under the First Amendment, this should have been a moot point, but as these free speech fights exemplified, there was and still is a yawning gap between theory and practice when it comes down to who is actually allowed to exercise that right. Before the advent of television and radio, soapboxing—setting up a literal box to stand on while speaking to a crowd—was a popular means of mass communication used by politicians, actors, preachers, and activists alike. Major free speech fights broke out in Spokane, Washington; Missoula, Montana; Kansas City, Missouri; Sioux City, Iowa; and San Diego, California; as well as in Portland, Oregon, where the IWW caught wind of the cannery strike and showed up with soapboxes at the ready. It was here that Marie Equi's leftist political awakening, her memories of a working-class childhood, and the scars of systemic inequality she saw etched into her patients' bodies each day, fully crystallized. She threw her lot in with the Wobblies, and while the cannery strike failed, the movement writ large gained a giant.

When the U.S. entered World War I, Equi's fiercely antiwar stance set her apart from her peers in Portland, but as per usual, she rejected the calls to moderate her message in the face of public disapproval. A pro-war parade saw Equi join uninvited, incendiary banner in tow: "Prepare to die, workingmen, JP Morgan & Co. want preparedness for profit." Those bold actions earned Equi a target on her back, one that would ultimately land her in the same hot water that had burned Ben Fletcher. On May 16, 1918, President Wilson signed an amendment to the 1917 Espionage Act aimed at further curtailing dissent against the war. The silencing summer that followed saw Equi snatched up by police on June 30, 1918, the same day fellow Wobbly and socialist labor leader Eugene V. Debs was taken in for sedition. The state devoted considerable resources to secure a conviction for Equi, and her trial saw the worst of the era's homophobia and Red Scare hysteria.

Equi was determined to fight back on behalf of free speech, herself, and the right to live and love as one prefers. She launched a lengthy appeal that freed her to continue her work and set the stage for her "last hurrah," an armed confrontation between the IWW-backed striking shingle factory workers and vigilantes hired by factory owners in Everett, Washington, that left five Wobblies dead and saw Equi rush to the victims' aid. Less than a year later, with her appeal dead in the water, Equi began a year of incarceration in October 1920.

Though she defiantly told her supporters, "I'm going to prison smiling," the experience left her profoundly shaken. Equi continued to advocate for free speech and workers' rights throughout her life, even if at a lower volume than before. Her last recorded appearance as a labor agitator came in 1934, when a sixty-two-year-old Equi was spotted on the picket line of a multi-union Portland maritime strike. She said her hellos and headed down to the nearby union hall to donate $250 (more than $5,000 in 2021 currency) to the cause. The workers won the 1934 West Coast waterfront strike, and they remembered her dedication years later. In 1952, after they heard the news of then eighty-year-old Marie Equi's death from renal disease, the dockworkers' union passed a resolution in honor of their old friend. They declared Equi to have been a powerful fighter for the working class, who had braved "personal danger and hardships to preserve peace, freedom of speech, and the right of labor to organize." It was a fitting epitaph for this remarkable woman.

THE BLOODY RESPONSES TO REVOLT

As much as Equi, Fletcher, and Parsons suffered for their involvement with the IWW, they got off easy compared with the misfortunes that befell some of their counterparts. In 1915, Swedish-born songwriter and poet Joe Hill, perhaps the most famous Wobbly of them all, was executed by firing squad in Utah after being convicted of a murder he almost certainly did not commit. During his short life, he penned some of the Wobblies' most beloved labor songs, including labor movement mainstays like "There Is Power in a Union" and "Rebel Girl," which he dedicated to Elizabeth Gurley Flynn, and his last words to Big Bill Haywood have since been taken up as a rallying cry—"Don't waste any time in mourning. Organize!" At his request, his ashes were portioned out into hundreds of small envelopes that were then distributed to IWW members across the country (and as an official IWW delegate from Oregon, Marie Equi assisted in engineering the dispersal). Most of said ashes ended up scattered to the winds or on IWW graves, but some have had a more eventful afterlife, disappearing down the gullets of various Wobblies and Hill supporters (as legend has it, modern-day British musician and lefty activist Billy Bragg washed a portion down with a swig of union-made beer).

But few of these violent anti-IWW episodes stand up to the gruesome fate of Frank Little. Born in Oklahoma in 1879, Little was of mixed European and Indigenous heritage, and became known throughout the West for his success in organizing miners, lumberjacks, dockworkers, and farmworkers on the frontier, as well as for his lopsided grin—the disfigurement a jaunty reminder of a childhood accident. His life in labor began as a member and then organizer for the Western Federation of Miners, but in 1905 he joined the IWW and never looked back. Like Mother Jones, he agitated on the behalf of workers in many industries, but he had his most formative and impactful experiences working with miners. Like his predecessor Lucy Parsons, Little turned to personal embellishment when it suited him, playing up his Indigenous ancestry and styling himself a "half-breed hobo agitator" as he became more heavily involved in IWW organizing. Little used his alleged connection to the first Americans as a means of relating to workers of color, and to deflect criticism of the IWW as an "anti-American" organization. He had been raised in a diverse multiracial environment and was comfortable around people of different races and ethnicities, an asset during his first assignment for the WFM: organizing striking Mexican copper miners in Clifton and Morenci, Arizona.

There, the mine bosses (who would eventually consolidate under the Phelps Dodge banner) operated a racist two-tiered system in which Mexican laborers were forced to live in the most rundown, squalid dwellings available. Little overcame the workers' suspicion of the WFM—which it had earned through years of refusal to organize workers of color—by printing multilingual union literature, working hand-in-hand with Mexican-American organizers like Fernando Velarde, and engaging with local *mutualistas*, Mexican community aid societies, to reach more of the workforce. And it worked, cementing his reputation as a smart, resourceful labor organizer. Little then hit the road, becoming enmeshed in labor actions and free speech fights from Montana to Missouri, winning (and losing) strikes, infuriating bosses and cops, crossing paths with the likes of Elizabeth Gurley Flynn, and ascending to a leadership role within the IWW's General Executive Board.

Agitation ran in the family; his sister-in-law, Emma Harper Little, was a devoted Wobbly in her own right, juggling life as a miner's wife with a project to expand her political horizons. She was a constant source of support and solidarity throughout Frank's life, and broadcast her own views on socialism and the working class in IWW publications and local newspapers.

The spotlight made the Littles a target, both for labor work and their antiwar views. Frank was routinely threatened with political and physical harm. He was kidnapped and held at gunpoint during a 1913 dockworker strike in Minnesota, dealt a brutal beating two years later by company men in Wisconsin, and suffered a hernia after being jumped in El Paso, Texas, in 1917. He grew accustomed to the violence, and friends would later say that in life Frank saw his potential martyrdom as more fact than fancy.

The summer of 1917 would see Frank Little travel to his final labor action, in Butte, Montana, to help organize striking copper miners at the Anaconda Mining Company. He arrived already struggling—in terrible pain from the beating anti-union goons had dished out in El Paso, nursing a fractured ankle that saw him rely on crutches to move from meeting to meeting. He tucked them under his bed when he went to sleep the evening before August 1, 1917, when armed men burst into his room and dragged him out of his bed before daylight. He wore only underwear as the six assailants tied him to the rear bumper of their sedan and dragged Little along behind them down a granite-paved road leading out of town. He was likely unconscious, if not already dead, when they slipped a noose around his neck and left him to hang. None of his murderers were ever arrested, and Frank Little's body was laid to rest under a gravestone bearing his name and, in one final work of agitation, the inscription **"SLAIN BY CAPITALIST INTERESTS FOR ORGANIZING AND INSPIRING HIS FELLOW MEN."**

In the wake of Frank's violent end, sister-in-law Emma threw herself into extending the family's legacy in the labor movement. She tirelessly chronicled the IWW's history in scrapbooks and letters, a crucial exercise for an organization perpetually at risk of attack and erasure by state and corporate force. Federal agents would pester Emma, and raided her home and her records, even in front of her frightened children, frequently throughout her life. Nonetheless, Emma retained the signature Little fearlessness, ascending to her own era of labor leadership as head of the Women's Union Label League in Fresno, California. As Wobblies all around her were hunted down and charged with sedition, she wrote a letter directly to President Wilson demanding the return of a manuscript his agents had stolen during one of their raids on her home. While he never answered, the FBI never darkened Emma Harper Little's doorstep again.

5

THE MINERS

I prefer coal dust to a powder puff. And I'd rather use a crosscut saw than a golf club. That may sound unladylike, but every woman to her own desires. Mine is digging coal.

—Ida Mae Stull, pioneering Ohio coal miner

Ida Mae Stull always knew she was different. Born with what she'd later call a "twisted-up leg," the coal miner's daughter used leg braces to get around her hometown of Scio, Ohio, in her youth. Even when she was a grade-schooler, the independent streak that would make her famous was already on full display. She refused to be shamed for her disability, by her classmates or anyone else, and as she later told the *Chicago Tribune*, at just seven years old, Ida declared that she was finished with being disrespected at school. "Ain't nobody going to laugh at me."

Newspaper reports disagree on at exactly what age Stull first entered the mines herself; some say twelve, others say eight, and after her legend had grown, a few even claimed a tender age of six. Regardless of what the calendar said, it's a fact that she was only a little girl when she started following her father underground to help dig coal. At first she was a helper, carrying her dad's lantern and pushing the coal cart ahead at his side. But as she got older and stronger, she became a formidable miner in her own right, regularly hauling out six or seven carts a day for her $2 daily wage.

A teenaged Stull worked alongside her husband in a small eastern Ohio country bank "drift mine"—an independent operation dug out of the Appalachian hills by hand. By 1933, in her mid-thirties, she had become part owner of a mine near Jewett, Ohio—a first for a woman in the mining business. Things were going pretty well for her and her family; the mortgage was paid, the kids were thriving, and Stull was doing what she liked best—avoiding "women's work" around the house and digging coal. Photos of her from that period show a tall, statuesque woman with muscled forearms, a steely squint, and a determined set to her jaw.

But in late January 1934, word kicked up about federal mine inspectors sniffing around Ida Mae's business. She saw a mortal threat to everything she had worked for over the past two decades.

Stull wasn't working alone in the mines anymore; desperate for labor, operators had been forced by the Great Depression to (at least temporarily) suspend their prejudices and allow women underground to work alongside the men. Though Appalachian women like Stull had been quietly working in family-owned mines for decades, Ohio state law forbade "the weaker sex" from engaging in a host of manual labor jobs, coal mining included. Stull was both pioneer and outlaw, and she knew that the lawmen would find her eventually. When the day finally came in early February, her female coworkers hid while Stull prepared to give their visitor proper welcome.

"I knew he was coming to put me out, so I put some rotten eggs in my coal cart," she'd later explain. "I started throwing, and chased that inspector out of the mine to his car and covered the car besides. I really stunk him up!"

Ida Mae's valiant efforts notwithstanding, James Derry, chief of Ohio's Bureau of Mines, responded to her stunt with an order that she leave her job at once. Stull appealed the order and took the fight to court, where the press dubbed her the "Amazon of the coal pits" and seemed to regard her with a mixture of derision and awe. Her stern, snappy one-liners during interviews helped solidify her reputation as a woman it was best not to cross. (One choice sound bite: "I could show that mine inspector a thing or two when it comes to muscle"). Ultimately, Stull's ownership stake proved to be the determining factor, and she was allowed to return to work in 1935.

Despite the headaches and the hassles, Stull liked her job, and was furious at the implication that her time would be better spent in the kitchen doing what she termed "baby work." Moreover, she was good at it. A 1935 article marveled, "Any miner in the district will admit that she's his equal physically," and Stull herself took pride in her ability to outwork her male counterparts. She didn't mind the hard labor, the dirt, or the coal dust; to her, it was vastly preferable to a more traditional life indoors. "Overalls, boots, and a miner's cap suit me better than silks, slippers, and a butterfly hat," she told one reporter. "My face gets black, but I prefer coal dust to a powder puff. And I'd rather use a crosscut saw than a golf club. That may sound unladylike, but every woman to her own desires. Mine is digging coal."

Stull's mining career ended in 1944. Her husband died that year, and without her partner by her side, she found she'd lost her taste for coal. She spent the next forty years in peaceful obscurity, caring for her children, grandchildren, and great-grandchildren and scraping out a living on her farm in Scio. True to form, she prided herself on her self-sufficiency and ability to work well into her old age. In one of her last interviews, she made it plain that her fighting spirit had never faded. "I still got my strength," she told the reporter. "Ain't afraid of man or woman, and I can still find coal in these hills." Ida Mae Stull died on April 23, 1980 at the age of eighty-four.

WOMEN BREAK OPEN THE MINES OF APPALACHIA

Stull may have been the nation's best-known "lady coal miner," but she'd be far from the last. It did take several more decades and a federal ruling before women workers were legally (though not warmly) welcomed into the coal mines. The 1964 Civil Rights Act, which outlawed employment discrimination on the basis of race, color, religion, sex, or national origin, and President Johnson's 1967 Executive Order 11375, which strengthened enforcement of the policy barring hiring discrimination on the basis of sex, removed the last major legal hurdles for women who wanted to work in the mines.

Diana Baldwin and Anita Cherry of Kentucky were at the forefront of the mid-century battle to integrate women workers into Appalachia's coal mines, and are often erroneously cited as America's first women coal miners (one imagines that the ghost of Ida Mae Stull would like a word about that!). But they were trailblazers in their own right as the first women members of the United Mine Workers of America hired to work inside a mine. The year prior, four women had applied for work underground at the Clinchfield Coal Company in Cleveland, Virginia, igniting a debate within the local mining community over whether or not they should be accepted; reactions were mixed, but the women themselves held firm. "The people who say a woman's place is in the home are the people who can afford to," Catherine Tompa, one of the eight applicants, said in a 1973 issue of the *United Mine Workers Journal*. "We want these jobs for one reason: money. We work hard now and we expect to be given the same jobs as the men have. If we can't do it, we'll admit we're wrong."

The company simply refused to respond to their applications, and without the support of the union—who feared layoffs and whose seniority rules dictated that UMWA members be hired for whatever jobs were available—the women were put off. Their mission may have been thwarted by outside forces, but times had changed and attitudes had shifted too far to keep the dam from breaking. As Tompa said in 1973, when she was planning to send in her application to the mine, "I had been watching a show on television the night before. There was one of those women's lib people on from New York. When I thought of men making all that money in the mines, I figured we could, too." Less than a year later, two of Tompa's like-minded Southern sisters would prove her right and finally succeed in kicking open a door that had been wedged shut for centuries.

Diana Baldwin, a twenty-five-year-old former hospital receptionist, and Anita Cherry, a thirty-nine-year-old former practical nurse, began working at Beth-Elkhorn Coal Corporation's Mine 29 in Jenkins, Kentucky, in 1973. They applied for the same reason that most coal miners of any gender apply—the pay was good, and they needed the money. Several of their family members who'd previously worked in the mines tried to discourage them from applying. They thought tales of bloody accidents on the job and the black lung disease that had stolen their breath would put the notion to rest. But these women were resolute; they both had children to feed and bills to pay, and as Baldwin told a *New York Times* reporter in 1974, "We can make more than twice as much money in the mines as we could at the hospital."

In 2016, Baldwin's daughter, Lori, revealed how difficult the work environment had been for her mother, especially in the beginning. "I can remember times when my uncles had to take her to work because she was getting threats—threats of being tarred in the mines," she said. "But she was determined. She had three kids to support, and that's what she did."

Like Ida Mae Stull before her, Baldwin developed a particular affinity for the work, spending two decades working underground before eventually becoming a safety inspector for the Mine Safety and Health Administration. And she found no shame in the profession or the implications of being a woman doing "men's" work. Quite the opposite, in fact. "I was the first woman to operate a shuttle car with coal," she told the Associated Press in 1973. "There was one man who stood at one end and one who stood at the other and he says, 'Do you know you're making history?' That thrilled me to death."

The number of women working in the mines nearly doubled between 1970 and 1975, but legalization didn't mean that mine owners suddenly rushed to hire them. The scales were still weighted against them, but Betty Jean Hall, a lawyer from eastern Kentucky, was more than prepared to tip them back again. In 1977, Hall cofounded the Coal Employment Project, a nonprofit organization that sought to train women and extend employment opportunities in the Appalachian mining industry. Hall's survey of the communities local to the mines found demand still far outstripped the supply of mining jobs available to women.

So CEP got to work, and successfully used the courts to bring recalcitrant coal companies to heel. In 1978, Hall filed a complaint against 153 of the nation's largest coal companies, alleging mass hiring discrimination; when they lost the suit, coal bosses were forced to pay thousands of dollars in back pay to women who had been denied mining jobs, and to agree to balance out the gender disparities in their workforce.

Coal companies grudgingly implemented affirmative action programs as a result of that lobbying, but women remained unwelcome underground. They were given the hardest, dirtiest work to encourage them to quit, and "last hired, first fired" policies were poison to their cause. Those who did find steady work underground often saw the work itself as easier to handle than their coworkers. The laws barred sex discrimination at work, but it was rampant in the mines. Women miners in the 1970s and 1980s were subject to bullying, disrespect, sexual harassment, and even sexual assault. For many women, the route to their subterranean workplaces must have felt like heading straight down into Hell.

"I was attacked in the mine by a man, and he threatened to rape me," West Virginia coal miner Darla Baker told the Associated Press in 1982. "A supervisor and a group of men sat and watched the whole thing." One year prior, Baker and eight other women had sought damages from Consolidation Coal in Pittsburgh, Pennsylvania, for sexual harassment and invasion of privacy. In this case management had refused to act when a peephole was discovered in the wall of the women's bathhouse, but the culture of sexual harassment was already a widespread problem in the mines for years prior. Black workers like Baker's fellow plaintiffs Shirley Freeman and Mary Johnson were forced to contend with racist abuse as well; after rejecting the advances of her white supervisor, Freeman heard him swear, "I'll work that Black bitch until she quits." Instead, she and her sisters fought back, and won a settlement in 1982. They were part of a new wave of women coal miners who turned to collective action and the courts to combat the discrimination and harassment that was so prevalent in their industry, and sought to clear the path for the next generation.

BLACK LABOR AND THE COAL CREEK WAR

During her era, Ida Mae Stull was widely recognized as "the first woman to work in the coal mines," but as Roland L. Lewis's seminal 1987 book *Black Coal Miners in America: Race, Class, and Community Conflict, 1780–1980* notes, it's more accurate to say that she was the first woman who publicly *chose* to work there. As early as 1760, enslaved Black women were being forced to labor in the Virginia coalfields as domestic workers, handling the cooking, childcare, and cleaning while their male counterparts were sent underground. And there is evidence that some were even sent into the mines to dig coal.

For example, in 1821, a Virginia slave owner listed three Black women as laborers in his mine, and in 1864, the Shelby Iron Company in Shelby, Alabama, listed at least one Black woman among its enslaved workforce. It stands to reason that there were others, perhaps dozens or even hundreds of other enslaved Black women, who were sent down into the darkness to hammer away at the unforgiving rock below. History has forgotten their names—or, more likely, never cared to ask. Unlike Ida Mae Stull, they had no choice in the matter, and neither did the enslaved Black men who worked alongside them.

In the nineteenth century, the Appalachian coalfields were predominantly staffed by white men with ancestral roots in England, Ireland, Scotland, and Northern Europe, but Black coal miners made up a significant percentage of the workforce before, during, and after the Civil War. Following Emancipation, some formerly enslaved Black workers chose to continue working in the coalfields, but thanks to a diabolical practice called "convict leasing," many more found themselves sent back down into the mines against their will. Convict leasing—a racialized forced penal labor system in which incarcerated people were "leased" out to local industrialists or farmers and forced to work for free—spread throughout the South and became a major force in propping up its faltering post-Confederate economy. Coal mine operators in Georgia, Alabama, and Tennessee came to depend on convict leasing to provide cheap labor, and to uphold the white supremacist racial hierarchy that kept their prisons—and their mines—full of Black men.

Those incarcerated workers were treated horribly, fed poorly, frequently injured or killed on the job, and didn't see a dime of the hundreds of thousands (if not millions) of dollars their labor generated for rich white men. While politicians, like Georgia senator

Joseph E. "the Convict King" Brown, and mine owners raked in profits, incarcerated Black miners worked "in such places as rendered it necessary for them to lie on their stomachs . . . often in mud and water with bad ventilation, in order to get out the daily amount of coal that would save them from the punishment to be inflicted by the whipping boss," reported an 1890 Georgia legislative committee.

Black incarcerated workers were also used as leverage against attempts to organize workers in the mines. They were frequently brought in to act as strikebreakers during work stoppages, and their minuscule leasing fees helped bosses keep labor costs down at the expense of more highly paid union workers. For the mine owners, the cost savings came first, but the racial animus incited by moves like these was more than welcome. Between 1891 and 1892, Tennessee's Coal Creek War catapulted the issue of convict leasing onto the national stage. In April the Tennessee Coal Mining Company had rejected a suite of demands from its employees, and instead shut down its mine outside Briceville, Tennessee, in retaliation. Later that summer the company tore down miners' homes to build a stockade to house a new staff of involuntary, incarcerated laborers, and reopened.

Three hundred miners promptly rushed the stockade, released the incarcerated workers, and put them on a train headed out of town. Aided by the governor, the coal bosses ferried the convict laborers back—only to be met with two thousand miners this time. This game of cat-and-mouse continued for months, culminating in late October, when three stockades were burned and more than three hundred incarcerated workers were clothed, given food, and set free by the miners (most were recaptured, but 165 of them escaped to freedom). Hundreds of miners were arrested for the part they played in the Coal Creek War, but their point had been made, and a serious blow had been struck against convict leasing in Tennessee, which became one of the first Southern states to abolish the practice, in 1896.

Convict leasing continued apace elsewhere despite the wretched conditions and vocal opposition from abolitionists and reformers (as well as, one would assume, the incarcerated workers themselves, though few people thought to ask them their opinion on the matter). It was simply too profitable, and Black prisoners were seen as too expendable, to warrant changing a system that filled state coffers and funneled profits to a powerful elite. Georgia eventually did away with the practice in 1908, and most other states followed suit. But Alabama, whose economy was deeply dependent on convict labor, dragged its heels. The state did not formally abolish convict leasing until 1928, following public outcry over the brutal murder of James Knox, a Black man who'd been imprisoned for forging a $30 check and was whipped to death by overseers a few days after he was sent into the mines.

Outside of the coalfields, enslaved Black men, women, and children could also be found laboring in the salt mines of West Virginia, in an industry that also enthusiastically embraced convict leasing. As historian Cyrus Forman told the *Los Angeles Times*, at the height of the West Virginia salt industry, there were "sixty salt furnaces burning twenty-four hours a day, seven days a week. . . . three thousand enslaved people were working nonstop." Before embarking on his illustrious career as an educator and activist, Booker T. Washington, the son of enslaved parents, spent part of his childhood working in the salt furnaces of the Kanawha Salines. "Though I was a mere child, my stepfather put me and my brother at work in one of the furnaces," he explained in his autobiography. "Often I began work as early as four o'clock in the morning." At the time, Washington was nine years old. One of the area's largest salt furnaces, Dickinson & Shrewsbury, still exists today, now revived as the artisanally branded J. Q. Dickinson Salt-Works. Washington grew up a stone's throw away from where the company's original headquarters once stood; there's even a walking tour that guides intrepid travelers along the route between the old salt furnace and a re-creation of his childhood cabin, in case they feel some desire to retrace his small, weary steps.

Given the virulent racism and white supremacist rhetoric that underpinned much of post-Reconstruction society, it is a small wonder that Black workers were able to find a home within the traditional boundaries of organized labor. While the majority of unions in the U.S. remained segregated for a repulsively long stretch of time, there were notable exceptions; among them were the United Mine Workers of America, which operated on an industrial scale and organized Black workers alongside white ones. Racism and prejudice proliferated within the leadership as well as the rank and file, yet the very fact that Black members were welcomed into the fold (in theory if not always in practice) helped make the UMWA the largest and most diverse union in America for much of the nineteenth century. As tenuous as the ties between white and Black members may have been, all UMWA workers were outfitted with protections they'd have otherwise been denied, and one hopes that at least some workers made interracial bonds of brotherhood underground.

THEY CALLED HER MOTHER JONES

The UMWA had a number of big personalities and tough-talking bruisers at its disposal, but one of its most effective agitators was an old Irish woman in a black dress who prowled the picket lines and struck fear into the hearts of the corporate elite. This "John Brown in petticoats" was a militant socialist who breathed class war like a dragon and doted on her members as if they were her own children. She was born Mary Harris. They called her Mother Jones.

The woman who would become Mother Jones lived an entire life's worth of pain, struggle, and tragedy before she found her calling: organizing the working class, lifting up the unheard, and unseating those who would gladly earn their money by grinding the poor's bones to dust. A dressmaker by trade, left widowed with four deceased children in the 1871 yellow fever epidemic, Jones re-invented herself as a labor organizer and self-proclaimed hell-raiser. She grew famous for her signature billowing black dress, replete with lace collar, a severe white bun, and a pair of tiny eyeglasses perched on her fierce countenance. A century before Johnny Cash donned his all-black getup to symbolize his allegiance with the poor and downtrodden, Jones reached for widow's weeds to illustrate her status as the grandmother of a movement. She cultivated a matriarchal, sometimes impish image, fondly referring to grizzled miners and favored politicians alike as "my boys" and crusading against child labor. Only some of that came naturally; the rest was a theatrical flourish, cooked up to emphasize Harris's age and gravitas and add to her stature as the one and only Mother Jones, the bane of the coal bosses and a fighter to the core.

Unlike many labor figures of her day, Jones did not discriminate against women or Black workers (though her single-minded focus on building working-class power at all costs left some of her views shortsighted at best, in particular her silence as the American labor movement went on the offensive against Chinese immigrant workers). During labor clashes, her greatest weapon was the womenfolk. She was known for actively encouraging women and families to get involved in strikes and organizing wives into "mop and bucket" battalions to fight alongside their husbands on the picket lines and hold down the home front.

She never stayed put for long, perpetually hitting the road even in her advancing age, and sowing rebellion wherever she roamed. In Wilkes-Barre and Carbondale, Pennsylvania, Jones championed the cause of striking silk mill workers, many of them the daughters of coal miners; she returned to the state in 1903 to lead a group of one hundred young mill workers on a three-week journey from Philadelphia all the way to President Theodore Roosevelt's New York home to whip up public outrage around the scourge of child labor. At the time, 18 percent of American workers were under the age of sixteen, and as Jones herself once said, "The American people were born in strikes, and now in the closing days of the nineteenth century, even the children must strike for justice."

While she traveled around the country organizing and agitating, Jones—hailed in labor circles as "the miner's angel"—became a target, smeared in the press and relentlessly tailed by police and company men wherever she popped up. When she was called to the 1914 Colorado Coalfield War, her reputation preceded her—and landed her in prison during one of the most horrific massacres in labor history. After visiting the area several times and leaving to drum up support across the country, Jones was intercepted at the train station en route to the coalfields. Her imprisonment drew out thousands of local miners and their families to protest her arrest. Mexican revolutionary leader Pancho Villa, whom Jones had negotiated with to stanch the flow of immigrant strikebreakers into Colorado during the labor fight, even wrote to President Woodrow Wilson offering to free one of his American captives in exchange for her release. While Jones languished in prison, strikers fought for their lives against company-hired gun thugs and the U.S. military. The conflict came to a dreadful head on April 20, when company goons and the Colorado National Guard violently attacked a striking miners' camp, slaughtering twenty-one in the process. Most of the victims were women and children.

The Ludlow Massacre left deep, lasting scars on the United States' workers' rights movement, serving as another stark reminder of the potentially deadly retribution that can await workers who dare to fight back. Its last living survivor, Ermenia "Marie" Padilla

Daley, walked the earth as recently as 2019. Just three months old when the militia set her home ablaze, she was a coal miner's daughter who had been born in the Ludlow mining camps; after the massacre, her parents split up, and she and her siblings were sent to various orphanages around Colorado.

THE WEST DIVERSIFIES THE WORKFORCE

The Colorado showdown (and Jones's fateful meeting with Pancho Villa) reflected the changing racial and cultural makeup of America's mine workers and its workforce at large. As the nineteenth century entered its second act, new immigrants from China, Japan, Mexico, Latin America, Scandinavia, Eastern Europe, and the Mediterranean could be found laboring in mines throughout the West. Coal companies actively recruited workers from various European and Asian countries, wagering that ethnic and cultural differences among the groups would keep any one group from building collective power. They bet wrong.

In 1890, the Union Pacific Coal Company hired Black mining leader James E. Shepperson to attract new recruits to its Dana, Wyoming, mines. Unbeknownst to the new recruits, they were being brought on explicitly to act as strikebreakers in an ongoing labor conflict between the mine and its white workforce. That plan failed when the Black miners, who were union men, refused to cross the picket line or help break the strike, and instead forced the company to set higher wages for all of the mine's workers.

In Ludlow, the twelve hundred striking miner families spoke two dozen different languages; Black workers, Mexican workers, immigrant workers from Greece, Italy, and Eastern Europe, and native-born white workers fought side by side against the bosses, supported by militant miners' wives and family members and led by organizers like Louis Tikas, a Greek immigrant who was later murdered in a massacre by National Guard troops. The Western Federation of Miners (WFM), a precursor to the UMWA that later changed its name to the International Union of Mine, Mill, and Smelter Workers and was active in founding the Industrial Workers of the World (IWW) and the Congress of Industrial Organizations (CIO), organized on an industry-wide scale, and counted immigrant workers and Black workers among its members.

After the discovery of gold in the hills of California, the 1848 Gold Rush drew floods of hopeful workers of every stripe. Those frontier boomtowns created new economic opportunities for the thousands of women who headed west. While immigrants from coal-rich countries like Japan and England were familiar with seeing women working in the mines back home, the practice was frowned upon in the American West. Instead, women—who were a minority in early Western mining towns, which were overwhelmingly male—found employment in hospitality, food service, sex work, and domestic work for the mines. In towns like Butte, Montana; Bisbee, Arizona; and Cripple Creek, Colorado, the influence of the WFM helped women workers organize into small local trade unions.

William "Big Bill" Haywood, the WFM's secretary-treasurer, began working in an Idaho silver mine at the age of nine; as an adult, he was one of the most fearsome and effective union organizers in America, a strapping frontier socialist with a missing eye and a booming, powerful voice that carried throughout the nation's union halls and picket lines. He went on to help cofound the IWW, lead influential strikes in the Northeast (including the 1912 Lawrence Textile Strike), fight for the eight-hour workday, and later flee the country for Russia after decades of state persecution, but his time with the WFM is what first honed his radical sensibilities and his fervent belief in industrial unionism, the necessity of organizing the entire working class into "One Big Union." In 1894, the WFM led a miners' strike in Cripple Creek that erupted into an armed struggle replete with dynamite and bloodshed. It got so violent that the state intervened on the miners' behalf, which marked the first and only time that a state militia was called out in support of a strike. After five months, the WFM triumphed, and the victory helped the union begin to build power throughout the region. The same year, the fledgling United Mine Workers of America launched a massive general strike in the bituminous coal mining industry that was initially a success, but broke down after months of hammering from police, militias, and National Guard troops and left the union deeply weakened. It would take several decades before the UMWA found its footing, by which point the WFM would be dealing with setbacks of its own.

INDIGENOUS AND LATINO WORKERS HOLD THE LINE

But even as unions worked to improve conditions for their members and to gain a foothold in the Western labor landscape, not everyone was happy about all those new mining towns cropping up around the country. Their arrival brought nothing but trouble to the Indigenous mine workers who had already been at war with the U.S. government for a lifetime; once the streams of greedy white settlers began to pour in, native miners were exploited, assaulted, and saw their land decimated by the invaders. Indigenous workers have been mining various substances since time immemorial, from metals like silver, gold, copper, and lead to salt, coal, and valuable stones like hematite, turquoise, and quartz. In the modern era, they've also been involved in extracting more dangerous materials like asbestos and uranium, especially after World War II, when the demand for radioactive material skyrocketed; the Navajo Nation has been fighting to ban uranium mining on its lands since the 1970s.

In the Midwest, both lead and copper mines were cultivated by Indigenous tribes for generations before white settlers "discovered" their bounty. In southern Wisconsin, the women of the Ho-Chunk, Mesquaki, and Sauk tribes controlled the lead mines, and engaged in active mining only on a seasonal basis. The women successfully guarded their secrets from outsiders until the War of 1812 established a permanent American military presence on their land, and subsequently sent thousands of resource-hungry white settlers and heavily armed fur traders flooding into their territory. The copper mines of Michigan's Keweenaw Peninsula were first dug out more than seven thousand years ago by prehistoric native people, but it wasn't until 1842 that the federal government realized the peninsula's potential value and used a treaty to wrest it away from the Ojibwe people who were then stewarding the land. The Southwestern copper mines of Arizona and New Mexico underwent a similar fate; these ancient mines were discovered and cultivated by native tribes, newly "discovered" by settlers, and then brought under white European or American control.

The Keweenaw Peninsula was also the site of the 1913–1914 Copper County Strike, when the Western Federation of Miners led the area's predominantly Cornish immigrant workers on a strike that ended only a week before the Ludlow Massacre set Colorado aflame. Anna "Big Annie" Klobuchar Clemenc, the Slovenian American president of the Women's Auxiliary No. 15 of the Western Federation of Miners, was a coal miner's wife and domestic worker who stood six feet tall. She became one of the most visible faces of the strike by leading daily support parades for the strikers while waving a massive American flag on a ten-foot pole, and was arrested and jailed during the strike, allegedly for fighting with scabs. Known as "the American Joan of Arc," Clemenc remained fiercely devoted to the cause of labor throughout her life; when she was once asked if her arms got tired waving the heavy flagpole, she replied, "No, I would support it forever, just as I would my country."

The large-scale, often violent labor uprisings of the nineteenth century petered out as the mining industry began its decline and unions were weakened by federal labor laws and so-called right-to-work legislation. The coal industry and the labor movement both evolved significantly over the ensuing decades, but the tension between workers and bosses remained constant, and mass unrest was never more than a hair's breadth away. As new generations of miners in Appalachia and elsewhere in the nation continued to go down into the darkness in hopes of earning a decent living, their families and communities remembered those past battles—and their bodies kept the score.

Echoes of those past betrayals bubbled up on the Arizona borderlands in 1983, when thousands of Chicano, Mexican, and Indigenous workers at the Phelps Dodge copper mines in Morenci, Ajo, Clifton, and Douglas, Arizona, decided to walk out during contract negotiations. Instead of participating in "pattern bargaining"—a form of industry-wide standard-setting that was then common to the mining industry, in which multiple companies agreed to adopt the same basic union contract—Phelps Dodge instead decided to negotiate the contract on its own terms. Copper prices were down and the company was in debt, so in an effort to reduce its labor costs, executives elected to hike up health-care costs, eliminate cost-of-living increases, and freeze wages for its majority Latino and Indigenous workforce. It also resolved to continue operating the mines in the event of a work stoppage, instead of simply shutting down as it had during many previous strikes.

The miners, who were represented by the United Steelworkers, reacted with dismay; in their view, deviating from the established industry-wide bargaining system would hurt other workers across the industry, betray the sacrifices their ancestors had made to build up the mines into a place where they and their descendants could have a decent living, and allow their bosses to make even deeper cuts to their pay and working conditions. They were also shaken by the company's insistence that the mines would keep running, with or without them; in previous years, strikers' jobs had been there waiting for them once they returned, but now that guarantee had flown out the window. This already felt different from the other strikes, but the contract was set to expire on June 30, 1983, and a decision had to be made. As the hours ticked by, United Steelworkers treasurer Frank McKee turned to Alex Lopez, the union's chief negotiator, and said, "Alex, tell your people we're not getting anywhere. PD wants to try and bust us. Can you get your troops together?"

Union roots ran deep in Morenci and its satellite towns. The Industrial Workers of the World (IWW) and the Western Federation of Miners (WFM) had had a strong presence there since the early 1900s, particularly among the Latino laborers that the AFL refused to organize. The WFM led a 1915 "Strike of the Mexicans" work stoppage at a Ray, Arizona, copper mine that became one of the state's first strikes. The same year, four thousand miners at a Phelps Dodge mine in Clifton, Arizona, organized under the WFM banner and struck for higher wages and union recognition, but the company's anti-union ethos was already well developed, and they refused to negotiate. Governor George Hunt, who was known to be sympathetic to labor, traveled to Clifton to show support for the strike, and even called in the National Guard to help keep the company from bringing in strikebreakers. Mother Jones made an appearance as well, calling the action "one of the most remarkable strikes in the history of the labor movement." It didn't hurt that the strike ended in a settlement favorable to the workers, either—though the loss prompted Phelps Dodge to intensify its decades-long anti-union project, as well as its inequitable and racist treatment of workers of color, particularly those who had immigrated from Mexico.

In the Phelps Dodge mines (and throughout the Southwestern copper mining industry), Latino and Indigenous workers were regularly paid far less than their white coworkers. They were shunted into segregated locker rooms and eating areas, and were subjected to racist abuse and discrimination on the job. Women miners dealt with all of that plus sexual harassment and sexist discrimination; it's no wonder that these workers became some of the most militant union supporters and organizers. In 1917, during another Latino-led strike in Bisbee, Arizona, the company oversaw the largest forced migration by a private corporation in American history. At the behest of Phelps Dodge company president Walter Douglas, twelve hundred union members were rounded up at gunpoint, herded into cattle cars still loaded with manure, then left stranded in the New Mexico desert 173 miles away. Few ever made it back to Bisbee. "It was like the army had prisoners," Katie Pintek, a witness to the event, recalled later. "If they saw someone standing about to run, they were going to shoot. Two did get killed that day. . . . What kind of America was that?"

A HALF CENTURY LATER, BACK WHERE WE BEGAN

In the charged summer of 1983, only a few generations after the notorious Bisbee Deportation, the memory of that mistreatment was still fresh in the minds of those who'd endured unequal treatment themselves. When the decision was made for the mine's twenty-nine hundred workers in Ago, Bisbee, Douglas, and Morenci to go out on strike once again, Alex Lopez's troops answered the call. As midnight fell, workers gathered at the entrance to the Phelps Dodge mine in Morenci, the largest and most productive mine of the four. Among them were Lydia Gonzales Roybal, the only woman in her maintenance division and the daughter of a former miner, and Joe Sorrelman, a Navajo machinist and Vietnam veteran whose own father had been recruited from the Navajo reservation to work in the mines before him. "I couldn't betray the other people in the union," Sorrelman explained as he stood alongside his friends and coworkers. They were determined to hold the line, no matter what the company threw at them. None of them knew then that the ensuing strike would last for nearly three years, send shock waves throughout the Southwestern mining industry, and mark the beginning of a new era of blatant, hostile strikebreaking. At that moment, just after midnight, the only thought on the strikers' minds was of the long night ahead, and what would happen when the scabs' cars pulled up the next morning.

The Great Copper Strike of 1983, as it would become known, was a brutal slog that fractured entire communities, pitting neighbor against neighbor and, sometimes, wives against husbands. The local United Steelworkers Women's Auxiliary was initially organized as a domestic support group, tasked with cooking, holding bake sales, planning fundraisers, and caring for strikers' children. But as the days turned into weeks, and weeks turned into months, the women began to rebel against the patriarchal expectation that they'd stay home and concern themselves with the kitchen and the kids during the strike. "This isn't going to be a 'Ladies' Auxiliary,'" swore Toni Potter, an early member who was thoroughly uninterested in acting like a meek, submissive "lady" while her community went to war against the company. "Kiss that shit goodbye. This is going to be the Women's Auxiliary."

As the strike marched on, the Women's Auxiliary came into its own. The bake sales and burritos were left on the back burner as the women became a constant presence on the picket lines, antagonizing scabs and facing off against police. "If we could just get rid of these broads, we'd have it made," a frustrated state trooper was heard to complain in the thick of the fight. A series of court injunctions had severely limited the number of strikers allowed on the line, so their wives, mothers, sisters, daughters, and neighbors stepped in. Police responded with hostility, violence, and targeted arrests, but even after Arizona governor Bruce Babbitt sent in the National Guard to occupy their town and suppress the strike, the women of Morenci refused to be cowed. "These women made the scabs' lives miserable," Women's Auxiliary president Fina Roman later recalled. "It didn't help so much with the end result. But we reminded them that they didn't come and take over without a fight."

Roman was no stranger to labor organizing, or agitation. She'd been fired from her previous job at a construction company in Clifton when Phelps Dodge, who contracted through the company, accused her of trying to organize migrant farmworkers. She was on the town council at the time, and had hosted United Farmworkers union leader Cesar Chavez in her home when he came through Arizona as part of a longer Southwestern tour. Phelps Dodge caught wind of it and pressured her boss to fire her. Years later, when she heard about the strike, Roman thought about her own mistreatment at the company's hands and began attending auxiliary meetings to see if she could help out. She ended up being elected president, and was part of a delegation of Morenci women who would later crisscross the country on a speaking tour, spreading the word about the strike to union halls and conventions from Tucson to Wall Street.

Jean Lopez was among those who joined her. Her grandfather Brigham Hernandez had emigrated from Mexico and fought to organize a union at the mines in Morenci decades earlier, and was a victim of the 1917 Bisbee Deportation as a result. Her father followed him into the mines, and Lopez later became a miner's wife. When she stood up in front of a union hall full of strangers, she was terrified, but Lopez was able to draw strength from those family memories, and from her own experiences on the line. "I was motivated by what I had seen here [in Morenci]," she explained. "I felt angry about the police brutality I had seen. I saw my own friends chained and beaten. Just being here made me so angry, I could find the courage to do anything."

Public speaking—to say nothing of raising hell on the picket lines—was still a new skill for many of the women, who had been raised in traditional patriarchal family structures and were generally expected to be seen and not heard. Women who were raised for a life of domestic servility, who had never worked or socialized outside the home, suddenly found themselves organizing rallies, attending weekly meetings, handling floods of donations, flipping off scabs, giving interviews to TV cameras, and surviving violent interactions with the police. By the time the strike finally ended, some of them found that their lives and relationships had been irrevocably altered. The newfound independence and autonomy of the women pulled some husbands along for the ride, but others saw their relationships break down under the strain and end in divorce. The action took a heavy toll and, thanks to the company's mass recruitment of replacement workers, ultimately resulted in the largest decertification (a majority vote against the union) in U.S. history, affecting thirty-five chapters of thirteen different unions representing Phelps Dodge workers in Arizona, New Mexico, and Texas. The United Steelworkers may have been driven out of Phelps Dodge, but Morenci was still a union town, and there was simply no going back to the way things were.

"To these women, defending the union is a means of defending the family and home, because through the union they've elevated living standards and brought dignity into those homes," Fina Roman told author Barbara Kingsolver in her 1989 book on the strike.

"We're striving so that the children are not wholly dependent on Phelps Dodge. . . . They will be able to offer something to the employer other than brawn. And to have some choice about what they do. We don't just want to raise people to feed to this machine."

THE 2021 WARRIOR MET COAL STRIKE

In April 2021, coal miners and their families in rural Alabama found themselves carrying on that time-tested tradition when the UMWA's District 20 called a strike against Warrior Met Coal.

Warrior Met had come to Brookwood in 2016, swooping in to buy up the mines after their previous owner, Jim Walter Resources, went into bankruptcy. Mass layoffs followed, and Warrior Met rehired many of the laid-off workers on the condition that they accepted a subpar union contract with hefty cuts to their pay, vacation time, and health-care benefits. The miners sucked it up, confident that the company would cut them in once it became profitable. "If somebody saved your life, it would seem like to me that you would be indebted to them," Moses Moore, a Warrior Met miner, told me. "And us as union workers, we saved Warrior Met. So it would seem to me that it should be a no-brainer. You helped me, now I'm gonna help you guys."

But five years later, Warrior Met was in the black, but it had no interest in sharing its bounty with the people who'd dug it out of the cold dark ground. When contract negotiations began and the company offered the workers a new agreement without any major improvements, they overwhelmingly voted it down. The strike was on.

While many of this latest crop of workers hadn't been around (or even alive) the last time coal miners in the area went on strike, their fathers, grandfathers, and great-grandfathers surely were. The UMWA has been active in the state since 1890, and Alabama's coal miners have a history of both pushing back against unfair labor practices and acting in interracial solidarity. The state's history is littered with major strikes and labor actions, many of them undertaken by interracial groups of coal miners in the greater Birmingham area. That's not to say that the union or the mines were a utopian beacon of anti-racism; while the UMWA in Alabama prided itself on being a "biracial" union and installed some Black leaders, racial tensions frequently ran high, and some racist white members rejected their Black union brothers outright.

The Great Strike of 1894 saw nine thousand miners strike in protest of low wages and the convict leasing system. In 1908, eighteen thousand miners near Birmingham struck against U.S. Steel, which had recently purchased the Tennessee Coal, Iron and Rail Company (TCI) and drastically cut wages. For two months, white and Black workers held the line, even after U.S. Steel evicted them from their company-owned houses and led them to erect a makeshift tent city. Alabama governor Braxton Bragg Comer called in the state militia to crush the strike, and the company used the opportunity to enforce strict segregation in its mines. In 1920 and 1921, Birmingham's miners went on strike again, this time to win union recognition, and activity ramped up in the 1930s and early 1940s until the 1943 Bradford Act severely hampered the union's ability to organize.

The Warrior Met strike lasted twenty-three months, far longer than the miners or union officials had anticipated. As of this writing, the workers have gone back to work with no clear resolution in sight. Like the Morenci women of the 1983 copper strike (as well as the 1973 Brookside strike portrayed in the documentary *Harlan County USA*), the miners and their families made several trips to New York City to confront Warrior Met's shareholders and bring their message to a wider audience. "Going to a place like New York that is a union city restores your drive to fight," Haeden Wright, the president of Brookwood's UMWA Auxiliary and wife of a striking Warrior Met miner, told me about her trip up north. "When you have the opportunity to witness brothers and sisters you have never met coming to stand in solidarity and amplify the voice of their fellow workers, it is overwhelming."

As the strike passed its eight-month mark, a judge in Tuscaloosa County heeded the company's request to grant a restraining order against the strikers, effectively banning the picket line. This marked an escalation in Warrior Met's ongoing use of the court system to advance its goal of breaking the strike. Moreover, it was a chilling suppression of the inalienable rights of free speech and free assembly. "The Constitution of the United States protects American citizens' rights to stand on the side of a road and call a scab a scab," UMWA International president Cecil Roberts said in a statement shortly after the decision was handed down. "It protects their rights to peacefully assemble and air their grievances with an employer or any other person or entity. It protects their rights to seek redress from the government. We intend to continue to exercise our rights."

He emphasized their resolve during a November 4 rally in front of BlackRock's New York City headquarters. That day, hundreds of UMWA members from multiple states were joined by supporters from UNITE HERE, SAG-AFTRA, NWU, and the city's labor community to demand that BlackRock—which owns a 14 percent stake in the company—send Warrior Met to the bargaining table. "We must stand and take back what is rightfully ours, brothers and sisters, and I want you to know something," he boomed, entreating them to be strong and stand together despite the violence, the injunctions, and the hardship. As he closed the rally (and before he and six other UMWA leaders blocked an intersection and were arrested for disorderly conduct), he channeled the spirit of Dr. Martin Luther King, hollering to the heavens in his West Virginia twang. "Ain't nobody gonna turn us around!"

6

THE HARVESTERS

We were not "given" our rights. It is not even "we took our rights." Instead, we created our rights.

—Gerardo Reyes, farmworker and Coalition of Immokalee Workers member-organizer

The harvesters—those who work in the United States' fields, farms, and food production factories—remain one of the country's most precarious and exploited workforces. The devaluation of their labor and the ignorance of their sacrifice stems from a legacy of exploitation that stretches all the way back to the enslaved African captives who powered the Southern agricultural economy throughout the pre-Emancipation period.

Today's agricultural worker is still likely to have arrived from another country; 73 percent of all American agricultural workers are foreign-born, with 69 percent hailing from Mexico. Those workers, nearly half (47 percent) of whom are "undocumented," are part of a continuing struggle—one that, given the gross exploitation endemic to the sector and its laborers, faces an uphill battle to equity. But as over a century of organizing has shown, these workers have always been ready to fight for what they deserve.

HAWAI'I'S MASTERS AND SERVANTS

The exploitative agricultural practices of the U.S. did not start within, and have not been limited to, its own borders. Forty years before the U.S. forcibly annexed the Kingdom of Hawai'i, the Hawai'ian Legislature passed the 1850 Masters & Servant Act. The law formalized the islands' "Perquisite System" that enshrined contract labor—in which workers "bound" themselves to a "master" for a predetermined period of time—as the norm on the islands' vast sugarcane plantations.

In 1835, William Hooper, a wealthy Massachusetts industrialist, leased land from King Kamehameha III to establish Hawai'i's first large-scale sugar plantation in the village of Kōloa. Several dozen Native Hawaiians were hired to work on the plantation from its outset, and Hooper—in a preview of practices to come for Henry Ford and the Appalachian coal companies, constructed a "company town," complete with housing, company medical clinics, and a company-issued "currency" that workers received instead of cash (women were paid the equivalent of 6 "cents" per day, while men got 12 and a half). The Native Hawaiians, proud and accustomed to their traditional way of life, soon became openly defiant toward their employers. They took every opportunity to stop working in order to smoke and tell stories instead, a habit that Hooper's neighbors found "amusing" and the landowner was infuriated by. Finding the native workforce insufficiently cooperative, Hooper then turned to a new pool of labor: China.

Chinese traders had had a presence in Hawai'i since they first became interested in its sandalwoods in 1789 (in China, the islands were known as Tan Heung Shan, "Sandalwood Mountains"), and Chinese-owned companies had been running sugar mills there since 1802. The first group of Chinese laborers arrived in 1852 after signing contracts to cut cane on the island's rapidly expanding sugar plantations, driven by poverty and attracted by promises of steady work and decent wages. Ninety-five percent of them were men, and by 1884, 5,600 of the 13,200 Chinese "male agriculturalists and rural laborers" on the islands worked on sugar plantations. Other available work included rice production and agricultural work on fruit and vegetable farms. Hawai'i's industrial powers reveled in the fruits of the Chinese immigrant labor that came to compose the lion's share of the islands' working class, but the presence of growing "outsider" influence made the white land-owning class nervous.

In 1882 the U.S. government saw fit to pass the Chinese Exclusion Act, a law restricting Chinese immigration and permanently barring the country's immigrants from citizenship. Taken in concert with the Scott Act three years later, the new law legally banned Chinese entry to the country, and up to thirty thousand U.S.-based Chinese living outside the country were barred from returning to their homes. Japanese workers arrived to Hawai'i in large numbers to replace the excluded Chinese, and before long planters grew concerned about their "excess" numbers as well. In a cynical bid to diversify the plantation workforce, white business agents began traveling farther and farther afield to entice job-seeking young men with no agricultural experience to sign away their lives. They actively recruited immigrants from Korea, Portugal, the Philippines, Puerto Rico, Norway, Russia, and Germany; in 1901, two hundred Black workers were shipped in from Tennessee. These contracts legally bound workers to specific plantations for three to five years. Japanese, Chinese, and Filipino workers were given different wages for the same work, and most overseers, called *lunas*, were white or European. This system of ethnic segmentation was deliberate. "Keep a variety of laborers, that is different nationalities, and thus prevent any concerted action in case of strikes, for there are few, if any, cases of [Japanese], Chinese, and Portuguese entering into a strike as a unit," George H. Fairfield of the Makee

Sugar Company recommended to his fellow planters. The great multiethnic strikes of the early twentieth century would prove him wrong, but they were still decades away.

No matter where they'd originated, the workers were united by their arduous labor. "The sugar cane fields were endless, and the stalks were twice the height of myself," one Korean woman worker remembered. "Now that I look back, I thank goodness for that height, for if I had seen how far the fields stretched, I probably would have fainted from knowing how much work was ahead." Under the contract labor system, "deserters" could be imprisoned; many workers, tired of the backbreaking workload and barbarous mistreatment from the plantations' whip-cracking overseers, fled to the mainland anyway. Others found different ways to resist. Mioshi, a Japanese field hand, took the Hilo Sugar Company to court in 1891, alleging that the conditions he was working under constituted a form of "involuntary servitude" that violated his rights under the U.S. Constitution (the all-white judges ruled against him). The lynching of Katsu Goto, a plantation worker turned shopkeeper who had been part of the first wave of Japanese emigration to Hawai'i, further underscored how high the stakes were for workers who tried to push back against the contract labor system. After he finished his three-year plantation contract and opened up a store of his own, Goto, who was by then fluent in English, became known for providing counsel and legal advice to plantation workers. He was often called to act as an interpreter between Japanese workers and plantation management during disputes. Plantation owner Robert M. Overend hated Goto so much that he once threatened to shoot him if the man went anywhere near the Overend plantation. On October 28, 1889, Katsu Goto's body was found hanging from a telephone pole.

Seven years after a violent American- and European-led coup d'état against Queen Lili'uokalani overthrew the Hawai'ian monarchy, two years after the independent nation of Hawai'i was formally annexed by the United States, and two years after Katsu Goto's murder, 1,160 Japanese immigrant field hands on the Lāhainā plantation organized the new territory's first successful strike in 1900. Once the new U.S.-backed territorial government went into effect on June 14, the oppressive Masters & Servant Act was nullified, and more major sugar workers' strikes followed in 1906 and 1909. The 1909 strike involved five thousand Japanese workers and stretched on for three months; it was broken when plantation owners hired Chinese, Korean, Portuguese, and Hawai'ian workers as scabs at double the daily rate. Later, bosses would lean on Filipino and Puerto Rican workers as strikebreakers, but efforts to divide workers on racial and ethnic grounds would ultimately fail as the islands' labor movement began to embrace a strong multiethnic solidarity that reflected its diverse workforce.

Those lessons stuck; on the mainland, Japanese and Chinese workers with experience in the Hawai'ian struggles would help found the Japanese Mexican Labor Association (JMLA) to rail against exploitation in the California sugar beet fields and notch the first major victory against a California agricultural giant when they successfully struck against the Western Agricultural Contracting Company in 1903. But that glow faded when the AFL refused to recognize their charter unless they expelled their Japanese members, and the union, horrified, refused. The response from JMLA's secretary, J. M. Lizarras, spoke volumes about the power of multiracial organizing, and of what true solidarity looks like: "Better to go to hell with your family than to heaven by yourself."

SUGAR AND BLOOD

By the 1920s, Chinese, Japanese, Korean, and Filipino immigrants to Hawai'i had become a significant part of the agricultural workforce alongside native workers, and the ensuing decades would see a burst in labor militancy culminating in the islands' largest mass labor action to date, the Great Sugar Strike of 1946.

The ramp-up to the biggest strike in Hawai'ian history took decades. In 1920, three thousand members of the Filipino Labor Union went on strike against the Hawaii Sugar Planters Association, joined by the Japanese Federation of Labor, a coalition of Japanese workers from neighboring plantations throughout the Hawai'ian Islands. By its end, this strike's ranks grew to 8,300 laborers from six O'ahu plantations. The multicultural effort held, forging a path for future labor advancement that achieved both immediate success—the pressure resulted in a 50 percent wage increase—and progress toward long-term goals, with the creation of the islands' first multiethnic labor union, the Hawaii Laborers' Association.

Labor had won the moment, but capital would not stand down for long. The next major action, the Filipino Piecemeal Sugar Strike of 1924, collapsed into extreme violence with little provocation. Police gunned down sixteen striking Filipino sugar workers in Hanapēpē, Kaua'i, in what became known as the Hanapepe Massacre. After counting the dead, the state arrested and deported many of those who survived, including Filipino labor leader Pablo Manlapit. Blood would flow again in 1938, when a demonstration in support of striking Inland Boatmen's Union members was swarmed by police. "They shot us down like a herd of sheep," Chinese Hawai'ian labor leader and massacre survivor Harry Lehua Kamoku would tell a friend the next day. "We didn't have a chance. . . . They shot men in the back as they ran. They shot men who were trying to help wounded comrades and women. They ripped their bodies with bayonets. It was just plain slaughter." The Hilo Massacre would count fifty injuries, including two women and two children.

The toxic intersection of corporate violence and worker dissent raised the stakes to an unsustainable boiling point, with all players reaching deeper and deeper into their bags of tricks. In 1944 sugar's

"Big Five" companies—Alexander & Baldwin, American Factors, Castle & Cooke, C. Brewer, and Theo. Davies—embarked upon a two-year plan to cut the heart out of Hawai'i's domestic workforce, hoping to demoralize its Japanese employees by recruiting six thousand new laborers from the Philippines. In the midst of World War II, Japan had been an occupying force in the Philippines, and planters assumed the divide would translate to their workers. Having caught wind of the plan, the sugar workers' union, the International Longshoremen's and Warehousemen's Union (ILWU), infiltrated the labor importation apparatus and sent union organizers to take jobs as cooks and stewards aboard ships sailing from the Philippines to Hawai'i. By the time the new recruits stepped ashore on January 30, 1946, they had already signed union cards, and arrived to a hero's welcome, complete with a union-provided brass band. "When those employers saw those [union] buttons, man, their faces dropped a foot-and-a-half, you know?" union organizer Frank Thompson later recalled. "So then we raised a lot of hell because the accommodations the planters had for these people were the same as you'd do cattle, only worse."

That year, the sugar plantations' union drew up a list of goals to help raise its membership out of poverty, including wage increases and a forty-hour workweek. Conditions for plantation workers at this time had stagnated, and the Big Five ruled over Hawai'i's multiethnic agricultural workforce with a level of control almost unimaginable today. The Hawaiian Sugar Planters' Association, as the Five's organizing cartel was known, employed more than one-fifth of the state's population, and wealthy white sugar industrialists from the mainland controlled nearly every aspect of the islands' economy. A 1939 report for the Bureau of Labor Statistics noted this hegemonic condition in stark detail, writing, "The position of the individual plantation worker is especially vulnerable. The house in which he lives, the store from which he buys, the fields in which he finds his recreation, the hospital in which he is treated, are all owned by plantation management." The union wanted to limit the owners' control over the workers' personal lives by converting "perquisites" like segregated company-owned housing, company-run medical care, and company-provided fuel into actual cash, so that workers would no longer be held captive to the sugar barons' whims.

The Big Five balked at these demands and refused to negotiate. In response, on September 1, 1946, about twenty-six thousand sugar workers and their families, seventy-six thousand people in all, walked out of the fields and into the streets. The ILWU had foiled the bosses' racist "divide and conquer" approach by treating all of its members as equals. It had empowered community leaders to act as union stewards, conducting meetings in workers' languages like Japanese, Ilocano, Tagalog, and Vasayan, and emphasized interracial and multiethnic solidarity in its strike planning. The union also looked after the strikers' material needs; they set up soup kitchens at twenty-five plantations and organized a shipment of rice to help calm the strikers' fears that planters might try to starve them out, as had been done during strikes prior. They told them, "You are all economically exploited, whether you are Japanese, Chinese, Filipinos or whatever it is, and working people recognize that," Ah Quon McElrath, an influential Chinese Hawai'ian organizer with the ILWU, later explained. "All of the information that was given to them was, look, you are exploited, what are you going to do about it?"

What they did was kneecap the sugar industry for three months, and show the bosses who really ran the business. Instead of acting as strikebreakers, Filipino workers made up a crucial part of the strike planning and execution. "The Filipino workers who started working on the sugar plantations said look, we went through several years of extreme privation in the Philippines—we lived in the mountains, we ate roots, we ate whatever insects we could catch, and if we were to go on strike here, we can live the same kind of life as we did in the Philippines," McElrath explained. "At one time there was a severe question, because our membership was largely Japanese and a lot of them were in positions of leadership because by that time the Japanese were about 40 percent of the total population. They said it makes no difference to us, we are on strike, we will fight together."

The strike shut down thirty-three of the thirty-four sugar plantations on the islands for seventy-nine days, and cost the Big Five more than $15 million (about $209 million in 2021 dollars). It ended in resounding victory: sugar plantation workers won a higher wage increase than they'd achieved in the past twenty years, as well as other wins, like sick pay and an end to company-controlled "perquisites." They also helped elect labor-endorsed candidates to the Hawai'ian Legislature, and cleared a path for a follow-up, the 1947 Pineapple Strike (which ended in a stalemate). Seventy-plus years later, Hawai'i remains heavily unionized, boasting the highest rate of union membership in the nation at nearly 24 percent.

LOS BRACEROS, THE DUST BOWL, AND THE GREAT MEXICAN-AMERICAN MIGRATION

While the sugar strike roiled Hawai'i, over on the mainland, a young field-worker named Maria Moreno was busy trying to keep her family's heads above water. Born to a Mexican father and Mescalero Apache mother in 1920, Maria Torres Martinez began working in the fields alongside her parents when she was eight years old. She married twenty-one-year-old Luis Moreno when she was fifteen, and their family spent years trying to eke out an existence from the drought-ravaged fields at home in Texas. By 1940, she and Luis had joined the Dust Bowl migration and, alongside hundreds of thousands of others, moved to California in search of more fertile ground.

The Morenos and thousands of other Latino migrant workers picked produce in the Golden State's endless fields and orchards, and farther afield in Utah and Arizona as they followed the harvest to survive.

U.S.-born workers like Maria and her family were not the only people chasing those seasonal jobs, either. In 1942, the U.S. created the Bracero Program, an agreement with the Mexican government that allowed Mexican workers to fill seasonal jobs on U.S. farms and railroads, out of fears that World War II would sap the labor force and weaken the all-important agricultural industry. This program expanded on World World War I–era efforts to effectively import temporary Mexican workers to fill holes in the wartime labor market, exempting them from the restrictive Immigration Act of 1917. Employers welcomed the influx of cheap, exploitable labor, but labor organizations like the AFL, then led by xenophobic president Samuel Gompers (who had also lobbied for the Chinese Exclusion Act), resisted what they saw as an invasion of low-skilled competition for (white) American jobs. The AFL ceased its work with majority-Latino unions in the Southwest, and refused to organize Latino workers for decades afterward. Thanks to pernicious anti-immigrant rhetoric echoing out from politicians, unions, and the media, Mexican workers were met with racism, xenophobia, and violence, scorned for "taking American jobs," and enthusiastically exploited by employers.

During the 1930s, President Herbert Hoover enacted a massive deportation raid on people of Mexican descent, in which up to 1.8 million Latinos—nearly 60 percent of whom were U.S. citizens—were forcibly removed to Mexico. (President Eisenhower would reprise this racist campaign in 1954, when more than 1 million more Latino people were violently rounded up and deported.) As all this state-sponsored chaos played out, the AFL-CIO finally began to warm up to the idea of organizing Latino workers again. Union leaders were moved by the deplorable conditions that farmworkers were being forced to labor under, as well as growing public outrage over the situation. On a more cynical note, with the Second Red Scare in full swing, conservative union leaders also wanted to prevent labor's own radicals from making further inroads into the workforce. The anti-capitalist IWW and industrially focused CIO had been successfully organizing in the Latino community for years under the leadership of organizers like the CIO's first Latina council member, Guatemalan Communist labor activist and cannery union organizer Luisa Moreno (no relation to Maria). Moreno spent her storied career advocating for Latino workers' rights, organizing thousands of Louisiana sugarcane workers, Texas pecan shellers, Colorado sugar beet workers, and a multiethnic union of thirteen thousand cigar makers in Florida.

Luisa Moreno and her peers were well aware of the AFL's superficial interest in organizing Latino workers, and it made establishment leaders nervous to see those workers, especially those with unapologetically leftist politics, organize in spite of the barriers traditional labor had thrown up. Communist Mexican-American labor activist Emma Tenayuca, "the Passionflower of Texas," led protests, walkouts, and demonstrations to protest the deplorable working and living conditions that Latino workers faced in her native San Antonio. After dabbling in organized labor's mainstream, she formed the left-leaning coalition Workers Alliance and, with support from Moreno, led twelve thousand Latina pecan shellers in the heart of Texas on a successful three-month strike in 1938. It was a stunning early victory for the Latino workers' rights movement, and later organizers would build on that foundation to launch worker-led actions of their own. Like many labor activists of her generation, Tenayuca was later blacklisted for her political affiliations, but there was no erasing the impact she'd made on San Antonio and the labor movement as a whole.

The formalization of the bracero program only complicated matters. From 1942 to 1964, 4.6 million braceros came to the States from Mexico to work on short-term, primarily agricultural labor contracts. In theory, employers were obliged to hire braceros only in areas of certified domestic labor shortage; in practice, many growers ignored the rules and benefited from the cheap, exploitable labor of the migrant workers. Braceros suffered under terrible working conditions and were often called in to act as strikebreakers and scabs, which exacerbated tensions between them and other farmworkers who were trying to unionize. On top of that, this exploitative system depressed wages for all agricultural workers, a sector of the workforce that was already wildly underpaid and subject to rampant wage theft. Still, when the bracero program ended in 1964, so did an important legal pathway for migrant workers to attain seasonal employment in the States. According to the Farm Bureau, at least 50 to 70 percent of today's farm laborers are undocumented, which deprives them of essential labor law protections and the opportunity to formally organize. Agricultural work remains one of the most dangerous occupations in the United States and, with its off-book workforce, manages also to be among the least scrutinized.

"CRUSADER IN RUBBER BOOTS AND A BIG SKIRT"

Back in Texas, by 1958, Maria Moreno's family had expanded to include four sons and eight daughters. No matter how hard Maria, Luis, and their two adult sons worked, they still brought home only as little as $114 a week, and survival had become a Herculean effort. The last straw came after a massive flood in Tulare County, California, displaced them and over three thousand other farmworker families. "Everything was gone," her eldest daughter, Lilly DeLaTorre, remembered. "My mom went to ask for help, and no one would help." Her youngest was still a baby, and all she had to feed her was water and sugar. Their suffering was acute, and Maria's eldest son, nineteen-year-old Abel, who himself had begun working in the fields when he was five, eventually stopped eating so that his younger brothers and sisters would have a little more food on their plates. As a result, Abel temporarily lost his sight, and had to be hospitalized. Maria had seen enough, and began speaking out publicly about her family's plight and the dire situation into which all of the farmworkers' families had been thrust. "I see the people that buy delicious apples, bananas, all kinds of good foods, and then I take a look at my table—beans and potatoes!" she cried in one speech. "How do you think that I feel, seeing my son blind because we don't got nothing to eat, while some other tables are full and wasting food!"

Her story caught the ear of *Fresno Bee* reporter Ron Taylor, whose exposé on her son's sacrifice and her industry's misery pushed the state welfare board to reverse its policy and extend food assistance to the farmworkers. News of Moreno's victory spread to the Agricultural Workers Organizing Committee (AWOC), a pilot project of the AFL-CIO led by Dolores Huerta and Larry Ilitong that had been founded in 1959 to organize the diverse farmworker labor force. When director Norman Smith, who had been an autoworkers organizer in the thirties and forties, began building out the team, Moreno was one of his first hires. In accepting, she became the first female farmworker in U.S. history to be hired as a union organizer, and immediately got to work. "Our only option is to get organized," she told a meeting of workers in Spanish. "Like it or not, we've got to struggle, and we won't stop fighting until we've won."

Moreno was a respected and effective messenger for the union. Whether out in the fields or speaking to college students in Berkeley, when she spoke, people listened—and sometimes, they cried. Laurie Coyle, producer of 2018 documentary *Adios Amor: The Search for Maria*

Moreno, described her as "a crusader in rubber boots and a big skirt," and her reputation as an engaging, charismatic, often blunt public speaker won her fans (as well as a few detractors; fellow farmworker organizer Cesar Chavez allegedly couldn't handle her "big mouth").

AWOC was not without its troubles, and power struggles behind the scenes made it even harder to keep the project afloat. Dues-paying members were scarce, and AFL-CIO president George Meany was already less than enthusiastic about the project. In 1960, agribusiness giant DiGiorgio Farms sued AWOC for libel after screening a Hollywood-produced film on a 1947 DiGiorgio workers' strike that had previously been pulled from circulation, and Maria Moreno, a speaker at the event, was named as a defendant. As more legal issues began to mount, Meany pulled the plug on the union's funding. In a panic, AWOC hit upon what they thought would be a foolproof strategy: they would send Maria to the 1961 AFL-CIO convention to plead their case. Moreno was elected to head up AWOC's delegation, and she spoke from the same stage as President John F. Kennedy, Martin Luther King, Jr., Eleanor Roosevelt, and Walter Reuther, the president of the United Auto Workers. She used her time to describe the desperate conditions under which she and her children labored—the starvation, the poverty, the lack of health care—and to ask the labor movement to stand with the farmworkers as they struggled to organize. "Don't you think that our children had their stomachs full like the rest of you people that have a union or a decent wage," she told the crowd forcefully. "We don't. I hope that you people help us."

The plan worked. Her words resonated far outside the California fields where she had spent so many long, brutal days, and the delegates voted overwhelmingly to reinstate support for the AWOC. However, their win was not unconditional and came at the cost of reorganization and a leadership shakeup that claimed Moreno's position. "She wasn't afraid to say whatever she had to say, whether it was a politician or a worker or whatever," Gilbert Padilla explained in *Adios Amor*. "And I assume that's why they got rid of her." The year of Moreno's ousting, Padilla cofounded the Farm Workers Association with luminaries Cesar Chavez and Dolores Huerta. The organization would evolve into the United Farm Workers, a powerhouse agricultural workers' union that would build on AWOC's work to become the mighty force for justice it still is today. But unfortunately, Moreno herself wouldn't be there to see it.

After her ousting from AWOC, she disappeared from the labor movement and dedicated the rest of her life to religion. Faith had always formed the bedrock of her commitment to bettering the lives of others, and this daughter of a Baptist minister became a Pentecostal preacher. She founded a mission in Mexico where she and her family ministered to the poor until her death from breast cancer in 1989. Maria Moreno left behind her beloved children, forty-six grandchildren, twenty-nine great-grandchildren, and an immortal legacy of resistance. "I've been a worker all my life," she'd told a rapt audience all those years ago. "I know how to handle a man's job like a man, and I'm not ashamed to say it. I'm an American citizen, and I'm talking for justice."

Maria Moreno's was not the only name to be obscured as the United Farm Workers rose to prominence and its complex, visionary leader, Cesar Chavez, became a global symbol of the struggle for Latino workers' rights. History will not forget Chavez or his compatriot at the UFW, Dolores Huerta, a formidable Mexican-American union organizer who helped negotiate the closing terms of the epic five-year Delano Grape Strike. Huerta, now in her nineties and a global labor icon, continues to be a venerated advocate for farmworkers' rights. "These are the people that have to feed us, and to get out there every single day in the cold weather, planting and pruning and preparing the earth for the harvest, and then, during the harvest, being out there in the hot sun, doing the work to bring the food to our tables," Huerta told me in a 2020 interview for *Teen Vogue*. "We have to look at farmworkers as a very special occupation, just the way that we respect our firemen and our policemen."

However, key organizers like Larry Itliong and Nagi Daifullah are all too often relegated to a footnote in their better-known comrades' stories, or left out entirely. Without them, two of the most important labor actions in U.S. history might have never even gotten off the ground.

"SÍ, SE PUEDE!"

President Calvin Coolidge's signing of the 1924 Immigration Act severely limited the number of immigrants who could legally enter the United States. It limited the number of immigrants each year to 2 percent of a given nation's existing citizenry in the country, favoring Western European émigrés and essentially banning Asian immigrants, a group that had previously been banned from naturalization. But as always, businesses' interests in exploitable labor knew no such bounds. Employers turned to recruiting Filipino workers to fill their ranks, a group excluded from the new law due to the Philippines' then status as a U.S. territory. Once onshore, these workers were afforded few options for employment besides agricultural and factory labor, and became part of a seasonal migrant labor circuit that took them up the coast from the California fields through Washington's orchards to Alaska's fish canneries, and back again. This migratory experience exposed them to unions, and gave rise to a militant Filipino American labor tradition. "They saw the possibility of extracting themselves from the oppression of the workplace," Matt Garcia, author of *From the Jaws of Victory: The Triumph and Tragedy of Cesar Chavez and the Farm Worker Movement*, explained.

The tradition continues unabated; in 1981, Filipino American union organizers Silme Domingo and Glen Viernes would make the ultimate sacrifice, brutally murdered inside a Seattle union office as they stood up against a corrupt faction in their ILWU local on behalf of Filipino and Indigenous cannery workers.

Larry Dulay Itliong was born in the Philippines in 1913, and emigrated to California in 1929. By 1930, he'd already been involved in his first strike, joining lettuce pickers in Washington State. Itliong spent the next few decades organizing those workers, scattering the seeds of resistance wherever he went like a seven-fingered Johnny Appleseed. He'd lost three while working in an Alaskan cannery, and later founded the Alaska Cannery Workers Union, which is now Local 7 of the International Longshore and Warehouse Union (ILWU).

By the time he traveled to Stockton, California, in 1948 to help ILWU Local 37 organizers Chris Mensalvas and Ernesto Mangaoang lead asparagus workers in the first major agriculture strike after World War II, Larry was a seasoned, cigar-chomping rabble-rouser. He spoke three languages (and nine Filipino dialects), had run for union office—and won—on the slogan "militant, frank, capable," and served as vice president of Local 37 during the early 1950s. He founded the Filipino Farm Labor Union in 1956, and then years later, he and fellow Filipino organizers Philip Vera Cruz and Pete Velasco partnered with the AFL-CIO to create the Agricultural Workers Organizing Committee (AWOC). Emboldened by a successful strike they'd led against Coachella Valley grape growers in 1965, Itliong and Velasco aimed to bring that fire to Delano, where the majority of the country's table grapes were grown.

As president of the AWOC, Itliong called the September 7, 1965, meeting at Filipino Community Hall that led to the Delano Grape Strike and brought thousands of Filipino and Mexican workers together in a five-year work stoppage and nationwide boycott. Three days after that meeting, more than two thousand Filipino farmworkers walked off the job, demanding a wage of $1.40 an hour, 25 cents a box, and the right to form a union. Cesar Chavez was initially reluctant to get involved, in the moment preferring incremental measures with broader support, but he brought his National Farm Workers Association along for the fight after seeing the growers' violent reaction to the striking Filipinos. "[The growers] were beating them real bad, shutting off water," Roger Gadiano, a seventy-two-year-old Filipino American who grew up in Delano in the 1960s, recalled.

Within two weeks, twelve hundred Latino farmworkers had added their voices to the chorus of "*Sí, se puede!*" ("Yes, you can!") on the picket lines. The Filipino Community Hall became a strike kitchen where Filipino and Mexican workers cooked for one another and built a durable multiracial coalition. "The social and economic revolution of the farmworkers is well underway and it will not be stopped until we receive equality," key NFWA organizer Dolores Huerta told a crowd in 1966. "The farmworkers are moving. Nothing is going to stop them!"

She was right. The Delano strike ended in 1970 with significant wins for the farmworkers: a substantial pay increase, higher safety standards, and union rights. It also ushered in a new era of farmworker organizing when the AWOC merged with the National Farm Workers Association to create a new organization, the United Farm Workers Organizing Committee (UFWOC), which would ultimately become today's United Farm Workers.

NAGI DAIFULLAH AND THE LARGEST FARMWORKER STRIKE IN HISTORY

The new age of alliance was promising, but uneasy. With Chavez at the UFW's helm and Itliong installed as vice president, disagreements between the two powerful personalities over the direction of the new union, which had become majority Latino, were almost inevitable. The NFWA's largely Mexican immigrant membership had continued to grow, but most AWOC members were *manongs*, older bachelor Filipino farmworkers who had been unable to marry or have families due to racist anti-miscegenation laws. In 1934, the Tydings-McDuffie Act had limited the number of Filipinos who could enter the country each year to just fifty, effectively ending Filipino immigration and isolating those who had already arrived.

The union would launch another big action in 1973, known alternately as the Grape and Lettuce Boycott of 1973 or the Salad Bowl Strike, but instead of pitting workers against their bosses, this conflict was a turf war between rival unions. The UFW faced off against the Teamsters, who were attempting to gain a foothold in the California fields by cutting sweetheart deals with growers to keep the UFW out. A series of bitter strikes, mass pickets, boycotts, and secondary boycotts escalated into the largest farmworker strike in U.S. history, a massive undertaking that saw Chavez embark on hunger strikes that brought him to the brink of death and directly led to the first farmworkers' labor rights legislation in U.S. history. It was also a deeply diverse conflict, as this time the Mexican and Filipino majority were joined by Yemeni workers.

In the late 1960s and 1970s, political turmoil in Yemen led thousands of young men to emigrate to the U.S. to find work and some measure of peace. Most of them ended up in Detroit auto factories, but about five thousand made their way to California, where they joined

Mexican and Filipino agricultural workers in the verdant fields of the San Joaquin Valley. The Yemenis were initially welcomed by employers who assumed the Arab workers would be "docile," but as with the Filipinos before them, surviving unrest and revolution at home had left them with a politically radical outlook and a fearless hunger to organize. Among them was a slim twenty-four-year-old anti-imperialist named Nagi Daifullah, who had once dreamed of becoming a doctor but instead became an organizer and translator for the UFW. "He was very courageous, encouraging us and telling us, 'This is democracy, and if you want your rights, this is how you do it,'" said Ahmed Yahya Mushreh, a former grape picker and UFW member who marched alongside Daifullah and now works as a janitor with SEIU Local 87. "You fight for your rights. This is the United States."

As tensions among the strikers, the Teamsters, and the police ratcheted up, Daifullah took on a greater role as a strike captain. He spoke Arabic, English, and Spanish, drawing praise for his versatility from Cesar Chavez, who said, "He . . . gave himself fully to the grape strike and farm worker justice." The young organizer's courage took him out onto the front lines, but also painted a target on his back. On August 15, 1973, as he stood outside a cafe shooting the breeze with a group of farmworkers, three Kern County sheriffs pulled up and started hassling them. Deputy Gilbert Cooper turned his attention on Daifullah, who had spoken up in the workers' defense, and gave chase as Daifullah tried to leave. The deputy smashed his heavy flashlight into Daifullah's head, severing the much smaller man's spinal cord from the base of his skull. The two other deputies then dragged Nagi's limp body across the pavement, by his feet, bumping his head along the ground and leaving a smear of blood on the concrete. They left his mangled body in the gutter, and arrested three of the workers he'd been trying to protect. Daifullah would not survive his injuries, passing away as thousands of supporters held a vigil outside the hospital.

Seven thousand people accompanied Daifullah's casket on a funeral procession that stretched for eleven miles, and his body was sent home to Yemen for a much-deserved rest. UFW president Cesar Chavez spoke at his funeral and later wrote to his father in Yemen, saying, "So long as farm workers struggle to be free, Nagi's memory will burn bright in their hearts." The murder galvanized the strikers, and he became the first a martyr for *la causa*. (Juan De La Cruz became the second when he was shot dead on the picket line on August 16, just a few days after Daifullah had drawn his last breath.) Two years later, California passed the 1975 California Agricultural Labor Relations Act, which established collective bargaining rights for farmworkers, and in 1977, the UFW and the Teamsters finally made peace with a stable jurisdictional agreement. Labor peace arrived just a little later, as the UFW ended its boycotts of lettuce, grapes, and wine in February 1978. When farmworkers gathered to vote in those first legal union elections, there were many Yemenis from the Joaquin Valley among them. They cast their votes in honor of Nagi Daifallah.

During all of this action, Larry Itliong had remained out of the spotlight but was still active in the greater struggle, albeit from afar. Tired of clashing with Chavez, Itliong resigned from the UFW in 1971, but continued organizing and advocating for Filipino workers until his death in 1977. He spent time organizing workers in Brazil and Chile, and founded the Filipino American Political Association. He was also instrumental in establishing Paolo Agbayani Village, a retirement community for Filipino farmworkers in Delano, and negotiated a deal with the growers to have them donate a percentage of each grape box picked to support the village residents. In 2019, the state of California officially declared October 25 to be Larry Itliong Day.

That history—of struggle, dedication, and hope—has been shared by generations of harvesters, from Hawai'ian sugar plantations to Californian asparagus fields to Alaskan canneries to a few miles down the road from where you're sitting . . . and so has violence, abuse, and enslavement. In a direct continuation of the exploitative sharecropper system that kept Black and poor white tenant farmers in a state of feudal bondage after the Civil War, slavery still exists on American farms. Today's migrant workers are recruited with promises of work and driven out to unfamiliar remote areas where their passports and legal documents are confiscated and where they may be unable to understand the language spoken (for example, a significant percentage of workers from the Mexican states of Oaxaca and Guerrero speak indigenous languages like Mixteco, Zapoteco, or Triqui). There, they are held in bondage to a debt that they'll never be able to repay, or are simply forced to work for no pay under the threat of deportation or further violence. Like the braceros before them, the seasonal workers who arrive in the U.S. via the H-2A visa program (roughly 10 percent of the workforce, according to a 2020 Economic Policy Institute article by Daniel Costa and Philip Martin) are tied to an employer who is responsible for providing their housing, food, transportation, and immigration papers, a situation that leaves workers even more vulnerable to monsters like Global Horizons CEO Mordechai Orian, who alongside six others was accused of holding six hundred Thai guest workers against their will in what prosecutors called "the largest human trafficking case in US history."

Though these enslaved workers are compelled to labor in the shadows, they are not alone. The Coalition of Immokalee Workers (CIW), a worker-led grassroots farmworkers' rights organization based in the major agricultural hub of Immokalee, Florida, has been investigating and assisting in the prosecution of modern slavery cases since 1992. Thanks to the CIW's tireless efforts, the U.S. government has successfully prosecuted eight cases of slave labor on Florida farms, ultimately liberating over twelve hundred workers. The coalition, which operates under the slogan "*Todos somos lideres*" ("We are all leaders"), was born out of the Southwest Florida Farmworker Project, and has been a guiding light for the modern farmworkers' rights movement since its founding in 1993. Led by immigrant farmworkers from Haiti, Mexico, and Guatemala, the CIW has undertaken a number of campaigns aimed at addressing specific needs and issues facing its members, and harnessed the power of boycotts, hunger strikes, public pressure, and—years before it became commonplace—the Internet to win what at first seemed like impossible battles against agricultural Goliaths. By organizing horizontally and allying closely with local religious leaders and students' groups, the CIW built a sustainable, ground-up, community-based movement that has resulted in higher wages and safer workplaces, and raised industry standards across Florida, while providing a blueprint for other worker-led labor groups.

It took years of struggle (and a highly publicized series of boycott campaigns against fast-food behemoths like Taco Bell and Burger King) to get there, but now the CIW's Fair Food Program provides workers with education and resources to understand their rights, has created a mechanism through which workers can confidentially report misconduct and abuse, mandates a penny-per-pound premium to benefit workers' pay, and, via regular third-party inspections from the Fair Food Standards Council, ensures that safety standards are met on participating farms. Certain violations of the program's code of conduct trigger the suspension of membership—and the farms lose the ability to sell their produce to the coalition's participating buyers, which include fourteen major corporations, like McDonald's, Subway, Trader Joe's, Whole Foods Market, and Walmart. "This is the best workplace-monitoring program I've seen in the U.S.," Janice R. Fine, a labor relations professor at Rutgers, told *New York Times* reporter Stephen Greenhouse in 2014. "It can certainly be a model for agriculture across the U.S. If anybody is going to lead the way and teach people how it's done, it's them."

The CIW has also been a leader in addressing sexual harassment and assault in the Florida fields. "We took deep experiential knowledge of what the issues are and turned that into a code of conduct and then went on to create all the necessary mechanisms to really change that power dynamic," Nely Rodriguez, a former farmworker who is now a senior CIW staff member, told the *Atlantic* in 2018. On top of the myriad pay and health issues and the backbreaking conditions that all farmworkers labor under, women and gender-nonconforming workers face the additional threat of sexual violence at work. According to the CIW, an estimated four in five women in the U.S. agricultural industry suffer sexual harassment and assault on the job. They make up only 32 percent of farmworkers and work in a male-dominated industry that devalues their labor as well as their physical health and safety; many are also domestic abuse survivors, and have to navigate additional trauma. According to the Southern Poverty Law Center, undocumented women "are often the primary caregivers for children, making them less likely to assert their rights for fear of being fired or, worse, being deported and separated from their families. And because of their fear of being reported to immigration authorities, they are reluctant to report wage violations, sexual violence or gender discrimination, or to take legal action to stop it."

"WE WANT DIGNITY AND RESPECT"

When the COVID-19 pandemic first hit the U.S. in early 2020 and people were told to stay six feet apart and hunker down at home to avoid spreading the virus, agricultural workers across the country reported to work as usual. With faces swathed in bandanas and fingers crossed, they continued to plant, pick, cut, gut, and package the food that was destined for millions of tables, feeding a country that still denies many of them the most basic labor rights or medical care. "The threat to farmworkers is a threat to us all—not only because, to quote Dr. Martin Luther King, Jr., we are all 'tied up in a single garment of destiny,' but also because farmworkers feed us all," CIW cofounder Greg Asbed wrote in a 2020 *New York Times* op-ed. "No food workers, no food. It's that simple."

The vast majority of farmworkers in this country remain unable to unionize, so for those who do have the benefit of a union thanks to state laws, the extra layer of protection is critical for both physical safety and morale.

"It has given me extra strength to fight against injustice, what has been and still is," José Martinez, a Mexican mushroom farmworker in Washington State's Yakima Valley who now works ten-hour days enforcing the farm's COVID-19 safety precautions, told me. He first heard about the UFW in the 1970s, but became involved with the union after he moved up to Washington and began hearing about it on Radio Cadena, a nonprofit radio station with ties to the farmworker community. As his workplace is not yet unionized, Martinez is currently an associate member, but he still spends a lot of his time talking with his coworkers about how to make things better. As he tells me, ultimately it all comes down to equality and respect.

The quest for those same essential qualities is what has driven the harvesters to organize for generations, and is what led twelve farmworkers in upstate New York to form the state's very first farmworker union in 2021. After the state passed the 2019 Farm Laborers Fair Labor Practices Act, which grants agricultural and farm workers the right to collectively bargain, workers at Pindar Vineyards in Peconic got to work. Two years later, Local 338 RWDSU/UFCW was officially certified, and farmworkers had once again made history. "My coworkers at Pindar and I joined Local 338 because we want dignity and respect," Rodolfo M. said in a union press release. "We know that being a union member will help us get the recognition we deserve for all of our efforts."

When I spoke with Martir Zambrano Diaz, another of the freshly minted union members, he also emphasized the importance of bargaining for sick days, paid time off, and safer staffing levels. Originally from Honduras, Diaz spoke in Spanish as a union staffer translated, and asked that the consumers who benefit from their labor support both the laws that protect agricultural workers and efforts to secure a pathway to citizenship for those who lack documents. Mostly, he sounded relieved, and excited about the possibilities that organizing had opened up for him and his coworkers, after so many years of toiling in the shadows. "I'm very, very happy," he said. "And thankful."

7

THE CLEANERS

Domestic work—the work of caring for children, elders, and homes—is the work that makes all other work possible.

—Ai-Jen Poo, cofounder and executive director, National Domestic Workers Alliance

Women have always been expected to clean. Whether they were housewives tidying up their own homes, enslaved prisoners forced to care for a master's house, or waged workers who were called upon to clean up someone else's shit, women (and gender nonconforming people; just because they may have been rendered invisible in historical documents doesn't mean they weren't there) have traditionally done society's dirty work.

Their labor was often invisible, or at least they themselves were encouraged to be—relegated to separate entrances, separate bathrooms, shooed out of sight lest they mar the view and remind more privileged people of who was really keeping things running.

When Marxist feminist scholar and activist Silvia Federici wrote her 1974 treatise *Wages Against Housework*, she was already involved in the wages for housework movement, a grassroots network of women founded by anti-racist feminist Selma James in 1972. The campaign was international in focus and gave rise to multiple other impactful organizations, including the English Collective of Prostitutes and Black Women for Wages for Housework, which was cofounded by Margaret

Prescod and is now known as Women of Colour in the Global Women's Strike. Federici's razor-sharp analysis pulled no punches, and rang true to the frustrations of an invisibilized workforce. "The unwaged condition of housework has been the most powerful weapon in reinforcing the common assumption that housework is not work, thus preventing women from struggling against it," she wrote. "We are seen as nagging bitches, not workers in struggle."

The group's principle demand was simple: that people who work in the home doing the invisible work of cooking, cleaning, childbearing, caring for children and elders, catering to a spouse, running the household, growing and gathering food, and all manner of other unwaged domestic labor *should* be paid. Their view was that so-called women's work was an essential cog in the capitalist machine, and that only by demanding wages for that work could we get to a point where we can withhold that labor entirely. As Selma James said in a 2011 interview, "There is waged work in the society, and there is unwaged work in the society, and they're both absolutely crucial to the accumulation of capital and to its destruction." The original campaign has changed and evolved over the past four decades, but it's far-reaching political vision remains a vital part of ongoing conversations over gender, labor, and capitalism. "It was such a revelatory power even just to name 'wages for housework,'" Silvia Federici reflected in 2015. "It said, 'these homes are the factories in which we work.' It was a question of denaturalising housework and showing the social, historical character of the work."

The work itself has changed little over the years, nor has the reality of the people doing it. In this chapter, I've grouped domestic workers alongside their sisters (because it is so often sisters) in the wider cleaning world—the laundry workers, janitors, and housekeepers—because of the nature of their work and because they all occupy a dissonant space in which they are both utterly essential and treated as if they were entirely disposable.

WAITING TO WORK

"Twice I was hired by the hour at less than the wage asked by the women of the market. Both times I went home mad—mad for all the Negro women down through the ages who have been lashed by the stinging whip of economic oppression," the woman wrote, fury emanating from the page, the memory fresh in her mind's eye, and her deadline for the *New York Daily Compass* fast approaching. The writer, Marvel Cooke, had just completed her first day as a domestic worker, and had experienced firsthand what it felt like to be treated like "a strapping, big animal" purchased by the pound to do someone else's bidding.

Cooke's bad day took place in 1935, but this scenario will sound all too familiar to her modern counterparts. One hundred and twenty thousand day laborers, many of whom are Latino immigrants, some of whom are currently undocumented, still spend hours each day waiting outside American job centers, gas stations, and Home Depots for a potential employer to beckon them forward. That system of contingent work, in which a worker's time is literally bought by the hour or the day with no promise of further employment, is common within the construction and agricultural worlds (and will ring familiar to today's app-based "gig workers") but is not constrained to one industry—or one gender. Employers in search of housekeeping or cleaning services still frequent places like la Parada—"the Place"—in Brooklyn's South Williamsburg neighborhood to recruit *jornaleras*, or women day laborers, from the groups of immigrant Latinas who gather there, and the city itself has a long history of forcing hardworking women of color into the streets to beg for a shot at earning a few dollars and carfare.

Prior to the stock market crash of 1929 and the resulting economic devastation that defined the era, Black women had the market cornered on domestic labor simply because they had been barred from almost every other form of employment, especially in the South. During the 1920s, between 65 and 85 percent of Black women worked domestic service jobs—double the workforce participation rate of American-born white women, and triple the rate for immigrant women.

When Black women did move into industrial jobs in power laundries in the North, railroads in the Midwest, and factories in the South, they were only offered the hottest, heaviest, most hazardous positions. It's important to note that despite the misery and exploitation inherent in the work, these jobs were still considered preferable to working as domestic servants in private white homes, and were celebrated by the National Urban League as a sign of economic and social advancement. Black home laundry workers had long experienced greater autonomy by taking in laundry on their own terms, but the power laundries that appeared in the industrial North during the 1920s soon muscled them out of the market. (In the South, where white women intent on upholding racialized master-servant-style power dynamics would spend their last dollar to avoid the labor and indignity of washing their own dirty clothes, the abundance of home laundry workers kept the machines at bay until the 1930s.) Women who went to work at said laundries suffered under deplorable conditions, but Florence Rice, a Harlem domestic worker turned power laundry employee, insisted that it was still "better than domestic work, certainly."

Otherwise, many Black women workers found that the only option available to them, besides industrial labor or domestic work, lay in the informal sex work economy, in which they could potentially bring home much higher wages but faced increased risks of police brutality, imprisonment, and social stigma. For example, Black women made up more than half of Chicago's total arrests for sex work during that period, a number that soared to more than 78 percent as the Great Depression set in and more women struggled to find employment. In the Northern cities, Black domestic workers and laundry workers also had to contend with more competition, as newly unemployed white women and white women who were seeking employment outside the home for the first time swelled the ranks of available domestic labor, and many other white housewives sucked it up and did their own chores to save money instead of hiring out. In the power laundries, employers cut wages, implemented speed-ups, and fired workers, especially those who were older or disabled. Sometimes bosses fired Black women in order to hire white women, and others replaced white women with Black women, knowing they could pay Black workers less and work them harder with impunity.

"THE BRONX SLAVE MARKET"

The Depression hit domestic workers especially hard, as they had no federal safety net to fall back on (they and farmworkers were the two groups, predominantly Black, excluded from the 1935 Social Security Act). In New York City, Black domestic workers could be seen gathered on street corners in the Bronx, Harlem, and Brownsville every day, holding their work clothes in paper bags and accepting below-market rates, wage theft, and abuse out of sheer desperation. White housewives would cruise by each morning, peering out their car windows trying to pick out the strongest, "nicest" workers to exploit for the day. When civil rights icon Ella Baker and journalist Marvel Cooke visited those corners to talk with their occupants, they were horrified at what they found. They dubbed it "the Slave Market."

Following their investigation, Cooke and Baker cowrote an article about it for the November 1935 issue of the *Crisis*, the NAACP's magazine. Years later, Cooke went undercover, joining the "paper bag brigade" and hiring herself out to several employers to get a taste of what domestic workers were expected to endure to earn their 75 cents per hour (the women taught her to always start out asking for a daily wage of $6 and carfare, but employers inevitably bargained them down to the lowest possible rate). She was hired twice during her excursion, and received $3.40 for a full day of strenuous labor, including scrubbing floors on her hands and knees. "I gathered strength as I scrubbed that floor," Cooke wrote afterward. "I cleaned it with the strength of all slaves everywhere who feel the whip."

Cooke, the daughter of a teacher and a Pullman porter, was an educated professional woman who had enjoyed a relatively comfortable middle-class upbringing and was active in the Harlem Renaissance. She usually spent her days reporting stories for the *New York Daily Compass* as the white-owned paper's first full-time Black female staff writer, and her evenings discussing art and culture with the likes of poet Langston Hughes, her mentor W. E. B. Du Bois, and singer, actor, and activist Paul Robeson. Before landing at the *Compass* in 1950, she had worked at the Black-owned *Amsterdam News*, where she organized one of the first chapters of the Newspaper Guild—the first such local newspaper union at a Black newspaper—and was summarily fired in an anti-union purge (she was later jailed—twice!—for picketing the *News* office). After an eleven-week lockout, the paper was sold off to new owners, who promptly rehired the staff and gave them a raise. Around the same time, Cooke broke off her engagement with Roy Wilkins of NAACP and March on Washington fame (she found him to be "too conservative," and Cooke, a dedicated Communist, was anything but). It is doubtful that she had ever imagined she would find herself standing outside in the rain begging for work, or scrubbing a white woman's bathtub for mere pennies, but that was the daily reality for thousands of the Black women she lived alongside in her Harlem neighborhood.

She published her findings in a five-part series for the *Daily Compass* entitled "The Bronx Slave Market," and used her platform to advocate for reform. When Mayor Fiorello LaGuardia responded with a half-baked plan to enlist hiring halls and redirect workers to state employment services, Cooke responded with devastating effect, stating that LaGuardia's proposal would "merely put a roof over the Slave Market." While hiring halls had long been an established means for unions to find work for their members, the real problem was the systemic racism, discrimination, and misogynoir (anti-Black misogyny) that defined the way that the "paper bag brigade" workers were treated. Still Cooke continued on, speaking to workers and organizers to see what they felt was the best path forward. "Our primary aim is to bring these women into the union," Nina Evans, president of Local 149 of the independent Domestic Workers Union, told Cooke. "But other things must be done, too. We must carry on a continuous and militant fight to bring domestic workers under the protection of the minimum wage and minimum hour laws, and under the workmen's compensation and social security acts."

In her series, Cooke reports the story of a woman who is too afraid to use state services and instead tries her luck on the corner, fending off sexual harassment from men and cruelty from her employers. Each day, she is joined by more and more hopeful faces, and each day, she sees the bosses haggle a little harder over pennies. "Now she may get 7 cents an hour," Cooke determined. "But as more and more workers join her 'brigade'—as the supply of domestic labor surpasses the demand—wages are bound to be depressed even further. Her security lies in decent legislative safeguards, in employer education and employee training, and, above all, in unionization. These, and these only, will make Slave Markets disappear."

BUILDING POWER IN THE POWER LAUNDRIES

By the time Cooke's series was published in 1950, domestic workers and their sisters in the laundry business had been organizing among themselves for decades. In 1864, Irish immigrant women working as "collar laundresses" in the shirt-making hub of Troy, New York, formed the Collar Laundry Union; led by Kate Mullany and Esther Keegan, it was the first all-female labor union in the U.S. The CLU's three hundred members successfully agitated for and won raises in 1866, 1868, and 1869 before dissolving in 1870 after years of fierce opposition from laundry bosses. Mullany, however, remained active in the labor and women's suffrage movements, and was elected assistant secretary of the National Labor Congress in 1868, marking the first time a woman had been appointed to a national labor union office. There was of course the previously mentioned Washerwomen of Jackson's historic 1881 work stoppage, and in 1901 the Working Women's Association launched on behalf of three hundred domestic workers in Chicago.

In 1912, six thousand New York City laundry workers—a mix of Jewish, Italian, Irish, and German immigrants and native-born white women led by Irish immigrant laundry worker Margaret Hinchley—struck for more than a month to protest a proposed scheme that would have consolidated power in the hands of the city's leading laundry owners and, they feared, resulted in job losses. The city's chapter of the Women's Trade Union League (WTUL) furnished organizational resources as well as material support in the form of a strike fund.

The strike was ultimately broken thanks in no small part to the laundry delivery drivers, all white men, who disregarded their coworkers and crossed the picket line, but it did set the stage for large-scale laundry-sector organizing in the 1920s. In 1921, New York's shirt ironers—who at that point were predominantly Jewish men—endeavored to found their own Laundry Workers International Union Local 280, and sought help to do so from WTUL president Rose Schneiderman. Schneiderman saw an opportunity to advance her causes of labor solidarity and social progressivism at once, advising her union to take on "family ironers," a largely Black and female contingent who were employed on a freelance basis by hand laundries around the city. Schneiderman had long pushed for cross-racial engagement in the laundry sector, recognizing the power in numbers and the symbolic advantage of a fully integrated labor effort. Unfortunately, her rank and file's appetites for such an effort were limited. In contemporary terms it was a classic case of misogynoir, and not an uncommon response for even majority-immigrant shops of the time.

The labor movement was already rife with unequal "Jim Crow locals" that split white and Black workers into separate unions, but thanks to the shirt ironers slamming the door in their faces, the WTUL was left with no other option than to assist the women in forming their own parallel, de facto segregated union (LWIU Local 284). With veteran Black laundry worker Delia Haren as president, Local 284 soldiered on, holding meetings with more than four hundred workers at more than three hundred hand laundries around the city. As time passed, they would be boosted by cameos from people like A. Philip Randolph and ILGWU organizer Frank Crosswaith (whose nickname, "the Negro Debs," underscored the Caribbean immigrant's deep commitment to class struggle), but their campaign did not really take flight until 1934 when a Black domestic worker named Dora Lee Jones founded the Domestic Workers Union of New York. The Harlem-based union circulated literature and news clippings about domestic workers' issues, pushed to standardize private employment, and warned workers to avoid the exploitative "Slave Market."

The DWU also chipped away at the isolation of domestic work by setting up a library and reading room, making space for the women to socialize in their precious little time off. The DWU eventually affiliated with the predecessor to today's Service Employees International Union (SEIU) and grew to more than one thousand members. But growth did not unstack the deck against Jones's vulnerable membership. DWU workers often came from disadvantaged backgrounds, struggled with poverty, and were subject to unsteady employment from a host of clients. The regular dues payments that fueled other unions were not feasible for the DWU's membership. In an ugly preface to the modern debate around valuing the "hidden labor" of managing a household, the AFL's and CIO's member unions were in many ways impediments to establishing the legitimacy of domestic workers, the AFL deeming theirs to be "unskilled work" and the CIO declaring the home to not be a workplace. Frozen out of the traditional trade union structure, worker-organizers like Jones had to instead depend on intra-communal bonds to create networks of solidarity.

The same year Dora Jones founded the DWU against a vibrant Harlem backdrop, an interracial group of four hundred laundry workers across the bridge in Brooklyn would strike over their bosses' refusal to pay them the new state-mandated 31-cent-per-hour minimum wage. Once again, the WTUL arrived on the scene ready to offer support and resources, and Eleanor Roosevelt, a member of the league, offered the workers the use of her Secret Service agents to protect them from police (and had them arrest at least one laundry boss for hurling insults). The "mink brigade" certainly played an important role in this and other strikes, but there was an obvious gulf in terms of race, class, and economic status between the wealthy white housewives and society women who made up the WTUL's membership and the impoverished, predominantly Black working-class women they endeavored to support. While the WTUL contributed crucial support and was especially effective in pulling political strings for workers' benefit, fundraising from rich friends and securing publicity for important actions, there was also a tendency among some of its members to take a patronizing tone when engaging with workers, to police Black women's tone and behavior, and to push their own ideas around respectability and "ladylike" deportment on the picket lines.

Internal fissures were also beginning to divide the WTUL, little by little. The Progressive Era was rife with well-meaning white feminist groups who centered gender over race and class, and the WTUL was no exception. (Their liberal descendants today have made only so much progress; as writer and activist Grace Chang noted in her *Disposable Domestics*, "Efforts to improve conditions and wages for domestic workers and child-care providers have historically drawn a poor response from mainstream women's groups." That was written in 2000, so one can imagine how bad things were a century prior.)

The once radical Rose Schneiderman herself had become an established mover and shaker in the country's labor leadership. Appointments to New York's Minimum Wage Advisory Board and FDR's National Recovery Act (NRA) Labor Advisory Board were evidence of her mellowing politics, and Schneiderman also drew criticism from the long-running Communist paper the *Daily Worker* for being an "ally" of "the A. F. of L. machine." Schneiderman's close relationship with the Roosevelts and discomfort with the emerging radical movements that would define the 1930s political landscape were another factor. The ideological gap between different eras of the WTUL would lead to its eventual dissolution in 1949.

DORTHY LEE BOLDEN AND THE WORLD AHEAD

A world away from the WTUL's swanky Manhattan clubhouse, a young, visually impaired leader-to-be named Dorothy Lee Bolden was waiting in the wings. Bolden would later grow into a powerful organizer and activist, but in 1934, she was only an eleven-year-old girl. She was already a seasoned domestic worker, though; she had joined her mother in service at the age of nine, taking the bus to and from work each day. Bolden would spend forty-nine years as a proud domestic worker, but she occasionally held other jobs as well. She got her first taste of union power while working at the National Linen Service; when she and her coworkers unionized, her daily wage rocketed from $3 to $23. During the early 1960s, she volunteered with Ella Baker's Student Nonviolent Coordinating Committee and organized urgent protests against police brutality. "I went to rallies, I was the most vocal person there," she recalled. "I stayed that way and Dr. King sent SNCC and all the rest of them: 'Look Bolden up down there, she'll help you.'" In 1964, she organized a boycott of Atlanta schools to protest the school board's refusal to treat Black students fairly. And she worried about the conditions she and her fellow domestic workers labored under, especially how their low wages might impact their ability to participate in the broader fight against segregation. "We couldn't be going to integrate the schools out there barefooted," she explained in a 1995 interview. "I didn't want to integrate my child into a society like that [if they] didn't have no shoes or decent clothes to put on." She decided they would need a union.

In those days, Dr. Martin Luther King was her next-door neighbor on Auburn Avenue in Atlanta, and when she came to him asking for advice on how to organize domestic workers one day, he told her, "You do it—and don't let nobody take it. I know they will have a fight on their hands if they try to take it." Bolden was born a fighter; she was once briefly committed to a psychiatric institution when police couldn't believe she'd dared to refuse her white employer's orders. So when Dr. King spoke, she took his advice and ran with it. She had been riding the bus to work since she was a child, and knew that those hot, uncomfortable rides were often the only time that domestic workers had to socialize among themselves. Bolden started to hold conversations with them about wages, long hours, brutish employers, and aching bodies, building community while also laying the bedrock for a new organization. The other women trusted her, because she was one of them; she knew the pain of a thirteen-hour day, the pinch of low wages, and the prickle of constant disrespect. Bolden traveled every inch of Atlanta she could, with a word for every domestic worker who would listen—especially about the power of their votes. All the while she fended off harassment from the Ku Klux Klan, who would call her house and threaten her life. "I never told anybody because it didn't scare me, didn't bother me," she later recalled. "It made me angry, it made me determined to do what I had to do." She poured as much energy into the project as she could spare. For a mother of seven with a full-time job, juggling it all was a challenge. But she did it anyway.

Those conversations bore fruit when, in 1968, after getting a few last pieces of advice from a few trusted voices within organized labor, she put out a call on the radio and in Black-owned newspapers inviting domestic workers to the first meeting of the National Domestic Workers Union. Eight women came to the first meeting, but many more followed, and Bolden was elected the group's first president. The Atlanta Urban League, a community organization, had its own plans to organize domestic workers, but Bolden (who had mentioned her project to them previously and received little interest) came to their second meeting on the subject, took control of the room, and told them in no uncertain terms, "I already got a group together. If y'all want to do this, you can join my group." So they did.

Bolden's firm belief in the power of civic engagement, especially for Black women, meant NDWU membership required two things: a fee of $1 and a completed voter registration form. This would not be a traditional labor union, and Bolden was cognizant of Black people's suspicions of striking and organized labor, thanks to the hostile response they often received from racist all-white unions. Rather, she framed the NDWU as a training, advocacy, social services, and educational group, a sisterhood that also taught its members how to negotiate for higher wages and better treatment. The NDWU developed programs specifically targeted toward lifting Black women workers out of poverty, and promoted "Maids Honor Day" to publicly recognize and honor them for their labor. The group's eight original demands revolved around economics and the right to rest—minimum wages for various types of work, paid vacations, Social Security contributions from their employers, time off, sick leave, an eight-hour workday—and were intended to prevent Atlanta from developing its own Bronx-style "Slave Market."

Within the first two years of the NDWU's existence, Atlanta's domestic workers saw their daily wages rise from less than $5 to an average of $13.50 to $15, a seismic shift that was still less than they deserved, but so much more than they'd had before they organized. Membership grew rapidly, and soon numbered thirteen thousand across ten cities. Bolden led the organization for the next thirty years, and became a political power player and beloved Atlanta icon. She was called to advise three presidents on social services and workers' rights, and used her own money to keep NDWU afloat in the 1980s after federal funding dried up. The NDWU proper folded in 1996, but by then more organizations aimed at aiding domestic workers had sprung up, and their cause had gained global attention.

Bolden's emphasis on voting rights and equality was also heard loud and clear by another generation of community-minded Black leaders like voting rights activist and politician Stacey Abrams, whose 2018 gubernatorial campaign was strongly supported in Atlanta by the National Domestic Workers Alliance. "She didn't back down to anybody," Rep. Nikema Williams, former director of NDWA's political arm in Georgia, told journalist Laura Bassett for *HuffPost*. "She stood up to make sure workers had contracts and base wages, some of the same things we're fighting for today, just to have dignity and to be heard in order to do their jobs. We absolutely ground ourselves in the work of Dorothy Bolden and her vision in everything that we do."

Bolden's legacy would manifest in more ways—and more industries—than one. Black workers and workers of color now see more open avenues for employment, but they are still too often relegated to the "dirty work" of unpleasant or hazardous labor like cleaning, hauling, caring for the ill or elderly, and picking up others' soiled clothes, kitchen scraps, and bodily fluids. Even now nearly a third (28 percent) of Black women are employed in service jobs compared with just one-fifth of white women. The Economic Policy Institute found that in 2019, a majority (52.4 percent) of domestic workers were Black, Hispanic, or AAPI women—more than a quarter (27.2 percent) were Latinas, and nearly one in five (19.7 percent) were Black women. Most house cleaners (58.9 percent) are Latinas and more than a quarter (27.2 percent) of agency-based home care aides are Black women.

There have been significant legal strides for these workers' rights, though domestic workers (and farm workers) remain excluded from the 1935 National Labor Relations Act. In 2010, New York passed the Domestic Workers Bill of Rights, the first statewide law to extend basic labor protections to domestic workers. Hawai'i, California, Washington, and several other states followed suit, expanding on the initial legislation with greater protections like overtime and a minimum wage. The year 2020 saw Philadelphia pass the strongest domestic-worker legislation in the nation, a bill to protect the city's sixteen thousand nannies, house cleaners, and home care workers—many of whom were excluded from federal assistance due to their documentation status. These were necessary steps forward, but there is still so much further to go.

Black domestic workers were once told they were impossible to organize—and then formed their own unions, and struck by the thousands. Throughout the late 1980s and 1990s, Latino janitors were told the same thing. Up until the 1970s, the industry had been heavily unionized (the Service Employees International Union even got its start as the Building Service Employees International Union), but that changed when investors began pouring money into commercial real estate and expanding their portfolios throughout the country. Subcontracting out to the lowest bidder was cheaper for building owners, businesses, and retailers, and carried the added benefit of insulating employers from liability; instead of hiring janitors outright, they could outsource the human costs of cleaning their real estate properties to a web of contractors, who then hired from a primarily Latino, largely immigrant pool of independent contractors. The decline of unions in the industry dovetailed with a huge drop in wages, and the workers themselves were told once again that the white leadership of local unions just didn't know how to organize them. Those workers ended up launching one of the largest worker justice campaigns in recent U.S. history.

When a young man named Stephen Lerner arrived in Denver in 1985, the city's janitors were making an average of $4 per hour. His boss, SEIU president John Sweeney, had authorized a national campaign to organize the nation's janitors, and as the newly appointed head of the union's janitorial division, Lerner set out for Colorado. A year later, more than eight hundred had joined the union, and word was spreading fast. Sweeney's first visit to check on the campaign moved him in a way he hadn't expected. The workers' testimonies from the ground, and the hope they had derived from the organizing efforts that had been devoted to their work space, was incredible. Latino immigrants, once dismissed as being "too hard" to organize, became a priority for the union. "Everyone said you can't win in building services because people work part-time, many are undocumented, and Latino immigrants don't want to unionize," Lerner later recalled. "After Denver, everyone said we won because undocumented Latino workers were ripe for unionization!" Time and care had paid off.

SEIU moved next to Washington, D.C., and Los Angeles, and the latter became a hot spot for more direct and confrontational action. In L.A. they used street theater and public protests to stir sympathy, and then they went straight to the sources of power. Building bosses started to see protestors lined up ready to chat at their favored restaurants and golf courses. The mood shifted during a peaceful protest on June 15, 1990, when striking janitors and their allies were viciously attacked by the Los Angeles police; one protestor suffered a miscarriage as a result of the scrum. The workers still held firm, singing out a rallying cry borrowed from their siblings in the United Farm Workers, another predominantly Latino immigrant union, "*Sí se puede!*," as they continued to fight. It worked; between 1987 and 2000, area-wide contracts covering up to ninety-five hundred janitors included increased wages and full health coverage for five thousand workers. By the time they were done, 90 percent of the building services market in downtown Los Angeles and the Century City business district were union, and the campaign had set its sights on new targets in Houston, Boston, and Miami, where things would *really* heat up.

The 2006 Miami Justice for Janitors campaign was a knockdown, drag-out fight. The standoff saw the University of Miami, led by its president, former Clinton cabinet member Donna Shalala, pitted against its janitorial staff and a host of the workers' allies—Miami's student body, local religious leaders, and the surrounding community. The janitors held a historic nine-week strike, lasting from February 28 to May 3, 2006, that saw labor leaders Dolores Huerta, Eliseo Medina, and Jimmy Hoffa, Jr., head south to pitch in. Clergy from the South Florida Interfaith Worker Justice (SFIWJ) association hit the streets alongside striking workers who used every trick in the book—they blocked traffic, they chanted while holding signs (demanding "Justice for Janitors!"), and they lambasted Shalala in the press. The face of the anti-union efforts had done herself no favors by agreeing to a fluffy *New York Times* piece on her luxurious lifestyle in the midst of the strike, and Ana Menendez, a *Miami Herald* columnist, seized on the opportunity to contrast the UM president's existence with the brutal reality campus cleaners faced. "I have worked hard all my life, but the situation in this country has changed," Zoila Garcia, a striking janitor, told Menendez. "The cost of living is so high and no one can live with these salaries. These millionaires just don't understand the struggles of working people."

A month in, a group of ten workers and six students raised the stakes by launching a hunger strike. As one worker, Feliciano Hernandez, explained, "They are treating us like dogs. We can't allow that to continue." After three more weeks without progress, hunger strikers Isabel Montvalo and Odalys Rodriquez were rushed to the hospital in desperate need of medical attention. In their stead, SEIU president Andy Stern and executive vice president Eliseo Medina—who had just led five thousand janitors in Houston to victory—stepped up and volunteered to continue the fasts. More than 150 other labor and political leaders joined to take part in a "rolling fast" in solidarity with Isabel and Odalys.

Faced with intensifying opposition and a public relations nightmare, the university caved. Wages were raised, workers' share of health-care costs were reduced, and the janitors' union was formally recognized. Justice for Janitors had notched its first big victory in one of the South's trickiest states to organize, and had earned its laurels as one of the new century's most visible and impactful campaigns linking immigrants' rights and workers' rights.

Echoes of that progress would ring out a decade later, when members of Local 1877 in Orange County, California, would take an even bigger—and more difficult—leap toward progress.

"*YA BASTA!*" ("ENOUGH IS ENOUGH")

In 2015, a PBS *Frontline* documentary, the Emmy-nominated "Rape on the Night Shift," shed a harsh light on the endemic nature of sexual violence within the janitorial industry. It is an exceptionally risky field for women workers—one often worked in isolation by recent immigrants who may have uncertain immigration status or language barriers that make it more difficult to seek aid against exploitation. A 2021 Cornell University report found that "women janitors are more likely to experience unwanted sexual behavior than men; they are also much more likely to be targeted by supervisors and to switch jobs due to harassing behavior," and "many survivors do not trust existing channels for reporting and responding to sexual harassment."

Journalist Bernice Yeung, lead reporter for the PBS film and author of *In a Day's Work* on the topic, explained further in her book: "If there is a perfect storm of factors that put workers at risk, night-shift janitorial work is at its epicenter," she wrote. "Nearly every office building in America relies on janitors, but we rarely see the people who do the vacuuming and mopping. The work is scheduled to happen at night or during the early morning, when few people are around. They are expected to be invisible."

The union representing the janitorial workers shown in the film, the Service Employees International Union—United Service Workers West (USWW), was caught flat-footed. In a pre-#MeToo world, sexual harassment hadn't been on the (predominantly male-led) group's radar. They'd been focused on "bread-and-butter" economic issues and had overlooked the specific dangers facing their female members. But USWW represents twenty-five thousand janitors across California, the majority of whom are immigrant women of color. Clearly, a significant part of the membership was suffering in silence, and the documentary sent a shock wave through the entire union.

To the group's credit, the missteps were taken as a lesson, and the USWW immediately began work to make things right. In 2016, the Ya Basta—Spanish for "Enough Is Enough!"—campaign was born; an all-out, worker-led fight against sexual harassment in the workplace. Ya Basta centered the thoughts and opinions of survivors, taking their cues as it directly engaged in peer-to-peer organizing, training, and mentorship. Since then, Ya Basta has grown into a social justice juggernaut—with demonstrations, marches, hunger strikes, and speak-outs pushing the issue of sexual harassment even further into the public sphere. Upon passage of California's Ya Basta–inspired 2017 Property Service Workers Protection Act, which protects janitors from wage theft and sexual harassment on the job, a janitor named Georgina Hernández spoke up before her coworkers to share the stomach-churning details of her own sexual assault on the job. "I share this because I know this is happening every day," she explained to journalists Sanjay Pinto, Zoë West, and KC Wagner for a *New Labor Forum* article. "This isn't just in the janitorial industry, it's in all industries. . . . And as a woman, one lives and fights out of necessity, to support your family. To survive."

The women of Ya Basta have also trained more than a hundred *promotoras*—community-based trainers who go into workplaces to share knowledge and resources with fellow workers—to continue the work on the ground. In doing so, they adopted the bottom-up organizing model that has worked so well for other worker-led labor groups, like Janitors for Justice or, even further back, Dora Jones's Domestic Workers Union. In October 2019, Ya Basta notched another legal victory when the Janitor Survivor Empowerment Act was signed into law and expanded the legal framework for the *promotoras'* mission—requiring that employers make qualified peer-to-peer trainings on workplace sexual violence available to every janitor in California.

Ya Basta's continuing success provides a powerful blueprint of the kind of real-world progress that can be won when a union commits its resources to campaigns for communities, led by those communities. Labor's most sacred task is to protect its most vulnerable workers at all costs, and poor and working-class women, especially Black women and immigrant women of color, are still frequently placed in the most unsafe environments. The Depression-era "paper bag brigade" in Harlem, janitors in 1990s Miami, and even more recently, the thousands of Marriott Hotel housekeepers who secured protections from sexual assault through a nationwide strike in 2018, all had their labor devalued, their bodies abused, and their very humanity questioned or disregarded.

By sharing their burdens and utilizing common ground to forge collective action, each obtained some semblance of relief. Each drew upon the work of those who came before—domestic workers, laundry workers, janitors, and hotel housekeepers alike—in a chain that has enabled each new cohort to translate empathy into action, reclaim their own power, and hand new workers the tools to fight back on their own terms.

All of them—from Kate Mullany and Marvel Cooke to Dorothy Bolden and Georgina Hernández—were told over and over again that certain types of workers—domestics, laundry workers, and countless other women who were expected to shut up, scrub, and remain invisible—were "unorganizable." It was a drumbeat of discouragement surrounding the labor movement then, and it continues to color perceptions of who can and should organize now. But each time, those workers proved that conventional "wisdom" wrong.

There are certainly circumstances in which it is more difficult or complicated to organize. And America's obsolete labor laws, the most impactful of which were passed back in the 1930s, remain ignorant to the diversity of people, circumstances, and industries this country has developed over the past century. Still, as of 2020, 65 percent of Americans said they approve of labor unions, and 48 percent of workers who were polled in 2017 said they would join a union if allowed; but far too many don't even have the option. So-called right-to-work states like Georgia, Texas, and Alabama (and their Republican legislatures) hamstring organizing at every turn, and even workers in states with more liberal labor laws still see union-busting bosses swoop in to crush their efforts to organize. But as we've seen (and will see again later), "difficult" has never meant impossible.

8

THE FREEDOM FIGHTERS

The colored men who went to war for this democracy returned home determined to emancipate themselves from the slavery which took all a man and his family could earn, left him in debt, gave him no freedom of action, no protection for his life or property, no education for his children, but did give him Jim Crow cars, lynching and disfranchisement.

—IDA B. WELLS, *THE ARKANSAS RACE RIOT*

One of the bloodiest racial massacres in U.S. history started with a union meeting. In the years following the Civil War, formerly enslaved Black people in the South gravitated to agricultural work or domestic service, both in order to take advantage of their previous work experience and because of the profound lack of other options. It just so happens, of course, that these were also two of the lowest-paid occupations. Southern white elites were happy to see Black workers in a familiar subordinate setting, but chafed at the new requirements to actually pay them for their labor and treat them as full-fledged human beings.

In response, landowners came up with a work-around. Much like the convict leasing system, which was born of the same urgent desire to subjugate and extract free labor from Black people, a new innovation—sharecropping—was an inherently unequal partnership that upheld the prevailing white supremacist power imbalance and forced generations of emancipated Black agricultural workers to, again, work for next to nothing.

Sharecroppers and their families were bound to the soil. They signed agreements with landowners to rent acreage, supplies, and tools to grow crops like cotton, rice, and tobacco. In exchange, sharecroppers would theoretically receive a share of the profits. But in reality, white landowners devised means to force their sharecropping partners into vicious cycles of debt. Black workers and their families were compelled to shop on credit at the plantation store, overcharged for needed supplies, crushed under interest payments, and then denied the ability to see how much they actually owed. Itemized accountings of the Black farmers' debts were difficult to obtain, if they existed at all. It was illegal for Black sharecroppers to leave a plantation until their debts had been paid, and they were highly discouraged from selling their crops to anyone besides the landowner with whom they'd initially contracted.

Debt slavery had technically been outlawed in 1867 when Congress passed the Peonage Abolition Act—but the news somehow failed to reach the white landowners of the Arkansas Delta, who continued their aggressive economic exploitation of the Black sharecroppers who worked their land. Some formerly enslaved sharecroppers even found themselves working for their old masters, further alienating them from the alleged promise of their freedom. As Frederick Douglass observed in his autobiography, under this system of modified serfdom, the Black sharecropper was "free from the individual master," but was now "the slave of society."

By 1918, Black farmers returning from military service overseas in World War I had hit upon a plan to close this terrible addendum to the era of chattel slavery. That year, Robert L. Hill founded the Progressive Farmers and Household Union of America (PFHUA) with the stated aim to "advance the interests of the Negro, morally and intellectually, and to make him be a better citizen and a better farmer." The union recruited hundreds of sharecroppers to its ranks through lodges across Arkansas, including in the towns of Elaine, Ratio, and Hoop Spur. The cotton business was booming, with prices at record highs; sharecroppers finally had a potential opportunity to pay off their debts and throw off the shackles of peonage—but first, landowners would have to be made to play fair.

"SHOOT TO KILL ANY NEGRO WHO REFUSE[S] TO SURRENDER IMMEDIATELY"

By 1919, the union felt strong enough to take action on behalf of a group of Black cotton farmers in Elaine who wished to sue their employers for their fair share of that year's bumper crop. White lawyer Ulysses S. Bratton, known to be sympathetic to the Black workers' plight and credited with years of work suing Delta landowners for violations of the Peonage Act, took the case. On September 30, 1919, Bratton sent his son, Ocier, an accountant and World War I veteran, down to the Ratio lodge to meet with union organizers and collect his lawyer's fee. Less than an hour into the younger Bratton's roadside meeting with the two dozen Black men and women sharecroppers behind the lawsuit, a group of armed white men rode up and kidnapped him. An angry mob chained him to a storefront and rifled through his pockets, further enraged when it found he had an IWW newspaper tucked away. Ocier was labeled a labor agitator, thrown onto a train, and transported twenty-five miles to Helena, where he remained in jail for thirty days.

While this particular drama played out, a far bloodier altercation unfolded in a Hoop Spur church, where the local PFHUA chapter met to decide whether to hire Bratton, Sr., to represent them as well. Suddenly, the sound of gunshots pierced the air, as a white mob gathered outside and began firing into the church. W. A. Adkins, a white special agent of the Missouri Pacific Railroad, was caught in the crossfire as Black PFHUA guards returned fire, and his accomplices rushed to get help. Phillips County sheriff Frank F. Kitchens immediately deputized a posse of three hundred men to put down this "insurrection," as they'd decided to term a simple case of Black self-defense. By the next morning nearly a thousand more white men from throughout the Mississippi and Arkansas Delta joined Kitchens's posse; "low-down" sorts spoiling for a fight and a chance to vent their racist spleen on as many Black folk as they could get their hands on.

But this was still not enough. Governor Charles H. Brough arrived with his own contingent of 538 federal troops, including a twelve-gun machine gun battalion, who came to nearby Elaine riled up and ready with orders "to shoot to kill any negro who refused to surrender immediately." The multiday onslaught that followed took the lives of an untold number of Black people of every age and gender. The death toll is believed to have stretched into the hundreds, with another 285 Black people arrested and jailed until their employers could be found to vouch for them (PFHUA president Robert L. Hill was hidden by friends during the massacre and fled to Kansas).

Officials scrambled to deflect focus away from the carnage in the Elaine streets, drawing attention to their efforts to punish those responsible for the deaths of five white people also killed in the melee. They circulated an unfounded conspiracy that the PFHUA had recruited Elaine's Black workers into a plot to massacre Elaine's white residents, foisting responsibility for the violence on the Black residents who'd been its primary victims.

Local elites had not yet had their fill of Black pain. A secretive cabal of prominent white businessmen met and saw to it that 122 more Black citizens were arrested and charged with offenses ranging from nightriding to murder. The first twelve men to be tried—Frank Moore, Frank Hicks, Ed Hicks, Joe Knox, Paul Hall, Ed Coleman, Alfred Banks, Ed Ware, William Wordlaw, Albert Giles, Joe Fox, and John Martin—were given biased white attorneys who made little effort to defend their clients, and were quickly sentenced to the electric chair. Those still waiting to be processed saw the writing on the wall and jumped to accept sham plea bargains carrying exorbitant sentences. Allies up North finally took notice as word got out about the Elaine Twelve's plight. The National Association for the Advancement of Colored People (NAACP) launched its own investigation, and pioneering investigative journalist and anti-lynching crusader Ida B. Wells sprang into action on receiving letters from several of the Elaine Twelve begging for her help.

"Because we are innercent men, we was not handle with justice at all Phillips County Court. It is prejidice that the white people had agence we Negroes. So I thank God that thro you, our Negroes are looking into this truble," wrote one man, who also described in gruesome detail the torture and mistreatment he and his fellow prisoners had suffered. Wells's work covering the 1917 East St. Louis riots may have struck a chord with the victims, whose experiences being hunted by white mobs mirrored those of their brothers in Missouri.

The St. Louis massacre had been labor-related as well, an outgrowth of Black workers being brought in as strikebreakers to replace white laborers at the Aluminum Ore Company. Incensed white workers revolted and quickly overran the city, murdering dozens of the Black workers and burning their homes to the ground. Ida B. Wells's *The East St. Louis Massacre: The Greatest Outrage of the Century* brought national attention to the slaughter, and now she would do the same in search of Elaine's bloody truth.

By the time of her arrival in 1921, the NAACP's legal appeals for the Elaine Twelve had already dragged on for years. Relations between the area's white and Black communities had grown even rawer and tenser in the interim period, and Wells knew she was walking straight into a maelstrom. The Elaine jail would be her first stop, where she would seek an audience with plea-bargained PFHUA prisoners still held there; what she found was almost inconceivable. Ed Ware, prominent sharecropper and secretary at the PFHUA's Hoop Spur lodge, shared threats of being lynched while in custody. The church where this had all begun—the site of the shoot-out that kicked off the bloodletting—had been burned down later that night, forever obscuring the full number of murdered Black men, women, and children who lay inside. As the massacre raged, their families had no way of knowing where they were or whether they had survived at all.

Wells also learned that the union arrestees had been tortured and coerced into false confessions of their alleged roles in planning the Elaine violence, meaning that *all* were now sentenced to death. The NAACP's legal efforts to free them finally succeeded in 1925, when outgoing Arkansas governor Thomas McRae freed the final six Elaine prisoners. And it was not a moment too soon, because McRae's successor was Thomas Jefferson Terral, a confirmed member of the Ku Klux Klan.

"It was a Declaration of Economic Independence, and the first united blow for economic liberty struck by the Negroes of the South!" Wells later wrote of the landowners' reaction to Black sharecroppers' efforts to unionize and bargain for higher prices. "That was their crime and it had to be avenged." Her masterful report on her findings in Elaine, *The Arkansas Race Riot*, helped cement the massacre and its legacy in the public consciousness, but the work of properly commemorating the Elaine Twelve themselves continues to this day. Lisa Hicks Gilbert, descendant of Elaine Twelve defendants Ed and Frank Hicks, made her case in a 2021 interview with the *Guardian*: "This group of resilient men and women who organized, who wrote by-laws to govern themselves by, only wanted what was promised and only asked for what they had earned," she said. "I'm convinced resilience was in their DNA, and I plan to honor their lives and tell their stories like it's in mine."

That resilience has been a hallmark of the long and continuous struggle for Black liberation and self-determination in this country, and as Gilbert says, those who fought for that freedom survived unimaginable trauma and unspeakable horrors in their pursuit of something more. As an investigative journalist, Ida B. Wells acted as a documentarian of those atrocities, risking her own life many times over to force Americans to recognize the scourge of lynching. "If the Southern people in defense of their lawlessness, would tell the truth and admit that colored men and women are lynched for almost any offense, from murder to a misdemeanor, there would not now be the necessity for this defense," she wrote in her book *The Red Record: Tabulated Statistics and Alleged Causes of Lynching in the United States*. "But when they intentionally, maliciously and constantly belie the record and bolster up these falsehoods by the words of legislators, preachers, governors and bishops, then the Negro must give to the world his side of the awful story."

Wells devoted her life to sharing those stories, and as her career went on, she also became involved in a number of other social, political, and cultural organizations aimed at uplifting her community. In 1925, the same year the last of the Elaine Twelve walked free, Wells invited A. Philip Randolph to her home to speak to the Chicago Women's Forum. He was on something of a publicity tour for his ambitious—and sorely needed—new project, a union for the Black railroad workers who served as porters and maids on Pullman's luxury cars. It would become the first all-Black union to successfully negotiate a contract with a major American corporation, as well as the first of its kind to receive a charter from the American Federation of Labor.

THE PULLMAN RAILWAY PORTERS

By the early 1900s, the Pullman Company was the largest employer of Black workers in the United States. Founding oligarch George Pullman was personally unmoved by the fight for racial equality; rather, he was a detail-obsessed, pragmatic ultra-capitalist who had devised a specific formula for how he wanted his workforce to look and act—and took pains to maintain it. He knew that white-led railway unions were apathetic at best and openly hostile at worst to the idea of organizing Black workers, and that Black workers themselves had very few options for decent-paying, respectable jobs, especially in the Deep South, where he sent agents to recruit his first class of porters. The company's hiring policy hinged on stereotypes around the supposed "docility" of Southern men when compared with their Northern and Western counterparts and, in its early days, extended this theory to include formerly enslaved workers out of the assumption that they would be instinctively more deferential and accustomed to menial labor.

The company also specifically placed a premium on dark-skinned men as a means of enforcing the color line between servant and served. No porter would ever be mistaken for a passenger on Pullman's watch or, worse, become too friendly with a passenger's wife. Porters' daily duties ran the gamut from making beds, hauling luggage, and shining shoes to caring for patrons' children, providing simple medical care, and offering a sympathetic ear to whiskey-soaked passengers' late-night ramblings. Their labor was essential to upholding Pullman's reputation for luxury, yet they still depended on tips to pad out their meager salaries and were forbidden to eat alongside passengers or even sleep during their long overnight shifts (George Pullman is often credited with hastening the widespread adoption of tipping as a customary practice in America—thanks for that one, George).

Racist white passengers already accustomed to calling Black men "boy" used the term to summon porters, or demanded their attention with a cry of "George!" since, in their eyes, the workers "belonged" to George Pullman. It was an often degrading occupation, but under Jim Crow, the Pullman porter's life of travel, steady pay, and proximity to the Gilded Age glitterati was dearly coveted. Without a union, the porters had to grin and bear it in order to keep their jobs.

On the job, they may have been ordered around like servants, but back home, the porters were regarded as paragons of Black manhood. They helped forge the foundations of a nascent Black middle class, passing down to relatives jobs with decent pay and exposure to an otherwise inaccessible world; many prominent Black leaders got their start riding the rails. Malcolm X spent time on the railroads as a youth selling sandwiches and washing dishes, but lasted only about a day with Pullman. He undoubtedly found Pullman's well-padded rule book and demand for obsequious service intolerable. But while he was there, the revolutionary observed, "We were in that world of Negroes who were both servants and psychologists, aware that white people are so obsessed with their own importance that they will pay liberally, even dearly, for the impression of being catered to and entertained."

Pullman porters had attempted to organize since 1890, when a group of workers calling themselves the Charles Sumner Association (named after a prominent white abolitionist) threatened a strike. Porters continued their organizing efforts throughout the late 1890s and early 1900s, though typically excluding the maids who worked alongside them. In 1915, Robert L. Mays broke through and founded the Railway Men's International Benevolent Industrial Association, an organization that fought for higher wages, integration of all railway unions, and an end to segregated train cars. Mays's group dissolved in the shadow of World War I, but a decade later and to the dismay of their staunchly anti-labor Pullman bosses, the porters would finally get their union.

The International Brotherhood of Sleeping Car Porters and Maids (BSCP) was formed in 1925 by three Pullman porters, Ashley Totten, Roy Lancaster, and William H. Des Versey, and labor organizers Milton P. Webster and A. Philip Randolph. Randolph, a socialist and president of the short-lived National Brotherhood of Workers of America, had already earned his labor stripes organizing elevator operators in New York City and dockworkers in Virginia, and was quickly elected the Brotherhood's first president. As publisher of the *Messenger*, the country's most prominent radical Black newspaper, Randolph had both a keen head for publicity and a space to host secret union meetings away from the prying eyes of Pullman operatives. The latter quickly proved necessary as the company struck back with a vengeance. Spies were deployed to monitor porters for pro-union sentiments, and sympathizers were fired en masse. Brotherhood cofounder Ashley Totten suffered a fractured skull at the hands of a Pullman-connected assailant, and the company hired a wave of Filipino porters, to warn Black workers that their monopoly over the profession wasn't set in stone. Nonetheless, more than half of eligible Pullman porters had joined the union by the end of its first year.

A. Philip Randolph more than earned his larger-than-life profile in labor history and, later, the civil rights movement, but he and his fellow Brotherhood organizers did not make their uphill climb alone. As Rosina Tucker, a pivotal player in the Brotherhood-affiliated Women's Economic Council, once said, women made the union: the spouses and daughters of porters, and the Pullman maids, who were ultimately funneled into auxiliaries rather than offered full membership in the union itself. Their contributions have long been overshadowed by their male counterparts in the

Brotherhood's proud mythology, but the truth is that the union could not have launched—or notched half of the victories it won—without their fervent support and untold hours of unpaid labor.

THE PULLMAN MAIDS' DOUBLE BIND

Pullman maids suffered the same—and, often, even worse—indignities their male counterparts encountered on the rails. Sexual harassment from customers and gender discrimination, even from the porters themselves, ran rampant. Aspiring Pullman maids were subject to strict hiring criteria, and the position was open only to Black female applicants until 1925, when the company also began hiring Chinese women to work its Western routes during its initial anti-union blitz. By 1926, the company employed two hundred maids to its ten thousand porters, and their duties were to clean the cars and provide intimate services to female passengers, from hairdressing and mending clothes to giving free manicures on demand. Like the porters, maids were also expected to provide free childcare and eldercare on their routes, and to purchase their own supplies, from sewing needles to nail files. They were often the only female crew member on their car, and were forbidden to socialize with passengers or even porters. Their isolation was a stark contrast from the valuable camaraderie Brotherhood members shared to ease their burdens. Pullman maids' wages were higher than what Black women in other domestic service jobs could expect, but still less than porters'.

The double bind of sexism and racism they faced as Black women workers set the Pullman maids apart from their railroad brothers. In addition, their relationship with the porters' wives was complicated by spouses' belief that the union's first priority should be to economically empower their men so that they could gain access to the benefits of a bourgeois middle-class existence. There was far less consideration extended to the Black women who already worked alongside those men for lower wages, but outspoken Pullman maids like Josephine Puckett, Ada V. Dillon, Tinie Upton, and Frances Albrier became organizers in their own right, ensuring the maids' concerns would not go unheard.

To be clear, the porters' wives were no monolith. A rare few saw fit to break with their respectability-minded sisters and stand with the Black women workers toiling alongside their husbands, supporting both groups in the cause for equity. One, Rosina Bud Harvey Corrothers Tucker, would become a potent weapon in the Brotherhood's fight. Tucker served as a liaison to A. Philip Randolph, collecting dues and delivering messages between him and the Washington, D.C., branch. "If the management found out, they would fire people," she once recalled. "That's why, in one sense, it was easier for the wives to do the work. That's how I got involved."

Her enviable position came after heroic recruiting efforts on the Brotherhood's behalf, visiting at least three hundred porters' homes in the D.C. area alone. She had also cofounded the Colored Women's Economic Council (CWEC), a precursor to the union's Ladies' Auxiliary that went on to spawn chapters wherever the Brotherhood had a presence. Tucker became the Colored Women's Economic Council's first president with Randolph's endorsement and, despite her slight stature, became known for her commanding presence at union meetings and conferences. She would spend the rest of her life in labor, serving as the Ladies' Auxiliary secretary-treasurer, organizing Black women workers, and throwing herself into labor's close relationship with the Civil Rights Movement.

Tucker's emphasis on organizing Black women workers across various industries ran afoul of Halena Wilson, devoted unionist and president of the Ladies' Auxiliary. The two women worked together more or less harmoniously for years, but those ideological rifts over organizing women and the primacy of the porters' concerns over the maids' was further magnified by the uncomradely behavior of their union brothers. When the BSCP finally ratified its groundbreaking first contract with the Pullman Company in 1937, it made significant gains for porters—but signed away maids' seniority rights and treated their welfare and wages as an afterthought. After Pullman maids had spent years fighting to establish the union and to improve conditions on the rails, their own union cast them aside. That same year, the union officially dropped the "Maids" from its name.

In those early days, Tucker was joined by Lucy Bledsoe Gilmore, the president of the St. Louis CWEC and an electrifying public speaker whom a shaken company agent once described as "a second Emma Goldman" when she laid into Pullman at a Brotherhood meeting for mistreating her porter husband. They and other auxiliary women redoubled the auxiliary's fundraising efforts for the Brotherhood, a task they hoped would serve the dual purpose of filling the union's coffers and soothing fragile male egos. Through their work, a number of high-profile radical and progressive women were brought into the fold in support of the Brotherhood; names like A'lelia Walker, Harlem socialite and heir to Madam C. J. Walker's hair salon empire; Floria Pinkney, the first Black organizer for the International Ladies' Garment Workers' Union; Rose Schneiderman of the Women's Trade Union League; and the IWW's Elizabeth Gurley Flynn all were enthusiastic boosters for the Pullman porters.

The women's economic support for the union didn't end there; A. Philip Randolph's wife, Lucille, for example, was a Howard University graduate and salon owner and used her extensive social connections to help bankroll both the Brotherhood at large and Randolph himself, who worked without a salary until 1936. Auxiliary efforts even extended to door-to-door "Union Maid" cosmetics sales and "bobbed hair contests" at Madam C. J. Walker–branded salons. These principled women gave everything they had to the union, and their menfolk's outdated chauvinism paled before fighters like Gilmore, whose militancy rivaled any man's. "If we never have another bite to eat, we will still fight for the Brotherhood," she told a crowd in St. Louis. "I am like a rubber ball; the harder you throw me, the higher I bounce."

As the porters' wives organized and agitated from the sidelines, Frances Mary Jackson Albrier was one of the Pullman maids who found themselves in the thick of the battle between the company and the union. In the 1920s, Albrier, a single mother and graduate nurse from Howard University, had taken a job with Pullman under the assumption that she would be using her medical training to care for ill passengers; instead, she was handed a manicure kit and compelled to pay for someone to teach her how to use it.

As she began trying to organize her fellow maids, Albrier struggled to convince them—many of whom were single heads of households who had families to feed and who dreaded the alternative of having to find a job drudging in a white woman's house—that the risk was worth it. Pullman maids typically quit their jobs as soon as they married, and in terms of the Brotherhood, their hope was that increasing wages and bettering conditions for male porters would allow them to leave the workforce altogether (which, considering how wretched their job opportunities were as Black women in the Jim Crow 1920s and 1930s, seems eminently reasonable). "Our responsibility was trying to educate the Black public and the Black women on these things," Albrier explained. "They didn't understand the economics; they only understood the need for the job."

For his part, Randolph hovered between the union's two ideological poles. He was a firm believer in fighting for Black manhood and economic power, and shared the view that Black women were best served by embracing the respectable domesticity of housewives, but his support was also crucial in preserving the freedom of the

WEC and Ladies' Auxiliary to pursue their own political and educational agendas. "Organization is not only necessary for the economic emancipation of men, but it is also necessary for the economic emancipation of women," he told the BSCP's New York City convention in 1926. His openness to women's leadership would serve him well in the next chapter of his career as a leader for Black civil rights at large.

In 1941, Randolph announced the union's intention to sponsor a thousands-strong march on Washington calling for full citizenship rights for Black people, an end to racial discrimination in the defense industry and in unions, and Black self-government in colonized Africa and the Caribbean. The White House shuddered at the prospect of a (somewhat) radical Black organizing action in the heart of the nation's racially segregated capitol. It was here that Randolph and the Brotherhood's immense and growing stature came into play; the union leader received direct pleas from President Franklin Delano Roosevelt's office, offering to sign Executive Order 8802—a ban on discriminatory employment practices in all federal agencies and unions—in exchange for postponement of the march. Randolph took the offer, but this win merely set the stage for the bigger, bloodier battles to come, where he and the Brotherhood were assured to be in the thick of it all. The women would be there, too.

"YOU'RE SUPPOSED TO BE SCARED WHEN YOU COME IN HERE"

When A. Philip Randolph first met Bayard Rustin, Rustin was a young man fresh off a flirtation with the Communist Party and ready to cause some good trouble. Twenty-three years Randolph's junior, Rustin appeared on his doorstep in the spring of 1941, hoping to work with the Brotherhood. Randolph turned him away then due to the younger man's membership in the Young Communist

League, as the veteran saw the party as being insufficiently committed to racial equality and disruptive to his own reformist stance. Rustin soon became disillusioned with the party as well, and reconnected with Randolph shortly thereafter to begin a partnership that would end up moving mountains.

Young Bayard was well versed in the virtues of persistence and self-esteem. He was born one of twelve children, and raised by his Quaker grandparents in West Chester, Pennsylvania. His grandmother, Julia Rustin, was a charter member of the NAACP, and frequently opened her home to Black leaders like W. E. B. Du Bois, James Weldon Johnson, and Mary McLeod, who shaped young Bayard's political education. By the time he was fourteen, Rustin knew he was gay, and when he told his grandmother about his realization, she accepted the news without judgment. As a result, he never felt shame or guilt around his sexuality, even when his identity was used against him by his detractors, or after he was arrested and imprisoned in 1953 for engaging in consensual sexual activity with other men.

After establishing his rapport with Randolph, Rustin turned his attention to the antiwar movement, joining the Fellowship of Reconciliation (FOR) and cofounding the Congress of Racial Equality (CORE). In 1943, Rustin had been sent to federal prison for refusing to register for the draft, and he used his three years inside to organize fellow prisoners to agitate against the prison's segregationist policies. After he was freed in 1947, he became deeply involved in FOR and rose to a leadership position. The group sent him to California to defend the property of the more than 120,000 Japanese Americans who had been imprisoned in internment camps by the U.S. government, overseas to multiple colonized countries in Africa and Asia to advocate for pacifism, and to India to learn more about Gandhi's nonviolent teachings.

In the midst of his global travels, Rustin also helped organize the Journey of Reconciliation, a series of civil disobedience actions undertaken by an interracial group of activists, which marked Rustin's first major foray into nonviolent resistance. In order to test a recent Supreme Court decision barring segregated seating in interstate travel, a group of fifteen men—eight white, seven Black, Rustin among them—traveled through fifteen Southern cities in an early precursor to the Freedom Rides; white men sat at the back of the bus and Black men sat at the front, daring authorities to enforce the law. Twelve of the fifteen were arrested, with Bayard himself doing thirty days on a chain gang as punishment for crossing Jim Crow. At one point, an arresting officer, frustrated by Rustin's composure in the face of intimidation, spat, "N-gger, you're supposed to be scared when you come in here!" Rustin's answer may as well sum up his entire lifetime of service: "I am fortified by truth, justice, and Christ. . . . There is no need to fear."

"THERE WAS NO ONE MORE ABLE TO PULL IT TOGETHER THAN BAYARD RUSTIN"

That fearlessness came in handy later in Rustin's career, as his personal life became more of an issue among his colleagues in the labor and civil rights movements. When the news of his 1953 arrest for "lewd conduct" hit, he was outed to the world, and tendered his resignation from FOR to its furious director. A. J. Muste, a former union organizer, was a longtime mentor who had been tolerant of Rustin's identity as a gay man, but chose the path of least resistance when he forced Bayard out of FOR rather than risk damage to the group's reputation. This situation would repeat itself several times throughout Rustin's life; homophobic prejudice gave others an excuse to sideline him, disregard his talents, or cut him out entirely.

Similar fears saw the NAACP object to Rustin's inclusion in a 1956 trip to Montgomery to school Black Southern leaders, among them a young preacher named Dr. Martin Luther King, Jr., in the ways of nonviolence. Randolph stood up for him, though, and Rustin spent much of that year leading workshops and advising the members of the Montgomery Improvement Association (MIA) on the practical applications of nonviolent civil disobedience. It was Rustin, for example, who convinced Dr. King to give up his stockpile of defensive firearms, after pointing out the contradictions of preaching nonviolence while being armed to the teeth. That productive period was not to last; after a Black reporter threatened to publish an exposé on Rustin's sexuality and past ties to Communism, he had to be smuggled out of Alabama in the trunk of a car. Dr. King felt Rustin's knowledge and political prowess outweighed any potential controversies, but other MIA members disagreed, and Rustin had to cheer on the Montgomery bus boycotts from the relative safety of his Harlem, New York, apartment. But Rustin would have the last laugh, when another march loomed and some of those leaders who had once rejected him needed his help.

One of the chief architects of the 1963 March on Washington for Jobs and Freedom was a gay Black man. That revolutionary moment, both in creation and in execution, would not have happened without Bayard Rustin. During planning stages for the march, Rustin was brought in by the "Big Six" leaders—the Brotherhood's Randolph, at the time also the sole Black member of the AFL-CIO Executive Council and the Negro American Labor Council; John Lewis, president of the Student Nonviolent Coordinating Committee (SNCC); CORE cofounder James Farmer; NAACP executive secretary Roy Wilkins; Whitney Young, the executive director of the National Urban League; and SCLC (Southern Christian Leadership Conference) chairman the Reverend Dr. Martin Luther King.

There was no denying that Rustin's direct organizing experience and understanding of nonviolent tactics put the rest of the group to shame; as John Lewis later recalled, "This was going to be a massively complex undertaking, and there was no one more able to pull it together than Bayard Rustin." Wilkins (the man who had been too conservative for Marvel Cooke's tastes) still initially protested Rustin's inclusion in the event, fretting that his "controversial" personal life would detract from their mission, but Wilkins's objections were overruled by the rest of the committee. Rustin soon got to work, drawing up an agenda and orchestrating every tiny detail of an event that would ultimately see 250,000 people peacefully assemble on the National Mall.

As author William P. Jones explained in his book *The March on Washington: Jobs, Freedom, and the Forgotten History of Civil Rights*, Rustin's interest in the march was rooted in economics. His goal was to draw attention to "the economic subordination of the Negro" and advance a "broad and fundamental program for economic justice." He had just seven weeks to plan the event, and save for a few hiccups, it went off without a hitch. Even Malcolm X, generally kept at arm's length due to his Black nationalist leanings, saw fit to attend. In retrospect, the only sour note was the shameful exclusion of women like Rosa Parks, Addie Wyatt, and Ella Baker, pivotal activists and organizers in their own right, who were robbed of the spotlight by their male counterparts' sexism.

For all his efforts, Bayard Rustin was never publicly named march director, and was instead identified as Randolph's "deputy." In the wake of the march's roaring success, Rustin was offered posts at the NAACP and SCLC, his "controversial" status momentarily forgotten. But he turned them down to instead lead the newly launched A. Philip Randolph Institute, an organization founded by Randolph in 1965 with a focus on racial equality and economic justice. The APRI sought to strengthen Black workers' presence in the labor movement, and Rustin embraced its mission with open arms, doubling down on his own belief that economic empowerment won through labor unions, not racial justice activism, was the answer to Black liberation. It is ironic to think that he had split with Communism all those years earlier over its perceived abandonment of racial justice, only to pivot toward class reductionism in his later years. "The problems of the most aggrieved sector of the Black ghetto cannot and will never be solved without full employment, and full employment, with the government as employer of last resort, is the keystone of labor's program," he wrote in a 1971 essay. "There is simply no other way for the Black *lumpenproletariat* to become a proletariat."

His focus on economic issues at the expense of race ruffled feathers and made Rustin enemies within the burgeoning Black Power movement; it also alienated some of his comrades in the civil rights struggle and marked the beginning of a descent into neoconservative thought. This second era of Rustin's public life saw him break with many of his old allies and form new bonds with groups the young Bayard would hardly have recognized. But even as his own politics were changing, Rustin continued to throw himself into the causes he personally felt were most essential. He traveled the world, calling out human rights abuses wherever he found them. He crossed back and forth over the Mason-Dixon Line at home to do the same for abuses in the American South. And he never did give up his commitment to the rights of workers against their corporate oppressors, as seen in his righteous, and ultimately heartbreaking, return to Memphis in 1968.

On February 12, 1968, nearly one thousand members of AFSCME Local 1733 went on strike after two sanitation workers, Echol Cole and Robert Walker, were crushed to death in a garbage compactor. The tragic fates of Cole and Walker lit a fuse, but the conflict had been a long time coming. Since T. O. Jones successfully organized Local 1733 of the American Federation of State, County, and Municipal Employees (AFSCME) in 1964, the workers had attempted to strike several times, but were always beaten back. This time, they'd finally had enough. Garbage piled up in the streets as strikers rallied under the slogan "I Am a Man!" and held firm in the face of police brutality. The city's other, predominantly white, unions shied away from the Black sanitation workers' public struggle, but Steelworkers Local URW 186, which boasted the largest Black union membership in Memphis, lent its firm support, and Walter Reuther, the president of the United Auto Workers, wrote the strikers a check for $50,000.

As the weeks went on, news of the strikers' militancy reached Rustin and other civil rights leaders, including his old comrades Wilkins and Dr. King. "If I were the mayor of this city, I would be ashamed," Rustin told a crowd of strikers on March 14, 1968, never one to mince words. "I wouldn't want these men to not be able to feed their families on the lousy pittance they are paid."

While Rustin's connections with labor were more prominent, Dr. King was a union man as well, speaking at multiple AFL-CIO conventions and sending his solidarity to various labor struggles. But unlike Rustin, he viewed the causes of labor and Black labor as inextricably interconnected, with economics as just one piece of a bigger puzzle. The reverend used his famed oratory skills to raise the spirits of workers across the country, saluting the United Farm Workers and leader Cesar Chavez for their "indefatigable work against poverty and injustice" during a 1968 hunger strike, and in 1962 writing to a group of striking laundry workers that "as I have said many times, and believe with all my heart, the coalition that can have the greatest impact in the struggle for human dignity here in America is that of the Negro and the forces of labor, because their fortunes are so closely intertwined."

On April 3, Dr. King stood in the pulpit of a Memphis church and delivered his famed "I've Been to the Mountaintop" speech in support of the sanitation workers. He spoke of the workers' struggle and the dire need to stand with them as they fought, challenging the crowd to answer the question, "If I do not stop to help the sanitation workers, what will happen to them?" Some have posited this speech marked a planned turn for King, expanding his purview more solidly beyond racial justice and on to the cause of economic justice as well.

But by the next day, he was dead, slain at his hotel by a coward's bullet. Bayard, who was in Memphis at the same time and was called on to comment following the assassination, was unable to keep the tears from streaming down his face. "It is up to us," he said then, "the living, the Black and white, to realize Dr. King's dream."

And on April 16, after weeks of mourning and meetings, the strike was finished, too. The dignity that the workers had demanded and that Dr. King had called out to the heavens for was won, for a time. The images of the striking Black men with placards around their necks proclaiming boldly "I Am a Man"—at a time when the Jim Crow South still sneeringly referred to Black men as "boys"—became powerful symbols of that struggle for dignity, for a fair wage, for bread and roses, too. It's no surprise that those words and those photos have resurfaced again and again, as Black people have been continually forced to reassert their humanity in the face of a system that devalues their very existence. "I Am a Man" predates "Black Lives Matter," but the sentiment remains the same: We are here. We matter. We are bloodied, but unbowed.

In the summer of 2020, another group of Southern sanitation workers followed in Memphis's footsteps. In hot, humid New Orleans, skilled "hoppers" kept the city's streets clean at great personal cost, braving the heat, heavy physical toll, and literal filth that characterized their job. The workers—all of whom were Black—earned $10.25 an hour, with no benefits or sick days, to haul away a major city's reeking trash amid a heat wave, a global pandemic that disproportionately struck cities and Black communities like their own, and America's 2020 nationwide uprising against police violence and racism. "If you know New Orleans garbage, it's real, nasty, and heavy," Kendrick Anderson, one of the striking hoppers, told me in an interview. "We work from sunup to sundown. . . . I got hurt several times on the truck where I would end up in the hospital. It's not right, it's not right. It's time for everyone to realize and know what's going on."

On May 5 of that year, twenty-six hoppers formed the City Waste Union and declared themselves on strike until their demands were met. Their employer, a staffing company called PeopleReady, fired them and brought in prison labor, exposing incarcerated workers to the same risks and dangers as the hoppers with none of the training or pay. The strike stretched on for months. A resolution was never officially reached, but the strikers took pride in standing up for themselves against an exploitative employer, and in finding their own place in the proud, complicated legacy of Black workers' struggle. "We, like many before us, feel downtrodden and left behind," hopper Jonathan Edward told me in 2020. "We deserve better, and we won't let up until we get what we need."

The City Waste Union was far from the only group of sanitation workers who saw its members stand up for their rights amid the turmoil of the United States in 2020. In that same month of May, Tuskegee, Alabama, sanitation workers struck, protesting in front of city hall for weeks. On June 20, the New Orleans hoppers joined the local chapter of the Movement 4 Black Lives at a rally calling to defund the city's police department and to "invest in Black Lives." And in Philadelphia, Pennsylvania, sanitation workers walked out as well, disgusted with the city's inadequate response to the COVID-19 pandemic that had left dozens of sanitation workers ill and thousands more in desperate need of protective equipment.

Each of these actions builds on those that came before, and each new generation finds its own version of Ida B. Wells, Rosina Tucker, or Bayard Rustin to follow and fight alongside. As King told the workers in Memphis in 1968, as their strike was beset by bloodthirsty police and politicians, "Nothing worthwhile is gained without sacrifice. The thing for you to do is stay together, and say to everybody in this community that you are going to stick it out to the end until every demand is met, and that you are gonna say, 'We ain't gonna let nobody turn us around.'"

9

THE MOVERS

Labor cannot stand still. It must not retreat. It must go on, or go under.

—Harry Bridges, ILWU union leader

When it comes to organized labor in the United States, the International Brotherhood of Teamsters surely has the market cornered on name recognition. In pop culture, the Teamsters are often used as a convenient stand-in for organized labor in general, and cracks about their brutally effective but notoriously corrupt former president Jimmy Hoffa and his 1975 disappearance (allegedly courtesy of the Mafia) linger despite the Teamsters' post-Hoffa reform efforts to clean up their act. While they may be the first example that comes to mind thanks to their long and colorful history (as well as their impeccable merch game), the Teamsters are only one part of a constellation of transportation workers who keep America running—and rolling, and flying.

At a basic level, the country's economic power has always been dependent on its transportation workers, and whenever those workers have chosen to withhold their labor the results have been, in a word, transformative.

The Great Railroad Strike of 1877 acted as a catalyst for the protracted workers' rights struggles and widespread sociopolitical change that would define much of the twentieth century. Transformative figures like anarchist organizers Emma Goldman and Lucy

Parsons, socialist labor leader Eugene V. Debs, Knights of Labor head Terence Powderly, and AFL founder Samuel Gompers were all inspired by the massive forty-five-day railroad strike that cost hundreds of millions in damage, resulted in one hundred casualties, and saw a thousand people imprisoned.

Almost 150 years later, Uber and Lyft drivers across the country went on strike in 2019 to protest low wages and poor treatment by their app-based bosses; in 2020, New York City's taxi drivers shut down the Brooklyn Bridge to demand relief from enormous debts they incurred for the right to operate a cab, and in 2021, they won their debt battle after a fifteen-day hunger strike. Immigrant worker–led groups like Rideshare Drivers United and the New York Taxi Workers Alliance have taken cues from the labor movement's past while working to shape its future in a way that translates corporate gain into material benefits for the workers off whose labor the corporations are profiting. These large-scale labor actions were but small examples of what can happen when the country's movers and shakers decide they've had enough. Some of them move cargo; others move people; and still others maintain and operate the machinery that moves both. But all of them wield considerable power when they work collectively. And as history shows, they're not afraid of using it.

Dockworkers have a rich history of radical dissent all their own, especially in terms of interracial solidarity. There is a direct line to be drawn between Ben Fletcher's Philadelphia Local 8 in the early twentieth century and those eight hours in 2020 when the International Longshore and Warehouse Union (ILWU) shut down the ports up and down the West Coast in honor of Juneteenth. The ILWU was born in blood during the 1934 West Coast waterfront strike, the same strike that honorary Wobbly Marie Equi had supported in Portland as her final public act as a labor agitator. On

May 9, 1934, every longshore worker on the West Coast downed their tools; the bosses brought in strikebreakers and the police met the strikers with violence. With support from other maritime workers and rank-and-file Teamsters, the strike held for eighty-two days, but conditions deteriorated along the way. On July 5 in San Francisco, police fired into a crowd of protesting strikers, killing workers Howard Sperry and Nick Bordoise, and injuring dozens more. The melee, now known as "Bloody Thursday," led Harry Bridges, a former Wobbly and later president of the ILWU, to draft plans for a general strike. Within two weeks, 150,000 workers from multiple San Francisco industries shut the city down for four days. The longshoremen's strike would settle that fall, with the ILWU gaining control of the hiring halls (and with them, the allocation of jobs) at every port on the West Coast.

The ILWU has since distinguished itself as a fearless, fighting union that has had no problem making public its disagreements with other factions within the labor movement or proudly throwing its support behind pressing political causes. Unlike many of its contemporaries, the union opened its arms to Black members in the 1930s, and the ILWU's Local 10 had become a majority Black union by the 1960s. Following the 1934 win, the union embarked on a "March Inland" campaign that expanded its reach beyond the docks, bringing thousands of warehouse workers into the fold and kicking up bitter disputes with the AFL, who considered it an encroachment on their territory. President Harry Bridges's vision of an industrial "Maritime Federation" saw canning and agricultural workers drawn into the ILWU fold, and the union extended its resources to the Mexican and Asian American workers in those sectors as well. It hired Mexican organizers to reach workers in the Los Angeles barrios, and brought in visionaries like Bert Corona, a CIO organizer and socialist whose Committee to Aid Mexican Workers (CAMW) went on to lend support to workers' struggles throughout the country. When the union offered its legal services to a group of striking lettuce workers in Salinas, California, who had been blacklisted by their employers, ILWU lawyers secured an injunction from a federal judge holding blacklisting to be illegal, a legal first that helped the lettuce workers regain their union. The union's tumultuous relationship with the Teamsters, with whom they shared an interest in organizing warehouse workers, reached a detente when Jimmy Hoffa rose to power and suppressed the anti-Communist red-baiting that had dogged the union during the 1950s and 1960s.

In more recent years, the ILWU (which changed its name in 1997, dropping the original "Longshoremen's" and "Warehousemen's" designations in order to be more gender inclusive) has become known for a willingness to harness its physical power to aid political movements. The 2020 port shutdown made headlines, as it came in the wake of the police murder of George Floyd and the ensuing national uprisings over racism and police brutality, but that was far from the ILWU's first foray into social justice. On May Day 2008, the union walked off the job to protest the Iraq War, and as far back as 1962, the union made waves by refusing to unload cargo from South Africa's apartheid regime. It backed the predominantly Filipino and Mexican American United Farmworkers in their Delano Grape Strike between 1965 and 1970, and organized Asian American farmworkers in Hawai'i. During the nineteen-month occupation of Alcatraz Island by Indigenous activists in 1969–71, Indigenous ILWU member Joseph "Indian Joe" Morris, who'd been born on a Blackfoot reservation in Montana, used San Francisco's Pier 40 as a base to ferry people and supplies back and forth to the island; the self-styled "Alcatraz troubleshooter and mainland coordinator" undoubtedly contributed to the occupation's staying power. Given the political and social overlap between the two entities' Oakland chapters, it was more than likely that there were some Black Panthers within the ILWU's ranks, too—and in 2021, legendary educator, author, and former Black Panther Dr. Angela Davis joined Paul Robeson and Dr. Martin Luther King, Jr., as honorary members.

The 2010 police murder of Oscar Grant led the ILWU's Bay Area locals to shut down the Port of Oakland to demand justice, and in 2015 the ILWU's Local 10 in San Francisco held a May Day work stoppage in honor of Walter Scott, another Black victim of police violence and friend of the International Longshoreman's Association (ILA) Local 1422 in South Carolina. For some, the memory of Bloody Thursday is still fresh, and is a wound that is reopened each time another union member is injured or killed by the police. "Longshore workers have a long tradition of protesting injustice in the community, and . . . recent events deserve a strong response from all Americans," ILWU Local 10 president Melvin Mackay said at the time of Scott's death. "The public shouldn't be afraid of the people who are supposed to protect them."

The ILWU's interventions on behalf of the marginalized didn't start or end at Latino and Asian American exploitation or police violence against Black Americans. The 1980s saw it take on an American institution—Colorado's Coors Brewing—on behalf of a multicultural coalition determined to recalibrate the balance of power in its workplace.

BREWING UP TROUBLE

The first rumblings of what would become a historic boycott came in 1957, when Coors brewery workers in United Brewery Workers Local 366 struck for 117 days. During the course of the strike, workers encouraged their supporters to boycott Coors's products, and labor leaders, including AFL-CIO president George Meany, entreated their members to do the same. The strike itself wasn't much of a success, but it planted the seeds of what would become a decades-long fight pitting the working class against one of Colorado's wealthiest and most powerful families.

The slavish devotion of the conservative, anti-union Coors family to the concepts of free market capitalism and anticommunism, coupled with its unsettling interest in worker surveillance (including preemptive polygraph tests for prospective employees) meant that organized labor faced an uphill climb whenever the two parties met at the bargaining table. But strikes broke out anyway, periodically resurfacing the boycott as a pressure tactic against a company that seemed too big to fail. Transportation workers—specifically, beer delivery drivers—got involved in 1974. San Francisco's Teamsters Local 888 had been locked in a bitter contract dispute with Coors ever since their master contract with beer and other beverage distributors across California expired in the summer of 1973. The union suspected Coors's attorney, Bud Lerten, had been rallying the support of other distributors to join Coors in refusing the union's new contract terms over wages and sick leave. The Teamsters called a strike, sending members to picket in front of noncompliant distributors and printing signs that labeled Coors "The Anti-Union Beer." As days stretched into weeks, and then weeks into months, the union reached settlements with distributors in several locations; but four hundred workers in the Bay Area and Sacramento remained out on the line. Not only did the Teamsters hire two full-time organizers to focus solely on the boycott, but the union's generally conservative-leaning leadership stepped back and allowed those organizers—Allan Baird, and Andris "Andy" Cirkelis, a Latvian refugee—to forge connections with unexpected corners of the community. At the time, the Teamsters were in need of good press. As Allyson P. Brantley writes in *Brewing a Boycott: How a Grassroots Coalition Fought Coors and Re-*

made American Consumer Activism, a nasty conflict with the predominantly Latino United Farm Workers had done the union's image no favors, nor had its alleged Mafia ties, corruption, and reactionary and racist sentiments from both leadership and the rank and file. Baird and Cirkelis first reached out to local communities of color to join the boycott, but they were quickly rebuffed, and informed it would take a great deal of dedicated organizing work to properly earn those communities' trust and support.

The two organizers drafted an ambitious affirmative action proposal aimed at bringing more "Black, Spanish Surname, Asian American, Native American, and Women" members into the fold at Local 888. When the proposal was sent around to local distributors, most of the recipients balked at its demands, and Baird and Cirkelis used the lukewarm (or outright hostile) response as ammunition to accelerate their efforts. Chicano activists had already been organizing around Coors's racist hiring policies for years, and Local 888 ramped up its outreach to leaders like Juan "Freddy Freak" Trujillo, a key organizer in the Chicano-led boycott in Coors's Rocky Mountain home state of Colorado. Those leaders had already done the work of building interracial solidarity among the Black and Indigenous workers harmed by Coors's racism, and when the Teamsters came knocking, they were able to share with the union a blueprint drawn from successful, real-life solidarity. Local 888's genuine efforts to address discrimination at Coors and within their own union convinced groups like the Native American Labor Advisory Council, the Latino Misson Youth Commission, and the Black Panther Party to join in on the boycott as well. Another critical blow was struck when the predominantly Palestinian American members of the Independent Grocery Association, who ran many of the smaller shops that stocked Coors, signed on to a letter promising to honor the boycott in their stores.

Baird then turned his focus on connecting with the LGBTQ community, a group that had been targeted by discriminatory policies at Coors that sought to weed out "subversive" elements in the company. Polygraphs and pointed multiple-choice tests were administered to employees with the goal of exposing—and punishing—any behavior deemed "abnormal" by the arch-conservative leadership of the company. To better reach those workers, Baird brought openly gay politician Harvey Milk and Bay Area Gay Liberation (BAGL), headed by the queer socialist organizer Howard Wallace, into the fold. (Baird and Milk forged a bond during the boycott, and Baird worked on several of the San Francisco politician's campaigns before Milk's assassination in 1978, a historic touch point in the queer liberation movement that shook the nation.)

The unlikely pairing of Teamsters and queer folks drew quizzical reactions from those who didn't understand the underlying issues that had brought them together, but those involved understood the need to support one another's struggles. As word spread and gay bars banned Coors from their premises, Local 888 worked to hire openly queer workers and add gay and lesbian employment protections to the contracts they negotiated. It was a mutually beneficial partnership that had enormous potential, but it was cut off at the knees by internal divisions and red-baiting. Local 888's coalition ultimately fractured under pressure from both the national AFL-CIO, which claimed the boycott was hurting other unionized Coors workers, and the Teamsters, who increasingly saw Baird and Cirkelis's multiracial, queer-affirming outreach campaign as too radical.

Two years into the boycott, Local 888 crumbled, but even after the Teamsters pulled out, the other activists in the fight stayed the course. The Chicano and LGBTQ communities kept the Coors boycott rolling for decades (and for some, it never ended at all). Organized labor officially jumped back into the fray in 1977, when the United

Brewery Workers Local 366 went on strike again over the same complaints that had spurred them to action in 1957. While their strike was broken after twenty months, the AFL-CIO finally backed the boycott, and continued to urge its members to honor it until 1987, when the AFL-CIO negotiated an agreement with Coors. Wallace went on to join members of the Gay and Lesbian Labor Activists Network in cofounding Pride at Work, the first national organization for LGBTQ labor activists; the group affiliated with the AFL-CIO as a constituency group in 1997 and remains a hub for queer organizers and rank-and-file workers within the movement. (And it's probably safe to assume that they still don't serve Coors at PAW events.)

"NO RED-BAITING, NO RACE-BAITING, NO QUEEN-BAITING!"

While unions were welcome allies in the fight with Coors (and the ILWU had already committed to organizing across racial and social barriers well before the Teamsters got the memo), there was another transport union whose members had already cut their teeth on the front lines of earlier battles for liberation. The San Francisco–based Marine Cooks and Stewards Union (MCS) was formed in 1901 to represent the workers who served the well-heeled guests aboard the era's hulking luxury liners and merchant ships. It was a grueling occupation characterized by low wages, poor sanitation, spoiled food, entitled passengers, and working conditions that gave rise to the ships' nickname: "floating tenements." Many of the cooks and stewards were Black or Asian; following the opening of Angel Island as an immigration hub, an influx of Chinese, Japanese, and Filipino immigrants joined San Francisco's maritime workforce, and were met with racism and naked hostility from entrenched labor organizations, MCS included.

Until the 1930s, the MCS accepted only white men as members; in 1921, the Colored Marine Employees Beneficial Association of the Pacific (CMBA) was formed to represent those workers the MCS rejected, and the two unions engaged in bitter competition over jobs and control of the waterfront. It would take the momentous impact of the Great Waterfront Strike of 1934 to illustrate how crucial it was for the labor movement to unite and organize across racial lines. As more leftists rose to power in the organization, the MCS embarked on an ambitious project to integrate its membership. The Congress of Industrial Organizations (CIO) was formed the next year by UMWA leader John L. Lewis, with a goal to compel the AFL to organize along industrial lines; the two groups' paths diverged considerably over the decades, especially as the Red Scare heated up, but in 1935 at least, the CIO represented a promising new vision of progress. Leftists were having a moment, and Communists in particular became deeply entwined with the more radical sectors of the movement. As Revels Cayton, a Black Communist MCS leader, later recalled, "Union leadership was reactionary, but the rank and file . . . fought to make it a democratic union, one in which discrimination did not exist."

In the MCS's case, that struggle for a united union explicitly included LGBTQIA workers, self-identified "queens" who composed a significant portion of the workforce at every level. Queer workers, from sailors to longshoremen to stewards, were drawn to the waterfront by an atmosphere of sexual freedom that was absent on land, and seafaring culture allowed space for intimate contact between men at sea, chipping away at the sexual binary that dominated on land. The MCS secured workplace protections for LGBTQIA workers decades before the gay liberation movement went mainstream or enshrined those rights in union contracts. As Allan Bérubé, a pioneering social historian on the lives of working-class lesbians and gay men who had extensively researched the MCS prior to his death in 2008, told *New Socialist* magazine in 1988, "You couldn't be fired for anything except for not doing your job—you had to violate something in the contract. So being gay was not a reason for being fired."

The MCS emerged as a beacon of interracial solidarity and a haven for LGBTQIA workers, who would occasionally raise money for union benefits by putting on drag shows and musicals. The playful, campy side of gay culture was also expressed in the union's newspaper, the *MCS Voice*, which mixed radical militancy and Marxist analysis with images of queer and interracial solidarity. Manuel Cabral, a ship's janitor known as the "Honolulu Queen," decorated the MCS union hall with flowers and hung up lace curtains; when the ILWU and other maritime workers gathered each year on the remembrance of Bloody Thursday, Cabral arranged the flowers at the sidewalk memorial. The union adopted the slogan "It's anti-union to red-bait, race-bait, or queen-bait," and during World War II provided a useful outlet for queer workers who wished to participate in the war effort but were barred from military service due to their sexuality.

The MCS continued to practice what it preached for the rest of its existence, even as the rising fear of Communist influence on the movement began to cause problems for its members. By 1949, the union's overwhelmingly white leadership had realized it did not accurately reflect its predominantly Black and Asian membership; within a year, that old guard stepped down to make room for a more diverse set of new leaders. Its membership remained overwhelmingly male, but the union went to bat for other genders as well. In 1950, when the Matson Navigation Company refused to allow Luella Lawhorn, a Black woman, to work on its luxury liner *Lurline*, to Hawai'i, all 311 stewards on board walked off in protest. The union held firm and saw to it that Lawhorn became the first-ever Black stewardess on a U.S. passenger ship in the Pacific.

Unfortunately, after World War II, the MCS got caught up in the same web of fear-mongering and repression that kneecapped so many other more radically inclusive and politically leftist unions during the Red Scare (especially those affiliated with the CIO, which refused to force its members to take an anti-Communism pledge). Shortly thereafter, in the 1950s, the union was kicked out of the CIO alongside the ILWU and other allegedly "Communist-dominated" unions, and absorbed into the more conservative Seafarers International Union. The now-defunct organization's multiracial, queer, leftist history would have been lost without the efforts of chroniclers like Bérubé. "What many of you younger people are trying to do today as queers—what you call inclusion and diversity—we already did it 50 years ago in the Marine Cooks and Stewards Union," Stephen "Mickey" Blair, a gay white MCS member who had served as the MCS's vice president, told him in the 1990s. Blair's partner, Frank McCormick, was a vice president of the California CIO, and they were both involved in the 1934 waterfront strike. "We did it in the labor movement as working-class queens with left-wing politics, and that's why the government crushed us, and that's why you don't know anything about us today—our history has been totally erased."

"WE PUT THE 'TRANS' BACK IN TRANSPORTATION"

LGBTQ workers and organizers have always been at the forefront of labor struggles in this country, whether they were leading the charge openly or behind the scenes, and the transportation industry is no exception. It's not a main feature of author and labor activist Miriam Frank's groundbreaking compendium *Out in the Union: A Labor History of Queer America*, but Frank's book does introduce a number of compelling transit-adjacent characters. Howard Wallace, a gay Teamster who was instrumental in building bridges between the queer community and the labor movement during the Coors boycott, later organized the first March on Washington for Gay Rights in 1979. Carol Ernst and Susan Schurman, a pair of lesbian bus drivers and members of AFSCME Local 693 in Ann Arbor, Michigan, became two of the first people to successfully negotiate a gay rights provision into a collectively bargained union contract, in 1974. More recent scholarship on the lives and livelihoods of working-class LGBTQ people has yielded even more examples of folks queering transportation work throughout history.

Author and professor Anne Balay's *Semi Queer: Inside the World of Gay, Trans, and Black Truck Drivers*, draws on her own experience as a queer trucker as well as interviews with sixty-six current and former drivers to paint a picture of the joys, sorrows, dangers, and affirmation that many queer and marginalized workers have found on the open road. Balay's writing points to the mobility inherent in the work itself as a major attractor for marginalized people, situating trucking as a sort of liminal space that spans geographical borders as well as sexual, racial, and gendered boundaries. The same isolation and loneliness that can make the job so difficult end up providing a kind of safety to queer and trans workers whose very existence is threatened at work and out in the world. "I think a lot of trans women choose this career because it's a place where we *can* work—we're by ourselves, no one's going to harass us in the truck," a trans woman with the pseudonym Sisyphus told Balay, describing the unending homophobic and transphobic harassment she's endured at other workplaces. "The fact that people hate me 'cause I'm trans, well, then they'll hate me, but say hello to my truck."

Long-haul trucking is not an easy job, and is seldom a worker's first choice for employment; the hours are long, the pay isn't great, and the physical, mental, and emotional toll can be staggering. Truckers are paid by the mile, not the hour, in a modern version of the piecework system that kept nineteenth-century garment workers hunched over their reams of fabric late into the night. Every aspect of the drivers' workdays—which can stretch up to fourteen hours—is tightly regulated and monitored, and so are their bodies; many truckers live with disabilities caused by their labor, lack health insurance, suffer from food insecurity, and are frequently tested by their employers for sleep apnea based on factors like BMI and medical history, then compelled to use expensive CPAP machines. Women and nonbinary truckers as well as gay men face an increased risk of sexual violence and assault by fellow drivers and other strangers, and trans drivers face the additional hurdle of having to locate safe restrooms at less-than-welcoming truck stops and in states that have passed anti-trans "bathroom bills." The industry remains dominated by straight cisgender white men with conservative politics (as of 2016, Balay reported that about 5.1 percent identified as women and 8 percent as people of color; there is no data available for queer or trans workers, though Balay estimated in *Rolling Stone* that trans women may make up as many as 3 percent of drivers). The truckers Balay interviewed either said—or showed—that sexism, racism, transphobia, homophobia, and anti-immigrant rhetoric are all too common. "While there are a lot of LGBT members out here driving a truck, even more are the old-school, rednecky, antigay types. . . . God forbid there be a f-ggot in the restroom with them," Alix, a trans man from the South, told her in a 2016 interview. "I have to watch myself; I'm always looking over my shoulder because of the attitudes and politics, especially in this past year."

Despite its downsides, trucking remains both a lifestyle and a livelihood for many workers who are shut out of other avenues of employment, and the workers who are in it are *really* in it. "A long time ago, once I accepted who I am, I chose not to hide who I am," explained Carolyn, an intersex and trans driver. "And the only way it's going to get better for myself and people who will come later is to be out there. . . . I'm trying to be more of a leader type, trying to set an example. Let the trucking industry know, hey, we put the 'trans' back in transportation!"

While some of the problems in the trucking industry are baked in (as one Black woman trucker observed to Balay, "Trucking as a whole is racist, but then America is, so it's no surprise"), it stands to reason that many of the issues these marginalized workers face could be resolved, or at the very least alleviated, through unions. In 2019, a group of conservative truckers calling themselves Black Smoke Matters attempted a weeklong strike to protest government regulations on the trucking industry, but only a few dozen people participated. It was a far cry from the militancy of 1934, when Teamster truck drivers shut down the streets during the Minneapolis General Strike and ended up in a bloody battle with the police, but these workers were at a severe disadvantage. Trucking used to be a heavily unionized industry, with high salaries and decent benefits to match. But that all changed after the Carter administration undertook a deregulation spree during the 1970s. The passage of the Motor Carrier Act (MCA) of 1980 cut costs for the consumer, but slashed drivers' earnings and shifted the onus for highway safety off of the federal government or the employers and onto the individual workers. While some truckers are still represented by unions like the Teamsters (who as of 2019 represented seventy-five thousand of the nation's 1.8 million long-haul truckers), many of them are classed (often improperly) as independent contractors, which strips them of the protections afforded to full-time employees under current U.S. labor law.

The deregulation of the trucking industry unfolded alongside the collapse of the Teamsters union under the weight of its various corruption scandals, the suspicious disappearance of Jimmy Hoffa, and its vicious squabbles over territory with other unions. Hundreds of unionized carriers went out of business during the first few years after the MCA was implemented, and as a result, the remaining carriers' desire to avoid using union labor in favor of paying cheaper wages eviscerated the membership. Deregulation was a perfect storm of complex and unfortunate circumstances, one that has continued to harm the current generation of marginalized truckers, and transportation workers in general. And things would only worsen when President Carter's successor, a flashy, hard-line conservative, took office.

REAGAN DECLARES WAR ON LABOR

Ronald Reagan, the former president of the Screen Actors Guild (SAG) and the only union member ever to have ascended to the presidency, came to power in 1980 and unleashed utter hell upon the United States' labor movement. Transportation workers would bear the brunt of his anti-labor, pro-business conservative agenda, and his attack on the airline industry would come to symbolize the Republicans' enduring hatred for unions. Though Reagan is infamous for the many terrible policies he inflicted on the American people, within the world of labor, his most reviled action remains his brutal evisceration of the 1981 Professional Air Traffic Controllers Organization (PATCO) strike. Prior to this event, even during the most contentious labor conflicts, it was uncommon for companies to hire permanent replacements for striking workers; most workers could count on their jobs being there waiting for them upon their return, which made strike activity far less of an existential gamble than it would soon become.

On August 3, 1981, when 11,359 PATCO members went out on strike for higher wages, safer working conditions, and a thirty-two-hour workweek, the air-traffic controllers were technically breaking a 1955 law that banned federal government employees from striking (much to unions' annoyance, the law was upheld by the Supreme

Court in 1971). It was a gamble, but one that they assumed they'd win, since other government unions had previously violated said law and called strikes without incident. The thought of the government hauling off and firing thousands of essential aviation workers seemed too far-fetched to be a real threat; the union reckoned that their members' jobs were too important to the economy and required too much high-level training for employers to be able to fill them with scabs on short notice, and decided that they held enough leverage to shrug off the law. PATCO was already known for its militancy, and for launching a series of smaller wildcat strikes (i.e., work stoppages and walkouts that are not sanctioned by union leadership) throughout the 1970s; they strove to personify the old labor maxim "There are no illegal strikes, just unsuccessful ones," which would later come back to bite them when they hit the bricks in a work stoppage that ended up ticking off both boxes. In 1981, following months of stalled contract negotiations, those earlier trial runs boiled over into their most spectacular—and ultimately doomed—effort yet. Until then, PATCO hadn't had to contend with Ronald Reagan.

The day the strike was announced, and after seven thousand flights had been canceled, the president held a press conference during which he declared, "They are in violation of the law and if they do not report for work within forty-eight hours they have forfeited their jobs and will be terminated." Two days later, after only thirteen hundred of the nearly twelve thousand strikers had returned to work, he followed through on the threat, framing their work stoppage as a "peril to national safety." Thousands of air traffic controllers were fired and barred from working in the industry ever again, and their employers began accepting applications from their replacements less than two weeks later. PATCO's president, Robert Poli, who had authorized the strike, was found in contempt by a federal judge and ordered to pay $1,000 a day in fines for each day the strike continued.

Ironically, PATCO was one of the few unions that had endorsed Reagan in the lead-up to his 1980 presidential campaign, and Reagan had sent the union a letter promising to look out for their interests. Instead, with Reagan's backing, the strike was broken in a matter of days. So was PATCO itself; the union was decertified the following October and ceased to exist. Worse, a terrible precedent had now been set, and the aftereffects of Reagan's war on PATCO would ripple throughout the labor movement for decades. Politically, Reagan's hard line against labor became a plank in the Republican platform and a loyalty test for the new generation of conservatives he helped spawn. Opposing unions—public sector and otherwise—has since become utterly entrenched in the Republican Party's policies and public image, even as it continues to attempt to paint itself as representing "hardworking blue-collar men and women," as Texas senator Ted Cruz (himself a millionaire married to an heiress) phrased it in one especially disingenuous 2021 tweet.

In terms of labor's relationship to capital, the PATCO affair emboldened employers to take harsher measures and a more combative posture against workers who went on strike, solidifying management's inherent advantage and tilting an already inequitable power dynamic squarely in the bosses' favor. During the 1970s, the labor movement had built up enough strength and influence to ensure that the mere threat of a strike was often enough to get a recalcitrant employer to back down, but post-PATCO, that power swung in the other direction. The number of large-scale strikes plummeted, declining by nearly 90 percent between 1977 and 2016; by 2020, that number had dwindled into the single digits, with only 8 strikes of more than 1,000 workers recorded by the Bureau of Labor Statistics. Comparatively, in 1970, there were 380 major strikes or lockouts, and nearly 200 in 1980, but the so-called PATCO Syndrome helped hasten that decline into mere double digits by the mid-1990s. There are still big strikes happening, but unions have had to adapt, and many now choose to focus their energies on winning at the bargaining table and in the boardroom instead of on the picket lines.

Some unions continue to relish a fight, though, and the aviation industry is still full of scrappers. While PATCO workers were fighting their battles on the tarmac, flight attendants were waging their own war for justice thousands of feet high in the air. Reagan was initially attracted to PATCO and sought its endorsement partly due to the composition of its membership, which skewed heavily white, male, conservative, and veteran. In contrast, the flight attendants' unions were the Gipper's worst nightmare. For decades, their militant, progressive membership was predominantly made up of women and gay men, and they elected feminist activist Patt Gibbs, an out lesbian, to the presidency of the Association of Professional Flight Attendants in 1977. There is a long history of LGBTQ workers within the flight attendants' unions and in that workforce, and the intersection between the women's rights and queer liberation struggles has been a major driver behind those unions' biggest wins and most heated battles.

The profession of flight attendant has evolved considerably over the past century, and so has the public perception of its workers. It was initially conceived as a man's job, and not only that, a specifically masculine, physically robust, implicitly heterosexual man's job. In the 1920s and into the 1930s, aviation was coded as a masculine, military-adjacent space, and its workers were expected to fit the part, whether they were piloting the plane or serving drinks in the cabin. Those expectations soon shifted, and the gender dynamic flipped entirely. After the Boeing Air Transport Office (a precursor to United Airlines) turned her down for a pilot job, Ellen Church, a trained pilot and registered nurse, became America's first woman flight attendant in 1930. Her new bosses liked the idea of having trained nurses on board to calm anxious fliers' nerves, and gave her a three-month trial to see how she and the seven other women she'd recruited—Jessie Carter, Cornelia Peterman, Inez Keller, Alva Johnson, Margaret Arnott, Ellis Crawford, and Harriet Fry—fared. These "sky girls," as they were then called, were required to be "single, younger than 25 years old; weigh less than 115 pounds; and stand less than 5 feet, 4 inches tall," and expected to handle luggage, take tickets, tend to sick passengers, help fuel the plane, and even tighten the bolts holding the seats to its floor. They passed the test with flying colors, and the long reign of the "air hostess" (and later "stewardess") had begun.

After World War II broke out and stewards were called up for service alongside millions of other male workers, the airlines grudgingly began hiring women in droves (and soon dropped the nursing requirement entirely, since so many nurses were needed for war work). The transmogrification of the once male-dominated profession into "women's work" was complete, and would remain that way for decades. In the beginning, they were also all white. Joan Dorsey, the first Black woman flight attendant in the U.S., was hired by American Airlines in 1963, and even then, it took her several tries to convince the boss to give her a chance. "I was interviewed five times," she said in a 2019 interview. "You know no one else had to go back that often. But I kept coming back and coming back. I think it was just courage. When you're that young, you just want to do what you think you should do and just get on with it." Dorsey went on to have a long and fruitful career with the airline, retiring in 1999. Some of her more memorable trips took her to Vietnam and to Kenya, and she worked on the charter flight for Hubert Humphrey, Lyndon Johnson's running mate, during an entire campaign season. Humphrey was one of the main authors of the Civil Rights Act, and the significance of their crossed paths was not lost on Dorsey. "Equality was a big issue and I was right there also pursuing equality for everyone," she said, looking back on her time as a trailblazer.

FREEDOM TO FLY

Only a few years after Joan Dorsey met one of its architects, the Civil Rights Act helped a man named Celio Diaz, Jr., strike a blow for workplace equality in an industry that could not have been less interested in the idea. Diaz was a straight, married father of two from Miami who worked as a truck driver but had always wanted to be a flight attendant, inspired by the exploits of an uncle who had served prior to World War II. In 1967, he decided to take the leap by applying for a job as flight cabin attendant with Pan American Airlines. Male flight attendants still existed post–World War II, but made up a tiny percentage of the workforce, and ironically, they had to contend with the new stigma that accompanied their chosen gig. At the time, only about 4 percent of flight attendants were men, and the gender reversal had become so thoroughly entrenched so quickly that male stewards were regarded as suspiciously feminine, or outright queer, especially during the aggressively hetereonormative 1950s. A gory 1954 Miami murder case involving twenty-seven-year-old William T. Simpson, a gay man who worked as a flight attendant for Eastern Airlines, unleashed a viciously homophobic Miami-area "gay panic" and further hardened homophobic attitudes against men who shared his identity as well as his profession—despite the fact that Simpson was the victim. Pan Am implemented a women-only flight attendant policy shortly thereafter.

Though the stereotypes about gay male flight attendants came from an ugly place of misogyny and homophobia, they stumbled into accuracy in one respect. Many of the men and women who chose a life in midair were queer, whether or not they chose to share their identities with the world. The constant travel and rootless existence that the job required allowed both straight cisgender women and queer flight attendants of all genders an escape from the rigid, gendered social expectations that would have otherwise governed their lives back on terra firma. The skies offered them freedom from the drudgery—or dangers—that may have otherwise defined their working lives. Those jobs also offered a sense of community, safety, and even sex and romance. Their love lives are well documented, and in his book, *Plane Queer: Labor, Sexuality, and AIDS in the History of Male Flight Attendants*, Phil Tiemeyer writes that "the aisles and galleys of airplanes, as well as crew hotels and crash pads, served the same role that other gays and lesbians found in bars: a place where they could meet others like themselves and even embrace their same-sex desires for the first time."

Many airlines were unabashedly up front about both their strictly gendered hiring preferences as well as their homophobia, and due to Pan Am's own strict policy of hiring only women, Diaz's application was rejected. Undaunted, he filed charges with the Equal Employment Opportunity Commission (EEOC) and eventually took the matter all the way to the Supreme Court. His argument was that the company had violated the Civil Rights Act's Title VII by discriminating against him on the grounds of sex. After four years of litigation, in which the company's lawyers argued that women were better suited for the job, attacked the idea of "male stewardesses," and insisted that the mere presence of gay men on a flight was unfair and potentially harmful to the customer, Diaz won his case in 1971. Unfortunately, by then he had passed the age limit to become a flight attendant, stymied by yet another form of discrimination. Diaz himself was never able to live his dream, but he had helped pave the way for the next generation of young men with eyes to the sky to realize their own. Whether or not he realized it, he also helped carve out a path for gay men to enter a heavily unionized labor force that would allow them to access the benefits and protections that every worker deserves, and that marginalized workers who would otherwise be at risk of arbitrary firings or workplace discrimination desperately need.

As Tiemeyer estimated, gay men have made up a considerable percentage of male flight attendants since the 1950s, and have consistently made up about 15 percent of the total flight attendant workforce. That percentage reached as high as 80 percent of male flight attendants in the 1970s, and remains significant, while the numbers of queer women and gender nonconforming workers has also increased. "A large contingent of the women who formed our union were lesbians, and they weren't out," explained Sara Nelson, a veteran flight attendant who began working in the industry in 1996 and now serves as the president of the Association of Flight Attendants (AFA-CWA). "You had to quit if you got married, or you got pregnant, [and] they couldn't come out to their families, so what could they do? They had to create a career where they could continue in this job, because it was their excuse not to have to go live the life of a 1950s housewife."

Those women—Ada Brown Greenfield, Frances Hall, Edith Lauterbach, Sally Thometz, and Sally Watt Keenan—who were all active flight attendants for United Airlines, banded together to form the Air Line Stewardess Association (ALSA) in 1945, and in doing so launched one of the most militant aviation industry unions this country has ever seen. In 1973 the Association of Flight Attendants split off from its parent union, then gained its own charter with the AFL-CIO in 1984, and later affiliated with the Communications Workers of America (CWA) in 2003. Throughout its history, the AFA-CWA has had to contend with rampant misogyny, sexism, homophobia, and all-around bad behavior from customers as well as from coworkers in the skies and on the ground, and has needed to fight to protect a membership that was and is predominantly composed of women and queer men. Combatting discrimination in the workplace has always been a necessary priority for unions representing flight attendants, given the culture of sexual harassment, abuse, discrimination, and disrespect that so many of these workers have been expected to shoulder (usually in high heels, and with their makeup applied just so). "I've literally had people say to me—and I broke down during the MeToo movement when I heard these stories directly, from six months to thirty years on the job—'At some point, Sara, we just had to recognize it as part of the job,'" Nelson said.

Nelson shared some of those stories, including her own, when she testified in front of the Congressional Caucus for Women's Issues in 2018. "Flight attendants, about 80 percent women, are ongoing victims of sexual harassment and sexual assault," she stated. "Our union was formed to give women a voice and to beat back discrimination and misogyny faced on the job. We defined our careers at the bargaining table, in the courts, and on Capitol Hill. We taught the country to leave the word 'stewardess' in the history books. . . . But the industry never disavowed the marketing schemes featuring short skirts, hot pants, and ads that had young women saying things like 'I'm Cheryl, fly me.'"

Airlines have been pushing the sexualization of flight attendants as a marketing tactic since the mid-1930s. As a rule, women were fired when they married, became pregnant, or reached the grand old ages of either thirty-two or twenty-five. The prim hemlines, sensible shoes, and modest caps of Ellen Church's day soon gave way to shorter shirts, higher heels, sassy little scarves, and increasingly Byzantine rules over weight, makeup, and hairstyles (even today, Black women's hairstyles are policed by "guides," like the one Emirates released in 2018, that show what is and is not acceptable—for example, natural dreadlocks and dyed hair are banned). These rules helped keep costs down—flight attendants' wages had gotten skimpier alongside their uniforms—and also ensured a quick turnover in the workforce, as many young women left to get married and start families after only a few years on the job. Advertising campaigns played up the youth and beauty of employees, featuring photos of dainty (or buxom) young women welcoming (presumably male) passengers aboard, and sporting suggestive slogans like the aforementioned "fly me" tagline courtesy of National Airlines. Thanks to decades of pressure from the union, airlines finally shelved the weight requirement in 1993, sixty years after Ellen Church worked her first flight.

That happened also three years before Nelson began flying with United Airlines, but everything didn't magically change overnight. She still remembers having to attend "makeup days," as well as witnessing a much more sobering aftereffect from all those years of mandatory weigh-ins. The stress of knowing that they could be suspended without pay or lose their job if their weight exceeded the limit took a heavy toll on workers in more ways than one. "My first two to three years on the job, it was like one funeral after another of a flight attendant that had a heart condition from anorexia or bulimia," she said. "As the weight program went away, that doesn't happen today. But I remember that vividly. . . . If you didn't know, you wouldn't know. But clearly, they had struggled, and they lost their lives from it."

Gay men escaped the worst of the appearance policing that women had to endure, but queer workers of all genders still faced an additional layer of discrimination. During the 1980s, the AFA-CWA became one of the first unions to explicitly advocate for the rights of workers living with HIV/AIDS, and to push back against prejudiced employers to ensure that those workers retained their health care benefits. In 1984, as the AIDS crisis ravaged the gay community and scientists struggled to figure out why, a French Canadian flight attendant named Gaëtan Dugas became enmeshed in the center of the controversy. A study published in the *American Journal of Medicine* showed Dugas to be part of an early cluster of sexually active gay men who were infected with the virus, and labeled his node "Patient O"; somewhere along the line, the "O" morphed into a zero, and a disastrous domino effect unfolded. In his bestseller about the AIDS epidemic, *And the Band Played On*, journalist Randy Shilts dubbed him "Patient Zero," and Dugas—who died from kidney failure the same month the study was released—was blamed for spreading the virus. Shilts, who was also gay, later expressed regret for his mistake and the role he played in the widespread demonization of an innocent man; he died from AIDS in 1994.

Efforts have been made to correct the record and exonerate Dugas, but in the 1980s, he may as well have been public enemy number one. The association only added to the stigma gay flight attendants faced at work and in the media, compounding their own fears and struggles as the crisis continued. Securing their health care was one small but crucial action that the union could take to support queer workers, and those workers also found strength in union contracts that protected them from discriminatory firings and guaranteed paid sick leave and vacation days that many needed for either their own health reasons or to take care of friends who were ill or dying. As Ryan Murphy notes in his 2016 book, *Deregulating Desire: Flight Attendant Activism and the Family Values Economy*, "Gay men in the airline industry were often single, and could not always count on parents, siblings, or partners for help as they suffered from a heavily stigmatized illness. As the AIDS crisis highlighted the importance of relationships that were committed but not legally recognized, activists pushed to broaden family benefits eligibility to include flight attendants' unmarried partners."

"We actually fought for men to be able to have the right to do the job, and then it was gay men who spoke up and said, 'Wait a minute, we want these issues in the contract bargaining,'" Nelson recalled. "And I remember the matriarchs of our union saying to them, 'Well, if you want that, you've got to get involved in the union. . . . If you want to make a change, then you better get involved for the next contract negotiations.' And they did."

In another effort to support their queer members, the flight attendants' union went all-in on securing domestic partner benefits for all of its members, which was a major demand from both queer workers and other workers who wanted those benefits for various reasons. In 1996, after the city of San Francisco passed a law requiring companies that did business with the city to provide domestic benefits for their employees, United Airlines, along with the Air Transport Association, the management lobbying group representing twenty-one other airlines, sued the city, arguing that they should be exempt from the running as nationwide businesses regulated by federal law. The local AFA chapter sprang into action, launching a public pressure campaign that soon turned to civil disobedience. At the San Francisco Gay Pride Parade, AFA members handed out leaflets reading "Is United really gay-friendly?" in full view of a United-sponsored parade float. The union and its coalition partners, Howard Wallace's Pride at Work, the Human Rights Campaign, and the Harvey Milk Democratic Club, held a raucous demonstration outside of United's downtown ticket office, blocking the entrances and handing out ten thousand more leaflets. The union was constrained by the Railway Labor Act, which governs airline labor negotiations and representations and prohibits members from engaging in actions that may cause financial harm to an employer, but their coalition partners weren't, and calls for a boycott began to build. United eventually caved in 1999, and within days of their announcement, both American Airlines and Delta Air Lines followed suit and offered domestic partner benefits for all of their employees as well. Domestic partner benefits soon became industry standard, and the AFA has continued to push for progress.

When President Trump's brutal 2019 government shutdown squeezed federal employees to the bone and left thousands of her members without paychecks, AFA-CWA president Sara Nelson shook the labor world by daring to stride up to the podium and mention labor's nuclear option—the general strike. In doing so, she evoked the large-scale labor battles of the past while offering a fresh, more militant vision for labor's future, and also scared the living daylights out of the craven government officials who'd been holding all those workers hostage. The shutdown ended a few short days later, and Nelson's speech is now acknowledged to have been a crucial tipping point. The mere mention of a general strike was enough to send more conservative labor leadership into a tizzy (and to get the rank and file buzzing with excitement), but few people realize just how close we came to seeing one.

"What gets lost in all the noise is that while we said that the labor movement should *talk* about a general strike, we were actually *preparing* to strike," Nelson explained. "The first question to me was, 'Sara, what are the pilots going to do?' And I would say, 'Yeah, airplanes don't take off without pilots, but they also don't take off without flight attendants—we made sure of that in the 1950s. We have just as much power, if we're willing to use it.' "

10

THE METALWORKERS

You have made the decision to do battle, and that is the only decision you will make. We *shall decide the arena and the time.*

—General Gordon Baker, cofounder of the Dodge Revolutionary Union Movement

The stereotypical image of the burly Midwestern white man swaggering through a construction site in a hard hat or wrangling slabs of metal on an assembly line has long defined what "union labor" looks like in the popular imagination. Those characters have always played an outsized role in the heavy manufacturing industries and continue to make up an important piece of that puzzle, but their experiences are far from universal. Whether they're welding auto parts on an assembly line, hammering nails, bending steel, or marching on the boss, American manufacturing workers have always come from diverse identities and experiences. And they've also been an integral part of the house of labor since the very beginning. After all, who do you think built it?

Women and workers of color have also been around to see its foundations crumble, and watch as its beams threaten to collapse—sometimes literally. After the September 11 attacks, people flooded in from across the country to offer aid and help with the cleanup efforts, and among them were a cohort of Mohawk ironworkers originally from the territories of Akwesasne (which comprises Ontario,

Quebec, and New York State) and Kahnawake, near Montreal. They had once helped build the Twin Towers, and now that the building had been reduced to ash and twisted metal, the men returned to help clear the wreckage at Ground Zero. By then, they and their fathers and grandfathers had been leaving their mark on the city of New York's most cherished landmarks for over a century. Mohawk ironworkers helped raise icons like the Empire State Building, the George Washington Bridge, Lincoln Center, the Chrysler Building, and the Waldorf Astoria. As Kyle Karonhiaktatie Beauvais, a sixth-generation Mohawk ironworker, told *Smithsonian* magazine in 2002, "There's pride in walking iron."

The tradition of Mohawk people taking on this very specific, high-flying, death-defying job stretches back to 1886, when they were hired by the Canadian Railroad to work on a bridge spanning the Saint Lawrence River into their ancestral land. During the 1920s Art Deco craze, skyscrapers popped up like mushrooms all over Manhattan, and Mohawk ironworkers traveled down from the Kahnawake Reservation in occupied Tiohtià:ke (also known as Montreal) to work on them, walking across two-inch-thick beams hundreds of feet in the air without so much as a tremble. At one point, officials from the U.S. Immigration Service bizarrely tried to deport them, alleging that the Mohawk workers who commuted between the U.S. and their reservation in Canada were "illegal aliens." The 1928 *Diabo v. McCandless* case slapped that down, affirming the Mohawks' right as citizens of a sovereign tribal nation to move freely across the imaginary line separating the now colonized tribal lands that they and their ancestors had occupied for millennia.

During the 1930s, hundreds of Mohawk workers and their families took advantage of that ruling and moved south, building up a community around the Ironworkers Local 361 union hall on Atlantic Avenue in New York. They created a little slice of home the locals called "Downtown Kahnawake" that lasted until the early 1960s. As New York City's building boom cooled down and the completion of the New York State Thruway slashed the commute between downtown Brooklyn and upstate New York, the skywalkers began to "boom out" in search of work elsewhere. The tradition persists, as Mohawk ironworkers continue traveling from work site to work site, walking iron and making superhuman feats of strength and agility look easy. In 2002, New York City paid its respects to those workers and their elders with an exhibit at the National Museum of the American Indian's George Gustav Heye Center called "Booming Out: Mohawk Ironworkers Build New York."

A MIDWESTERN REVOLUTION

As of 2021, the U.S. construction industry is still booming and the building trades are heavily unionized, but not all of the nation's builders have been so lucky. The country's manufacturing sector has declined severely since its post–World War II high point, and so has its union density. The auto industry's shuttered factories, jobs shipped to countries with lower wages, and weakened unions have become a symbol of the waning American empire. But things weren't always this dire. Unions once fought tooth and nail to establish a foothold in the country's automobile plants, factories, and steel mills. When those workers were able to harness the power of collective bargaining, wages went up and working conditions improved. The American Dream, or at least a stable middle-class existence, became an achievable goal for workers without college degrees or privileged backgrounds. Many more became financially secure enough to actually purchase the products they made, boosting the economy as well as their sense of pride in their work. Those jobs were still difficult and demanding and carried physical risks, but those workers—or at least, *some* of those workers—could count on the union to have their back when injustice or calamity befell them.

In Detroit, those toiling on the assembly lines of the Big Three automakers—Chrysler, Ford, and General Motors—could turn to the United Auto Workers (UAW), then hailed as perhaps the most progressive "major" union in the country as it forced its way into the automotive factories of the mid-twentieth century. The UAW stood out like a sore thumb among the country's many more conservative (and lily-white) unions, with leadership from the likes of former socialist and advocate of industrial democracy Walter Reuther and a strong history of support for the civil rights movement. But to be clear, there was still much work to be done; Black representation in UAW leadership remained scarce despite its membership reaching nearly 30 percent Black in the late 1960s.

The Big Three had hired a wave of Black workers to fill their empty assembly lines during World War II, often subjecting them to the dirtiest and most dangerous tasks available and on-the-job racial discrimination. And then, of course, once white soldiers returned home and a recession set in, those same workers were the first ones sacrificed. Production picked back up in the 1960s, and Black workers were hired in large numbers once again. Black workers grew to become a majority of the workforce in Detroit's auto plants, but found themselves confronting the same problems as before. In factories where the union and the company had become accustomed to dealing with one another without much fuss, a culture of complacency set in, and some workers began to feel that the union was more interested in keeping peace with the bosses than in fighting for its most vulnerable members. Tensions were rising, both in the factories and the world at large. By May 1968, as the struggle for Black liberation consumed the country, the memory of the 1967 Detroit riots remained fresh, and the streets of Paris were paralyzed by general strikes, a cadre of class-conscious Black activists and autoworkers saw an opportunity to press the union into action.

They called themselves DRUM—the Dodge Revolutionary Union Movement. DRUM was founded in the wake of a wildcat strike at Dodge's Detroit plant, staffed by a handful of Black revolutionaries from the Black-owned, anti-capitalist *Inner City Voice* alternative newspaper. The *ICV* sprang up during the 1967 Detroit riots, published with a focus on Marxist thought and the Black liberation struggle. DRUM members boasted experience with other prominent movement groups like the Student Nonviolent Coordinating Committee and the Black Panthers, combining tactical knowledge with a revolutionary zeal attuned to their time and community.

General Gordon Baker, a seasoned activist and assembly worker at Chrysler's Dodge Main plant, started DRUM with a series of clandestine meetings throughout the first half of 1968. By May 2, the group had grown powerful enough to see four thousand workers walk out of Dodge Main in a wildcat strike to protest the "speed-up" conditions in the plant, which saw workers forced to produce at dangerous speeds and work overtime to meet impossible quotas. Over the course of just one week, the plant had increased its output 39 percent. Black workers, joined by a group of older Polish women who worked in the plant's trim shop, shut down the plant for the day, and soon bore the brunt of management's wrath. Of the seven workers who were fired after the strike, five were Black. Among them was Baker, who sent a searing letter to the company in response to his dismissal. "In this day and age under the brutal repression reaped from the backs of Black workers, the leadership of a wildcat strike is a badge of honor and courage," he wrote. "You have made the decision to do battle, and that is the only decision you will make. *We* shall decide the arena and the time."

Their next battle came quickly. DRUM led another thousands-strong wildcat strike on July 8, this time shutting down the plant for two days and drawing in a number of Arab and white workers as well. Prior to the strike, the group had printed leaflets and held rallies that attracted hundreds of workers, students, and community members, a strategy DRUM would go on to use liberally in later campaigns to gin up support and spread its revolutionary message.

Men like Baker, Kenneth Cockrel, and Mike Hamlin were the public face of DRUM, but their work would have been impossible without the work of their female comrades, whose contributions were often overlooked. Hamlin admitted as much in his book-length conversation with longtime political activist and artist Michele Gibbs, *A Black Revolutionary's Life in Labor*. "Possibly my deepest regret," Hamlin writes, "is that we could not curb, much less transform, the doggish behavior and chauvinist attitudes of many of the men."

Black women in the movement persevered despite this discrimination and disrespect at work, and they also found allies in unexpected places. Grace Lee Boggs, a Chinese American Marxist philosopher and activist with a PhD from Bryn Mawr, met her future husband James Boggs in Detroit after moving there in 1953. She and James, a Black activist, author (1963's *The American Revolution: Pages from a Negro Worker's Notebook*), and Chrysler autoworker, became fixtures in Detroit's Black radical circles. They naturally fell in with the DRUM cadre, and Grace fit perfectly when Hamlin organized a DRUM-sponsored book club discussion forum in order to draw in progressive white and more moderate Black sympathizers. Interest in the Marxist book club was unexpectedly robust, and it grew to more than eight hundred members in its first year. Grace stepped in to help lead its discussion groups, and allowed young activists to visit her and James at their apartment and talk through thorny philosophical and political questions until the wee hours. She would go on to become one of the nation's most respected Marxist political intellectuals and a lifelong activist for workers' rights, feminism, Black liberation, and Asian American issues. As she told an interviewer prior to her death in 2015 at the age of one hundred, "People who recognize that the world is always being created anew, and we're the ones that have to do it—they make revolutions."

Further inside the DRUM orbit, Helen Jones, a printer, was the force behind the creation and distribution of their leaflets and publications. Women like Paula Hankins, Rachel Bishop, and Edna Ewell Watson, a nurse and confidant of Marxist scholar and former Black Panther Angela Davis, undertook their own labor organizing projects. In one case, the trio led a union drive among local hospital workers in the DRUM faction, hoping to carve out a place for female leadership within their movement. But ultimately, these expansion plans were dropped due to a lack of full support within DRUM. "Many of the male leaders acted as if women were sexual commodities, mindless, emotionally unstable, or invisible," Edna Watson later told Dan Georgakas and Marvin Surkin for their *Detroit: I Do Mind Dying*. She claimed the organization held a traditionalist Black patriarchal view of women, in which they were expected to center and support their male counterparts' needs at the expense of their own agenda. "There was no lack of roles for women . . . as long as they accepted subordination and invisibility."

By 1969, the movement had spread to multiple other plants in the city, birthing groups like ELRUM (Eldon Avenue RUM), JARUM (Jefferson Avenue RUM), and outliers like UPRUM (UPS workers) and HRUM (health-care workers). The disparate RUM groups then combined forces, forming the League of Revolutionary Black Workers. The new organization was to be led by the principles of Marxism, Leninism, and Maoism, but the league was never an ideological monolith. Its seven-member executive committee could not fully cohere the different political tendencies of its board or its eighty-member-deep inner control group. Most urgently, opinions diverged on what shape, if any, further growth should take.

Some promoted the creation of a Black Workers Congress that sat above individual workplaces or industries. Advocates envisioned the arc of a BWC developing into a viable national party, but nuts-and-bolts unionists inside shops and plants themselves vehemently opposed the idea, asking that they refocus on their original mission: workers and building the revolution on the shop floor. The schism deepened until the League came apart at the seams in a 1971 leadership purge. One faction was absorbed into a group called the Communist League while others pressed on with the BWC vision. An inaugural BWC conference was held on September 5, 1971, with plans drawn up to recruit Latino, Indigenous, and Asian affiliates, but enthusiasm for this new organization was short-lived.

BUILDING MULTIRACIAL ALLIANCES IN THE MICHIGAN AUTO INDUSTRY

The formal structures of DRUM and the League of Revolutionary Black Workers may have been short-lived, but the seeds of change planted in Detroit weren't going anywhere. DRUM's pressure campaigns led anxious employers to boost outreach to recent Arab immigrants, assuming that a looming fear of deportation would keep the workers "docile" and unlikely to cause trouble for the bosses. But instead of serving as a meek and obedient counter to the more militant Black workers intent on spreading their revolutionary message on the factory floor, Arab workers quickly found common ground with Black workers as exploited minorities in a majority-white setting. The Black workers, especially those who were active in revolutionary circles and Black nationalism, were familiar with Islam and sympathized with the anti-Zionist, anti-colonial struggle of Palestinian coworkers. Like their Black coworkers, Arab immigrants were paid the least and worked the hardest. They, too, were denied opportunities to advance off the assembly line due to the bosses' racism and favoritism, and many first-generation Arab workers faced the barriers of language and religious accommodation at work. "Chrysler hopes to make conditions worse for all of us by first attacking the conditions of the Arab workers," read a flyer circulated by the radical caucus SPARK at the Dodge Main plant. "They count on turning us against each other so they can do this. . . . Chrysler figures that no one else will try to help an Arab worker when Chrysler attacks him."

Events far outside Detroit quickly put Chrysler's assumptions about the Arab character to the test. The 1968 Battle of Karameh, a military conflict between the Israeli Defense Forces (IDF), the Palestinian Liberation Organization (PLO), and the Jordanian Armed Forces (JAF) sharpened political consciousness in Arab communities around the world, including Detroit's. Local organizations sprouted up in the area, seeking to combat the discrimination and racism that had plagued Arab neighborhoods since the first wave of immigrants from Palestine, Yemen, and Lebanon emigrated to the region in the early 1900s. Palestinians became more vocal about their opposition to Israeli occupation, holding sit-ins and protests on college campuses that spread into nearby Arab neighborhoods. Yemeni workers formed the Committee to Support the Liberation of the Occupied Arab Gulf, a trade union with dual focus on labor power and opposition to monarchical control of the Arabian Peninsula. Organizations like the Arab Community Center for Economic and Social Service (ACCESS) opened. (Many years later, a Palestinian American lawyer and immigrant autoworker's daughter named Rashida Tlaib would spend time at ACCESS before becoming the first Palestinian American Muslim member of Congress a decade later.) By 1971, workers at a Chrysler automobile factory in Warren, Michigan, had taken a page out of DRUM and the League's book, and formed the Arab Workers Caucus (AWC).

As organizer and former AWC chairman Ismael Ahmed recalled in a 1999 interview with the Arab American National Museum, the group soon spread to twenty different plants in the Detroit area. The AWC, he said, was less of an official organization than a movement based on addressing the treatment of Arab workers—until a murder, and a war.

ARAB SOLIDARITY IN DEARBORN, MICHIGAN

When twenty-four-year-old Yemeni United Farm Workers organizer Nagi Daifullah was murdered by California police during the Salad Bowl Strike in August 1973, Detroit's Arab diaspora rallied to demand an inquiry into his death. One demonstration in South Dearborn, Michigan, drew about five hundred people, most of them Arab autoworkers. There, Patricia Proctor, a Detroit-area UFW organizer, noted that many of the Arab immigrants staffing the auto plants had started out as farmworkers in the California fields, underlining the strong connections between the two communities. A few months later, the 1973 Arab-Israeli War erupted, and Dearborn's Arab population, some of whom undoubtedly still had family in the impacted regions, followed the action as closely as they could from thousands of miles away. A coalition of Arab community leaders held a two-thousand-person demonstration at the Ford Rouge Union Hall Local 600 in which speakers outlined the corporate interests of the Big Three auto companies and their business connections to Israel.

When the Arab autoworkers in attendance learned that their own union, United Auto Workers (UAW) Local 600, had used their dues money to purchase $300,000 in State of Israel bonds, they were furious. Three thousand of them and their neighbors marched to the union office in Dearborn, holding signs reading "Stop US-Israeli Terror Against Arab People" as they demanded that the union dump their Israeli investments. A new, revitalized Arab Workers Caucus was formed with seventy representatives from nearly every auto plant in Detroit, and saw an opportunity to take its grievances to the source: UAW International president Leonard Woodcock was soon set to appear in downtown Detroit to receive a humanitarian award from B'nai B'rith International, a Zionist charitable organization.

That day of Woodcock's celebration, November 28, would see a monumental wildcat strike. In the weeks prior, seventy thousand leaflets in Arabic and English were passed around encouraging people to make the workers' concerns heard loud and clear. And on the day of, Arab high school students were stationed at the plant's entrance to make sure workers knew of the demonstration to be held that day. When the call came, twenty-five hundred Arab workers downed their tools and walked out. "We actually shut down the [Dodge Main] plant," Ahmed remembered, and production slowed at multiple others. Later that evening, as Woodcock tried to enjoy his $100-a-plate dinner, more than a thousand people protested outside. As labor historian Jeff Schuhrke wrote in *Jacobin*, the protestors—the majority of them Arab autoworkers who'd participated in the day's work stoppage and their Black coworkers—chanted slogans like "Don't abuse workers' dues" and held signs reading "Dispose of the Bonds" and "Jewish People Yes, Zionism No." Instead of facing the crowd outside, Woodcock—who had ascended to UAW leadership on the back of his perceived support for women's and minorities' rights—escaped out a back door.

UAW leadership initially dismissed the protests that day as a "Communist conspiracy," standing aside as the company disciplined or fired more than five hundred workers in its aftermath. But the undeterred Arab Workers Caucus took its demands to the friendlier grounds of the 1974 UAW constitutional convention in California; the same state in which their Yemeni brother Nagi Daifullah had lost his life to a cop's baton one year prior. Union leadership still wanted no part of the conversation, but the AWC had anticipated their response and instead went local—convincing multiple UAW subchapters around the country to divest from Israel on their own. By 1975, the UAW proper had been pushed to drop $48,000 of Israel-linked investments, and the Arab Workers Caucus had notched a crucial victory for justice. Collective action had lent a voice where decades of ignorance and oppression had preferred there would be none.

Small victories like these, while significant, would of course fall short of solving all the toxicity around race and representation inside the auto industry. Heavy industry at large has never been particularly kind to its workers, and can be especially callous to those it deems vulnerable or disposable. Two decades after the League of Revolutionary Black Workers and the Arab Workers Caucus had set these issues front and center in the Motor City, a twenty-three-year-old Black woman named Suzette Wright discovered just how much work was left to be done.

FIGHTING SEXUAL HARASSMENT ON THE ASSEMBLY LINE

It was 1993, and Wright was stretched thin: she was a single mom to a four-year-old while trying to squeeze college classes in between shifts at Chicago Assembly, the Ford Motor Company's oldest continuously operating automobile manufacturing plant. Against her Ford employee father's wishes—he had wanted her to finish college, not follow him onto an assembly line—Wright had passed the required tests and earned a place in the plant, where she was immediately taken aback by the way some of her new coworkers responded to her. "As we're walking through the plant, the men that are on the floor are talking to each other about the women they see," she told me in a 2021 interview. "They're chanting, they're calling out 'Fresh meat!' as we walk the aisle, they are pointing to the one they think will be their conquest, they are saying it loud enough for us to hear as we walk by, and it's super-intimidating. So you already get the sense before you ever pick up a tool that you are going to be in an environment like this, that you will have to protect yourself against. That's how it started."

Wright spent six years working at Ford, rising through the ranks to become a general utility manager (a high classification meaning she could do any number of different jobs). "I was hanging full-size tires on a Ford Taurus at five months pregnant!" she remembers, but a toxic work environment—and the aggressively misogynistic behavior of her coworkers—eventually did push her to a breaking point. The sexual harassment she had experienced on that first day never stopped, and only intensified as the years went on. Wright tried to keep her head down and think of her paycheck, her good health-care benefits, and her daughter's private school tuition, hoping that those pluses would outweigh the mental and physical torment she endured each day. "Every time something would happen, it was like a little pinch would be taken away from my personage, like I would just feel less than," she explained. "When [the harassment] is consistently every day, all day long, before you look up, there's nothing left of you."

The final straw came when her supervisor called her up in front of a roomful of men and offered her $5 to perform fellatio on him. When the president of her plant's union, UAW Local 551, found out that she was preparing to file a complaint, Wright says that he met her at her car and persuaded her not to go forward. "He looked me in the face and said, 'You're a pretty girl, take it as a compliment.'"

Throughout her entire ordeal, Wright says that she never felt supported by the union, characterizing it as a boys' club that protected its own at the expense of more vulnerable workers. "These are people that worked together for years, and so when you go to a union rep, and you have to say, 'One of your friends did this to me,' he's not looking out for you. He's looking out for his friend who voted him in that he goes to barbecues with."

Wright sought help dealing with her trauma and stress, eventually attending an intensive outpatient program at a mental health facility. "I was not even telling people I was going to the hospital. They thought I was going to work every day, but I was checking into a mental health facility, because it was so difficult." Though she had paperwork from Ford confirming that she was out on medical disability, Wright's insurance company refused to cover her claims, until finally, after several months, she returned to Ford out of economic desperation. Her only request upon return was to be moved to a different section of the plant, far away from the supervisor who'd harassed her. The company refused. The next night, after seeing a local news story about women dealing with sexual harassment in another local factory, Wright called the station—and hired an attorney.

The resulting lawsuit ended with Ford paying a substantial settlement to Wright and another female worker who had joined her in the harassment suit, setting up a $7.5 million fund to be split among nine hundred women workers who'd experienced harassment at the plant between 1996 and 1999. When she first met with her attorney, Wright told the lawyer that she wanted two things: an apology and her job back. The former would come from James J. Padilla, Ford's group vice president for manufacturing, only after Wright interrupted his news conference announcing the settlement, but she would never get to return to the job she'd fought so hard to keep.

Wright used the settlement money to build a new life for herself and her children outside the factory gates; she opened a salon and began hosting a local talk show. For nearly two decades, she buried the traumatic memories of her time at the plant, but 2017's #MeToo moment brought all those emotions rushing back again. "I was ecstatic," she recalled. "Because twenty years ago, yes, my story was all over the news for about five minutes, and nobody cared. But this seemed to be gaining some traction."

Ford has since been hit with multiple other lawsuits. In 2014, thirty-three women at the Chicago Assembly Plant filed a class action sexual harassment suit against the company. In 2019, Andrea Bush, a worker at Ford's Dearborn Assembly Plant, sued Ford for sexual harassment, retaliation, and a hostile work environment; her story mirrors Wright's, down to the denial of her simple initial ask to be moved away from a sexually aggressive supervisor. Wright keeps an eye on these developments, but now spends most of her time with speaking engagements, leading workshops—and driving for Lyft. "Men typically get in my car and say, 'Is there anything else that you do?' And I love it when they ask that," she says with a mischievous chuckle. " 'Yes, I travel the country talking about ways to eradicate workplace sexual harassment!' And then some men lean right in, and some men I work on, in the car, and I end up having really incredible conversations that I really do think ripple out into the world. I do."

STEEL PRIDE

Breaking the silence brought Suzette Wright to a place where she can now spend her time educating and advocating instead of wrestling with massive slabs of steel, but not every manufacturing worker gets such a happy ending. Some, particularly those whose sweat and blood powers one of the most white-male-dominated, traditionally masculine heavy industries of all, can't even tell their coworkers who they really are. As author Anne Balay illustrates through conversations with forty queer and trans LGBTQ steelworkers in her 2014 book, *Steel Closets: Voices of Gay, Lesbian, and Transgender Steelworkers*, there is no safe way to be gay in the mills, and those who do choose to step outside the closet are gambling with their lives.

There's a certain romance to steel and its place in the American imagination. My own grandfather was a steelworker, a millwright to be exact, and he used to tell me stories about all the red-hot furnaces and heated union meetings that shaped his experience in the steel mills of New Jersey. His death from mesothelioma—an extremely aggressive cancer of the lungs caused by asbestos exposure—uprooted my entire universe, but it's an all too common reward for those who sacrifice their lives on the altar of steel. The job is incredibly dangerous, even if you make it to retirement with your lungs intact (and to be clear, few do). Steel itself is on its way out, too, limping along at a fraction of its former glory. The steel industry began its precipitous decline in the late 1970s and early 1980s, when demand plummeted amid a ten-year recession and layoffs gutted the workforce; in the years between 1979 and 1982, hundreds of plants closed, and more than 150,000 steelworkers lost their jobs.

It was a tumultuous period for workers, a time of economic upheaval, social reorganization, and rebellion. The Reagan administration's war on labor had already begun chipping away at unions' power, and the ones that survived became single-mindedly focused on saving their members' jobs, in the process sacrificing some of the militancy and vision that had made them such a potent tool of the working class. This dissolution affected some workers more than others, particularly those whose identities stood out in their traditional, cis-male-dominated workplaces; there, queer and trans workers were more easily targeted and ostracized than in a more consciously progressive workplace. The post-Stonewall gay liberation movement stands out as a successful action that rose outside of, and sometimes even in opposition to, the bounds of formalized union activism.

A 1974 ruling against nine of America's largest steelmakers ordered the industry to address decades of discriminatory hiring and wage practices, demanding back pay to make existing workers whole after a decade-plus of wage theft, and outreach to attract more women and people of color to its workforce. Progress to be sure, but in places like majority-white Gary, Indiana, where Balay focused her research, efforts to address those shortcomings focused primarily in the areas of gender identity and sexual orientation. Most of the new hires at those mills were women, and many of them were lesbians; since union contracts protected workers only on the basis of sex, race, and creed, those women, and other queer workers, were left out to dry.

That lack of vital workplace protections was only one of the reasons that lesbians, gay men, and transgender workers felt compelled to hide their sexuality at work. Steelworkers work in pairs or teams and depend on one another to complete their labors safely. Closeted queer and trans workers who don't feel safe sharing details about their lives find themselves isolated. Balay's research shows a workplace soaked in homophobia, misogyny, and transphobia and makes evident the social costs of coming out—even today. Many remain closeted at work, and keep the details of their personal lives quiet. Elise, a trans woman who spoke with Balay in 2010, began working at U.S. Steel's Gary Works in 1967. She finally came out to her coworkers in 1994, and was immediately assailed with death threats. Her car and locker were vandalized, and she was assaulted, threatened, and sexually harassed by men she'd worked alongside for decades. The plant had to assign her a bodyguard. "You have to rely on your coworkers in the steel mill," Athena, a middle-aged lesbian worker using a pseudonym, told Balay in 2011. "And in the back of your mind, are you thinking, if something happens, are they gonna turn their back, 'cause they kinda wish you were dead anyway?"

In recent years, the United Steelworkers have expressed public support for LGBTQ rights as well as other progressive causes, taking part in the AFL-CIO's Pride at Work caucus and its own Steel Pride program for members. Union contracts have been amended to contain specific language aimed at LGBTQ inclusion—including nondiscrimination clauses. Whether those changes have been felt on the shop floor is another matter, but it is absolutely a positive development within the labor movement that issues of race, gender, identity, and sexual orientation have become an intrinsic part of the conversation. Saying "better late than never" veers dangerously close to letting various unions and their leaders off the hook for excluding or outright abandoning the workers who have needed the most support, though, so instead, let's call it a decent step forward, and acknowledge how much further the movement needs to go to ensure that all workers are actually heard, valued, and protected by strong union contracts and collective power.

As union leadership stumbles over itself to catch up, it's important to remember that workers themselves have always been at the forefront of these struggles. These queer and trans steelworkers who had to stay confined in the closet for their own safety but found their own ways to resist and thrive are part of the same radical legacy that saw Mohawk skywalkers demand the right to free movement across their stolen lands; DRUM, the League of Revolutionary Black Workers, and the Arab Workers Caucus take on racist discrimination in the Motor City; and Suzette Wright blow the lid off of Ford's vile culture of sexual harassment. The image of the white, blue-collar, cisgendered male manufacturing worker may persist in some imaginations as the classic avatar of the American working class, but as these stories and the many others before and after them have shown, this country's blackened temples of heavy industry have always been the site of multiracial, multigender, and queer labor conflicts, campaigns—and sometimes even victories.

11

THE DISABLED WORKERS

When other people see you as a third-class citizen, the first thing you need is a belief in yourself and the knowledge that you have rights. The next thing you need is a group of friends to fight back with.

—Judy Heumann, disability rights movement leader

Benjamin Lay trembled with fury as he waited for his turn to speak. Surrounded by his fellow Quakers at that September 19, 1738, meeting, he could feel the sword pressing into his side and the anticipation for yet another righteous showdown surging in his veins. When he finally got his chance, he leapt up and began delivering a dark prophecy, one that shamed and condemned the slaveholding landowners among the congregation to Hell. "Thus shall God shed the blood of those persons who enslave their fellow creatures!" he cried, and plunged the sword into a book he carried. Red liquid spurted out into the "Man-stealers" faces, and several women fainted; it was pokeberry juice, not blood, but Lay had succeeded in delivering his message with characteristic aplomb. No truly godly person would engage in or profit from the "Hellish Torments" of slavery, and Benjamin Lay had taken it upon himself to confront the sinners in his midst.

As the eighteenth century's most outspoken white abolitionist, Lay was accustomed to such confrontations and relished every opportunity he got to spread the gospel of abolition. Like the great nineteenth-century radical abolitionist John Brown after him, he fought for the freedom of his fellow human beings with a wild religious fervor. He had been kicked out of countless meetinghouses in his native England as well as in his adopted home in Pennsylvania for his "troublemaking" ways and eccentric, theatrical attitude. While American Quakers later became firm allies to the abolitionist cause, during the 1730s and 1740s, many prominent members of the community held slaves and profited handsomely from their dealings with the slave trade. The fiery, fearless Lay was an outlier even among religious radicals. His militant opposition to slavery and penchant for confronting powerful Quakers about their sinful human holdings won him few friends, and his short stature made him a target for ridicule by those who sought to delegitimize his message. Lay was a little person, standing just over four feet tall, and his spine was curved due to kyphosis, which gave him a hunched appearance. America's first white revolutionary abolitionist was a working-class disabled immigrant.

Born in Essex, UK, Lay had honed his class consciousness by working with his hands from a young age. He'd worked as a shepherd, a sailor, a glove-maker, and a bookseller, and he developed an enormous appetite for works of philosophy and religion, publishing his own book, *All Slave-keepers that keep the Innocent in Bondage, Apostates*, in 1737 with the help of his friend Benjamin Franklin. His wife, Sarah, was also a little person, and was often away working as a traveling minister. They had previously spent time living in Barbados, where nine in ten people were enslaved on vast sugar plantations and were subjected to barbaric torture; the horrors they witnessed and close relationships they formed with enslaved people there hardened the Lays' resolve to fight for abolition. As Franklin once put it, "Sugar was made with blood." Lay remains a marginal figure in the history of the abolitionist movement due to several factors: his unpopularity (his "zeal" was not entirely welcome among the straightlaced Quakers, and he loved to make a scene), his insistence on total abolition decades before it became a widespread demand, and his disability, which isolated and othered him nearly as much as his radical views. He did not live to see himself vindicated, but at the age of seventy-seven, he witnessed the Quakers' first big move toward abolition: beginning to discipline and disown members who traded slaves. "I can now die in peace," he told the friend who'd delivered the news, and so he did, on February 3, 1759, after forty-one years of uncompromising, unrelenting agitation against the evils of slavery. "Is there any eviler Fruit in the World than Slave-keeping?" he had thundered. "Any thing more devilish? it is of the very Nature of Hell itself, and is the Belly of Hell."

The cause to which Benjamin Lay devoted his life would not see initial resolution until more than a century after his death, and even now, almost three hundred years later, there are still people in this country forced to labor in bondage. During the eighteenth century, when Lay lived and agitated, six to seven million enslaved people were kidnapped from various African countries and brought to labor in the American colonies, and the population of enslaved people only grew as time went on. Many of those people were disabled, whether by birth or at the cruel hands of enslavers and overseers. Harriet Tubman, a revered leader who led dozens of enslaved people to freedom on the Underground Railroad, had a seizure disorder and would periodically fall into "spells" as a result of brain damage sustained from being struck in the head with a two-pound weight as a child.

Enslaved African people often suffered a high rate of physical, mental, and sensory disabilities. Escapees were frequently punished with torture and mutilation, which left people with missing limbs or other body parts. People who were born with disabilities were regarded as worthless by slaveholders who saw them only as property, yet those same people were often valued sources of support for their fellow workers, providing cooking, childcare, and healing. During the colonial era, disability was defined solely by one's ability to work, and free disabled people were generally able to count on their families and communities for support if needed. Enslaved workers, deprived of their ability to build their own support networks, found other ways to care for those who needed it.

As the nineteenth century dawned, industrialization took root, and formerly self-sufficient agricultural workers and artisans began migrating into the cities to search for waged labor. This caused a profound shift in the lives and labor of disabled workers. "Before the Industrial Revolution, disabled workers were more included in the work of their family farms because every possible talent had to be utilized," Kathy Martinez, a queer Blind Latina who currently serves as the president and CEO of Disability Rights Advocates and is a former assistant secretary of the Office of Disability Employment Policy for the U.S. Department of Labor, told me. "If they didn't kill us first—we were often left to die."

Northern factories and workhouses soon became responsible for a tidal wave of work-related injuries—and a new generation of disabled workers. The cruelty, dehumanization, and deprivation that had already become routine on Southern plantations found a second home within the factories, slaughterhouses, and "dark Satanic mills" of the industrial North, then expanded west via the railroads and mines; in every case, the workers were left to pick up the pieces. Those who were able to find even a scrap of work despite their new disabilities were lucky; many others found themselves consigned to poverty and hopelessness.

During this same period, millions of soldiers were overseas rotting in trenches and dodging bullets in World War I, and 224,000 of them came home injured or permanently disabled. They faced a confusing social cocktail of hero worship and stigma, and as memories of the Great War faded, so did the public's sympathy for the wounded warriors they saw begging on the street or selling newspapers to get by. The government stepped in with a number of pension benefits, soldiers' homes, and rehabilitation programs like the 1917 Smith-Hughes Vocational Rehabilitation Act. Since the Civil War, veterans had been the first disabled people to benefit from federal legislation and government employment programs, and each new bloody military conflict has been followed by leaps in medical science and military technology that have also benefited disabled civilians, from advancements in surgical techniques to increasingly sophisticated prosthetics.

However, those advances come with a price tag that has often left them out of reach for those who need them most. As writer Britt H. Young, who was born with a limb difference and uses a prosthesis, noted in a 2021 piece for *Wired*, "The most sophisticated and expensive prosthetic technologies have long been completely free for veterans—and extremely expensive for anyone else." Great War–era rehabilitation efforts cushioned the blow for many disabled veterans when they came home and found themselves competing with seasoned war workers for jobs, but many of them—particularly Black veterans, and those whose disabilities were less visible than an empty sleeve or a missing leg—were left behind. During this era, rehabilitation programs and pension funds were generally reserved for white men; women, people of color, and people with severe disabilities were typically excluded.

CIRCUSES FOR BREAD

Meanwhile, those who had come by their disabilities by birth instead of on the factory floor or on the fields of battle were seldom given the chance to earn a wage, and those whose families could not or would not support them were instead shunted off into institutions, hospitals, or the workhouse. During the nineteenth century, there were very few options for disabled people to find employment. Social stigma, along with a lack of medical understanding around physical and cognitive differences, made it difficult for them to participate in society at all. There was an option for those whose disabilities were deemed exotic, wondrous, or horrific enough, though. Attitudes toward physical differences were far from enlightened, and vaudeville had ushered in a new thirst for live entertainment. In order to avoid either a dull, hidden life in the care of their relatives or the barbarism of institutionalization, some people decided to take what seemed like the best option available: joining the sideshow.

Hundreds of performers, from conjoined twins Daisy and Violet Hilton to William Henry Johnson, a Black microcephalic man also known as Zip the Pinhead, made their living on the sideshow circuit. It became a viable and hyper-visible career path where the luckiest performers found a fiercely loyal community and a steady paycheck, and some even found love. It became a big business, too, and at the U.S. sideshow's peak in the 1940s, there were more than one hundred independent sideshows rolling through America's cities and small towns at any given time. Some sideshow performers made handsome livings by performing for big crowds, while others displayed themselves at intimate high society gatherings; Laura Bridgman, a Deaf and Blind nonverbal woman who was the first child with her condition to be taught to read and write, was exhibited to curious onlookers from within the Boston institution where she lived. The famous folk carved out their own unique niches in show business, like Annie Jones, a nineteenth-century superstar "bearded lady" who used her fame to advocate against the word "freaks," or General Tom Thumb, a three-foot-four phenomenon who was instrumental in launching the career of Ringling Bros. founder and legendary showman P. T. Barnum. Thumb—born Charles Stratton—became a millionaire, toured Europe, was invited to Abraham Lincoln's White House, and enjoyed an audience with the queen of England. Thumb saved Barnum from bankruptcy twice and married a fellow little person, Lavinia, a genteel New Englander who stood less than three feet tall and had a lucrative public career of her own.

But despite the potential for adventure and the lure of the midway, it wasn't all roses, and not every disabled sideshow performer had run away to join the circus. Others were sold into it as children by their parents, or were "discovered" by predatory agents. Joice Heth, an elderly Black Blind woman whose performances as "George Washington's 116-year-old nurse" helped launch circus impresario P. T. Barnum's career, was sold to him by promoter R. W. Lindsay. There is no way to discuss the sideshow (and the history of freak shows more generally) without bringing up the exploitation, racism, and ableism that characterized so much of its existence, as well as the tarnished ethics of exhibiting disabled people's bodies for other people's amusement and titillation. It's unsurprising that the disability rights movement has an uncomfortable relationship with this part of its history. "Sideshows set the stage for modern conceptions of disability—identifying people with disabilities as objects of scorn and pity, as inherently 'other' from mainstream society," Maria Town, the president of the American Association of People with Disabilities, told me when I first wrote about this for *Vox* back in 2019. "However, even though sideshows were exploitative, they were spaces where people with disabilities, like famed [conjoined] performers Chang and Eng, began to assert their worth and curate how individuals looked at them. . . . As people with disabilities work to reclaim sideshows and identities like 'freak,' modern sideshows become important sites for the development and proliferation of disability culture."

That exploitation was infinitely worse for Black people, Indigenous people, and other people of color, who were not only subjected to horrific racism, but were sometimes outright enslaved by the showmen who took them out on the road, forcing them to perform in minstrel shows as well as so-called ethnic shows, which played up racist and xenophobic stereotypes. Many disabled sideshow stars were skilled performers in their own right, yet they were hauled up on stage to be gawked at, compelled to perform degrading dances and pantomimes, or, in an extra level of dehumanization, locked in cages like animals. Black and Brown women were also viewed through an exoticized, hypersexualized lens. In the sad case of Julia Pastrana, an Indigenous woman born in Mexico and billed as the "Ape Woman," mistreatment followed her from life into death; after she died, her body—along with that of her child—was taxidermied and displayed for profit. Appearing in the U.S. as late as 1972, Pastrana's remains were finally repatriated in 2012. Even in death, she was treated like more of an object than a person.

The metric that dictated the difference between a wonder and a monster was capricious, to say the least. Those who were deemed aesthetically pleasing or who possessed special talents or skills were elevated above their fellows. Sideshow celebrities of color like William Henry Johnson, conjoined Thai-born twins Chang and Eng Bunker, and Millie and Christine McKoy, a pair of Black conjoined twins who were born into slavery but ended up traveling Europe performing as the Two-Headed Nightingale, were fêted as entertainment royalty and racked up considerable fortunes. Conversely, Sara Baartman, a South African Khoikhoi woman whose appearance was sensationalized and sexualized by European audiences, was subjected to forced medical examinations and other cruelties. Baartman was an accomplished musician and polyglot but was kept as an indentured servant who "belonged" to her manager, William Dunlop. It's likely she was forced into sex work at the end of her stage career, and she died at the age of twenty-six. Her brain, skeleton, and sexual organs remained on display in a Paris museum until 1974. For Baartman, her career was not a choice, and her sad story is a prime example of the brutal exploitation that dominated the lives and deaths of many sideshow performers of color. Most of the disabled people who weren't drawn (or yanked) into the sideshow spent their lives in institutions, and the rise of the eugenics movement held dire consequences for people whom society's so-called elite had deemed undesirable. The term "feebleminded" was primarily used to convey intellectual disability, but it became a catchall to further pathologize and stigmatize a wide variety of people (especially women who refused to conform to strict middle-class definitions of feminine chastity and virtue—or to apologize for their careers) and thereby justify their incarceration and institutionalization. During the early 1900s, various authorities categorized sex workers as "feebleminded" and incarcerated them in institutions alongside an array of other people with various medical, social, or wholly imaginary issues. There, many were sterilized against their will, as in the case of Carrie Buck, the woman behind the notorious *Buck v. Bell* Supreme Court case. After she was sexually assaulted by her employer's nephew and became pregnant as a result, Buck—who was poor and uneducated, but did not have any intellectual or cognitive disabilities—was deemed a "middle-grade moron" by several prominent eugenicists and confined to an institution until her forced sterilization years later. Her case set a precedent through which the state was able to sterilize thousands more "undesirable" people, predominantly the disabled, sex workers, Black women, Indigenous women, and other women of color. In 1961, civil rights icon Fannie Lou Hamer, a disabled Black woman, was forcibly sterilized without her knowledge; the procedure was so common at the time that it had its own nickname, the "Mississippi appendectomy." *Buck v. Bell* has never been overturned.

In the mid-twentieth century, public attitudes began to change thanks in part to the presence of injured and disabled World War I and World War II veterans, and medical advancements opened up more employment opportunities for disabled people in general. Eugenics and scientific racism fell out of vogue (at least publicly), appetites for live entertainment shifted, and laws were passed targeting the exhibition of human beings. Not everyone is glad it's gone, and the modern sideshow community continues to thrive in pockets like Coney Island, where disabled sideshow stars like Xander Lovecraft still tread the boards. "It wasn't many years ago where we still weren't welcome or allowed in regular society," Lovecraft told me in a 2019 interview. "We're the performers that we are today because of those who came before us."

Disabled people now make up the largest minority group in the U.S. According to the CDC, one in four U.S. adults—sixty-one million people—have a disability "that impacts major life activities," and that percentage increases as people age, reaching two in five people aged sixty-five and older. They are also a major presence within prisons, with the Bureau of Justice reporting that 32 percent of federal prisoners and 40 percent of those in jail report at least one disability, and as of 2019, 25.9 percent of people with disabilities were living in poverty. The wage gap between disabled workers and those the disability justice movement refers to as "temporarily abled" is massive, with disabled women earning $.46 on the nondisabled male dollar and $.65 on the nondisabled female dollar.

While organized labor has often served as a strong ally during disabled workers' protests and campaigns (and some individual unions have been especially stalwart supporters), labor's overall track record within the disability rights movement is certainly not without its stains. During the 1970s, while some groups of disabled activists were busy fighting the power in Appalachia, San Francisco, and Washington, others were fighting for their freedom from an institutional nightmare. The rise of the deinstitutionalization movement (which advocated for the removal of cognitively, psychiatrically, and intellectually disabled people from public mental hospitals and similar carceral institutions in favor of community-based care and independent living) saw disabled activists and their allies clash with labor unions who opposed the closing of institutions over fears it would cost their members' jobs. Law enforcement and corrections officers belong to unions that protect them from repercussions when they abuse or kill disabled people; as disability rights activist Vilissa Thompson, a disabled Black social worker and creator of Ramp Your Voice, notes, "50 percent of people killed by law enforcement are disabled, and more than half of disabled African Americans have been arrested by the time they turn twenty-eight."

"Those of us that are deemed American Indian and Alaskan Native have the highest rates of disability of any other ethnic or racial group in this country," Jen Deerinwater told me. Jen is a citizen of the Cherokee Nation of Oklahoma and a bisexual, Two Spirit, multiply disabled journalist and organizer whose work focuses heavily on the intersections between disability and the issues Native communities face. That group also faces the highest rate of police violence per capita, and even the lowest-quality medical care remains inaccessible to wide swaths of their population. As Jen expounded, the same spirit of resistance that has sustained Indigenous communities through centuries of genocide and colonial violence has also been weaponized against them, often by unionized state agents, to cause further harm. "Any time you have an oppressed group of people who rise up, the state and the corporations are going to come down on you," Jen explained, citing the number of permanent injuries suffered by water protectors involved in the Dakota Access Pipeline protests. Deerinwater pointed to Vanessa Dundon, a member of the Navajo/Diné Nation who was left partially blind after police shot her in the face with a tear gas canister during a 2019 attack on the Standing Rock camp. "We've seen this with labor struggles, obviously, and you see that with Native communities, and that violence creates more illnesses that create more disabilities."

"HANDICAPPED WORKERS MUST LIVE, GIVE US JOBS"

Employment has long been a central pillar of the disability rights movement, and one of the first groups to make that explicit in a public and militant way was the League of the Physically Handicapped. In 1935, six young disabled New Yorkers who were fed up with the Works Progress Administration's (WPA) informal policy of not hiring people with disabilities decided to take their grievances directly to the city's Emergency Relief Bureau (ERB), and started raising hell. After ERB director Oswald Knauth refused to meet with them, the group staged a sit-in inside the ERB's office, drawing widespread attention and support for their cause. As occupier Hyman Abramowitz told Knauth, "We don't want charity. We want jobs!"

After nine days, the occupiers were dragged away and arrested. After the trial, the group named themselves the League of the Physically Handicapped, and continued to hold demonstrations, picket, and recruit more members. After three weeks of protests, the WPA offered jobs to forty League members, but the group refused to be placated by scraps, and continued their campaign. Over the next year, they successfully forced the WPA office to hire more than fifteen hundred disabled New Yorkers. The League then took the fight to Washington to challenge the WPA's stance on "unemployable" workers itself—and ended up occupying the agency's federal headquarters. "You have to understand that among our people, they were self-conscious about their physical disabilities," League member Florence

Haskell later recalled. "I think [the protests] not only gave us jobs, but [they] gave us dignity, and a sense of, 'We are people too.'"

In 1940, Paul Strachan founded the American Federation of the Physically Handicapped. Unlike the LPH, which was centered on people with physical disabilities, the AFPH brought together people across the disability spectrum, including disabled veterans, to push for federal disability policy reform, making it the first cross-disability organization in the U.S. Instead of focusing on individual efforts at inclusion or rehabilitation, Strachan instead saw disability as a class and labor issue, a framework that would be echoed by the later disability justice activists. The AFPH sought to forge a path to economic security and equal citizenship, lobbying for greater access to government employment, employment placement assistance, and legislation requiring employers to hire people with disabilities. Strachan also spearheaded initiatives like National Employ the Physically Handicapped Week, which Congress recognized in 1945 and which now exists as National Disability Employment Awareness Month. (In a nice bit of foreshadowing, the President's Committee on National Employ the Physically Handicapped Week would eventually be led by disability activist Justin W. Dart, Jr., who would go on to play an important role in the passage of the Americans with Disabilities Act of 1990.)

The AFPH also received funding from labor organizations and unions, like the AFL, the CIO, the UMWA, and the International Association of Machinists (IAM); the latter would prove to be an especially stalwart ally to disabled workers. Strachan himself had previously worked as a labor organizer, at the Bureau of War Risk Insurance (the predecessor of the Veterans Administration) during World War I, and as a lobbyist for the AFL. It was only natural that the AFPH found allies within the mainstream labor movement. As Audra Jennings explains in *Out of the Horrors of War: Disability Politics in World War II*

America, "The AFPH agenda offered a concrete link between traditional union concerns about health and safety and newer goals of expanding the protections offered by the welfare state and helped focus labor's attention on both union and nonunion disabled people." AFL representative Lewis G. Hines noted during a 1944 hearing in front of the House Committee on Labor, "A great many of these [disabled] folks are members of our organizations," and as such deserved labor's backing—and the government's support.

Meanwhile, in Cleveland, Henry Williams and a group of other Black World War II veterans were developing rehabilitation programs for their fellow disabled GIs, and organizing "wheel-ins" and "body pickets" in front of the mayor's office to demand adequate rehabilitation centers and housing for returning injured veterans. Post–World War II, Black disabled veterans were often shut out of the job training and rehabilitation programs that were their rightful due under the GI Bill and Public Law 16, thanks to the racist and discriminatory practices upheld by medical doctors, psychiatrists, and government officials. But Williams and his fellow veterans refused to quietly accept unequal treatment. During the same era, the Blind Veterans Association was busy advocating for its members' rights to rehabilitation, employment, and accessibility. Formed in 1945 by a group of young soldiers who were recovering from their injuries together at an army hospital in Connecticut, the organization took an explicitly antiracist stance by welcoming Black and Jewish members, and speaking out against racism and antisemitism during a time when all of the largest veterans' associations excluded Black veterans or had racially segregated chapters. These groups recognized that disability spans class, race, and gender, and were determined to ensure no one was left behind in the struggle. "Though broken in body, I was fighting with those millions to stamp out those same principles that we fought against during the war," Williams later reflected, on his time battling discrimination on multiple fronts. "I was fighting for the civil rights of every disabled citizen."

As the 1970s dawned, another generation of American troops was being sent off to suffer, sicken, and die in yet another bloody war, this time in Vietnam; more than twenty-five thousand young men registered as conscientious objectors to avoid taking part in the slaughter, and some of them joined the Volunteers in Service to America (VISTA) as an alternative. Founded as part of President Johnson's War on Poverty campaign and envisioned as a civilian answer to the Peace Corps, VISTA had volunteers spread out all over the country to help bring education and resources to neglected, poverty-stricken communities. Some of those volunteers headed to Appalachia, where they became enmeshed in local struggles and provided support for pivotal grassroots organizing, especially in West Virginia. There was trouble brewing in the coalfields of Boone County, where miners had spent centuries fighting for decent wages and health-care benefits but were now seeing the results of those hard-fought battles evaporate before their eyes.

At that point, "coal workers' pneumoconiosis," an irreversible respiratory disease better known as black lung, had been quietly ravaging generations of miners. Despite coal bosses' insistence that the dust was actually beneficial, or at least not actively harmful, by 1968 a Public Health Survey had found that one in ten working miners and one in five retirees had a coal dust–related lung ailment, making up one hundred thousand people who had been left partially or fully disabled by their dirty, hazardous working conditions. As modern medicine finally caught up and properly identified their ailment as an occupational disease, miners and their families began pushing for justice. That year, a coalition of disabled coal miners, local union leaders, and other mine workers founded the

West Virginia Black Lung Association, but by then, a man named Robert Payne had already gotten the ball rolling.

Robert Payne started working in the West Virginia coal mines as a child of fifteen and joined the UMWA as soon as he was able. As he once said, "I was born a union man because my daddy was a union man," and Payne would more than live up to that legacy. Before he became an activist, though, he was a coal miner, one who was repeatedly injured on the job. First he lost several fingers, and then he lost his ability to work after being severely burned in a mine explosion. It was bad timing on his part, though of course it wasn't his fault; the corrupt mismanagement of UMWA president Tony Boyle had tanked the UMWA-controlled Welfare and Retirement Fund, which previous UMWA president John L. Lewis had implemented in the 1950s to provide for workers who had given their bodies (and often, their lives) to the mines. As a result, by 1964, nearly 20 percent of the fund's beneficiaries—disabled miners and their widowed spouses—had lost their benefits, and Robert Payne was far from being alone in his determination to make things right.

In 1967, he and other miners who'd been shafted formed the Disabled Miners and Widows of Southern West Virginia, and petitioned UMWA leadership to have their benefits restored. When they received no response, Payne drew upon his experience as an evangelical preacher and started calling upon his people to mobilize. They led a series of rallies and wildcat strikes across West Virginia to draw attention to the desperate conditions coal miners continued to face. Even after mine operators took out restraining orders against them and got the police involved, the Disabled Miners held firm. Payne and three others were eventually jailed for their trouble and charged with contempt of court. Meanwhile, UMWA president Boyle refused to meet with them. The Disabled Miners ended up suing the union, and as a result of their litigation, $11.5 million was paid out to disabled miners and miners' widows, and those who'd lost benefits saw them reinstated. The miners had won this first round, but a larger battle was already brewing.

On November 20, 1968, disaster struck, and brought the miners' plight out from underground and into the national spotlight. On that day, a massive explosion consumed the Consol No. 9 coal mine outside of Farmington, West Virginia; 78 miners lost their lives, and the bodies of 9 of the victims were never recovered. That year alone, 311 coal miners died in work-related accidents. "Today is four months since the terrible tragedy, and 78 men are still entombed—our husbands, fathers, and sons," Sara Lee Kaznoski, whose husband was killed in the explosion, told a roomful of senators during a congressional hearing on mine safety following the disaster. "You must all see that the laws are strengthened for the future of coal miners. It's up to each and every one of you."

As families mourned and politicians pontificated about safety regulations, rank-and-file miners were busy battling an old foe with a newfound sense of urgency. Mine operators were still doing little or nothing to control coal dust inside their mines (or were actively working to flout safety regulations), and the Black Lung Association began organizing around a new state legislature bill they hoped would force companies to meaningfully tackle the coal dust problem and provide compensation to black lung victims. They brought three thousand miners to Charleston in January to hear the first draft of a potential black lung bill, but by February 18, 1969, it had become clear that more persuasion was needed, and the miners began to walk out on their jobs. Beginning at Westmoreland Coal's East Gulf Mine, the wildcat strike spread like wildfire throughout the state, jumping from mine to mine as one by one the workers downed their tools. By the following week, forty thousand coal miners had shut down virtually all the coal mines in West Virginia in the largest political strike in U.S. history. On February 27, the streets of the state's capital, Charleston, filled with one thousand miners and their families as they marched to the statehouse to urge legislators to pass legislation addressing their concerns. Led by organizers from the Black Lung Association, they chanted "No law, no work!" as they marched; as the *Charleston Gazette* reported, one young boy, Mark Legg, carried a sign reading, "My daddy is a coal miner. He need's protection." Finally, on March 12, Governor Arch Moore signed a bill into law that set strict safety standards on coal dust levels inside the mines and provided compensation for black lung victims and their widowed spouses. It was the first legislation in the country to recognize black lung as a compensable occupational disease, but it would not be the last, and the black lung crisis would continue to claim new generations of miners to come.

However, the miners' success and the increased visibility their strike had brought to the black lung crisis made a marked impact, and their tireless work advocating for improved safety regulations undoubtedly saved countless lives. (In their free time, the BLA would later become involved in the Miners for Democracy movement, which challenged internal corruption in the UMWA and eventually sent Tony Boyle packing). Their actions spurred the passage of a series of important federal mine safety laws, including the 1969 Federal Coal Mine Health and Safety Act, its expansion with the Black Lung Benefits Act in 1972 (which Nixon signed only grudgingly), and the 1977 Federal Mine Safety and Health Act, which strengthened and expanded miners' rights, required mine rescue teams to be established, and created the Mine Safety and Health Administration. "The strike's the onliest weapon the rank and file has. . . . There wasn't no one person responsible for what happened in 1969," Robert Payne, the founder of the Disabled Miners and Widows of Southern West Virginia, reflected in a 1972 interview. "Everybody was responsible for it. It was all the miners and disabled miners striking to get this Black Lung law passed."

SECTION 504, A CIVIL RIGHTS ACT FOR THE DISABLED

As disabled coal miners and their allies were raising hell in Appalachia, another group of disabled workers—or, to be more specific, disabled people who were being prevented from working by discriminatory policies and a lack of accessibility—were gearing up for a battle of their own. In 1970, a young Jewish woman named Judy Heumann made headlines when she sued the New York City Board of Education for discrimination after her teaching license was denied on the basis of her disability. When she was a little girl, she had been forbidden to attend school with her friends because school administrators dubbed her wheelchair "a fire hazard." After winning her case in 1970, she became the first wheelchair user to work as a teacher in New York City, and that same year, she and a few friends started Disabled in Action (DIA), a direct action group focused on disabled people's civil rights. As President Nixon repeatedly shot down the Rehabilitation Act of 1973, DIA mobilized, and eighty activists shut down Madison Avenue to protest his veto. "If you believe in something, do whatever you have to do to get your point across," Heumann later wrote in her 2020 memoir. She didn't know it then, but she and her comrades would change the world by spending the next few years doing exactly that.

When the act finally passed, disabled activists were thrilled with the inclusion of Section 504, the first federal civil rights protection for people with disabilities. It was modeled on the Civil Rights Act and explicitly aimed at protecting disabled people from discrimination.

However, the government dawdled on implementing the necessary regulations that would have actually made Section 504's sweeping provisions enforceable. Fed up, disabled activists began organizing to ensure that Nixon's Health, Education, and Welfare secretary, Joseph A. Califano, Jr., did not try to neuter the regulations. As their letters and phone calls were ignored, months turned into years, and activists turned to more direct action. Their campaign culminated in a twenty-five-day occupation of HEW's fourth-floor offices in the San Francisco Federal Building (with smaller sit-ins taking place at the agency's offices in Atlanta, Boston, Chicago, Denver, Los Angeles, Philadelphia, and Seattle). The 504 Sit-in, as it was dubbed, was organized by seasoned activist Kitty Cone, a wheelchair user with a long history of involvement in various social justice movements, while Judy Heumann led on-the-ground operations in San Francisco. They and one hundred other disabled protesters, interpreters, and personal care aides held the line and cared for one another as government officials shut off the building's water, tried to block food and medication deliveries, and cut the phone lines. In response, local churches, community groups, Vietnam veterans, and political organizations came to the activists' aid.

Among the occupiers was Brad Lomax, a Black Panther who had multiple sclerosis, and his aide, a fellow Panther named Chuck Jackson. Lomax, a Howard University graduate, had previous experience linking his two communities; in 1975, he had connected the Bay Area's Center for Independent Living with the Black Panthers in an effort to better serve the city's Black disabled community. During the 504 Sit-in, he and Jackson coordinated with their local Black Panther Party, who stepped in to provide daily hot meals and other supplies to the demonstrators. Without those provisions, fellow occupier Corbett O'Toole later wrote, "the sit-in would have collapsed."

That relationship would prove even more fruitful two weeks into the sit-in, when a delegation of activists (including Lomax, Heumann, and Cone) was sent to Washington, D.C., to meet with senators Alan Cranston and Harrison Williams and drum up public attention for their cause. The Black Panthers picked up the tab for their plane tickets. Organized labor also contributed crucial support once they got to D.C. The International Association of Machinists rented a U-Haul truck with a lift on the back to transport the group's wheelchair users around the city. As Cone remembered, the union went above and beyond to support the disabled activists. "[The IAM] allowed us to use their union headquarters to organize demonstrations, so we had access to telephone lines, copy machines and other things necessary for organizing," she recalled.

A special congressional hearing was convened, and the activists testified, one by one, about what Section 504 meant for them and their comrades. "We want the law enforced," Heumann thundered. "We will accept no more discussion of segregation." Frank Bowe, a Deaf man who was the director of the American Coalition of Citizens with Disabilities, spoke last. His remarks left the crowd in tears as he said somberly, "Senator, we are not even second-class citizens, we are third-class citizens." The sit-in, the media coverage, the community support, and the strength and determination of the activists themselves made their mark. On April 28, 1977, Califano quietly signed the regulations, bowing to the activists' demands and ending what had become the longest peaceful occupation of a federal building in U.S. history. As the occupiers finally walked and wheeled out of the San Francisco Federal Building two days later, they sang "We Shall Overcome" at the top of their voices. They had won. "The sit-in was a truly transforming experience, the likes of which most of us had never seen before or ever saw again," Cone wrote on its twentieth anniversary. "For the first time, many of us felt proud of who we were. And we understood that our isolation and segregation stemmed from societal policy, not from some personal defects on our part, and our experiences with segregation and discrimination were not just our own personal problems."

Section 504 did have its limits. For one, it applied only to federally funded buildings. But its implementation laid the groundwork for the 1990 Americans with Disabilities Act, which expanded its protections to include workers in private institutions and workplaces. The passage of that law took more organizing efforts and another round of militant protests, this time led by a group called ADAPT, then known as Americans Disabled for Accessible Public Transit. One of the most impactful direct actions of their entire campaign came on March 13, 1990, when more than a thousand people marched from the White House to the Capitol to demand the ADA's passage. When they reached the building, sixty disabled protestors got out of their wheelchairs and mobility aids and slowly crawled up the Capitol steps on their hands and knees. They were led by an eight-year-old girl with cerebral palsy named Jennifer Keelan, who had attended her first disability rights protest when she was only six years old. "I wanted to make sure that not only my generation of kids with disabilities would be represented, but future generations of kids with disabilities as well," she explained in a 2020 interview.

They won their battle, too. The ADA was another watershed moment for the nascent disability rights movement, and for the hundreds of disabled activists who'd laid everything on the line to fight for their right to be treated as equal citizens under the law, instead of as "third-class citizens." One of the first big chapters in the modern disability rights movement had begun with a little disabled girl in Brooklyn who just wanted to go to school with her friends, and one of the later ones was led by another little disabled girl who wanted to make sure her own generation's voices would be heard. "We looked beyond how we each spoke and moved, how we thought and how we looked," Judy Heumann reflected as she looked back on that era of protest and power-building. "We stood for inclusiveness and community, for our love of equity and justice—and we won."

That galvanizing moment led to an ongoing wave of disability rights activism that culminated legislatively in the passage of the ADA and has evolved into a vibrant and complex grassroots movement for disability justice that is being led by a new, even more diverse generation of leaders: people like Alice Wong, Imani Barbarin, Lydia X. Z. Brown, Mia Mingus, Keah Brown, and Jen Deerinwater, among so many others. "The disability movement was founded by white middle-class men and women, and they had their privilege already, so they were fighting for disability rights as if we were one-dimensional people," Martinez said. "Now there is an understanding that people enter this conversation from multiple points of entry; race, being queer, being a woman—it all has an impact on your process."

Employment, working conditions, and accessibility still remain key focuses, alongside intersecting issues like racial justice and LGBTQIA rights, and despite the legal victories of the 1970s and 1990s, disabled workers with intersecting identities continue to face additional layers of oppression and discrimination on the job. "I enter every professional space as a Black disabled person, and even though I freelance, sometimes my needs are not met and I have to advocate for myself," journalist and author Keah Brown told me. "It's an extra hurdle on a racetrack full of hurdles." As Kitty Cone wrote, "People with disabilities experience discrimination as a class, irrespective of diagnosis." Brown echoed Cone's analysis, telling me that the reality for so many of today's disabled workers is still one of barely making ends meet, "because we aren't even seen as fully human" by corporations and employers.

"THEY KNOW WE'RE DESPERATE FOR WORK": TAKING ON THE SUBMINIMUM WAGE

A major contributing factor is the continuing existence of the subminimum wage, a carve-out in the 1935 Fair Labor Standards Act that allows employers to pay "individuals whose earning or productive capacity is impaired by a physical or mental disability, including those related to age or injury" at a much lower rate than even the paltry $7.25 federal minimum wage. (This also applies to the country's nearly six million tipped workers, like restaurant servers, bartenders, nail salon workers, parking attendants, and many more; teenage workers; and incarcerated workers, and has now become a problem for app-based gig workers.) For disabled workers like Frances Mablin, a Black woman with cerebral palsy who found herself working at Goodwill for $1.50 an hour after being hired at the standard minimum wage, the devaluation of her abilities cut deep. "The reason they get away with it is because no one has spoken up," Mablin told author and labor activist Saru Jayaraman in Jayaraman's book *One Fair Wage: Ending Subminimum Pay in America*. "They know we're desperate for work, that other people won't hire us."

Some of the responsibility for this current inequitable reality dates back to the New Deal, and can be laid at the feet of trailblazing labor secretary Frances Perkins, whose illustrious career included at least one critical misstep. During the hearings for the FLSA, the secretary proposed the legislation include a subminimum wage for what she termed "substandard workers," whom she described as those "who by reason of illness or age or something else are not up to normal production." It's likely she was thinking of returning war veterans who'd been left injured or disabled and were struggling to find civilian employment, and of the employers who needed a little extra enticement to hire workers they saw as damaged goods. Unfortunately, the "something else" line was soon stretched to include a wide range of people with a variety of disabilities, and the subminimum wage was here to stay.

And so were the segregated workplaces it spawned. "When [President Franklin Delano] Roosevelt passed the National Handicapped Act, they gave a certain chunk of money from the WPA to help disabled people work," Kathy Martinez explained. "The idea was that people with disabilities would be allowed to work in segregated settings, and if somebody wanted to create opportunities for people with disabilities, they could get these government contracts." Those contracts would prove to be very lucrative for some employers, who saved money thanks to the subminimum wage loophole. It created an entire cottage industry of so-called sheltered workshops that were intended to serve as temporary job training programs but functioned as little more than glorified daycare centers where workers were paid pennies on the dollar for their labor. Roosevelt, himself a wheelchair user who hid his disability from the public, would have never been caught dead in such a place, but there were still limited options for most disabled workers to find employment.

This system also led to some truly horrifying cases of worker exploitation. In 2009, the *Des Moines Register* broke the story of a group of men with intellectual disabilities who had been kept in squalor in a dilapidated old schoolhouse in the tiny Iowa town of Atalissa and ordered to work in a turkey processing facility from sunup to sundown, six days a week, for decades. Their story ended happily, with the men relocated to independent living facilities and given proper medical and psychological support to heal from their ordeal, but they were lucky. There is no way of knowing how many more disabled workers are being mistreated and abused throughout the country at this very moment, and as long as the subminimum wage remains on the books, employers will continue to have more opportunities to perpetuate the cycle of exploitation. "People with disabilities should be treated as equal to other people," Mablin told Jayaraman. "We have to buy clothes, buy food, things we need or things we like, like everyone else."

The COVID-19 pandemic and the rise of remote work illuminated yet another insidious way in which disabled workers have continued to be cast aside, marginalized, or treated as an afterthought: their offices. Disabled workers who had spent years explaining remote work as an accessibility issue to unyielding employers suddenly saw flexible work-from-home policies proliferate across various white-collar industries and become a new norm. Unlike their bosses, the virus did not discriminate, and the kind of workplace accommodations for which disabled workers had long been advocating apparently no longer seemed "unreasonable" once they became necessary to protect their abled coworkers. "This second year of the pandemic has solidified what a lot of disabled people already knew—that [even] if people who are not disabled don't care about us, they need to care about what the workspace will look like for everyone," Brown, who has been vocal about how the shift to remote work has left disabled workers behind, told me.

Until every single one of those interlocking barriers is smashed, all the curb cuts or legislative victories in the world won't level the playing field for disabled workers. When ADAPT activists flooded into the halls of the U.S. Capitol in 2017 to protest Trump's attempts to cut Medicaid and the Affordable Care Act, police yanked them out of their wheelchairs and dragged them away in handcuffs, a stone's throw away from the steps that their predecessors had crawled up in an earlier fight for justice almost three decades ago. "That's what we have to remember," Martinez said. "Any kind of justice fight is a work in progress."

And some of those workers aren't even interested in playing a bigger part in a capitalist economic system built on white supremacy and colonialism that has made space for them only grudgingly, and only after years of fervent struggle. By finally winning the ability to work in this country, disabled workers also ultimately gained the option of refusing to engage with a system that still sees no value in their labor or their lives. "I don't think we should be fighting to have shitty, dangerous jobs that undermine the rights of others," Jen Deerinwater told me. "Especially as a disabled person, I know that we're fighting to get jobs—but at the same time, I don't *want* those jobs. I don't want to be in that system. I want to see that system go the fuck away."

12

THE SEX WORKERS

Here's to the Ladies of the Night—Carry on! Save your money, make wise investments, and above all—love yourself.

—Sunny Carter, *Sex Work: Writings by Women in the Sex Industry*

On Saturday, June 28, 1969, during a police raid on a New York City gay bar called the Stonewall Inn, a group of gay men, lesbians, drag queens, and transgender revelers shocked the world by refusing to allow themselves to be arrested and abused like they'd been so many times before. The police were back for the latest "routine" raid of a gay bar, but this time the patrons fought back—hard. Among them (and some say leading the charge) were Marsha P. Johnson, a Black disabled trans woman; Sylvia Rivera, a Latina trans woman; and Miss Major Griffin-Gracy, a Black trans woman. The three women were part of a number of overlapping communities in queer New York City, and also shared a profession: like many trans activists then and now, they had engaged in sex work as a matter of economic survival at varying points in their lives. "You say 'get a job' like we can get one, but there's no such thing if you can't get work to maintain yourself, wash your body, have clean clothes, and feed yourself," Griffin-Gracy, who like many of her peers had periodically experienced homelessness and incarceration, told Jessica Stern in a 2009 interview. "What are you going to do if you have no way to pay for these things? You have to find something that's outside of the law."

That money also directly funded their activism work supporting poor and unhoused queer and trans youth and sex workers. When Johnson and Rivera founded Streets Transvestite Action Revolutionaries (STAR) following the Stonewall uprising, they immediately began fundraising to purchase a building in the East Village to serve as a haven for unhoused queer youth. "We fed people and clothed people," Rivera explained in a 1998 interview. "We kept the building going. We went out and hustled the streets. We paid the rent." The work was of course treacherous, as Johnson, proudly brandishing a can of Mace, once said: "It's very dangerous being a transvestite going out on dates because it's so easy to get killed." She and her sisters had to protect themselves and each other, because they knew no one else would.

STAR was more than a mutual aid project, as Marsha P. Johnson once said. "We believe in picking up the gun, starting a revolution if necessary. Our main goal is to see gay people liberated and free and have equal rights that other people have in America." Johnson and her comrades innately understood the intersectional nature of their struggle, even if those who should have been their natural allies did not. Sex workers like them provided crucial material and organizational support to the early trans rights movement as well as the broader gay liberation movement, yet due to the stigma attached to their labor, even the most pivotal activists were scrubbed from the narrative. In 1973, only a few years after the Stonewall uprising, Rivera was excluded from the speakers' list at a gay pride rally organized to celebrate its anniversary because the crowd was uncomfortable with her profession. Furious, Rivera got onstage anyway and castigated the crowd for abandoning their queer sex worker brothers and sisters who had been arrested and jailed for their means of survival. "I will not put up with this shit," she shouted. "The people are trying to do something for all of us, and not men and women that belong to a middle-class white club. And that's what you all belong to!"

Rivera and STAR went on to join the Young Lords, a Chicago-based Latino street gang turned political powerhouse and radical self-determination organization akin to the Black Panthers, and met with Panther leader Huey P. Newton in Philadelphia, where Rivera was delighted at Newton's pronouncement that she and her trans sisters at STAR were part of the shared struggle as "revolutionary people." She died in 2002, but her remembrances of Stonewall still radiate with a fierce pride: "I remember when someone threw a Molotov cocktail, I thought, 'My god, the revolution is here. The revolution is finally here!' "

Stonewall was a watershed moment in the queer liberation struggle, but it also marked a turning point in the sex workers' rights movement. A brave number of their own had publicly faced off against a wall of riot police to stand up for their siblings. They fought like hell for every single one of the trans people, gender-nonconforming people, queer people of color, unhoused queer people, and queer sex workers who'd been pushed too far for far too long. Whether or not they threw those bricks and Molotovs themselves, the actions that Johnson, Rivera, and Griffin-Gracy took that night and for many years after would set the world on fire. They weren't the first, and certainly wouldn't be the last, but they helped light a spark that continues to burn—and did it all while looking absolutely spectacular. "I would want my legacy to be: If it ain't right, fucking fix it, whatever it takes," Griffin-Gracy said in a 2018 interview. "I'd want to be remembered for trying to do the right thing and care for all people. We're all part of one another."

SAN FRANCISCO'S "BARBARY COAST"

A century before Stonewall or any of the nationwide and international sex worker activism that came after, thousands of sex workers had made their way west, into the newly occupied states and territories the U.S. had stolen from the area's original Indigenous inhabitants. Women in search of economic opportunity set up shop in frontier towns and mining camps, where some found the independence they'd sought, and others—especially those who were Black, Indigenous, Latina—found only poverty, abuse, and desperation. At least one, a sex worker turned brothel owner from Alabama named Laura Evans, managed to work her way up to owning an entire red-light district in Salida, Colorado. She'd previously worked sixty miles north in Leadsville, but had been run out of town by the Cloud City Miners' Union after helping to break an 1896 miners' strike (she had smuggled the strikebreakers' wages underground, hidden in her bustle, secretly undermining the union's negotiating position).

Mine bosses had already invited Evans and her brothel employees to ply their trade in the mines to help keep the scabs happy. This arrangement was acutely felt by the union miners who had composed Evans's client base before the strike, the betrayal so raw that Laura saw fit to skip town entirely after collecting her $25,000 union-busting bounty. The Old West was a tough place to make a living, but Evans's adventure in scabbing was still not the norm. Sex workers across the region were already beginning to build up their own networks of solidarity.

As the nineteenth century marched on, the continued westward expansion lured more settlers across the Rockies and toward a freshly conquered coast. A new generation of sex workers would set down roots in California, an eventual geographic home base to the sex workers' rights movement. By the turn of the century, San Francisco had earned a reputation as a lawless den of debauchery, drugs, and desperation. Due to the steady influx of sailors, gamblers, and pleasure-seekers who poured into the area each evening, sex work made big business for those who owned or worked inside its brothels. Law enforcement was more or less nonexistent, and efforts to "clean up" San Francisco's infamous "Barbary Coast," as the red-light district was named, did little to dent the thriving sex trade. The Progressive Era's white middle-class Christian women activists turned their attention to "rescuing" sex workers, in a convenient dovetail with the temperance movement, the nascent feminist movement, and the women's suffrage movements, all swirling in the nation's psyche at the same time. But this issue was different. For all the speaking these women did about what rights they felt that they and their sisters deserved, they didn't do much listening—particularly when sex work was involved.

Purveyors of this buttoned-up sense of Victorian morality tried to "save" sex workers through charity, or worse, by sending them to female reformatories—a gendered version of the workhouse in which women suspected of being immoral were incarcerated and taught rudimentary skills to prepare them for a new life as domestic drudges. The Bedford Hills Correctional Facility for Women, for example, which is currently the largest women's prison in New York State, was originally founded in 1901 as a reformatory for female offenders, including those who were convicted of "habitual drunkenness, prostitution, or vagrancy."

Outside of these plush clubhouses and wretched cells, a wider moral panic gripped the nation. Sex work, abortion, "obscenity," and alcohol were all criminalized, with the poor and working class disproportionately ordered to pay the price for disobeying the new moral order. World War I set off a wave of paranoia about the supposed dangers of "promiscuous" women, and American government officials launched a program aimed at protecting newly arrived army recruits from acquiring sexually transmitted infections, a move that further criminalized and abused thousands of sex workers. To this end, police and health officers gained the power to arrest, imprison, and perform crude physical examinations on anyone (though the people they arrested were almost always women) they "reasonably suspected" of carrying an STI.

A disproportionate number of those arrested were women of color and working-class women; Black women were often kept segregated from white women and jailed in subpar facilities and, alongside other women of color, were subject to racist violence in addition to sexual assaults. Some were even sterilized against their will or without their knowledge. They called it the American Plan, and it became one of the largest and longest mass quarantines in U.S. history. The program operated more or less continuously from the 1910s through the 1940s, and in some places was enforced as late as the 1970s; laws passed under the plan were used during the 1980s and 1990s to forcibly quarantine HIV/AIDS patients. Its influence can also be traced to the Tuskegee Syphilis Study and the World War II–era internment camps, and helped to lay the groundwork for the current mass incarceration crisis. As I reported in a 2018 piece for the *New Republic*, the same Civilian Conservation Corps (CCC) camps later used to imprison Americans of Japanese and German descent during World War II originally functioned as "concentration camps" for sex workers and other women incarcerated under its auspices. These American Plan–era laws are still on the books in multiple states.

It was against this ominous backdrop that the question of what to do about the Barbary Coast percolated among the city's gilded classes. The men in power embraced plans to shut down its sex trade and transform the area into a squeaky-clean business district; the hypocrites among them felt secure in the knowledge that vice raids generally skipped over the high-end brothels the rich frequented in favor of busting establishments that served working-class customers. Reform-minded San Francisco mayor James "Sunny Jim" Rolph began cracking down on vice in 1911, but it was only in 1917, after the passage of the Red Light Abatement Act, that the city finally banned brothels. A century into running their own affairs, San Francisco's sex workers had the rug pulled out from under them with little recourse—except, of course, for the power of collective action. On January 25, 1917, madams Reggie Gamble and Maude Spencer organized the first known sex workers' rights protest in U.S. history, and brought the fight straight to their opponents' doorstep.

"ALL I ASK IS FOR A LIVING WAGE AND I'LL GET OUT OF IT MYSELF"

The Reverend Paul Smith, pastor of the Central Methodist Church, was one of the loudest voices spurring on the city's campaign against vice, and was known for delivering fiery sermons from his pulpit about the evils of sex work. He was offended at the sight of women dancing, and complained that his flock ran the risk of being "corrupted on their way to and from church" due to the city's obsession with vice (local sex workers rebutted that his parishoners didn't seem to mind their presence; in fact, Smith's impassioned sermons allegedly helped ramp up demand). As with many so-called enlightened men of his era, Smith's pledge to "save" women from sex work never came with any real alternatives or acknowledgment of working-class women's economic plight. He was undoubtedly delighted to learn of the city's plans to close down the red-light district, and rallied his followers to attend a mass meeting just before the ban's start date, which had been ironically set for Valentine's Day 1917.

Madams Gamble and Spencer found a friendly ear in Fremont Older, editor of the *San Francisco Bulletin*, who had recently run the serialized memoirs of a sex worker (or potentially a composite of multiple sex workers) named Alice Smith in his paper. The memoirs were a sensation, and remain a valuable glimpse into the daily life and perspectives of a Barbary Coast sex worker. They told the story of an Illinois farm girl who moved to Oakland, California, in hopes of finding a more exciting future, but found herself laboring in laundries and restaurants for minuscule wages. Broke and exhausted, she found success moving among roles as a "freelance" sex worker, a brothel employee, and a madam until she eventually found her way out of "the life,'" as she explained in her writing. Smith's options as a single, working-class woman uninterested in marriage were already limited, and poverty had forced her to leave school at a young age. She described her path as almost inevitable, writing of how precarious women workers moved "from poverty to charity, from charity to drudgery, from drudgery to—this."

The *Bulletin* received more than four thousand letters in response to Smith's memoirs, many from sex workers with stories of their own to share. Their letters shared a common message: it all came down to money. If "respectable" jobs paid women more than the then standard $6 per week, the vast majority would readily change professions in a blink. "I don't want sympathy or a helping hand out of this life," one of them wrote. "All I ask is a living wage and I will get out of it myself." Another, who signed her letter "One of Society's Victims," offered a solution to those intent on moralizing her out of a job. "To the good people who are really interested in us I say, you cannot save us unless you overthrow the system of society that made us what we are."

The "fallen women" of San Francisco weren't going down without a fight. At the madams' behest, Older used his media connections to spread the word, while two staffers, Bessie Beatty and Rose Wilder Lane (daughter and collaborator to *Little House on the Prairie* author Laura Ingalls Wilder and influential member of the early libertarian movement), helped Gamble write out a speech for the next day's events—a final, high-stakes meeting with the Reverend Smith.

Smith was aghast when Gamble arrived, accompanied by a crowd of three hundred other sex workers. She swept past him and strode straight up to the pulpit, where her words made clear that this was a labor demonstration, and that these workers had gathered to discuss wages and their own social and economic oppression. They were not there to convince hard-hearted reformers of the morality of their profession, but were instead there to castigate them for their own role in perpetuating the conditions that left sex workers poor and desperate. "You want the city cleaned up around your church—but where do you want the women to go?" she asked him. "Men here in San Francisco say they want to eradicate vice. If they do, they better give up something of their dividends and pay the girls' wages so they can live."

Gamble called on Smith to use his influence to lobby for higher wages for women workers and improve their educational opportunities. Three-quarters of the women there that day, she explained, were also single mothers working to support their families. Gamble implored him to do something, anything, besides just hand down judgments, reminding him that Jesus did not scorn Mary Magdalene. "One of the girls told me that her brother, a Methodist minister, when she applied for help to him only told her to trust in God," she scoffed. "You can't trust in God when shoes are $10 a pair and wages are $6 a week."

The *San Francisco Chronicle*'s account of the protest called it "one of the strangest gatherings that ever took place in San Francisco," which shows just how young the city still was. The protest certainly publicized the workers' cause, but the damage had already been done; the Reverend Smith, though shaken, remained unmoved, and the San Francisco vice squads prepared to carry out the mass evictions that the women had tried so hard to prevent, which soon came with brute force. February 14, 1917, saw fourteen hundred women thrown out of their homes and left without shelter or employment. As anarchist feminist Emma Goldman witheringly noted, "The girls found themselves on the streets, absolutely at the mercy of the graft-greedy police." Madam Reggie Gamble's place was one of the first establishments to be shut down, undoubtedly as punishment for her bold protest and refusal to allow the workers to suffer in silence.

A century later, in 2017, sex workers gathered on the steps of San Francisco's Central Methodist Church once again to remember that history and affirm their community's onging struggle for basic human rights. As representatives from the Erotic Service Provider's Union, the Sex Worker's Outreach Project, and the US PROStitutes Collective, a multiracial sex workers' rights network founded in 1982, read out a new list of demands for sex workers' rights in the twenty-first century, those assembled held signs reading "No Bad Women, Just Bad Laws!" and "Outlaw Poverty, Not Prostitution!" Their words bore a deep similarity to those that had been spoken in that same spot one hundred years before. "[Women] will always be coming into [sex work] as long as conditions, wages and education are as they are," Madam Reggie Gamble had raged from that pulpit a hundred years before. "You don't do any good by attacking us. Why don't you attack those conditions?"

As sex workers' rights activist Kaytlin Bailey wrote in a 2021 article on the protest, "You cannot help people by hunting them." Even as the world changed and San Francisco burnished its rough-and-tumble frontier image to take on a mantle of progressivism (Gamble, ironically, found religion), attitudes toward sex work remained static. The madams and their comrades had flung the first stone in a long and bitter fight to live, work, and love freely, and San Francisco would continue to be a proving ground for the sex workers' rights movement. The battle had only begun.

AH TOY AND THE CHINESE IMMIGRANT WORKERS' STRUGGLE

Chinese women made up a significant percentage of workers in the nineteenth-century San Francisco sex trade, and as author Judy Yung writes in *Unbound Feet: A Social History of Chinese Women in San Fran-*

cisco, the majority of their labor was secured through kidnapping or outright enslavement in China before being transported to the U.S. The first working-class Chinese woman to step foot in San Francisco of her own accord was a twenty-year-old named Ah Toy, a native of Hong Kong who arrived with nothing more than the clothes on her back and the valuable ability to speak English. Despite her language skill, a glaring lack of opportunities made for a quick crash course in survival. Ah Toy evaluated her scanty options and chose sex work, setting up shop in what would later become known as the Barbary Coast. The launch of California's gold rush in 1848 at Sutter's Mill supplied her with a steady stream of clients, miners drawn west by the promise of endless riches. Mexican, Chilean, and Panamanian sex workers had been the first arrivals to the fledgling city, soon followed by white European counterparts—but for a time, Ah Toy was one of few Chinese sex workers in the city, attracting patrons with her perceived novelty as well as her beauty. Men would eagerly stand in line and pay an ounce of gold merely "to gaze upon the countenance of the charming Ah Toy." Their admiration went only so far, though; white sex workers could charge as much as twenty.

Ah Toy arrived in San Francisco during a time when the laws were elastic and the sex trade was in high demand. Women represented a distinct minority, and those who desired their companionship generally had to pay for it. Chinese men who made it to the U.S. were typically unable to afford to bring their families with them (or, considering their U.S. trip temporary, they had intentionally left them at home), giving rise to a "bachelor society." Racist politicians and employers posited that men left without romantic companions would be loath to lay down permanent roots in the U.S., and so they suppressed the incoming laborers' wages with the intent to rule out support for a spouse or family. (This scheme predated the Chinese Exclusion Act, which later explicitly forbade Chinese laborers from bringing their wives.) Together, these conditions meant that Ah Toy and other early Chinese immigrant sex workers were able to cash in, but that short window of opportunity—and the relative freedom that came along with it—didn't last.

While she worked independently, Ah Toy was able to capitalize on the city's noxious climate of lust, tokenization, exoticization, and racism to save up money to own and operate her own brothel. She became famous for appearing in court, both to press charges against those who tried to rob or swindle her, and to fight her own vice charges, all while dressed to the nines in the latest European fashions. In 1854, the California Supreme Court had stripped Chinese immigrants (as well as Black and Indigenous people) of the right to give testimony in cases involving a white person, so Ah Toy's insistence on taking her enemies to court made her even more of an anomaly. She bucked convention, but still adhered to and profited from her industry's most indefensible practices. To staff her establishment with young Chinese women, she did as the other Chinese brothel owners did: she bought them. Ah Toy, the resourceful immigrant, glittering courtesan, and infamous madam, was a slave owner. "Men were not the only ones who exploited Chinese [sex workers] for profit," Judy Yung explains in *Unbound Feet*. "When given the opportunity, Chinese women promoted themselves from the rank of oppressed to oppressor, preying on younger women in a vicious circle of traffic and procurement." A profound lack of labor protections and criminalization of the profession had bolstered the ability of pimps and madams to enslave and abuse sex workers on the Barbary Coast and elsewhere.

Ah Toy's influence soon faded, though the damage she inflicted on the women she held in bondage surely didn't. By the 1850s, the majority of the city's sex trade was run by pimps and brothel owners who continued to use force and intimidation to police and profit off female workers' labor. Madams, who were often former sex workers themselves and occupied a role akin to a combination landlord, manager, and boss, despised their male competition. As infamous San Francisco madam (and later mayor of Sausalito, California) Sally Stanford wrote in her 1966 memoir, pimps were the "crabgrass of prostitution." In the Chinese-run sector of the industry, Chinese secret societies and gangs soon moved in and wrested control of the sex trade away from the women whose labor had built it. "Race and class dynamics created the need for Chinese [sex workers] in America, while gender and class made poor Chinese daughters the victims of an exploitative labor system controlled by unscrupulous men denied gainful employment in the larger labor market," Yung writes.

Like the Black, Indigenous, and Latina sex workers with whom they shared a city and a profession, Chinese sex workers were particularly vulnerable to violence from all sides, triply bound by race, gender, and class, and further shackled by the legal constraints of indentured servitude. Many early Chinese sex workers, forbidden by their overseers from turning customers away and unable to access medical care, contracted severe venereal diseases and were left to die. As Professor Yen Le Espiritu wrote in her 2000 book *Asian American Women and Men: Labor, Laws and Love*, "Although immigration provided some benefits for women, it provided men many more opportunities to control and exploit them."

Racism and anti-Chinese rhetoric had plagued the West Coast's immigrant Chinese communities since the moment they stepped foot on U.S. soil. As Erika Lee writes in *America for Americans: A History of Xenophobia in the United States*, California politicians made numerous attempts to stem the flow of immigration by levying heavy taxes on Chinese workers and passing exclusionary laws, like an 1870 one (later ruled unconstitutional) targeting sex workers that barred the entry of any "Mongolian, Chinese, or Japanese female for criminal or demoralizing purposes." Anti-Chinese associations sprang up and were supported by labor leaders like Workingmen's Party leader Denis Kearney and AFL president Samuel Gompers, who blamed Chinese immigrants for lowering wages and labor standards. Foreshadowing the rhetoric that would later be used against Mexican and Latin American immigrants, these lions of labor used their platforms to rail against the "Chinese invasion" for snatching jobs away from white American workers (though in fact, Chinese laborers generally performed the most hazardous jobs and were paid less than white workers because white employers knew they could get away with it). When J. F. Janes, a political gadfly with a checkered past, founded the Anti-Chinese Union as an umbrella organization for California's various xenophobic lobbying groups, it quickly attracted state senators, congressmen, and labor leaders as members. In 1881, the San Francisco delegation to the Federation of Organized Trades and Labor Unions (a precursor to the AFL) successfully passed a resolution calling for the expulsion of the Chinese; the resolution lacked teeth and the Anti-Chinese Union dissolved after a few short years, but both are representative of the general anti-Chinese sentiment that had taken hold throughout the labor movement, and just how mainstream those views had become within California's political landscape.

The fight officially made its way to the halls of Congress in 1875, when California representative Horace F. Page introduced the Page Act, which aimed to "end the danger of cheap Chinese labor and immoral Chinese women"—in other words, male laborers and female sex workers. It was the first federal immigration law, and it relied in part on a series of intensive and invasive interrogations to ensure that prospective immigrant women were "virtuous." Inspectors relied on physical appearance (assuming, for example, that "real wives" were "prettier" than sex workers), and generally assumed that their subjects were lying. This cruel legislation effectively barred all East Asian women from immigrating, and was followed in 1882 by a blanket ban on all immigration from China. The Chinese Exclusion Act remained in effect until 1943, when the U.S. entrance into World War II left Americans hungry for allies against Japan.

This would not be the last time the U.S. government used its considerable might to bar or expel groups of people from its borders based on race, nor would it be the end of its propensity for using race, gender, and physical appearance to repress groups of marginalized workers. During Ah Toy's day, Chinese women bore the brunt of it, but those targets would shift throughout the decades, zeroing in on Black, Indigenous, Latina, and Asian workers in turn, and placing additional scrutiny and threats of violence on those who were trans and gender-nonconforming. Policing sex workers' bodies in order to control, exploit, or imprison them is a time-honored tradition, as American as apple pie . . . or the Salem witch trials.

MARGO ST. JAMES'S COYOTES AND THE HIV/AIDS CRISIS

In the 1970s, an explosion of activism led an entire generation to join the movements for feminism, Black civil rights, Indigenous civil rights and sovereignty, queer liberation, and disability rights, and also coincided with an upswing in militancy within the labor movement. The year 1970 saw the largest strike wave since 1946, during which one in six union members went out on strike, and also ushered in the birth of organizations written about previously like DRUM and the Coalition of Labor Union Women, which fought racial and gender discrimination on the shop floor. It was a thrilling, turbulent time that must have felt pregnant with possibilities, but not everyone was invited to the party. Even as radical ideas hit the mainstream and a wide array of liberation-minded organizations hit the streets in the name of revolution, the most marginalized workers were, as usual, left to fend for themselves. By 1973, one of them had a name: Call Off Your Old Tired Ethics, or COYOTE. It was the first sex workers' rights organization in U.S. history, and its charismatic founder, Margo St. James, believed that it was long past time to bring sex workers' issues out of the shadows and into the spotlight.

St. James was born on a farm outside of Seattle, Washington, in 1937. When she turned twenty-one, she followed a path taken by many bold, adventurous young women of her generation and decamped to San Francisco, where she became part of the much-documented Beatnik scene. She was first arrested for prostitution in 1962, though at that time St. James was not involved in the sex trade. Her robust social life had attracted the cops' attention, and their assumptions landed her in court. Her resulting conviction came from a judge who, when she assured him that she'd "never turned a trick in [her] life," decided that her knowledge of the term meant she must be a professional sex worker. St. James was infuriated, and that first spark of indignant rage provided fuel for what would become her life's work. She enrolled in law school and further familiarized herself with the legal system by working alongside criminal defense attorney Vincent Hallinan and picking up odd jobs from a bail bondsman (all while finding time to become California's first female private detective).

She eventually got that conviction overturned, but in the meantime, money was tight, and the mark on her record severely limited her employment options, so St. James began actually doing the sex work she'd been accused of. After she won her appeal, she decided she wanted to help other women push back against a skewed and unjust system. The result, COYOTE, was formed as "a loose union of women—both prostitutes and feminists—to fight for legal change." The group provided a safe space for sex workers to gather and find support, and cobbled together a menu of social programs and legal services that included establishing a bail fund, hosting consciousness-raising "rap sessions," organizing sex worker conventions in the U.S. and Europe, and providing immediate legal assistance to sex workers who called COYOTE's emergency number, which was often answered by St. James herself. COYOTE's first big public education campaign was launched in 1973, and sought to draw attention to the racist and sexist biases driving prostitution arrests in San Francisco. They called out law enforcement's blatant double standard when it came to enforcing the state's allegedly gender-neutral law against soliciting for prostitution, in which sex workers, who were predominantly women, made up 90 percent of the arrests, while their customers, who were predominantly men, routinely had their charges dropped.

The campaign also highlighted the double bind that Black sex workers and other sex workers of color were caught in, in which they faced much higher rates of arrest as well as racist discrimination within the industry itself. After Gloria Lockett was arrested in a raid in 1983, St. James helped her fight her case, and Lockett became involved with COYOTE. As she explained in a 2007 interview with Dr. Siobhan Brooks, her primary motivation to join the organization, which she described as "just too white," was to use its platform to elevate the voices of Black sex workers. "I felt it was important for me to be a part of COYOTE to let people know that Black women's issues were different from white women's issues," Lockett said, laying out the myriad ways in which white sex workers were privileged over sex workers of color. One example she noted was that white sex workers tended to work inside, in hotels, while Black sex workers were relegated to the far more dangerous street corners, were arrested at a much higher rate, and faced harsher charges and more jail time. "I knew that there had to be a voice for people who were working the streets and getting arrested—which meant mostly Black people," she explained.

Lockett went on to become COYOTE's codirector in the 1990s, and served on San Francisco District Attorney Terence Hallinan's Task Force on Prostitution, which included representatives from the National Lawyers Guild, the National Organization for Women, the Transgender Services Coalition, and the US PROStitutes Collective. During her COYOTE days, Lockett was a firm proponent of street organizing, and worked to reach San Francisco's most vulnerable people to educate them about safer sex and HIV/AIDS while also recruiting new members for COYOTE. In 1984, she cofounded the California Prostitutes Education Project (CAL-PEP), an HIV/AIDS prevention and education nonprofit that focused on street-based sex workers, and she served as its executive director for many years.

St. James was less inclined to the minutiae of grassroots organizing, but she was a born schmoozer and a public relations genius. She used her connections and verve to reel in support from high-profile names and donors, and to finagle invitations to come spread the gospel of decriminalization in print and on national TV. A glittering, irreverent annual gala she dubbed the "Hookers Ball" helped bring in crucial funding for COYOTE's work and became a major date on the San Francisco social calendar; in 1978, she greeted the event's twenty thousand attendees from the back of an elephant. St. James's flair for the dramatic aside, she took her work very seriously, and COYOTE became a lifeline for the San Francisco sex worker community as well as a blueprint for sister organizations around the country, including HIRE (Hooking Is Real Employment) in Atlanta, the ASP (Association of Seattle Prostitutes), PUMA (the Prostitutes Union of Massachusetts), PONY (Prostitutes of New York), and DOLPHIN (Dump Obsolete Laws, Prove Hypocrisy Isn't Necessary) in Hawai'i.

When the HIV/AIDS crisis hit, COYOTE and other sex worker–

led organizations found themselves at the forefront of another fight for survival, one that treated their members as an afterthought while simultaneously scapegoating them as vectors of disease. The classic World War I–era political tactic of painting sex workers as wanton superspreaders, and using their presumed role in an epidemic to further surveil, criminalize, and incarcerate them, reared its ugly head once again. This time, fanned by feverish War on Drugs rhetoric, even more marginalized people were swept into the dragnet. Gay men, intravenous drug users, and street-based sex workers bore the brunt of the increased scrutiny (as well as being more vulnerable to contracting the virus itself). COYOTE joined forces with groups like Larry Kramer's AIDS Coalition to Unleash Power (ACT UP) to advocate for the inclusion of women in AIDS research, and lobbied against the passage of new laws that sought to criminalize and discriminate against sex workers and HIV-positive people.

Sex-worker organizers Priscilla Alexander and Gloria Lockett shifted their focus toward HIV awareness and prevention work. Lockett reorganized CAL-PEP around harm reduction, and while the organization still provided resources to sex workers, she also retooled its outreach program to better meet the Black community's needs and to serve hard-to-reach, high-risk populations. In 1992, Alexander, after spending time in Geneva with the World Health Organization, came home with a plan for a much-needed sex worker–focused health clinic. Alongside COYOTE's St. James and Carol "Scarlot Harlot" Leigh (who coined the term "sex worker" and also founded the Bay Area Sex Worker Advocacy Network) and with support from the Exotic Dancers Alliance and San Francisco's STD Prevention and Control Department, she finally opened the St. James Infirmary, a "peer-based, full spectrum medical and social service organization serving current and former sex workers of all genders and their families," in 1999.

It remains an invaluable resource for the Bay Area's sex worker community and has expanded its services to include mental health counseling, harm reduction programs for intravenous drug users, a robust transgender health services program, and in 2020 its first transitional housing program for transgender and gender non-conforming adults, the Bobbie Jean Baker House.

Leigh is now retired from sex work, but remains extremely active in sex worker activism. When she coined the term "sex worker" itself in the 1970s, she was heavily involved in the feminist movement, and became interested in reworking the language used to describe herself and her coworkers. "I didn't want the discussion of this kind of activity to be a euphemism," she told me. "Prostitution is just not a good word, and it had come to also have another meaning, of trading oneself for an unworthy cause. I knew that we can't have our main title be an insult!" As she recounts, the term did not necessarily become politicized or enter common usage until the late 1980s, but its acceptance has slowly grown until now, when it is preferred by the wide variety of workers it describes. "I use the term 'sex work' to establish this work as labor," she explains. "I wanted to use this term to supplant the reference to the individual activities, because I wanted it to stand for all those."

THE MOVEMENT TAKES CENTER STAGE

As the Reagan then Bush then Clinton years dragged on and periodic moral panics over sex work popped up like clockwork, the West Coast would continue to be a locus for the sex workers' rights movement. Forty years after COYOTE began to howl, it would also be the site of erotic labor's first successful attempt to join forces with the more mainstream world of organized labor, in 1996, when San Francisco's own Lusty Lady became the first unionized strip club in America.

As with every great stride in labor history, the Lusty Lady workers' pathbreaking win came about thanks to years of previous organizing. In 1993, Dawn Passar and Johanna Breyer called a meeting of their fellow workers at the Market Street Cinema, a notoriously seedy strip club that was a favorite target of anti-porn crusader turned senator Dianne Feinstein, to discuss unsafe working conditions and the exploitative "stage fees" their bosses had implemented. The Exotic Dancers Alliance (EDA) was born. The group initially tried writing letters to the club's owners asking that they reduce the stage fees and improve scheduling, but upon receiving no response, they decided to escalate their campaign. But California's labor commissioner immediately put up another roadblock. "When we told the people that we were strippers, they hung up on us," Passar, who was born in Thailand and spent ten years working in the U.S. sex industry, recalled in an interview with Dr. Siobhan Brooks. "This was one of the main reasons EDA was started, so that when we were asked by people at the Labor Commissar if we are part of an organization, we could say that we're part of the Exotic Dancers Alliance organization. That way these people will listen to us."

And they did; the EDA invited representatives from COYOTE and the Service Employees International Union (SEIU) to their second meeting and, after learning that their independent contractor status prevented them from unionizing, filed wage and hour claims with the State Labor Commission against Market Street Cinema for employment status, back wages, return of stage fees, and tip theft. The EDA won the initial ruling, but an appeal sent them back to square one. A subsequent class-action lawsuit against Market Street Cinema resulted in the club having to pay out more than $600,000 in back wages and stage fees to more than sixty workers. Dancers in other states followed their lead, and by the time workers at the Lusty Lady hit their breaking point in 1997, they knew exactly whom to call.

Unlike the vast majority of dancers in the U.S., workers at the Lusty Lady, which was women-owned and regarded as a "feminist" establishment, had the distinct advantage of being properly classified as employees. This provided a steady hourly wage, but also came with an even bigger perk: the right to unionize. The workers didn't immediately act on it, but Dr. Siobhan Brooks, then a queer twenty-two-year-old women's studies major who used the stage name "Naomi," took up the charge. Brooks had noticed an atmosphere of blatant racism and colorism toward herself and the other Black dancers at the club, with Black dancers and other workers of color denied stage time and earning opportunities equal to their white counterparts'. "I would say that my actions kicked off the movement, but because the racism affecting Black dancers wasn't viewed as affecting everyone, it was very much seen as a marginal issue, which is often the case with racial discrimination cases," Dr. Brooks, now an associate professor of African American studies at California State University, Fullerton, and author of *Unequal Desires: Race and Erotic Capital in the Stripping Industry*, told me.

"When I asked [Lusty Lady manager] Josephine why Black women didn't work the Private Pleasures booth, she told me that the company lost money on Black women because white customers would rather pay a quarter than $5.00 to see a Black woman," Dr. Brooks wrote in a 2005 paper titled *Exotic Dancing and Unionizing: The Challenges of Feminist and Antiracist Organizing at the Lusty Lady Theater.* "Not satisfied with management's response to the racism I was noticing, I filed a racial discrimination complaint with the Department of Fair and Equal Housing to put pressure on the company to hire more women of color. After an investigation, and in an apparent attempt to avoid unionization, the management of the Lusty Lady did hire more women of color, most of whom, initially, were Black."

While Dr. Brooks and her Black coworkers were pleased to see more racial diversity onstage, the hiring spree did not solve the club's tremendous underlying problems. One of the workers' biggest safety concerns was the Lucky Lady's use of one-way windows, which customers often used to photograph or record the performers and sometimes sell or post the results online without the dancers' knowledge or consent. After an incident in which a customer was caught filming a dancer and assaulted another staffer as he was leaving, management dismissively told the dancer, Star, that if she couldn't handle it, she should find another job. She and the other workers were furious, and reached out to the EDA for help. Passar and Breyer advised them to contact SEIU, and on August 30, 1996, dancers at the Lusty Lady made history in heels by officially joining SEIU Local 790.

In 2000, Julia Query, a former Lusty Lady dancer and queer Jewish comedian, made a documentary called *Live Nude Girls Unite!* about the conditions at the club, the workers' quest to unionize, and the process of bargaining their first contract. "Margo St. James and Carol Leigh, a.k.a. Scarlet Harlot, paved the way by arguing that sex work isn't shameful," Query says in a voice-over. "Now they were supporting our organizing efforts. . . . They said our union was a win for sex workers everywhere!" In the documentary, shots of women spending long hours at the bargaining table tussling with management over sick days and union security are interspersed with interview footage of workers like a young Dr. Brooks, who echoed generations of sex workers with her blunt assessment that "what we all have in common is that we're all in it for the money. I wouldn't be standing in heels for a bunch of strangers if I wasn't getting paid."

Money was a big sticking point for Local 790, as were safety and basic respect on the job—in other words, the same things any group of workers tries to solidify in their first union contract. During bargaining, they also had to contend with SEIU union men who didn't necessarily understand or respect their work or their demands. "Our rep, Stephanie Batey, was supportive, but we faced a lot of sexism from the men in the union who didn't take us seriously," Dr. Brooks told me. "[They] would sometimes even laugh while we were speaking about our situation at meetings." After a grueling six-month negotiation that included a two-day "No contract, no pussy!" work stoppage over the firing of a pro-union worker named Summer, the workers got Summer her job back and voted in their first contract 71–1. "We received four paid sick days, basic contract language regarding sexual harassment and racial discrimination policies, wage increases, free shift trades, and a grievance procedure," Dr. Brooks recalled. "With unionization, there was an overall feeling that as a sex worker, one had rights, and one couldn't just be fired without a voice, which had happened frequently at the Lusty Lady."

They had achieved their goal of unionizing, but it wasn't all sunshine and sparkles after the contract was ratified. As anyone who has undergone the process of forming a new union knows, getting a contract can be just the beginning; building up a fledgling union and making it strong enough to enforce that hard-won legal agreement can be another struggle in and of itself. Dr. Brooks, who became a shop steward (a rank-and-file union member elected to represent workers in dealings with management), discovered that the same old racial disparities and lack of solidarity between white and Black workers continued to be a problem when it came to equal access to union benefits and discrimination at work. "The situation faced by women of color in the sex industry has a profound effect on the health status, immigration situation, child rearing practices, and future of all communities of color in the United States," Brooks wrote. "Sex worker activists need to challenge racism and white supremacy within the sex worker movement, while at the same time activists of color need to challenge sex phobia and sex worker phobia within movements of people of color."

When I spoke to her in 2021, Dr. Brooks was frank about the

challenges she and her fellow workers, especially other Black women, faced during and after they won their union. She described facing hostility from white workers over her insistence on addressing racism and colorism at work, and even the racial discrimination complaint she'd filed with the EEOC, which had effectively started the entire campaign, was dismissed as concerning a marginal issue. She believed unionization was the answer to effectively combating the club's racist and colorist policies, but it was not a silver bullet. "Many of the white dancers started to feel marginalized or attacked by my focus on racism, some requested not to work with me, and I was taken aside by management a few times to talk about how some white dancers didn't feel comfortable working with me," she recalled. "My response was I wasn't creating a hostile work environment for them, they weren't used to working with more dancers of color."

As employees, the Lusty Lady workers had had an advantage over most other workers in their industry. The massive U.S. worker misclassification problem means that most sex workers are categorized as independent contractors. Even most exotic dancers, who work inside brick-and-mortar establishments and have the terms of their labor dictated by bosses, remain categorized this way, and as a result, these workers have precious few protections under labor law, and no right to unionize. That hasn't stopped them from taking matters into their own hands—or from withholding their labor. Since the dawn of the striptease, strippers have been going on strike.

Self-proclaimed "high-class stripper" Gypsy Rose Lee, one of the most famous burlesque entertainers of her day and a pioneer of the striptease, was also known to be a leftist and friend of labor. Often heard speaking at local union meetings, she was one of the only female members of the short-lived Burlesque Artists' Association and helped orchestrate a three-day strike that shut down several New York City theaters in 1935. When the Minsky Brothers' theater locked out its stagehands for asking for higher wages, Lee rallied two hundred burlesque dancers in a solidarity picket outside the theater. "Gypsy called out to the theater and asked for some pickets," remembered former "burlesque striptease artist" Red Tova Halem. "All of us strippers put robes on over our G-strings" and "paraded outside the theater flashing passersby and shouting, 'Don't go in there, boys!'" The strike was settled that night, and the stagehands got their raise. Halem, a Jewish woman whose high earnings as a stripper enabled her to help thirteen of her relatives escape Nazi Germany, later went on to work alongside legendary ILWU leader Harry Bridges and serve as a delegate for the Culinary Workers Local 923.

In 2018, sex workers' rights activist and stripper Gizelle Marie spearheaded the NYC Stripper Strike. It began as an awareness campaign to call out club owners for allowing bartenders to siphon away strippers' wages, and soon saw thousands of workers unite to push back against racism, colorism, and exploitation in the city's strip club industry. The groundwork Marie and her fellow workers in New York City laid that year provided a blueprint for their siblings in other cities to kickstart a renewed wave of sex worker–led organizing that continues to redefine the movement. Dancers in New York, Georgia, Michigan, Nevada, California, and Massachusetts have brought class action suits against clubs over misclassification since 2009, but the California Supreme Court's 2019 *Dynamex* decision marked a sea change for the state's independent contractors, reclassifying many of them—including exotic dancers—as employees overnight. Strip club management frantically tried to find ways to duck compliance. The ruling also kicked off a debate within the state's stripper community over whether or not reclassification was the right move. Leading the charge on the pro side was Soldiers of Pole, a sex worker–led organization that aims to unionize the strip club industry. In 2019, Soldiers of Pole picketed outside

Hollywood's Crazy Girls Club to call out worker abuse at the club. "We have a right to force management to come to the table and abolish stage fees and wage theft and racist business practices and make a safe and sane work environment for dancers," stripper, sex worker, writer, activist, and SoP cofounder Antonia Crane told *Los Angeles* magazine. "The only way to do that is to unionize." SoP also reached outside its industry for support and partnered with the Communication Workers of America (CWA) Local 9003 for a solidarity pledge stating their shared interest in reaching "our goals of equality and labor rights for all strippers—not only in California—but in every strip club in America."

PERFORMERS' RIGHTS AND COMMUNITY CARE

The COVID-19 pandemic hit sex workers as hard as—and in many cases, harder than—workers in other professions. As their workplaces shuttered, they struggled to make ends meet; in a further blow, when the CARES Act was passed, sex workers were explicitly excluded. As workers nationwide responded to the crunch by walking out and withholding their labor in pursuit of safety, respect, and better wages, sex workers found their own ways to fight back. Cat Hollis, a Black nonbinary femme, was working as an exotic dancer in Portland, Oregon, when the COVID-19 pandemic caused the city's clubs to shut down. The sex workers there had initially launched the Haymarket Pole Collective in 2020 as a community resource for Portland's Black, Indigenous, and trans sex worker community, but the project quickly evolved into its first major action, the PDX Stripper Strike. As a result of their protest, nearly thirty Portland clubs agreed to adopt nondiscrimination policies and hold cultural sensitivity trainings, and the movement soon spread to other cities like Chicago and Philadelphia. When the city's clubs closed in

2021, the Haymarket Pole Collective mobilized again and received two grants from the Oregon Health Authority that enabled them to distribute up to $790,000 in rent, food, and medical assistance to members of the local BIPOC sex worker community.

According to Hollis, despite its name, the Stripper Strike isn't necessarily about withholding labor. It's more about mutual aid, community care, and justice at work. Exotic dancers' status as independent contractors and their lack of protections under current labor law precludes them from participating in traditional strikes, and since they aren't unionized, they don't have access to the kind of support and resources available to those who are. "It's really hard to be like, 'Hey, man, go up against your boss at the only place that's ever hired you when you don't even have diapers for your kids,'" they explained. "It doesn't take work stoppages to strike at the core of businesses, and to strike at the core of bosses, and at the wage gap. I think that it really is truly a verb, to stripper strike."

Farther down the West Coast, in 2021 the California-based Adult Performance Artists Guild (APAG) became the first federally recognized labor union for adult performers in the United States, and as of this writing it represents more than thirteen hundred members in the adult film industry. APAG was formerly known as the Adult Performers Actors Guild and originally affiliated with the International Entertainment Adult Union (a nonprofit labor organization that also represents the Exotic Dancer Guild and Adult Film Crew Guild), but split from its parent union in May 2021 and is now a fully independent union representing adult film performers, content creators, phone sex operators, webcam performers, adult performance artists, content streamers, and platform workers. "For the first time in history, workers in the adult industry are represented by a union with the right to collective bargain on their behalf," the union announced in 2021. "All too often, because of the stigma associated with sex workers, the needs of our community go ignored for the sake of others. As unionized workers, we bring legitimacy to our trade and a collective voice to demand change." Sex work has of course always been legitimate work, but unionization has aided those involved in establishing their status as workers. APAG has since emerged as a safe harbor for performers who have been exploited or mistreated on the job. "No matter what field you're in, the bosses are always going to mess with your money if you're the Lone Ranger, and you don't have support," APAG president Alana Evans told me. "Now they can't do that."

OnlyFans, an online content platform first popularized by sex workers, announced on August 19, 2021, that it was changing its content guidelines to prohibit creators from posting explicit content on the site. Founded in 2016, the site saw its popularity (and profits) explode as the pandemic moved existing sex work professionals, as well as "amateurs" seeking supplemental income, online. Transactions rose sevenfold on the site from 2020 to 2021, reaching upward of $2.2 billion dollars. The news came as no surprise given how frequently sex workers have been targeted by online platforms, but the very real implications of removing a crucial source of earnings in the midst of the worst pandemic in a century pressed the sex worker community into action. APAG was there to lead the charge, and added a help center to its website for workers whose OnlyFans accounts had been suspended. Before the threat broke, APAG had been in open communication with the platform for years, stepping in to get its members' accounts restored and even sharing the union's model releases for OnlyFans to use as a template for its own. Evans and her team weren't surprised when the hammer fell. "People don't recognize that the attack on us is truly an attack on their free speech, because wiping us out means there's no more content for them to enjoy," she explained. "Obviously, people want our content; it's what keeps the Internet afloat. But people don't recognize that at first, until something like the OnlyFans move happens, and then it's global. And they're going, wait, why are you guys doing this to these people?"

Facing enormous backlash from the very people whose labor had created the bulk of the site's value, OnlyFans walked back its statement six days later, and reversed the decision to change its policy, promising to "continue to provide a home for all creators." Unfortunately, the OnlyFans debacle was just the latest entry in the U.S. elite's moralistic crusade against the oldest profession. Evans even has a term for it: "occupational discrimination." Websites like Tumblr, social media apps like Instagram and TikTok, and payment processors like PayPal, Venmo, Square, and Cash App have constantly updated their terms of service in ways that exclude or target sex workers."We are seeing very clearly how censorship targets Black and Brown, trans, and fat sex workers more than thin, cis, white sex workers," Mona Marbelle, a queer Arab sex worker, told me. "They are the most likely to be criminalized, to face violence or incarceration, and are the least likely to be making tens of thousands on OnlyFans. When sites like OnlyFans threaten to kick sex workers off their platform, the most affected will be those who are already the most marginalized."

In 2018, Backpage, a classified advertising website that many sex workers used to screen clients and advertise their services, was shut down by the FBI. Only days later, the Stop Enabling Online Sex Trafficking Act (SESTA) and the Fight Online Sex Trafficking Act (FOSTA) were signed into law and immediately began to impact sex workers, rather than helping the trafficked people the law was allegedly written to protect. A 2020 Hacking/Hustling study authored by Danielle Blunt and Ariel Wolf with advisement from Naomi Lauren of Whose Corner Is It Anyway found that the law drastically reduced workers' ability to screen clients, and post-SESTA/FOSTA, 99 percent of the sex workers they surveyed felt less safe. One respondent characterized it as "a bill that is aimed to stop sex trafficking but is making the sex work industry more dangerous." The nineteenth- and early-twentieth-century reformers who went around trying to "save" fallen women are reborn anew in each generation of powerful elites who believe that they alone hold the answer to an age-old question that journalist Melissa Gira Grant articulates in her book *Playing the Whore: The Work of Sex Work* as having shifted from "What do we do about prostitution?" to "What do we do about prostitutes?"

The ongoing efforts to criminalize and eradicate sex work have caused immeasurable harm to countless marginalized workers, many of whom are also survivors of sexual violence, domestic abuse, or childhood abuse. Racism, colorism, misogyny, transphobia, homophobia, fatphobia, xenophobia, ableism, and other intersecting forms of oppression all combine under the umbrella of whorephobia, and workers—not customers, not politicians, not tech bosses—continue to pay the price. Black trans women are disproportionately represented in the sex trade due to lack of economic opportunities and the overwhelming discrimination and threat of violence they face. Ninety percent of trans sex workers or trans folks suspected of being sex workers report being harassed, attacked, or assaulted by the police. As Grant wrote in *Playing the Whore*, cops' approach to sex workers is always clouded by suspicion, and always "about profiling and policing people whose sexuality and gender is considered suspect."

The interlocking layers of oppression trans sex workers face can have extreme consequences. Trans people are thirteen times more likely to experience sexual assault in prison, and 11 percent of trans people have worked in the sex trade. When Layleen Cubilette-Polanco, a twenty-seven-year-old Afro-Latina transgender woman, was arrested and carted off to New York City's Rikers Island on a prostitution charge in 2019, she may have fully expected the kind of disrespectful, abusive treatment that so many sex workers, especially those who are Black and trans, face at the hands of the state. When prison guards decided to throw her into solitary confinement, she may have walked into that cell with dread weighing on her heart. She never walked back out.

Cubilette-Polanco, who had a documented history of experiencing epileptic seizures while in police custody, collapsed during her confinement, and guards waited an hour and a half to call for medical help. In one final act of violence, the resulting New York City Department of Investigation report deadnamed her (referred to her by her birth name instead of the one she chose to use post-transition). Cubilette-Polanco's death devastated her family, both blood and chosen. Layleenn had been a member of the iconic New York ballroom dynasty House of Xtravaganza, performing as Layleen Xtravaganza, and was remembered fondly by her kin. At a vigil held for Cubilette-Polanco in Foley Square, her relative Melania Brown told the crowd, "They treated my sister like she was nothing for how she decided to be happy,"

Sex workers of color who come from immigrant backgrounds are also more vulnerable than their U.S.-born counterparts. Red Canary Song is an abolitionist grassroots organization that advocates for migrant and Asian American sex workers' rights across the diaspora in Toronto, Paris, and Hong Kong. The project was initially founded in 2017 to support the family of Yang Song, a thirty-eight-year-old Chinese massage parlor worker who had fallen four stories to her death during an NYPD raid at her workplace in Flushing, Queens. Prior to her death, Yang Song had been violently assaulted by customers, including a police officer, and arrested several times on prostitution charges. A practical, resourceful woman, she had worked tirelessly anyway, trying to save up money and doing her best to stay connected to her family at home in China. She loved butterflies. Like the women of the Barbary Coast a century earlier and so many other immigrant sex workers of color today, Yang Song's goal was to make it, and like too many of them, she had her life cut short for the crime of survival.

Red Canary Song has worked hard to keep her memory alive and has built a strong foundation of mutual aid, education, and solidarity within its intersecting communities. Tragedy shook those communities once again in early 2021, as COVID-19 began to wend its way through the country and racist fearmongering from a former president put Asians and Asian Americans on edge. In March 2021, a white gunman named Robert Aaron Long attacked three massage parlors in Atlanta, killing eight people; six of them were Asian women. Their names were Soon Chung Park, Hyun Jung Grant, Suncha Kim, Yong Ae Yue, Xiaojie Tan, and Daoyou Feng. "Whether or not they were actually sex workers or self-identified under that label, we know that as massage workers, they were subjected to sexualized violence stemming from the hatred of sex workers, Asian women, working-class people, and immigrants," Red Canary Song wrote in a statement, written in Chinese, Korean, and English, that called for solidarity and advocated against responding to the tragedy with more police. "Decriminalization of sex work is the only way that sex workers, massage workers, sex trafficking survivors, and anyone criminalized for their survival and/or livelihood will ever be safe."

Sex workers' enduring ability to survive, thrive, and lift one another up despite it all is true worker power in action. Those who have chosen to align with the traditional labor movement have brought an influx of essential knowledge, militancy, and energy into a space that has often been far too conservative for its own—or anyone else's—good. "Self-determination, bodily autonomy, workers' rights, and workplace labor protections are truly the only way forward," Red Canary Song wrote in an op-ed for *Tits and Sass*, a sex worker-run digital publication. "If we want justice for all (im)migrant sex working people, that means opening all borders, abolishing (pol)ICE and letting massage workers fucking live."

The efforts of sex worker–led organizations and sex worker activists to secure safety, dignity, and respect for themselves and their fellow workers has been a centuries-long fight, and the ongoing struggle for basic worker protections and decriminalization continues to occupy a new era of resistance. The resilience of the sex workers' rights movement, and of sex workers themselves, in the face of overwhelming structural barriers, violent repression, and sociopolitical stigma is one of the most important labor stories in U.S. history and will undoubtedly continue to inspire new organizing and new tactics as the playing field continues to shift. "The sex industry is the oldest industry for a reason," sex worker and OnlyFans creator Bobby LaBottom (a.k.a. Frankie Bouvier) told journalist Reina Sultan in 2021. "We'll just continue to adapt."

13

THE PRISONERS

It only takes one person to tell his cell-mate, "It's fucked up we're working for 19 cents an hour, and there's people trying to change it."

—Hybachi LeMar, Incarcerated Workers Organizing Committee (IWOC) cofounder

The many strikes, protests, and acts of resistance chronicled throughout this book have made clear how powerful it can be when a worker—or better yet, a group of workers—decide to withhold their labor in order to change an unacceptable status quo. In the unequal tug-of-war between the forces of labor and capital, refusing to participate is one of the worker's greatest weapons, and the strike itself, when executed successfully, has proven to be an enormously effective tool for social, economic, and political change throughout history. Even outside of organized labor, for many people, quitting their shitty job or walking out in protest is understood to be a culturally sanctioned act of rebellion. Whether we're on the couch rooting for the fed-up paper pushers in the workplace revenge fantasy *Office Space* or cheering on the Walmart cashiers and fast-food workers reading their managers for filth on TikTok, many of us secretly fantasize about doing just that. And, as you've read, thousands of others have already taken things a step further, participating in strikes, walkouts, and protests of their own. There's really nothing like the power of a picket line, or the righteous satisfaction of telling your boss to take this job and shove it.

But what if you can't? What if your boss controls every aspect of your life, from when you shower to where you sleep to whether or not you can make a phone call or see your family? What if you have no legal right to strike, or organize, or even meet with your coworkers outside of a rigidly supervised setting? What if you're threatened with violence or even torture if you refuse to show up for a shift? What if you have no option to walk out, no matter how bad your job gets, because you're locked in a cage? That is the stark reality for millions of people in this country. Welcome to the life of an incarcerated worker.

It is a simple truth that the U.S. was built on forced and stolen labor. First, by the millions of Indigenous people who survived European settlers' early attempts at genocide and were trafficked and forced into service during the first wave of colonization. Then, starting in 1619, millions more African captives were kidnapped and trafficked into the early American colonies, their mass enslavement simultaneously meeting and fueling the young country's dependence on involuntary labor. Throughout the nation's history, various forms of indentured servitude, debt bondage, and outright enslavement have powered the U.S. economy and enriched its owner class, building an empire on the backs of enslaved Black and Brown captives as well as poor and working-class immigrants from across Asia, Africa, Europe, and elsewhere. After the Civil War and Reconstruction, when slavery was de jure abolished, the forced labor system of choice shifted from chattel slavery to penal labor, and shockingly little has changed since. It may have been more visible in the early twentieth century, when convict laborers still peppered the fields of the Deep South, but today everything from military and police equipment to mundanities like artisanal cheese and lingerie may have been made by the hands of an imprisoned laborer.

The forced laborers working on these new American plantations are paid mere pennies on the hour—if at all. Meanwhile, prison labor generates an estimated $1 billion per year. Federal Prison Industries, also known as UNICOR, is a government-owned prison labor program that has begun marketing its incarcerated workers' services to companies who want to avoid the costs associated with outsourcing their business and flaunt a "Made in America" label while paying next to nothing for slave labor right here at home. Under current federal law, all "physically able" prisoners who are judged not to be a security risk or have a health exception are required to work, either for UNICOR or at some other prison job, like food service or maintenance. Roughly half of the people incarcerated in state and federal prisons work either for the prison or for outside contractors during their time inside, and are conveniently excluded from the Fair Labor Standards Act, which means their employers can get away with paying them far less than the federal minimum wage for their labor. While they are working full-time jobs, prisoners also do not have the benefit of basic labor protections, such as minimum wage, sick leave, or overtime pay, and are forbidden from forming labor unions (more on that later).

Modern prison profiteers have found even more creative ways to exploit their captive workforce, while also falling back on "the old ways" via agriculture. Food production has become big business for prison profiteers, and savvy marketing and corporate consolidation have enabled them to launder the true origins of their products. The *Counter* reported in 2021 that academics Joshua Sbicca and Carrie Chennault at Colorado State University found that at least 650 correctional institutions have some sort of food processing, landscaping, or farming operation, and that huge corporations like Cargill, the Dairy Farmers of America, and the $3 billion mozzarella company Leprino are quietly stocking high-end restaurant menus and shelves in stores like Kroger, Whole Foods, and Walmart with food products produced by prison labor.

When Congress passed the 1935 Ashurst-Sumners Act, it prohibited the sale of prison-made goods across state lines, but added a carve-out for agricultural produce that has since ballooned into a multimillion-dollar industry. These circumstances have also led to gruesome historical echoes like the one at the Louisiana State Penitentiary—better known as Angola, or "the Alcatraz of the South"—where incarcerated workers pick cotton in the same plantation fields once worked by Reconstruction-era convict laborers, and by enslaved Africans before them.

Private corporations' profits from prison labor have continued to rise, thanks to the government-approved dirt-cheap labor costs. The average wage in state prisons ranges from 14 cents to 63 cents per hour for "regular" prison jobs, and between 23 cents and $1.15 per hour for those who work for state-owned businesses. Wages for prison jobs have decreased since 2001, and even the highest-paid incarcerated workers, like firefighters in California, see their hourly pay top out around $2 per hour. It's all perfectly legal thanks to the Thirteenth Amendment, which outlawed slavery in the U.S. with one very important caveat: slavery and involuntary servitude are illegal "except as a punishment for crime whereof the party shall have been duly convicted."

No matter that the so-called criminal justice system is riddled with racial bias against Black and Brown people, who have been historically oppressed and exploited and are still heavily overrepresented within the prison walls; as activist and author Shaka Senghor said in Ava DuVernay's 2016 documentary *13th*, "Once you've been convicted of a crime, you are in essence a slave of the state." In states like Alabama, Arkansas, Florida, Georgia, and Texas, that condition is literal; prisoners are paid nothing for their work.

Like prison life itself, prison labor—or as some prisoners prefer to name it, prison slavery—is a complex system with its own specific conditions. Though the wages are minuscule, prison jobs do offer a small measure of economic autonomy, and allow incarcerated workers to purchase necessary items like food and hygiene products and to pay for phone calls or video chat time with their loved ones. "Jobs are, strangely enough, in high demand among prisoners, at least where I was," David Campbell, a former political prisoner at Rikers, who helped organize a work stoppage during his time there, told me. "They really help to pass the monotony of the day. . . . Some guys would work two or even three [extra, unpaid] jobs just to pass the time."

Victoria Law, abolitionist journalist and author of two books on incarceration and resistance, was quick to point out the coercive nature of work inside the walls of America's criminal justice system. "'Oh, you want that job that will pay $2? You cannot organize, you cannot agitate; if you're in a women's prison, and that guard is looking at you on the toilet—well, do you want that to stop, or do you want that $2 an hour job?' You'll put up with all sorts of things that people on the outside who have more choices might not."

Incarcerated people have always been a part of the workforce, and as such, a part of the labor movement, even if the movement itself has largely failed to recognize that. A direct line can also be drawn between the Reconstruction-era convict leasing system discussed earlier in this book to today's modern prison-industrial complex. The politically charged 1960s and 1970s saw an uptick in organizing activity and the rise of the prisoners' rights movement, which married aspects of the civil rights, Black Power, Chicano, and Puerto Rican independence movements and applied them in protesting the horrors of mass incarceration.

In 1971, as a nationwide prisoners' rights movement picked up momentum, the most infamous prison rebellion in U.S. history exploded over five bloody days at the Attica Correctional Facility in Attica, New York. The original demands laid down by its architects, the Attica Liberation Faction, or Attica Brothers, were never met—an outcome that belies the basic nature of those requests: one line implored that prisoners be given "more fresh fruit" at mealtime, while another asked for a prison doctor to be provided. As the opening lines of the manifesto emphasized, "WE are MEN! We are not beasts and do not intend to be beaten or driven as such." There were signs that the nascent nationwide prisoners' union movement had had an impact on the Attica rebels' thinking; they demanded the right to take grievances to the prison administrators on a quarterly basis, and tellingly, called on the powers that be to "apply the New York State minimum wage law to all state institutions" and, in all caps, to "STOP SLAVE LABOR!"

There was a significant precedent there. A year before the uprising, in 1970, 450 Attica prisoners had held a three-day strike for higher wages. The men (who were predominantly Black and Puerto Rican) worked in the prison's metal shop manufacturing lockers and library shelves for a paltry 29 cents per hour and were stuck paying the prison's inflated commissary prices for food and basic necessities. Jorge "Che" Nieves, a survivor of the 1971 rebellion and the 1970 strike, later recalled how for the strike he organized the almost entirely Black and Latino body by drawing connections between the U.S. colonization of Puerto Rico and the Black liberation movement. "I said, 'We need to organize a union. But I know that in order to do that, we need to strike. We need to have a metal shop strike.' My brothers said, 'Let's do it.' So we did it." The three-day work stoppage resulted in a lowering of commissary prices, but its organizers were met with swift retribution from prison management. Twenty-six strikers, among them multiple Black Panthers and alleged members of the Weathermen faction of Students for a

Democratic Society, were transferred to other facilities; fifty others were further disciplined by losing time off for good behavior. Nieves was temporarily moved to another New York facility, Green Haven, where he promptly founded a chapter of the Young Lords.

Nieves would return to Attica and its metal shop, finding a new cause in the wake of the death of incarcerated Black Panther and political activist George Jackson at the hands of guards in San Quentin Prison. "We started discussing what we could do to commemorate the brother," he recalled. "So we planned a hunger strike, where everybody would go into the mess hall. I said, 'Don't say anything.' There was total silence. Many of us had black armbands. . . . We didn't eat." A guard who was on duty during the August 22, 1971, protest later remembered being shaken by the sight of the seven hundred silent prisoners in their matching mourning bands. "We noticed that almost all [the prisoners] had some black on them," corrections officer Sergeant Jack English told the New York *Daily News*. "Some had black armbands, some had black shoe laces tied around their arms, others had little pieces of black cloth or paper pinned on them. . . . It scared us because a thing like that takes a lot of organization, a lot of solidarity, and we had no idea they were so well organized."

On September 9, 1971, the guards and everyone else in the U.S. who was paying attention to the news would find out just how organized those prisoners were. That day, 1,281 of the Attica prison's approximately 2,200 prisoners rose up in the best-known prison uprising in U.S. history, the consequence of a movement that had first stirred in a workshop where a group of underpaid workers wanted to form a union. George Jackson himself had organized a hunger strike back in 1962, well before he became a prominent figure within the prisoners' rights and Black Power movements, and a full decade before his murder. Incarcerated activists and their allies outside had spent years laying the groundwork for large-scale resistance, and while Attica remains the best-known prison work stoppage of the era, the 1970s were a high-water mark for labor organizing behind the walls.

THE RISE OF PRISONERS' LABOR UNIONS

In Che Nieves's short but significant time organizing at Green Haven, he had crossed paths with another monumental figure in collective action behind bars. Earl Smoake, Jr., had been hard at work organizing incarcerated workers there, who labored making hospital gowns, bathrobes, pillowcases, and United States flags for an average of 35 cents a day. In 1970, Smoake kickstarted the formation of the Prisoners' Labor Union at Green Haven, enshrining in its constitution the union's intent to "advance the economic, political, social and cultural interests" of its members and to equalize "the rights, privileges and protections of prison labor with those of free labor everywhere." The fledgling union sent letters to New York state officials and the prison's superintendent requesting recognition as the official collective bargaining agent of the prison's incarcerated workers. The New York Legal Aid Society's newly formed Prisoners' Rights Project would serve as the group's legal counsel, and the effort was all set to launch under District 65, an independent union representing low-wage workers. Within a year, more than half the prison's population had joined.

The question of whether or not incarcerated workers had the right to organize would come up again and again as prison union drives began to spread throughout the carceral system. Post-Attica, prison guards and officials were uneasy about seeing the people they imprisoned coming together to build power and advocate for themselves, and many attempted to repress and derail these organizing efforts. The workers pressed ahead anyway. During the early 1970s, prisoners' unions were organized in Rhode Island, Ohio, Massachusetts,

Maine, Michigan, Delaware, Wisconsin, Pennsylvania, North Carolina, Minnesota, and the District of Columbia, swelling the ranks of unionized incarcerated workers nationwide to about eleven thousand members. As Donald F. Tibbs noted in his book *Black Power to Prison Power: The Making of* Jones v. North Carolina Prisoners' Labor Union, "In virtually every prison where there was a union, more than 90 percent of the inmate population wanted affiliation."

Just as the wider labor movement itself is home to many diverse goals and viewpoints, so, too, were these early prisoners' unions. Some, like the Ohio Prisoners' Labor Union, focused on bread-and-butter issues like wages and working conditions, concerns that wouldn't have sounded all that unfamiliar to workers outside the prison walls. Others, like Rhode Island's abolitionist National Prisoners' Reform Association (NPRA), were explicitly political in nature. For three months in 1973, members of the Walpole, Massachusetts, chapter of the NPRA actually ran the prison themselves, following a guards' strike that provided them with an opportunity to seize control and demonstrate to the media and the public that the prison's infrastructure of external discipline below a suite of "overseers" was unnecessary. Prisoners Bobby Dellelo and Ralph Hamm led the NPRA as a completely nonviolent movement. Order was established via a volunteer system, and community observers were welcomed into the prison to witness daily life inside. The union handled day-to-day operations, conflict resolution, labor issues, and food production, creating a "complex society" that one observer noted had "its workers, its employers, its organizations, its cooks, craftsmen, educators, even its artists." The outsiders, from places like nearby Harvard University and the Massachusetts Chamber of Commerce, were impressed by how smoothly the NPRA handled its responsibilities, from day-to-day operations all the way down to its rich schedule of cultural and political programming on the cellblock. As one later remarked, "It's worth paying them to retire. The guards are the security problem." On March 19, the Massachusetts Supreme Court ordered the guards to return, which led to a swift resumption of the prison's brutal former conditions and a heavy-handed crackdown on the prisoner-led collective that had so capably rendered them unnecessary.

While it's difficult to pin down which in this spate of organizing efforts was the "first" (prisons weren't exactly thrilled to document these kinds of things), it's certain that California had played a pivotal role in launching the prisoners' union movement. Following a nineteen-day strike in November 1970, prisoners in Folsom, California, formed the influential United Prisoners' Union, which welcomed both currently and formerly incarcerated people as members, as well as their families, and used legislation and advocacy to work for their concerns. However, some members felt the legal system was a dead end, and instead wanted to take more direct action. A schism formed between the two approaches, and in 1971, the UPU fractured, with one faction remaining focused on legislative efforts and the newly spun-off Prisoners' Union embracing more militant activism. The UPU stayed local, but thanks to the proliferation of its newsletter, *The Outlaw*, the PU was able to establish footholds nationwide.

In 1972, when a worker named Wayne Brooks, incarcerated in North Carolina's Central Prison, was hoping to organize a union, he reached out to the local PU representative. His union's founding came in fits and starts, but once it successfully established a strong foundation, the North Carolina Prisoners' Labor Union would become the most significant such organization of its era, an interracial group of Black, white, and Indigenous Lumbee prisoners that would count about half of the state's entire prison population as members. The NCPLU successfully filed for incorporation in 1974, and affiliated with the North Carolina AFL-CIO, as well as the North Carolina chapter of the ACLU. It was a bread-and-butter-issues union, targeting higher wages and workers' compensation for prisoners who were injured on the job; at the time, incarcerated workers in North Carolina were expected to work outside, maintaining state highways, laboring in rock quarries, and serving on hurricane cleanup crews, and injuries were common. The union also looked outside the walls to advocate for unemployment insurance for formerly incarcerated prison laborers. "If free citizens, who labored daily, had access to unemployment benefits, so also should a prisoner who has been a continuous state employee as a result of their incarceration," the NCPLU argued.

WOMEN'S PRISONS AND REBELLION

Like most prisoner unions of its era, the NCPLU's membership was overwhelmingly male. As Robbie Purner, a NCPLU organizer, told *Scalawag* in a 2018 interview, in her experience as an organizer, women prisoners held deep distrust that men could act as trustworthy advocates. "So many of them were imprisoned due to domestic violence issues and rape issues," she explained. "Why would they believe that men, even fellow prisoners, would care about their rights? Men had caused most of them to be where they were." However, that reticence did not mean that incarcerated women were not engaged in work stoppages and other forms of resistance. Women may make up only about 10 percent of the U.S. prison population, but they have always engaged in their own forms of resistance—whether or not people outside have paid attention.

Just a few years after Attica, two prominent women's prisons were roiled by protests of similar import, if not notoriety: one near the organizing hotbed of Green Haven and another in North Carolina, just a few miles down the road from the NCPLU's Central Prison stronghold. In 1975, prisoners at the North Carolina Correctional Center for Women held a sit-down strike calling for better medical care and counseling services. When prison guards began attacking them in an attempt to end their protest, the women fought back; the uprising ended only after over one hundred guards from other prisons were hastily sent in to restore order. A year prior, prisoners at the all-female Bedford Hills Correctional Facility in New York State rebelled after one of their own, a queer Black woman named Carol Crooks, was brutally beaten and thrown into segregation in retaliation for filing—and winning—a lawsuit against prison authorities.

On February 3, 1974, Crooks was thrown into solitary confinement after an altercation with a prison guard. While there she was stripped, tormented, and denied basic necessities like food and blankets. Crooks's friend Efeni Shakur, a Black Panther, publicized the case and attracted the attention of an attorney willing to take Crooks's complaint to court. Crooks's successful lawsuit ensured that going forward all Bedford Hills prisoners would be allowed their full rights to due process before being placed in solitary confinement. Prison authorities were forced to release Crooks back into the general population, but not without a plan to send her away again shortly afterward. On August 29, 1974, the guards got their chance. After Crooks got into a scuffle with another prisoner at dinner, her neighbors witnessed a team of male prison guards from the nearby Green Haven Correctional Facility drag Crooks from her cell, throw her down the stairs, and carry her away "like a roasted pig on a stick," as Crooks would ruefully recount to the *Village Voice* years later. That evening more than two hundred prisoners responded and, led by Crooks's partner Cindy "Sid" Reed and Dollree Mapp, took control of the prison for two and a half hours.

By midnight, the women had agreed to return to their cells, and the August Rebellion ended without a drop of blood spilled. Reed and other suspected leaders were sentenced to solitary confinement for a year each; Crooks received two, and true to form, decided to fight back. The resulting lawsuit, *Powell v. Ward*, resulted in concrete gains for the women and those still locked inside Bedford Hills. The defendants were awarded $127,000 in damages, and used the money to improve material conditions within the prison by buying supplies for the prison law library. The 1970s were a flashpoint of dissent in Bedford Hills, but it was far from its first (or last). The "girls" of the Bedford Hills Reformatory—as it was once called—had been headline fodder as far back as 1920, when they protested their miserable treatment by keeping guards awake all night with a cacophonous "noise strike."

While there are some experiences that are universal to incarcerated people of every gender, women and nonbinary people in women's prisons have specific physical needs and face additional risks of violence and assault from prison authorities. Many enter prison with a history of trauma and abuse, and have experienced a disproportionate amount of violence at home or on the streets; trans and gender-nonconforming prisoners are even more vulnerable to discrimination and mistreatment in a system primarily constructed around cisgender men. The Silvia Rivera Law Project notes, "Over-policing and profiling of low-income people and of trans and gender-nonconforming people intersect, producing a far higher risk than average of imprisonment, police harassment and violence for low-income trans people." According to Lambda Legal, nearly one in six transgender Americans—and one in two Black transgender people—have been to prison.

It's important to consider these conditions when attempting to understand why so much less is known about protests within women's prisons, and why that resistance may look different from what one might expect to see in a men's prison. Instead of a strike, prisoners in women's facilities may turn to legal challenges, as Carol Crooks did. Others may use letter-writing campaigns, like the 223 prisoners at Alabama's Julia Tutwiler Prison for Women who blew the whistle on two decades of sexual abuse. In 2014, they contacted the Department of Justice, writing letters that detailed the widespread sexual abuse that was being perpetrated by prison guards and covered up by prison officials; their efforts resulted in a federal investigation and mandated reforms.

Much of the work of author and journalist Victoria Law has focused specifically on people in women's prisons and the gender-specific indignities and forms of violence they face, from access to personal hygiene products to rampant sexual abuse and assault within the walls. When it comes to work stoppages, rebellions, and protests, incarcerated women often have more to lose. "People in women's prisons tend to be the primary caregivers, and also tend to be the ones that are still trying to bear the financial burden of staying in touch with their family members," Law explained. For some, the meager wages a prison job offers can be the only means they have of calling their children or buying tampons, and going on strike demands they risk losing those precious few economic resources. It's a tall order, especially when Law says that organizers do not always put in the required effort to reach women's prisons. "I don't think it's intentional," she clarifies, "but I think that there is this overlooking of the fact that there are people in women's prisons who are not reached out to about many organizing things, not just work and labor strikes, and they should be, because they might come with their own perspectives on what that would look like inside of a women's prison."

During that 1970s prisoners' union boom, women found themselves sidelined from the conversation, and soon, so did everyone else. The NCPLU had achieved remarkable success during its first year and had avoided any major conflicts with prison authorities, but the honeymoon didn't last. Meetings were banned, prisoners were forbidden from recruiting new members into the union, and the prison removed access to bulk mailings. The North Carolina Department of Corrections summarily rejected the union and any notion that it had a right to exist at all, and Secretary of Corrections David L. Jones was actively hostile, telling a roomful of corrections officers in Raleigh that "there is no union, there has been no union, and there will not be so long as I am secretary." He pointed toward the prison's Inmate Grievance Commission as an appropriate avenue for prisoners to raise issues instead. The union was furious over what it saw as a stifling of its members' First Amendment rights to free speech and free association, and filed a lawsuit against the IGC.

They notched an initial win from a three-judge federal district court, which ruled in favor of the prisoners' union. But prison officials appealed the ruling, arguing that the organization was a security threat and implying its interracial character was a race war waiting to happen. The case ended up in front of the Supreme Court, which ultimately reversed the decision and set a devastating precedent that, even under the First Amendment, prisoners have no legal right to join a union. To his credit, Justice Thurgood Marshall dissented, writing, "The Court, in apparent fear of a prison reform organization that has the temerity to call itself a 'union,' takes a giant step backwards toward that discredited conception of prisoners' rights and the role of the courts."

It was cold comfort. Marshall's doomsaying analysis of the case's potential fallout was correct. After the *Jones* decision was handed down, it became far more difficult if not impossible for incarcerated workers to organize their own unions, at least under the traditional NLRB-certified structure. "It cemented this idea and this legal precedent that people in prison do not have the right to organize around their prison conditions," Law explained. "No matter what you do, we are not bound to recognize you." *Jones* was far from the first legal challenge mounted by a prisoners' union in the U.S., but it had the most wide-ranging effects, and proved to be a debilitating blow for the prisoners' union movement. "The Jones decision crushed the movement for prison workers' organizations; it said the state gets to determine security issues and that's how it is," Chuck Eppinette, a formerly incarcerated antiwar activist who had worked as a paralegal for Debbie Mailman, the NCPLU's chief attorney, told *Scalawag* in 2018. "Unless the people who are directly affected have a voice in what happens, then the type of change that needs to happen will never happen. The North Carolina Prisoners' Labor Union showed a possibility."

The people involved have no regrets. Changing the world takes time, and blood, and hope, and for all of its flaws, the 1970s prisoners' union movement had all three in abundance. "Organizing is not simple," Purner reflected in a 2018 interview. "A lot of people have died to preserve freedom and human rights. It's an ongoing battle. There will be advances and then retreats. Advances and then retreats."

THE INCARCERATED WORKERS ORGANIZING COMMITTEE

Decades later, in 2014, the Incarcerated Workers Organizing Committee (IWOC) was founded by a handful of former prisoners, and a whole new chapter of the prisoners' rights movement began to take shape. It started with a conference call among the Free Alabama Movement, a prisoner-led human rights group, and several other organizations. That year, FAM had organized a weeklong work stoppage involving twenty-four hundred people at the St. Clair Correctional Facility and the William C. Holman Correctional Facility, two of Alabama's most violent and dangerous prisons, and was looking for ways to expand its work. Briana Peril, a labor organizer with the IWW who had been imprisoned in North Carolina as a teen in the 1980s, piped up and suggested that the union should begin recruiting incarcerated people, and waiving its dues requirement in order to make it easier for them to join. She had been inspired by conversations with her friend, Black anarchist political prisoner and former Black Panther Lorenzo Kom'Boa Ervin, who encouraged her to find a way to bring prisoners into the union. At the IWW convention that year, delegates voted to ignore the legal ruling that forbade incarcerated people from forming unions, and IWOC got to work.

IWOC's model is similar to the United Prisoners' Union's in that it includes incarcerated workers as well as formerly incarcerated people and outside advocates among its members, but its ultimate goal—the total abolition of the prison-industrial complex—is certainly more revolutionary than its more policy-oriented predecessors'. Its formation signaled a new era in prisoner-led organizing that operated using anarchist principles of mutual aid, militant opposition to the state and its many linked systems of oppression, and horizontal, non-hierarchical structures. IWOC, which is still heavily dependent on snail mail to get its literature into the hands of members and prospective members, has the added advantage of a built-in radical communications network thanks to the IWW's many chapters and its close relationship with like-minded abolitionist organizations like the Anarchist Black Cross and Books Through Bars. Modern technological advances like cell phones, email, and social media provide further avenues of communication for those who have—or are able to acquire—access.

Peril had lit the spark in that first conference call, but the organization was built with plenty of help from other like-minded organizers. Among them was Hybachi LeMar, a Black anarchist community organizer from Chicago who has been living in and outside the prison system since he was fifteen years old and who joined the IWW back in 2008. When Peril asked him to get involved as a cofounder, he was all in, and immediately began reaching out to prisoners through the most reliable means available: handwritten letters. There is no law against prisoners receiving union-related literature in the mail (though as with all prison communications, your mileage may vary depending on the facility), and IWOC took full advantage of that loophole to establish contact with people stuck in cells across the country. "I was working at the IWW office in Chicago at the time, writing to prisoners and asking them if they'd like to join the Industrial Workers of the World's Incarcerated Workers Organizing Committee, and letting them know they could join without dues," LeMar told me over the phone from the Pennsylvania psychiatric hospital in which he was living as a condition of his parole. "What the IWW was doing was groundbreaking—well, wall-breaking."

LeMar, who is also a member of the Black Autonomy Federation, became aware of the IWW while he was incarcerated in 2008. He had been thrown into solitary confinement—a practice the United Nations has condemned as psychological torture—for twenty-two months straight after allegedly assaulting a prison guard (a charge LeMar characterizes as "bogus"). During that period, other prisoners passed him the address to the South Chicago Anarchist Black Cross zine distro, and as he told me, his ensuing introduction to the union as well as anarchism and abolitionist writings felt like "a light came on in the closet of my mind." LeMar was hooked, and began writing his own essays to be published in the IWW's newspaper, the *Industrial Worker*. In one 2021 piece, he reflected on the horrors he and so many others had survived inside the walls, and made the terms of engagement clear: "Many imprisoned union members, those who are working and those who are stored in cells for profit, have documented countless instances of torture, slavery, religious persecution, and many other forms of inhumanity in American prison cells. The institutions of torture need to be abolished. They need to be seen and understood."

That raw, basic need to be seen as humans, not numbers or chattel, has often led prisoners to take matters into their own hands. Whether they've expressed that desire through the riot, revolt, or strike, the stakes have remained incredibly high, and any prisoner who dares to stand up against a system designed to crush them into dust runs a heavy risk. Participating in a prison strike can be a matter of life or death, but for prisoners seeking justice, if not freedom, there is really no other option. Since prisoners have no legal right to unionize, they have no right to protected concerted activity, so the consequences for those who dare to strike anyway can be harsh and swift. “We're under the threat of being thrown in the hole, because if you refuse to work inside prison, you get written up for refusing to obey a direct order,” LeMar explained. “So you could go to the hole for like sixty days for refusing to work, and end up being there for six years, because of so many write-ups that get piled on.”

Victoria Law also outlined those risks in no uncertain terms. This is an environment in which a person's boss controls—or many bosses control—every single aspect of their life, from when they shower to how often they're able to speak to their family, and saying no is simply not an option. Instead of simply resulting in being fired or docked pay, pissing off the boss can also get incarcerated workers' mail delayed, their visits cut short, their living quarters ransacked, their precious few comforts further curtailed, and their bodies brutalized by unsympathetic guards (many of whom enjoy the protections of their own unions). “When you're in prison, you don't have that option to be like, ‘Oh, working conditions and living conditions are horrendous, and brutal, and violent and life-threatening, let me get up and move to a different place,” Law explained. “So for people to organize a work stoppage or work strike, or any type of labor organizing is, in itself, an incredibly dangerous action. And the fact that people do this speaks to the atrocity of the working conditions that they're organizing against.”

These conditions explain why alternative forms of resistance like hunger strikes, sick-outs, and slowdowns, as practiced by vulnerable workers outside the walls, are also so prevalent among incarcerated workers. With no way to form a picket line, hold mass meetings, or physically walk off the job, people in prison use whatever means are available to them to protest and organize. During the first wave of the 2020 COVID-19 pandemic, prisoners at Rikers Island struck over a lack of hygiene supplies and personal protective equipment, and echoed demands from outside advocates that the most vulnerable prisoners (i.e., those who were elderly or had preexisting medical conditions) be sent home. Conditions inside the jail complex were extremely hazardous, with endemic overcrowding and prisoners falling ill in droves. To the people suffering inside, striking—or engaging in a "stick-up"—felt like a Hail Mary at that point, but it worked; within eight hours of the participants refusing to leave their dorms for work or mealtime, guards began delivering cleaning supplies to the dorms. "A solid portion of the guys in my dorm actually wanted to do a full-blown hunger strike until everyone was released," David Campbell, who was incarcerated on Rikers at the time, explained. "We definitely spent time discussing the risks involved, but even guys who were a few weeks from going home decided to take those risks. They were scared of catching COVID and fed up with the Department of Correction for treating them like they were disposable."

Several years prior, this diversity of tactics had been on full display during IWOC's first mass action in concert with the Free Alabama Movement. On September 9, 2016, forty-six facilities in twenty-four states took matters into their own hands to make a point. The strike saw twenty-four thousand incarcerated workers take part in any way they could—some refused to work, others went on hunger strike or boycotted the commissary, withholding their economic power from their overseers. These disruptions to everyday life on the block were meant to commemorate Attica, but the real aims reached for much more: prisoner voting rights, an expansion of decrepit and actively defunded rehabilitation and educational opportunities, and an end to prison slavery once and for all.

"To every prisoner in every state and federal institution across this land, we call on you to stop being a slave, to let the crops rot in the plantation fields, to go on strike and cease reproducing the institutions of your confinement," the strike call read in part. "When we remove the economic motive and grease of our forced labor from the US prison system, the entire structure of courts and police, of control and slave-catching must shift to accommodate us as humans, rather than slaves."

That strike begat others, as strikes tend to do. In 2018, IWOC, FAM, and Jailhouse Lawyers Speak, a national collective of incarcerated people who provide legal education and resources to other people in prison and who also supported the 2016 action, organized another nationwide prison strike. Slated to begin on August 21 and run through September 9, the strike mirrored earlier demands to abolish prison slavery and improve conditions within the prison itself and drew a direct line between prisoners' current struggle and the struggles of those who had come before. The prisoners' demands emphasized the stark fact that very little had changed since the prisoners' movement's 1970s heyday in terms of conditions or opportunities for those who were locked up and held by the state, and the demands were, once again, left unmet. "I believe teaching about Attica is a powerful tool to motivate the people into action," Safear Quaswarah, a currently incarcerated Mexican-American Muslim, told me in an interview. "We just need more teachers."

This new era of incarcerated worker–led labor organizing lacks even the faint nod of institutional support that some of its predecessors in the pre-*Jones* prisoners' union movement enjoyed. Imagine what an impact it would have had if the AFL-CIO had spoken out in support of the striking prisoners, or even acknowledged their struggle.

"If we really take seriously that all labor has dignity and value, then, of course, that [includes] the most exploited sector," said Dr. Dan Berger, University of Washington professor, historian, and author of *Captive Nation: Black Prison Organizing in the Civil Rights Era*. "If that demand is leveraged without the exclusions of incarcerated people, and without the exclusions of farmworkers and domestic workers and other people who have been traditionally discounted or ignored by the mainstream labor movement, then we're not just having to fight for bigger cages and longer chains."

The 2018 prison strike was ultimately a more limited event than its predecessor, involving prisoners in only a handful of facilities, but it got far more media attention. As Law pointed out when I interviewed her about the strike back in 2018, this increased awareness of what was happening inside led to an upswing in support from activists and advocates on the outside. That additional layer of scrutiny and support has had an important impact on the way prisoners are treated during potentially risky protests and work stoppages; more eyes can mean more accountability. Those who choose to strike are potentially less likely to face LeMar's experience of being sent "to the hole" now that there is more visibility and advocacy. "[Prison guards] couldn't just sweep the incarcerated organizers into solitary confinement to shut them up," Law explained. "Now they knew that there would be repercussions if they did that."

CALIFORNIA'S INCARCERATED FIREFIGHTERS

When journalist Jaime Lowe was visiting her mother in Los Angeles a few years ago, she chanced upon a five-hundred-word obituary for a woman named Shawna Lynn Jones in the *Los Angeles Times*. Jones, twenty-two, had been a child of the desert, born and raised on the edge of the Mojave in Southern California's Antelope Valley. She died on the job, suffering a grievous head injury while fighting a blaze in the Santa Monica Mountains, and left behind parents, siblings, and a dog named Charlie. In the obituary Lowe read, Jones's life was reduced to two sentences that focused on her crime and her participation in the California Department of Corrections' Conservation Camp Program, which trains groups of incarcerated people as firefighters and sends them out to the front lines of the state's deadliest wildfires.

"I had no idea there were forty-four camps throughout the state and that 30 percent of on-the-ground crews in California were incarcerated firefighters making a tiny fraction of what free world firefighters make," Lowe told me. That curiosity led to five years of research and interviews with women who had been or were still currently incarcerated and involved with the fire program, and a book—*Breathing Fire: Female Inmate Firefighters on the Front Lines of California's Wildfires*—and transformed Lowe into an abolitionist. "Caging people not only does not work, it traumatizes people and their families," she told me. "We need to tear down the entire system and build something that is actually centered around rehabilitation and compassion and community involvement. Labor can be a part of that but not in the context of torture and punishment, which is what our current system is."

Lowe's reporting took place during a time when the public had come to realize the extent of California's prisoner firefighter program, and finally saw it as an increasingly urgent labor issue as climate change ravages the state's forests. When California governor Gavin Newsom took office in 2019, he announced a pilot program that would allow formerly incarcerated people to assist in emergency response units. This sounded like progress but ignored the stark fact that their felony records often bar them from finding work as civilian firefighters once they're released. Following additional pressure, he signed AB 2147 into law, which altered the state's penal code to make it easier for prisoners trained in the Conservation Camp Program or on a county hand crew to gain employment as professional firefighters after release. Prisoner advocates, activists, and sympathetic media coverage had coalesced to essentially shame the state into action, but other baked-in institutional barriers remained. "The ultimate hiring agencies—CalFire and municipal departments—still have the ability to do a criminal search and see that there once was a felony on an applicant's record," Lowe explained. "These are historically discriminatory agencies and there's no way to know if that will factor into their hiring."

State legislators have continued to debate this issue for years, and more recent attempts to create a real pathway toward employment for formerly incarcerated firefighters were shelved following opposition from, sadly, the California firefighters' association. This disappointing episode showed that some sectors of organized labor still have a long way to go in rectifying their lack of solidarity with incarcerated workers. "We know we can fight for meaningful, dignified unionized labor as a baseline demand for society, but the problem is that so many unions have made that demand in a way that discounts and excludes prisoners," Dr. Berger explained during our call. "To see prisoners as job competition, rather than as fellow workers, is something that can be overcome, but I think it is a crucial obstacle." Ending prison slavery and supporting incarcerated workers is an issue that should concern the entire labor movement, and pretending that workers inside the walls don't exist—or somehow exist in opposition to others laboring outside—is a harmful and pigheaded dereliction of duty. Just like the craven factory owners, plantation overseers, and coal barons who oversaw the deaths and degradation of previous generations, the companies who profit off of this modern-day slavery and the politicians who allow it to continue are stained with workers' blood. For people in prison, taking back their power, withholding their labor, and asserting their humanity is a revolutionary act.

"Watching the COs serve food in the mess hall and sweep and mop the floors was immensely satisfying for all of us," David Campbell told me as he reflected back on the prison strike he helped organize during the height of COVID-19. "I think that sense that the tables could turn, that the prisoners did in fact possess that power despite our circumstances, was always present, even if it was usually pretty muffled."

EPILOGUE

As I write this, eight hundred coal miners in rural Alabama are now one step closer to ending the strike they began on April 1, 2021. Their union, the UMWA, has offered to send them back to work in hopes of finally spurring some movement from the recalcitrant coal bosses at Warrior Met. Throughout the making of *Fight Like Hell*, the miners have never been far from my mind. When I showed up on the picket line on April 10, 2021, with a box of Krispy Kremes and a vague hope that someone might tell me what was going on, I hadn't the faintest idea of how important this strike—and the people behind it—would become to me, or to this book. I expected that first filed story to be followed by a deluge of others, analyzing the history and context and conditions behind the strike. Instead, there were crickets.

At first, I was puzzled by the lack of media attention given to the strike; fresh off covering the Amazon campaign in Bessemer, I'd grown accustomed to being in the midst of a big, nationwide story and had fully expected the Warrior Met strike to achieve similar status. When it didn't, the miners and I were both left asking why. My hypothesis is that the nature of their industry (in an age of rapidly intensifying climate crisis, coal is not exactly popular) and assumptions around who they are and what they believe made them unsympathetic protagonists. Coal miners from rural Alabama, many of whom identified as Christians and conservatives, were a hard sell to progressives, while a story about a proudly unionized, multiracial group of workers standing up to the boss was a no-go for the Republican audience. In fairness, I probably wouldn't have cared as much as I do if I hadn't been able to spend time with the flesh-and-blood workers leading the strike, and found common ground between our two worlds.

I was initially drawn in after learning of the injustices being perpetrated against these workers in a part of the Deep South where a tradition of militant labor action runs as far down as the mines themselves. I stuck around because of the workers themselves, and specifically, the women. They started out as sources, but as the months crawled by, they became my friends. Haeden, Cheri, Connie—coal miners' wives, daughters, and granddaughters who were going through hell, but determined to make the best of it, just as their foremothers had done. We were about the same age, and though our lives looked very different, our kinship was genuine.

I felt it every time I went down to Alabama to check up on the strike. With its grand pine trees, tiny mom-and-mom shops, and long, lonesome roads, Brookwood felt a little bit like home, and so did the people I found there. The men, with their beards and Realtree camo pants and gruff affect, reminded me of my dad; the women, who were resourceful, strong-willed, and sweet until you gave them a reason not to be (and then God help you) may as well have been my aunts or sisters. I couldn't imagine how difficult it was spending all those months on the picket line, counting pennies and worrying about company violence, but I could at least be there to help amplify their message.

Journalists are given the power to decide whose stories are told and whose are forgotten, and that responsibility carries heavy consequences. For whatever reason, the coal miners of Brookwood were among the latter, joining untold numbers of others throughout history and right this moment, the ones whose struggles remain shrouded in shadows. That makes them no less important or impactful than the ones who do grab headlines, and for the Warrior Met strikers, the lack of attention was just one more hurdle to overcome. They held the line anyway. They know that the media can be helpful, and public support is even better, but solidarity is the sturdiest weapon of all.

For all those reasons, their strike was the only ongoing labor struggle I allowed myself to really dig into for most of 2021 to 2023. I was also worried that if I let my attention wander any further, this book might never get written. Even on a bad day, there was news in the labor world—a new industry was organizing, another group of Teamsters was on strike, Twitter was dragging a newly outed union-buster to hell. As the year went on, that temptation only intensified as workers around the country began to stir (and deadlines be damned, I couldn't help but follow along).

The year 2021 will be remembered as a historic one for many reasons, some good, most bad, but as far as I was concerned, the biggest story of the year was the wave of protests, walkouts, resignations, and strikes that swept the nation. The toxic slurry of social, political, and economic inequities, deadly police violence, far-right terrorism, and soul-crushing capitalist brutality that has defined American life for so many got a deadly boost from the COVID-19 pandemic. The urgency and uncertainty of the moment threw an even harsher spotlight on the desperate realities of work in this country—especially for those who didn't have the option to stay home.

Delivery drivers, retail workers, warehouse workers, sanitation workers, and agricultural workers were among the millions thrust onto the front lines of a terrifying plague, and were certainly some of the worst protected. "Those people, not only do they not have a safety net, but no matter what is going on, they have to continue to put their bodies and lives on the line," Veena Dubal, a law professor at the University of California, Hastings, and a fierce advocate for marginalized workers, told me. "There's some great tragic irony that it's these 'essential workers' who are the most dispossessed: the people who are carved out of all [labor] protections, the people who do the most dangerous work, and the people whose life spans are the shortest as a result."

When the arrival of COVID-19 vaccines lessened the immediate threat of the pandemic, bosses saw no reason to keep pretending they valued their employees' role in keeping the country running (if they'd ever bothered to do so in the first place) or to raise their stagnating wages. As this all played out, the government continued to bolster the fortunes of the rich and fail everyone else. The American working class was being brought to its breaking point, and something had to give. "People are angry and fed up," Dubal told me. "I don't think that we can discount the role that those emotions play in the uprisings that we've seen among workers in this country [in 2021]."

As the year went on, the workers communicated that fact in no uncertain terms. Thousands took advantage of a tight labor market to walk away from low-paid, high-risk jobs. They marched on bad bosses, struck at callous, crooked corporations, and used their collective power to push back against a ruthless system that expected them to cheerfully accept exploitation with a smile. Some dubbed it "the Great Resignation," others insisted it was a slow-burning general strike. "After years of being underserved and taken for granted—& doubly so during the pandemic—workers are starting to authorize strikes across the country," Rep. Alexandria Ocasio-Cortez observed on Twitter. "Good."

Either way, it happened everywhere, even in places one might not expect. In Alabama, after the Amazon workers in Bessemer lost their union vote at the end of March, they won an appeal against the company's flagrant union-busting, and immediately began making plans to rerun the election. RWDSU organizer Michael "Big Mike" Foster celebrated in a tweet—"Here we go again, but this time with a win!"—and immediately got back to work. Farther north, another group of Amazon workers in Staten Island launched their own organizing campaign, the Amazon Labor Union. Led by Chris Smalls, a former Amazon worker who'd been fired for protesting the company's dearth of COVID-19 safety precautions, the workers filed for an NLRB election on October 25, 2021. "This is monumental for the workers," Smalls told Reuters. "This is proof that you can stand up, fight back and organize your workplace."

As October rolled around, so did a fresh wave of labor actions. In a pleasant surprise to those who regularly cover these conflicts, the mainstream media finally sat up and took notice, and "Striketober"—a tagline initially dreamed up in a labor group DM—was born. It was hard not to get wrapped up in the excitement of seeing more than one thousand Nabisco workers and fourteen hundred Kellogg's workers walk out for higher wages and weekends off, just before ten thousand John Deere workers hit the picket lines over a discriminatory two-tiered employment system, while at the same time sixty thousand IATSE members in Hollywood were threatening to strike. It was thrilling to watch from the sidelines, and those actually involved in these struggles found themselves becoming a part of something bigger, too. "So many people feared for their lives in a really immediate way over the last year," Dubal explained. "What emerged from that is fury and outrage—and outrage and fury and love are the roots of organizing and solidarity."

As Striketober bled into Strikesgiving, three thousand grad student workers at Columbia University hit the bricks over paltry wages from their Ivy League employers, while thirty-two thousand healthcare workers at Kaiser Permanente threatened a gargantuan strike over deep pay cuts. New York City taxi drivers held a fifteen-day hunger strike, and won millions in debt relief. Starbucks workers in

Buffalo, New York, bravely faced down the company's transparent attempts to bust their union, and McDonald's workers in ten cities held a one-day strike to protest rampant sexual harassment in their workplaces. It wasn't all new action, either; that October also saw more than seven hundred nurses at Saint Vincent Hospital in Worcester, Massachusetts, reach their seventh month on strike. They'd walked out over poor working conditions and unsafe staffing levels, and were part of a much bigger fight within the health-care sector that impacts workers as well as patients. "It is not lost on us how important it is for us to hold our ground," striking nurse Marie Ritacco told NBC News. "We are not going to back down." (After nearly ten months they finally won, ratifying a new contract on January 3, 2022.)

The Warrior Met coal miners had hit the picket lines less than a month after the Saint Vincent nurses, and mere days after Amazon workers in Bessemer heard the unhappy results of their union election. Miners showed up to an Amazon rally to show their solidarity, but stayed busy fighting their own battle just a few miles down the road in Brookwood. Out on an unfair labor practices strike against a company that seemed hell-bent on starving them out instead of negotiating a decent contract, the miners faced an uphill climb, but it was nothing the UMWA hadn't dealt with before. As you've already read in this book, miners are tough, resourceful, and stubborn as hell. We didn't even get into the Battle of Blair Mountain, the union's epic fifteen-month strike against Massey Coal in 1985, or the role the fearless miner's wife and expert saboteur Sarah "Ma" Blizzard played in the brutal 1912 Paint Creek–Cabin Creek strike, but trust me—you wouldn't want to find yourself on a union miner's bad side.

Warrior Met's executives apparently missed that day in history class, though, and went to war. Things quickly turned ugly, with tensions flaring each time the state police appeared to escort a bus full of scabs into the mines. Company employees have been caught on video driving their trucks into the picket lines; multiple strikers have been sent to the hospital, and some are still feeling the physical effects of their injuries. "I'm not going to give up, because that's what they want," striking miner Greg Pilkerton told me in an interview for the *Nation*. In June, he and his wife, Amy, were both struck and injured by vehicles driven by company men. "My dad and them picketed back in the '80s, and it was a whole lot worse than what is going on now. I'm not going to, but if I was to give up this spot, my dad would probably come back to haunt me."

As the state's craven Republican politicians sat by and local law enforcement made it clear whose side they were on, a group of miners' spouses and retirees sprang into action to support their loved ones on the line. They quickly built a mutual aid network that distributed food and hygiene items, and organized holiday events to bring a little joy to the next generation. "We're not just going to stand there silent on the sidelines and be at home with the kids in the kitchen," Haeden Wright, a high school teacher and president of the UMWA Auxiliary in Brookwood, whose husband, Braxton, was on strike, told me in April 2021. "The company needs to know that when a man works for Warrior Met, the entire family signs that contract. And women can be a whole lot more vicious when you attack our families than men can."

It is an uncomfortable feeling to be closing out this book without recording the end to the strike—and, ideally, celebrating their victory. It feels unfinished, literally as well as metaphorically, especially after having spent so much time immersed in labor's past, excavating its wins (and losses, and stalemates) and familiarizing myself with so many of its unheralded and unsung leaders. No author aims for obsolescence, but I dearly hope that the 2021 to 2023 Warrior Met strike concludes before this book reaches your hands, and that the workers and their families who fought so hard for two years and counting are already enjoying the fruits of their shiny new union contract as you read it. Like so many workers before them, they deserve at least that much, and really, so much more.

But that's also kind of the point of all this, isn't it? This history does not stop just because one strike ends, or one campaign wraps up, or one stressed-out writer needs to hit her deadline. There is always another fight, a new contract, a fresh adversary. There is always another struggle to join, and another picket line to walk. Labor's cause is eternal, and its work is never done. Collective working-class power was behind every stride forward this country has made, grudgingly or otherwise, and will continue to be the animating force behind any true progress. Once you've committed to the idea of building a better world, you can't clock out of the fight for justice.

My hope for this book is that it will educate a new generation of workers on their rights, their history, and the sacrifices that so many people have made to get us to even this imperfect point.

And even more than that, I hope that the stories and characters in *Fight Like Hell* inspire readers—inspire *you*—to take action if you feel that those rights are being trampled on by powerful politicians, corporate titans, or just a standard-issue bad boss. If others can do it—and as these past few hundred pages have shown, they very often have—anyone can. *You* can. If you've got a few friends ready to fight like hell right along with you, anything is possible.

Sí, se puede!

ENDNOTES

FOREWORD

xi *I remember clicking:* Kim Kelly, "Unions Aren't as Complicated as You Might Think," Teen Vogue, March 12, 2018, https://www.teenvogue.com/story/what-a-labor-union-is-and-how-it-works.

PROLOGUE

xix *"If it is meant to be":* Kim Kelly, "An Unholy Union," *Vox*, March 15, 2021, https://www.vox.com/the-highlight/22320009/amazon-bessemer-union-rwdsu-alabama.

xxviii *"What is a labour victory?":* Judith Anderson, "Elizabeth Gurley Flynn." In *Outspoken Women: Speeches by American Women Reformers, 1635–1935*, ed. Judith Anderson (Dubuque, IA: Kendall/Hunt, 1984).

CHAPTER 1: THE TRAILBLAZERS

1 *"We must have money":* William Moran, *The Belles of New England: The Women of the Textile Mills and the Families Whose Wealth They Wove* (New York: St. Martin's Press, 2002), 35.

2n1 *"Man must be pleased":* Coventry Patmore, Patricia Aske, and Ian Anstruther, *The Angel in the House* (London: Haggerston Press with Boston College, 1998).

2n2 *During the Victorian:* Susan M. Cruea, "Changing Ideals of Womanhood During the Nineteenth-Century Woman Movement," General Studies Writing Faculty Publications, 1, (2005) https://scholarworks.bgsu.edu/gsw_pub/1.

3 *102 young women:* Joey La Neve DeFrancesco, "Pawtucket, America's First Factory Strike," *Jacobin*, June 6, 2018, https://jacobinmag.com/2018/06/factory-workers-strike-textile-mill-women.

4n1 *eight local textile mills:* John Larrabee, "Slater Mill Exhibit Recalls the 'Mother of All Strikes,'" *Sun Chronicle*, May 22, 2014, https://www.thesunchronicle.com/devices/features/stories/slater-mill-exhibit-recalls-the-mother-of-all-strikes/article_68f6d792-bc36-5faf-bcfe-b4f0022c81cf.html.

4n2 *Joined by several hundred:* Ibid.

4n3 *the women blockaded the mills':* DeFrancesco, "Pawtucket, America's First Factory Strike."

4n4 *"tumultuous crowd":* "Riots at Pawtucket," *Rhode Island American* (Providence, Rhode Island), XVI, no. 70, June 1, 825: [3]–p4.

4n5 *the negotiation table:* Ibid.

5 *Slater's child laborers:* Ibid.

6n1 *"dark Satanic mills":* "Pastures Green and Dark Satanic Mills: The British Passion for Landscape," Princeton University Art Museum, 2021, https://artmuseum.princeton.edu/art/exhibitions/1758//.

6n2 *to be paid for their labor:* "Factory Girls' Association," *Encyclopedia.com*, 2019, https://www.encyclopedia.com/history/encyclopedias-almanacs-transcripts-and-maps/factory-girls-association//.

7n1 *Accidents were common:* "The Role of Women in the Industrial Revolution," Tsongas Industrial History Center at UMass Lowell, 2021, https://www.uml.edu/tsongas/barilla-taylor/women-industrial-revolution.aspx//.

7n2 *Brown lung disease:* Janet Greenlees. "Workplace Health and Gender among Cotton Workers in America and Britain, c. 1880s–1940s," *International Review of Social History* 61, no. 3 (2016): 459–85, https://doi.org/10.1017/S0020859016000493.

7n3 *Sarah Bagley:* Lowell National Historical Park, Massachusetts, April 27, 2021, https://www.nps.gov/lowe/learn/historyculture/sarah-bagley.htm//.

8n1 *"The Pleasures of Factory Work":* Lowell National Historical Park, Massachusetts.

8n2 *the Lowell Female Labor Reform Association:* Lowell National Historical Park, Massachusetts.

8n3 *In 1834, mill managers:* Lowell National Historical Park, Massachusetts, "Labor Reform: Early Strikes," National Parks Service, U.S. Department of the Interior, accessed November 16, 2021, https://www.nps.gov/lowe/learn/historyculture/earlystrikes.htm.

9 *"There are hundreds of young females":* Moran, *The Belles of New England*, 43.

10n1 *LFLRA: New England Historical Society*, "Sarah Bagley Avenges the New England Mill Girls," 2021, https://www.newenglandhistoricalsociety.com/sarah-bagley-avenges-new-england-mill-girls/.

10n2 *"As he is merely a corporation machine":* Ibid.

10n3 *congratulated voters:* William Moran, *The Belles of New England*, 87.

10n4 *"cosigning William Schouler":* Ibid.

10n5 Voice of Industry: "The Voice of Industry," http://www.industrialrevolution.org/complete-issues.html.

11n1 *Bagley raged in print: New England Historical Society*, "Sarah Bagley Avenges."

11n2 *"The whip":* Moran, *The Belles of New England*, 35.

11n3 *Bagley's fight for social justice:* Erin Arnesen, *The Human Tradition in American Labor History* (New York, Rowman & Littlefield, 2004).
11n4 *one detail:* Arnesen, *The Human Tradition in American Labor History.*
12n1 *"Are we torn from our friends and kindred":* Moran, *The Belles of New England*, 24.
12n2 *"When I've thought about what soil":* Lucy Larcom, *An Idyl of Work (1875)* (Montana: Kessinger Publishing, 2008), 135.
12n3 *these workers had very few outlets to protest their mistreatment*: Ken Lawrence, "Mississippi's First Labour Union," libcom.org, 2016, https://libcom.org/history/mississippis-first-labour-union-ken-lawrence.
13 *W. E. B. Du Bois did in his book:* W. E. B. Du Bois, *Black Reconstruction in America*, (New York: Simon & Schuster, 1995), 13.
14 *As their petition read:* "Laundry Workers' Strike: Black Laundry Workers in Jackson, Mississippi, Demand Living Wages in 1866," New York Historical Society, 2021, https://wams.nyhistory.org/a-nation-divided/reconstruction/laundry-workers-strike/.
15n1 *Throughout the Reconstruction Era of 1865 to 1877:* Tera W. Hunter, *To 'Joy My Freedom: Southern Black Women's Lives and Labors After the Civil War* (Cambridge: Harvard University Press, 1998), 76.
15n2 *The Great Railroad Strike of 1877:* Joseph Adamczyk, "Great Railroad Strike of 1877," *Britannica*, September 5, 2014, https://www.britannica.com/topic/Great-Railroad-Strike-of-1877.
15n3 *protest their low wages:* Philip S. Foner and Ronald L. Lewis, *The Black Worker, Volume II: The Black Worker During the Era of the National Labor Union* (Philadelphia: Temple University Press, 1978).
16n1 *the strikers:* Ibid.
16n2 *the Port of Galveston:* "Emigration, Immigration, and Migration," University of Texas at San Antonio, October 11, 2021, https://libguides.utsa.edu/c.php?g=515536&p=5730362.
16n3 *Chinese workers:* John Jung, "Washing Clothes Before Chinese (B.C.)," *Chinese Laundries*, March 31, 2014, https://chineselaundry.wordpress.com/2014/03/31/washing-clothes-before-chinese-b-c/.
16n4 *"At these laundries, all the women talked at once":* Foner and Lewis, *The Black Worker, Volume II.*
17n1 *a campaign:* Donna Patricia Ward, "Former Slaves Went on Strike in 1881 Weeks Before a World's Fair in Atlanta," History Collection, November 18, 2018, https://historycollection.com/former-slaves-went-on-strike-in-1881-weeks-before-a-worlds-fair-in-atlanta/.
17n2 *the New South:* Shereen Marisol Meraji, "Balls and Strikes," NPR, September 2, 2020, https://www.npr.org/transcripts/908305393.
17n3 *happy workforce:* Rosalind Bentley, "Black Woman Magic: The Atlanta Laundry Workers' Strike of 1881," *Atlanta Journal-Constitution*, Febru-

ary 11, 2019, https://www.ajc.com/news/black-woman-magic-the-atlanta-laundry-workers-strike-1881/FvNH0PZLejzsq4VYULejmN/.

17n4 *Black Atlantans:* Ward, "Former Slaves Went on Strike."

17n5 *the right to vote:* Olivia B. Waxman, "When Did Black Women Get the Right to Vote? Suffrage History," Time, August 17, 2020, https://time.com/5876456/black-women-right-to-vote/.

17n6 *Atlanta's laundresses:* "Atlanta's Washerwomen Strike," AFL-CIO, 2021, https://aflcio.org/about/history/labor-history-events/atlanta-washerwomen-strike.

18n1 *Summer Hill:* Sean Richard Keenan, "GSU Researcher Takes Deep Dive into Summerhill's Fascinating, Turbulent History," *Curbed*, June 27, 2019, https://atlanta.curbed.com/2019/6/27/18761209/gsu-historian-deep-dive-georgia-avenue-summerhill.

18n2 *daily meetings:* Meraji, "Balls and Strikes."

18n3 *National Hotel:* "National Hotel," Atlanta History Center, 2009, https://album.atlantahistorycenter.com/digital/collection/athpc/id/741/.

18n4 *"The washerwomen strike": Atlanta Constitution*, July-August 1881, from Tera W. Hunter, "African-American Women Workers' Protest in the New South," *OAH Magazine of History* 13 (Summer 1999), http://www.oah.org/pubs/magazine/gilded/hunter.html.

19n1 *$20 fine:* Hunter, *To 'Joy My Freedom*, 90.

19n2 *to pay the fees:* "Atlanta's Washerwomen Strike," AFL-CIO, 2021, https://aflcio.org/about/history/labor-history-events/atlanta-washerwomen-strike.

CHAPTER 2: THE GARMENT WORKERS

21 *Child labor:* "Child Labor in U.S. History," The University of Iowa Labor Center, 2021, https://laborcenter.uiowa.edu/special-projects/child-labor-public-education-project/about-child-labor/child-labor-us-history.

22 *"This is the place":* Dickens, Charles. *American Notes for General Circulation*. London, Chapman and Hall, 1850. Pdf. https://www.loc.gov/item/01026779/.

24n1 *"The worker must have bread":* Minerva Brooks, "Rose Schneiderman in Ohio," *Life and Labor*, (September 1912): 288.

24n2 *Another speech she gave in 1911:* Leon Stein, *The Triangle Fire* (New York: Carroll & Graf, 1962), 144–45.

25 *I am a working girl:* "Clara Lemlich and the Uprising of the 20,000," PBS, 2021.

26 *the "needle trades":* Tony Michels, "Uprising of 20,000 (1909)," *Shalvi/Hyman Encyclopedia of Jewish Women*: December 31, 1999, Jewish Women's Archive, https://jwa.org/encyclopedia/article/uprising-of-20000-1909.

28 *a United Press reporter:* "Eyewitness at the Triangle by William Shepherd," Remembering the 1911 Triangle Factory Fire, Cornell University, Kheel Center, 2018, https://trianglefire.ilr.cornell.edu/primary/testimonials/ootss_WilliamShepherd.html.

29 roughly $6 for each lost life: "Triangle Shirtwaist Fire: AFL-CIO," AFL-CIO, accessed January 7, 2022, https://aflcio.org/about/history/labor-history-events/triangle-shirtwaist-fire.

30 The Living Century: Barbra Streisand, *The Living Century: Rose Freedman* (United States: The Public Broadcasting Service, 2001).

31n1 *Rose died one year:* Douglas Martin, "Rose Freedman, Last Survivor of Triangle Fire, Dies at 107," *New York Times*, February 17, 2001, https://www.nytimes.com/2001/02/17/nyregion/rose-freedman-last-survivor-of-triangle-fire-dies-at-107.html.

31n2 *"I had to do something":* "Her Life: The Woman behind the New Deal." Frances Perkins Center, 2014, https://francesperkinscenter.org/life-new/.

31n3 *"People had just begun":* Ibid.

33n1 *the safe passage:* "Frances Perkins," FDR Presidential Library & Museum, accessed November 18, 2021, https://www.fdrlibrary.org/perkins.

33n2 *"Most of man's problems":* "Her Life: The Woman behind the New Deal." Frances Perkins Center, 2014, https://francesperkinscenter.org/life-new/.

33n3 *a queer feminist:* Loren King, "Maine's Frances Perkins Center Gives FDR's New Deal Architect Her Due," *Boston Spirit*, May 11, 2021, https://bostonspiritmagazine.com/2021/05/maines-frances-perkins-center-gives-fdrs-new-deal-architect-her-due/.

33n4 *"I came to Washington to work for God":* "Hall of Honor Inductee: Frances M. Perkins," U.S. Department of Labor, 2021, https://www.dol.gov/general/aboutdol/hallofhonor/1989.

34n1 *"The white shops":* Judy Yung, Unbound Feet: A Social History of Chinese Women in San Francisco (Berkeley: Univ. of California Press, 2000).

34n2 *"We have tried repeatedly":* Ibid.

35n1 *"You have to start":* Ibid.

35n2 *"In my opinion":* Ibid.

36n1 *Sylvia M. Trevino:* "Sylvia M. Trevino 1947–2020," *Express-News*, January 15, 2020, https://www.legacy.com/us/obituaries/sanantonio/name/sylvia-trevino-obituary?id=9005817.

36n2 *the Farah workers:* Laurie Coyle, Gail Hershatter, and Emily Honig, "Women at Farah: An Unfinished Story," in *A Needle, A Bobbin, A Strike: Women Needleworkers, in America*, eds. Susan Davidson and Joan Jensen (Philadelphia: Temple University Press), 227–277.

36n3 *I believe in fighting:* Coyle, "Women at Farah: An Unfinished Story," 337.

37 The People vs. Willie Farah *The People vs. Willie Farah*: Texas Archive of the Moving Image, 1973, https://texasarchive.org/2011_02871.

38n1 *"I'm working because I need the money":* Philip Shabecoff, "Farah Strike Has Become War of Attrition," *New York Times*, June 16, 1973, https://www.nytimes.com/1973/06/16/archives/farah-strike-has-become-war-of-attriton-the-worst-part.html.

38n2 *"For years I wouldn't":* Emily Honig, "Women at Farah Revisited: Political Mobilization and Its Aftermath among Chicana Workers in El Paso, Texas, 1972-1992," *Feminist Studies* 22, no. 2 (1996): 425–52, https://doi.org/10.2307/3178422.

39n1 *Willie Farah's incendiary racist statements:* Coyle, "Women at Farah: An Unfinished Story," 227–277.

39n2 *"I felt that I was inferior":* Ibid., 260.

40 *the exploitation of immigrant workers from Latin America and Asia:* Janna Shadduck-Herández, Zacil Pech, Mar Martinez, and Marissa Nuncio, *Dirty Threads, Dangerous Factories: Health and Safety in Los Angeles' Fashion Industry* (Los Angeles: UCLA Labor Center, 2016).

41 *wage violations in 85 percent of the California garment factories:* Ludwig Hurtado, "Garment Workers, Paid by the Piece, Say They'll Keep Fighting to Change the System," *NBC News,* September 17, 2020, https://www.nbcnews.com/news/latino/garment-workers-paid-piece-say-they-ll-keep-fighting-change-n1237810.

42 *the Garment Worker Center:* Nathalia Orquera, "SB62: Advocating for California's Garment Workers," *Fashion Revolution USA*, 2020, https://www.fashionrevolution.org/advocating-for-californias-garment-workers/#:~:text=U.S.%2520clothing%2520factories%2520employ%2520about,less%2520than%252025%252C000%2520garment%2520workers.

CHAPTER 3: THE MILL WORKERS

43n1 *"They'll have to kill me":* Mary E. Frederickson, "Wiggins, Ella May," NCpedia, 1996, https://www.ncpedia.org/biography/wiggins-ella.

43n2 *The strikes' original organizers:* Matilda Rabinowitz, *Immigrant Girl, Radical Woman: A Memoir from the Early Twentieth Century* (Ithaca, NY: ILR Press, 2017).

45n1 *"a day without parallel":* Moran, *The Belles of New England*, 213.

45n2 *"We resolutely set out to combat these notions":* Ibid., 194

46n1 *"One policeman":* Robert Forrant and Jurg K. Siegenthaler, *The Great Lawrence Textile Strike of 1912: New Scholarship on the Bread & Roses Strike* (London: Routledge, Taylor & Francis, 2017).

46n2 *"A group of enraged Italian women":* Spicuzza, Mary, "Metroactive Features: Women's History Month: Social Change," MetroActive Features, March 1999, http://www.metroactive.com/papers/cruz/03.10.99/women3-9910.html.

46n3 *"They say that she":* Ibid.

47 *"What an example":* Rabinowitz, *Immigrant Girl.*

48n1 *Ola Delight Smith:* "Ola Delight Smith," Wikipedia, September 13, 2021, https://en.wikipedia.org/wiki/Ola_Delight_Smith.

48n2 *Fulton Bag and Cotton Mill Company:* Nancy A. Hewitt and Suzanne Lebsock, *Visible Women: New Essays on American Activism* (Champaign: University of Illinois Press, 1993), 182–84.

48n3 *bouncing around the South before settling in Atlanta:* Ibid., 169–171.
49n1 *two hundred white women and girls:* "Negro Help Causes a Strike: Six Hundred White Operatives Leave Work in Atlanta Cotton Mills—Factory Forced to Shut Down," *New York Times,* August 5, 1897, https://www.nytimes.com/1897/08/05/archives/negro-help-causes-a-strike-six-hundred-white-operatives-leave-work.html.
49n2 *a big fan of surveillance:* Michelle Haberland, "Review," *International Labor and Working-Class History* 64 (2003): 214–16, http://www.jstor.org/stable/27672905.
49n3 *"unspeakable" conditions: Evening Herald,* "Strike Waged in Georgia Factory," Georgia Tech Archives, August 15, 1914, https://exhibit-archive.library.gatech.edu/fulton_bag/ms004/images/ms004-116.pdf .
49n4 *forcing Black workers to evict white families:* Greta De Jong, "Review of *Contesting the New South Order: The 1914–1915 Strike at Atlanta's Fulton Mills,*" *Journal of Interdisciplinary History* 33, no. 3 (2003): 502–3, https://muse.jhu.edu/article/39317.
50n1 *the conflict spilled over into the streets: Evening Herald,* "Strike Waged in Georgia Factory."
50n2 *nine hundred workers:* Ibid.
50n3 *evicted eighty-five striking families:* Ibid.
50n4 *Smith was new to the textile industry:* Hewitt and Lebsock, *Visible Women, 182–84.*
51n1 *"Thugs and spotters":* Ibid.
51n2 *The union had made other glaring missteps:* Haberland, *International Labor and Working-Class History.*
51n3 *engaging in divisive racist rhetoric:* De Jong, "Review of *Contesting the New South Order.*"
51n4 *'cast my bread':* Hewitt and Lebsock, *Visible Women.*
52n1 *"paralyzed giant":* Robert P. Ingalls, "Antiradical Violence in Birmingham During the 1930s," *The Journal of Southern History* 47, no. 4 (1981): 521–44, https://doi.org/10.2307/2207401.
52n2 *the national textile industry had begun its decline:* Jeremy Brecher, "The US National Textile Workers' Strike, 1934," libcom.org, September 4, 2013, https://libcom.org/history/us-national-textile-workers-strike-1934-jeremy-brecher#footnote4_cgi20k7.
52n3 *National Recovery Administration (NRA):* The Editors of *Encyclopedia Britannica,* "National Recovery Administration," Britannica, July 20, 1998, https://www.britannica.com/topic/National-Recovery-Administration.
53 *"A Mill Mother's Lament":* Pete Seeger, "Mill Mother's Lament," YouTube, June 23, 2015, https://www.youtube.com/watch?v=jlaO0AsteD4.
54n1 *"They'll have to kill me to make me give up the union":* Nicholas Graham, "This Month in North Carolina History," UNC University Libraries, 2004, https://web.archive.org/web/20090531012624/http://www.lib.unc.edu/ncc/ref/nchistory/jun2004/.

54n2 *The 1934 textile strike:* John A. Salmond, "'The Burlington Dynamite Plot': The 1934 Textile Strike and Its Aftermath in Burlington, North Carolina," *North Carolina Historical Review* 75, no. 4 (1998): 398–434, http://www.jstor.org/stable/23522092.

54n3 *"flying squadrons":* George W. Troxler, "Flying Squadrons," NCPEDIA, 2006, https://www.ncpedia.org/flying-squadrons.

55n1 *Fort McPherson:* Eugene Talmadge, "Martial Law in Georgia," *Georgia Journeys*, accessed November 12, 2021, https://georgiajourneys.kennesaw.edu/items/show/419.

55n2 *Civil War–era army base:* Bryant Simon, " General Textile Strike," in *South Carolina Encyclopedia* (Columbia, SC: University of South Carolina, Institute for Southern Studies, 2016).

55n3 *The general strike of 1934:* Kenneth Rogers, "General Textile Strike of 1934," Digital Library of Georgia, 2021, https://dlg.usg.edu/record/geh_rogers_1119.

CHAPTER 4: THE REVOLUTIONARIES

57 *"The time will come":* Henry David, The History of the Haymarket Affair: A Study in the American Social-Revolutionary and Labor Movements (New York: Russell & Russell, 1964).

62n1 *"A very large number of police":* Paul Avrich, *The Haymarket Tragedy* (Princeton, NJ: Princeton University Press, 2020), 62.

62n2 *"The time will come . . .":* Ibid.

62n3 *"red-mouthed anarchist":* Jacqueline Jones, *Goddess of Anarchy: The Life and Times of Lucy Parsons, American Radical* (New York: Basic Books, 2017).

64 *"the public have no right":* Ibid.

66 *"the father of Harlem radicalism":* Jeffrey Babcock Perry, *Hubert Harrison: The Voice of Harlem Radicalism, 1883–1918*, (New York: Columbia University Press, 2009).

67n1 *"[Industrial unionism]":* Peter Cole, "Benjamin Harrison Fletcher (1890–1949)," BlackPast, July 27, 2020, https://www.blackpast.org/african-american-history/fletcher-benjamin-harrison-1890-1949/.

67n2 *"replete with gross indifference":* Paul Heideman, *Class Struggle and the Color Line: American Socialism and the Race Question, 1900-1930* (Chicago: Haymarket Books, 2018.)

67n3 *"New Negro Movement":* Jeffrey Babcock Perry, *Hubert Harrison: The Voice of Harlem Radicalism, 1883–1918*, (New York: Columbia University Press, 2009).

69n1 *"very largely to put":* "September 4–10: The Kornilov Affair," World Socialist Web Site, September 4, 2017, https://www.wsws.org/en/articles/2017/09/04/twrr-j01.html.

69n2 *"The judge has been using":* Ibid.

71 *"She did most of it"*: R. S. Neale, "Working-Class Women and Women's Suffrage," *Labour History*, no. 12 (1967): 16–34, https://doi.org/10.2307/27507859.
72 *"I started in this fight"*: Ibid.
73n1 Lara Vapnek, *Elizabeth Gurley Flynn: Modern American Revolutionary*, (New York: Avalon Publishing, 2015), 96.
73n2 *"I'm going to prison smiling"*: Ibid.
74 *"personal danger and hardships"*: Ibid.

CHAPTER 5: THE MINERS

79n1 *"at just seven years old"*: Anne Keegan, "Ida Mae—She Preferred 'Coal Dust to a Powder Puff,'" *Chicago Tribune*, May 7, 1980.
79n2 *"I prefer coal dust"*: Suzanne E. Tallichet, *Daughters of the Mountain: Women Coal Miners in Central Appalachia* (Philadelphia, PA: University of Pennsylvania Press, 2006).
80n1 *federal mine inspectors: St. Louis Post-Dispatch*: February 2, 1934, 9.
80n2 *Stull had been quietly working:* Carletta Savage, "Re-Gendering Coal: Female Miners and Male Supervisors," *Appalachian Journal* 27, no. 3 (2000): 232–48, http://www.jstor.org/stable/41057390.
80n3 *she'd later explain:* Suzanne E. Tallichet, *Daughters of the Mountain: Women Coal Miners in Central Appalachia* (Penn State University Press, 2006), 5.
80n4 *"I really stunk him up!"*: "Ida Mae—She Preferred 'Coal Dust to a Power Puff,'" *Chicago Tribune*, May 7, 1980, 5.
81n1 *"I could show that mine inspector"*: Ibid.
81n2 *"Any miner in the district"*: Ibid.
81n3 *"My face gets black"*: Keegan, "Ida Mae."
81n4 *In one of her last interviews:* Ibid.
81n5 *Ida Mae Stull died on April 23, 1980:* "Ida Mae Stull (1896–1980)—Find a Grave Memorial," Find a Grave, accessed November 18, 2021, https://www.findagrave.com/memorial/131896794/ida-mae-stull.
82n1 *1964 Civil Rights Act:* Civil Rights Act of 1964, P.L. 88-353, 78 Stat. 241 (1964).
82n2 *1967 Executive Order:* 11375 EO 11246 of Sept. 24, 1965, 30 FR 12319, 12935, 3 CFR, 1964–1965 Comp., p. 339.
82n3 *Diana Baldwin and Anita Cherry:* Judy Klemerud, "In Coal Mine No. 29, Two Women Work Alongside the Men," *New York Times*, May 18, 1974, 16.
82n4 *"The people who say a woman's place"*: "Textile Workers Seek Jobs in Mines," *United Mine Workers Journal*, May 15, 1973.
82n5 *refused to respond:* Dona G. Gearhart, "'Surely, a wench can choose her own work!' Women Coal Miners in Paonia, Colorado, 1976–1987," *UNLV Retrospective Theses & Dissertations*, 1995.
83n1 *"I had been watching a show on television"*: George Vecsey, "4 Women

Seek Jobs as Miners, And Man's World Is in Conflict," *New York Times*, September 9, 1972.

83n2 "We can make": Klemerud "In Coal Mine No. 29."

83n3 *Baldwin's daughter, Lori, revealed:* Mountain Eagle Staff, "Nation's First Female Miner Remembered," Comments, June 01, 2016, https://www.themountaineagle.com/articles/nations-first-female-miner-remembered/.

83n4 *spending two decades:* Ibid.

84n1 *"I was the first woman":* Ibid.

84n2 *nearly doubled:* Harold Wool, "Coal Industry Attracts New Workers," *Monthly Labor Review*, 1981.

84n3 *affirmative action:* Associated Press, "Coal Company Will Pay 78 Women Denied Jobs," *New York Times*, November 26, 1978, 50.

85n1 *Darla Baker told the Associated Press*: Associated Press "Women Coal Miners' Suit Breaks New Ground," *Nevada Daily Mail*, April 26, 1982, 5.

85n2 *eight other women:* Associated Press, "Woman Miners Seek Damages in Harassment Suit," *New York Times*, November 26, 1978, 50.

85n3 *Freeman heard him swear:* Leon Daniel, "Women Coal Miners Fight Sexual Harassment" United Press International, June 17, 1985.

85n4 *won a settlement:* Ibid.

86n1 *listed three Black women:* Savage, "Re-Gendering Coal."

86n2 *forced penal labor system:* "Convict Leasing," PBS, accessed November 18, 2021, https://www.pbs.org/tpt/slavery-by-another-name/themes/convict-leasing/.

87n1 *"in such places":* Jane Zimmerman, "The Penal Reform Movement in the South During the Progressive Era, 1890–1917," *The Journal of Southern History* 17, no. 4 (1951): 462–92, https://doi.org/10.2307/2954512.

87n2 *abolish the practice in 1896:* James B. Jones, "Convict Lease Wars," Tennessee Encyclopedia, Tennessee Historical Society, March 1, 2018, https://tennesseeencyclopedia.net/entries/convict-lease-wars/.

88n1 *did away with the practice in 1908:* "New Exhibit Examines the History of Convict Labor in Georgia," University Libraries, University of Georgia, September 11, 2019, https://www.libs.uga.edu/news/exhibit-examines-convict-labor-in-georgia.

88n2 *Cyrus Forman told:* "Slavery Documents from Southern Saltmakers Bring Light to Dark History," *Los Angeles Times*, April 16, 2020, https://www.latimes.com/entertainment-arts/story/2020-04-16/huntington-slavery-collection-west-virginia-salt-works.

88n3 *childhood working in the salt furnaces:* James Fallows, "The Past Is Never Past: Slave Labor in the West Virginia Salt Works," *Atlantic*, March 15, 2015, https://www.theatlantic.com/business/archive/2014/12/the-past-is-never-past-west-virginia-salt-works-edition/383493/.

88n4 *Kanawha Salines:* Louis T. Harlan, "Booker T. Washington's West Virginia Boyhood," *West Virginia History Journal* 32, no. 2 (January 1971): 63–85.

88n5 *"Though I was a mere child"*: Ibid.

88n6 *J.Q. Dickinson Salt-Works:* "Our History," J. Q. Dickinson Salt-Works, November 8, 2017, https://www.jqdsalt.com/timeline/.

88n7 *company's original headquarters:* "Slavery Documents from Southern Salt-makers Bring Light to Dark History," *Los Angeles Times*, April 16, 2020, https://www.latimes.com/entertainment-arts/story/2020-04-16/huntington-slavery-collection-west-virginia-salt-works.

90n1 *Jones reinvented herself:* Elliot J. Gorn, "The History of Mother Jones," *Mother Jones*, May/June 2001, https://www.motherjones.com/about/history/.

90n2 *self-proclaimed hell-raiser:* Harlan, "Booker T. Washington's West Virginia Boyhood."

90n3 *child labor:* Gorn, "The History of Mother Jones."

90n4 *did not discriminate:* "Mother Jones," AFL-CIO, accessed November 19, 2021, https://aflcio.org/about/history/labor-history-people/mother-jones.

90n5 *views shortsighted:* Gorn, "The History of Mother Jones."

90n6 *"mop and bucket":* Ibid.

90n7 *championed the cause of:* Bonnie Stepenoff, "Keeping It in the Family: Mother Jones and the Pennsylvania Silk Strike of 1900–1901," *Labor History* 38, no. 4 (1997): 432–49, https://doi.org/10.1080/00236649712331387214.

90n8 *silk mill workers:* Bonnie Stepenoff, "Child Labor in Pennsylvania's Silk Mills: Protest and Change, 1900–1910," *Pennsylvania History: A Journal of Mid-Atlantic Studies* 59, no. 2 (1992): 101–21, http://www.jstor.org/stable/27773524.

91n1 *three-week journey:* "Mother Jones."

91n2 *18 percent of American workers:* Madison Horne, "These Appalling Images Exposed Child Labor in America," History.com, April 26, 2018, https://www.history.com/news/child-labor-lewis-hine-photos.

91n3 *Jones herself once said:* Janet Raye, "Hellraisers Journal: Whereabouts & Doings of Mother Jones for November 1900, Part IV: Found with Silk Strikers of Wilkes-Barre & Carbondale, Pennsylvania," *Mother Jones*, December 20, 2020, https://weneverforget.org/hellraisers-journal-whereabouts-doings-of-mother-jones-for-november-1900-part-iv-found-with-silk-strikers-of-wilkes-barre-carbondale-pennsylvania/.

91n4 *became a target:* Dale Fetherling, *Mother Jones, The Miners' Angel*, (Carbondale, IL: Southern Illinois University Press, 2010).

92n1 *three months old:* Adam Hammond, "Ludlow Massacre Survivor Turns 104," KMGH, January 13, 2018, https://www.thedenverchannel.com/thenow/ludlow-massacre-survivor-turns-104.

92n2 *actively recruited workers:* Brigada R. Blasi, *High Country News*, February 1, 2021, https://www.hcn.org/issues/53.2/north-people-places-how-wyomings-black-coal-miners-shaped-their-own-history.

92n3 *In 1890:* Blasi, *High Country News.*

93 *age of nine:* Doug Linder, "William D. Haywood," accessed November 19, 2021, http://law2.umkc.edu/faculty/projects/ftrials/haywood/HAY_BHAY.HTM.

94 *Indigenous workers have:* William Ascarza, "Native Americans Mined Variety of Minerals Early On," *Arizona Daily Star*, May 20, 2013, https://tucson.com/news/local/native-americans-mined-variety-of-minerals-early-on/article_8d64025e-b0a7-5c5a-920d-b67f53073ef5.html.

95n1 *HoChunk, Mesquaki, and Sauk:* "Lead Mining in Southwestern Wisconsin," Wisconsin Historical Society, August 3, 2012, https://www.wisconsinhistory.org/Records/Article/CS408.

95n2 *controlled the lead mines:* Lucy Eldersveld Murphy, "Economy, Race, and Gender Along the Fox-Wisconsin and Rock Riverways, 1737–1832," (PhD diss., Northern Illinois University, 1996), University Microfilms International.

95n3 *established a permanent American military presence:* Sterling Knoche, "Lead Mining: Wisconsin, United States (19th C)," Anthropocene in Objects, June 8, 2016, https://anthropoceneobjects.net/portfolio/lead-mining-wisconsin-united-states-19th-c/.

95n4 *seven thousand years ago:* Jennifer Errick, "Exploring 70 Centuries of Mining History," National Parks Conservation Association, September 26, 2019, https://www.npca.org/articles/2309-exploring-70-centuries-of-mining-history.

95n5 *allegedly for fighting:* Keweenaw National Historical Park, Michigan, "Anna Klobuchar Clemenc," National Parks Service, U.S. Department of the Interior, March 13, 2019, https://www.nps.gov/kewe/anna-klobuchar-clemenc.htm.

96 *she replied:* Absolute Michigan, "Calumet's Big Annie," August 31, 2006, http://absolutemichigan.com/michigan/calumets-big-annie/.

97n1 *"Alex, tell your people":* Jonathan D. Rosenblum, *Copper Crucible: How the Arizona Miners' Strike of 1983 Recast Labor Management Relations in America* (Ithaca, NY: ILR Press, 1998).

97n2 *"one of the most remarkable":* F. Kadel, "No. 33, Paterson, NJ," *Coopers International Journal* 23, 1913, 319.

98 *"It was like the army had prisoners":* Jonathan D. Rosenblum, *Copper Crucible: How the Arizona Miners' Strike of 1983 Recast Labor-management Relations in America* (Ithaca, NY: ILR Press, 1998), 6.

99n1 *"I couldn't betray the other people":* Ibid.

99n2 *"This isn't going to be":* Jeremy Mouat, Review of *Copper and Class Struggle*, by Philip J. Mellinger and Jonathan D. Rosenblum, *Labour / Le Travail* 39 (1997): 277–84, https://doi.org/10.2307/25144118.

99n3 *"get rid of these broads"*: Ibid.

100n1 *sent in the National Guard* James M. Bailey, "Keeping People from Being Killed: Arizona Governor Bruce Babbitt, Public Safety, and the Phelps Dodge Copper Strike, 1983–1984," *Mining History Journal* 3 (1996): 3–14.

100n2 *"These women made the scabs'"*: Rosenblum, *Copper Crucible*.

101n1 *"I was motivated by"*: Barbara Kingsolver, *Holding the Line: Women in the Great Arizona Mine Strike of 1983* (Ithaca, NY: Cornell University Press, 2012), 136.

101n2 *"To these women"*: Ibid.

103n1 *"biracial"*: Henry M. McKiven, "United Mine Workers in Alabama," Encyclopedia of Alabama, October 12, 2010, http://encyclopediaofalabama.org/article/h-2948.

103n2 *struck against U.S. Steel:* "On This Day in Alabama History: Mine Workers Went on Strike," Alabama NewsCenter, July 8, 2018, https://alabamanewscenter.com/2018/07/08/day-alabama-history-july-8/.

103n3 *enforce strict segregation:* Jeremy Gray, "The Week in Birmingham History: Coal Mine Strike of 1908; Birmingham's Deadliest Plane Crash," AL.com, July 6, 2014, https://www.al.com/news/birmingham/2014/07/the_week_in_birmingham_history_4.html.

103n4 *1920 and 1921:* McKiven, "United Mine Workers in Alabama."

104n1 *a statement shortly after the decision:* "Alabama Judge Issues Unconstitutional Order at Warrior Met Strike," UMWA, October 28, 2021, https://umwa.org/news-media/press/alabama-judge-issues-unconstitutional-order-at-warrior-met-strike/.

104n2 *"We must stand"*: Kim Kelly, "The Miners Take Manhattan," *The Real News Network*, November 10, 2021, https://therealnews.com/the-miners-take-manhattan.

CHAPTER 6: THE HARVESTERS

105n1 *"We were not 'given'"*: Susan L. Marquis, *I Am Not a Tractor! How Florida Farmworkers Took on the Fast Food Giants and Won*. (Ithaca, NY: ILR Press, 2017).

105n2 *Today's agricultural worker:* "Agricultural Worker Demographics," National Center for Farmworker Health, April 2018, http://www.ncfh.org/agricultural-worker-demographics.html.

106 *sandalwoods in 1789:* HawaiiHistory.org, accessed November 22, 2021, http://www.hawaiihistory.org/index.cfm?fuseaction=ig.page&PageID=292&returntoname=Short+.

107n1 *actively recruited immigrants:* "Hawaii: Life in a Plantation Society," Library of Congress, accessed November 22, 2021, https://www.loc.gov/classroom-materials/immigration/japanese/hawaii-life-in-a-plantation-society/.

107n2 *"Keep a variety"*: Ronald T. Takaki, *A Larger Memory: A History of Our Diversity with Voices* (Boston: Little, Brown, 1998).

108n1 *"The sugar cane fields"*: Ibid.
108n2 *could be imprisoned:* "Hawaii: Life in a Plantation Society."
108n3 *took the Hilo Sugar Company to court in 1891:* Ibid.
108n4 *Katsu Goto:* Valentina Martinez, "Katsu Goto : Murder in Honoka'a," Ke Kalahea 2016, no. 4 (October 10), https://hilo.hawaii.edu/news/kekalahea/KG-Murder.
108n5 *a telephone pole:* Ibid.
109 *"Better to go to hell"*: Justin Akers Chacón, *Radicals in the Barrio: Magonistas, Socialists, Wobblies, and Communists in the Mexican American Working Class* (Chicago: Haymarket Books, 2018).
110n1 *the Filipino Piecemeal Sugar Strike of 1924:* Shoshi Parks, "The Not-So-Sweet Story of How Filipino Workers Tried to Take on Big Sugar in Hawaii," Timeline, June 1, 2018, https://timeline.com/filipino-workers-sugar-strike-fa58953e78e.
110n2 *Harry Lehua Kamoku would tell a friend: William J. Puette, The Hilo Massacre: Hawaii's Bloody Monday, August 1st, 1938* (Honolulu: University of Hawaii, Center for Labor Education & Research, 1988).
111n1 *two-year plan* ILWU Local I142, *1946 Sakada Filipinos and the ILWU* (Honolulu, HI: ILWU Local I142, 1996), http://thesakadaseries.com/images/1946_Sakadas.pdf.
111n2 *arrived to a hero's welcome* ILWU Local I142, *1946 Sakada Filipinos and the ILWU.*
111n3 *Thompson later recalled:* Harvey Schwartz, "Frank Thompson: Islands Organizer, 1944–1946," ILWU, accessed November 22, 2021, https://www.ilwu.org/frank-thompson-islands-organizer-1944-1946/.
111n4 *in stark detail* ILWU Local I142, *1946 Sakada Filipinos and the ILWU.*
112n1 *"perquisites"*: "Ah Quon McElrath, Hawaiian Strikes, Esp. 1946," Crossing East Archive, November 9, 2017, http://www.crossingeast.org/crossingeastarchive/2017/03/26/ah-quon-mcelrath-hawaiian-strikes-esp-1946/.
112n2 *soup kitchens:* Ibid.
112n3 *a shipment of rice:* Schwartz, "Frank Thompson: Islands Organizer."
112n4 *ILWU, later explained:* "Ah Quon McElrath, Hawaiian Strikes, Esp. 1946."
113n1 *elect labor-endorsed candidates:* ILWU Local I142, *1946 Sakada Filipinos and the ILWU.*
113n2 *1947 Pineapple Strike:* "Center for Labor Education and Research." Clear's elibrary, accessed November 22, 2021, https://www.hawaii.edu/uhwo/clear/home/e-library.html.
114n1 *Bracero Program:* Philip Martin, "Mexican Braceros and US Farm Workers," Wilson Center, July 10, 2020, https://www.wilsoncenter.org/article/mexican-braceros-and-us-farm-workers.
114n2 *U.S. farms and railroads:* Lawrence A. Cardoso, "Labor Emigration to the Southwest, 1916 to 1920: Mexican Attitudes and Policy," *Southwest-*

ern Historical Quarterly 79, no. 4 (1976): 400–416, http://www.jstor.org/stable/30238403.

114n3 *expanded on World War I–era efforts:* Robert Lazo, "Latinos and the AFL-CIO: The California Immigrant Workers Association as an Important New Development," *Berkeley Law*, January 1, 1991, https://lawcat.berkeley.edu/record/1113982?ln=en.

114n4 *1.8 million Latinos:* Diane Bernard, "The Time a President Deported 1 Million Mexican Americans for Supposedly Stealing U.S. Jobs," *Washington Post*, October 28, 2021, https://www.washingtonpost.com/news/retropolis/wp/2018/08/13/the-time-a-president-deported-1-million-mexican-americans-for-stealing-u-s-jobs/.

115n1 *Emma Tenayuca:* Ella Wagner, "Emma Tenayuca (U.S. National Park Service)," National Parks Service, U.S. Department of the Interior, March 30, 2021, https://www.nps.gov/people/emma-tenayuca.htm.

115n2 *"the Passionflower of Texas":* Kyli Rodriguez-Cayro, "6 Latina Women Leading the Labor Movement You Probably Never Learned About in School," *Bustle*, November 2, 2017, https://www.bustle.com/p/6-latina-women-leading-the-labor-movement-you-robably-never-learned-about-in-school-3209474.

115n3 *twelve thousand Latina pecan shellers:* "A Latinx Resource Guide: Civil Rights Cases and Events in the United States: 1938: Pecan Shellers Strike," Library of Congress, accessed November 22, 2021, https://guides.loc.gov/latinx-civil-rights/pecan-shellers-strike.

116 *$114 a week:* "You Already Know Cesar Chavez. What About Maria Moreno?" *The Counter*, September 28, 2020, https://thecounter.org/cesar-chavez-maria-moreno-ufw-awoc-farm-labor/.

117n1 *Norman Smith:* Students for a Democratic Society, "Farm Workers and Organized Labor Postwar Organizing Drives," Wind in the Fields, accessed November 22, 2021, https://oac.cdlib.org/view?docId=kt5779n7dt&chunk.id=d0e509&brand=calisphere&doc.view=entire_text.

117n2 *"Our only option is": Adios Amor: The Search for Maria Moreno*, National Endowment for the Humanities, 2019, https://www.adiosamorfilm.com/.

118n1 *"a crusader in rubber boots":* Laurie Coyle, dir., *Adios Amor: The Search for Maria Moreno. Adios Amor*, PBS, 2019, https://www.adiosamorfilm.com/.

118n2 *"big mouth":* Sam Bloch, "You Already Know Cesar Chavez."

118n3 *"Don't you think": Coyle, Adios Amor.*

118n4 *was not unconditional:* Students for a Democratic Society, "Farm Workers and Organized Labor."

119 *"I've been a worker":* Coyle, *Adios Amor.*

120n1 *recruiting Filipino workers* Maria Quintana and Oscar Rosales Castañeda, "Asians and Latinos Enter the Fields," Seattle Civil Rights and Labor History Project, 2004–2020, accessed November 22, 2021, https://depts.washington.edu/civilr/farmwk_ch4.htm#_edn22.

120n2 *seasonal migrant labor:* Ibid.

120n3 *"They saw the possibility":* Adam Janos, "How Cesar Chavez Joined Larry Itliong to Demand Farm Workers' Rights," History.com, May 7, 2019, https://www.history.com/news/chavez-itliong-delano-grape-strike.

121n1 *Stockton, California: Angelo Lopez,* "Filipino Americans and the Farm Labor Movement," Portside, May 12, 2014, https://portside.org/2014-05-12/filipino-americans-and-farm-labor-movement.

121n2 *vice president of Local 37:* Ibid.

122n1 *in the 1960s, recalled:* Adam Janos, "How Cesar Chavez Joined Larry Itliong to Demand Farm Workers' Rights," History.com, May 7, 2019, https://www.history.com/news/chavez-itliong-delano-grape-strike.

122n2 *a crowd in 1966:* Dolores Huerta, "NFWA March and Rally—April 10, 1966," Archives of Women's Political Communication, accessed November 22, 2021, https://awpc.cattcenter.iastate.edu/2017/03/09/nfwa-march-and-rally-april-10-1966/.

123 *In 1934, the Tydings-McDuffie Act:* "Tydings-McDuffie Act of 1934," Immigration History, February 1, 2020, https://immigrationhistory.org/item/tydings-mcduffie-act/.

124n1 *"He was very courageous":* Tyche Hendricks, "Legacy of Yemeni Immigrant Lives on among Union Janitors / Farmworkers Organizer to Be Honored in S.F," San Francisco Chronicle, January 28, 2012, https://www.sfgate.com/bayarea/article/Legacy-of-Yemeni-immigrant-lives-on-among-union-2782183.php.

124n2 *Cesar Chavez, who said:* Nikhil Misra-Bhambri,, "Yemenis in the San Joaquin Valley: The Embodiment of Pride, Duty and Loyalty," *Arab-AmericanNews*, February 22, 2021, https://www.arabamericannews.com/2021/02/22/yemenis-in-the-san-joaquin-valley-the-embodiment-of-pride-duty-and-loyalty/.

124n3 *The deputy smashed:* Rua'a Alameri, "Brutal Killing That Made a Yemeni Immigrant Hero of US Labor Movement," *Al Arabiya English*, May 20, 2020, https://english.alarabiya.net/features/2017/02/15/Rediscovering-brave-but-tragic-legacy-of-Yemeni-immigrant-labor-leader-in-US-history.

124n4 *They left his mangled body:* Ibid.

125n1 *Seven thousand people:* Ibid.

125n2 *later wrote to his father:* "Viva Brother Nagi," Kerning Cultures, April 27, 2021, https://kerningcultures.com/viva-brother-nagi/.

125n3 *Juan De La Cruz:* Omar Mansour, "Nagi Mohsin Daifullah and the Yemeni Farm Workers of California," Arab America, May 20, 2021, https://www.arabamerica.com/nagi-mohsin-daifullah-and-the-forgotten-yemeni-farmworkers-of-california/.

125n4 *1975 California Agricultural Labor Relations Act:* "Agricultural Labor Relations Act," accessed November 22, 2021, http://doloreshuerta.org/wp-content/uploads/2020/04/Handout-CA-Agricultural-Labor-Relations-Act-1.pdf.

125n5 *UFW ended its boycotts:* "Today in Labor History: United Farm Workers Launch the Lettuce Boycott," *People's World*, August 24, 2015, https://www.peoplesworld.org/article/today-in-labor-history-united-farm-workers-launch-the-lettuce-boycott/.

125n6 *gathered to vote:* "Viva Brother Nagi."

125n7 *Paolo Agbayani:* Village Brown and Patricia Leigh, "Forgotten Hero of Labor Fight; His Son's Lonely Quest," *New York Times*, October 18, 2018, sec. A, 20.

125n8 *negotiated a deal:* Gayle Romasanta, "Why It Is Important to Know the Story of Filipino-American Larry Itliong," Smithsonian.com, July 24, 2019, https://www.smithsonianmag.com/smithsonian-institution/why-it-is-important-know-story-filipino-american-larry-itliong-180972696/.

126n1 *recruited with promises of work:* "Slavery in the U.S.," Food Empowerment Project, accessed November 22, 2021, https://foodispower.org/human-labor-slavery/slavery-in-the-us/.

126n2 *a significant percentage of workers:* Scott Soriano, "The Rape Crisis Among California's Farm Workers," *Capitol Weekly*, January 9, 2020, https://capitolweekly.net/the-rape-crisis-among-californias-farm-workers/.

126n3 *roughly 10 percent of the workforce:* Helena Bottemiller Evich, Ximena Bustillo, and Liz Crampton, "Harvest of Shame: Farmworkers Face Coronavirus Disaster," *Politico*, September 9, 2020, https://www.politico.com/news/2020/09/08/farmworkers-coronavirus-disaster-409339.

126n4 *Global Horizons* CEO Mordechai Orian: "Slavery in the Fields and the Food We Eat," Coalition of Immokalee Workers, accessed November 22, 2021, https://ciw-online.org/wp-content/uploads/12Slaveryin theFields.pdf.

126n5 *"the largest human trafficking case":* Ibid.

127n1 *report misconduct and abuse:* Coalition of Immokalee Workers, "Part Two: 'We Are Not Victims—We Are Not Asking for Charity, We Are Calling for Justice!,'" October 16, 2020, https://ciw-online.org/blog/2017/10/part-two-we-are-not-victims-we-are-not-asking-for-charity-we-are-calling-for-justice/.

127n2 *penny-per-pound premium:* Steven Greenhouse, "In Florida Tomato Fields, a Penny Buys Progress," *New York Times*, April 25, 2014, https://www.nytimes.com/2014/04/25/business/in-florida-tomato-fields-a-penny-buys-progress.html.

127n3 New York Times *reporter Stephen Greenhouse:* Ibid.

128n1 *told the* Atlantic: Ariel Ramchandani, "There's a Sexual-Harassment Epidemic on America's Farms," *Atlantic*, January 30, 2018, https://www.theatlantic.com/business/archive/2018/01/agriculture-sexual-harassment/550109/.

128n2 *According to the CIW:* Coalition of Immokalee Workers, "Announcing: Farmworker Women Launch 'Harvest Without Violence' Campaign to End Sexual Violence in Wendy's Supply Chain!," August 28, 2020, https://ciw-online.org/blog/2017/09/harvest-without-violence/.

128n3 *Southern Poverty Law Center:* "Women in Agriculture," NFWM, July 14, 2020, http://nfwm.org/farm-workers/farm-worker-issues/womens-issues/#harassment.

129 New York Times *op-ed:* Greg Asbed, "What Happens If America's 2.5 Million Farmworkers Get Sick?" *New York Times*, April 3, 2020, https://www.nytimes.com/2020/04/03/opinion/coronavirus-farm-workers.html.

130 *"My coworkers at Pindar":* "New York Agricultural Workers Make History by Joining RWDSU/UFCW," The United Food & Commercial Workers International Union, October 19, 2021, https://www.ufcw.org/actions/victories/new-york-agricultural-workers-make-history-by-joining-rwdsu-ufcw/.

CHAPTER 7: THE CLEANERS

131n1 *"Domestic work":* Sarah Jaffe, "Low Benefits, Temporary Jobs— Work Is Getting Worse . . . but Hope for Labor Rights Is Emerging from a Surprising Place," Alternet.org, November 28, 2020, https://www.alternet.org/2012/08/low-benefits-temporary-jobs-work-getting-worse-hope-labor-rights-emerging-surprising-place/.

131n2 Wages Against Housework: Silvia Federici, "4. Wages Against Housework—Warwick," accessed November 22, 2021, https://warwick.ac.uk/fac/arts/english/currentstudents/postgraduate/masters/modules/femlit/04-federici.pdf.

132n1 *"The unwaged condition":* Ibid.

132n2 *2011 interview:* Julie McIntyre, "Care Work and the Power of Women: An Interview with Selma James," *Viewpoint*, September 15, 2018, https://viewpointmag.com/2012/03/19/care-work-and-the-power-of-women-an-interview-with-selma-james/.

132n3 *reflected in 2015:* Raia Small, "Silvia Federici Reflects on Wages for Housework," *New Frame*, May 15, 2019, https://www.newframe.com/silvia-federici-reflects-wages-housework/.

133n1 *One hundred and twenty thousand day laborers:* Robin Vives, "Amid Shades of Great Recession, Day Laborers Struggle to Find Work During Coronavirus," *Los Angeles Times*, March 30, 2020, https://www.latimes.com/california/story/2020-03-30/coronavirus-day-laborer-struggle-employment.

133n2 *waiting outside:* Ibid.

133n3 *la Parada:* Gwynne Hogan, "Williamsburg Day Laborers Command Top Dollar on 'Day Without Immigrants,'" *DNAinfo New York*, February 17, 2017, https://www.dnainfo.com/new-york/20170217/williamsburg/hasidic-williamsburg-immigrant-day-labor-work-undocumented/.

133n4 jornaleras*:* Cole Stangler, "Organizing the Corner: How Williamsburg's

Female Housecleaners Are Fighting for Higher Wages," *Village Voice*, May 11, 2017, https://www.villagevoice.com/2016/08/08/organizing-the-corner-how-williamsburgs-female-housecleaners-are-fighting-for-higher-wages/.

134 *"better than domestic work"*: Gerda Lerner, *Black Women in White America a Documentary History* (New York: Vintage Books, 1973).

135n1 *excluded from the 1935:* Jessica Pearce Rotondi, "Underpaid, but Employed: How the Great Depression Affected Working Women," History.com, March 11, 2019, https://www.history.com/news/working-women-great-depression.

135n2 *November 1935:* Ella Baker and Marvel Cooke, "Bronx Slave Market," *The Crisis* 42, no. 11 (November 1935).

136n1 *"I gathered strength"*: Marvel Cooke, "'Mrs. Legree' Hires on the Street, Always 'Nice' Girls," *The Daily Compass*, January 11, 1950.

136n2 *Newspaper Guild:* "One of the Most Influential Black Journalists You Probably Never Heard Of: On the Media," WNYC Studios, June 9, 2021, https://www.wnycstudios.org/podcasts/otm/episodes/most-influential-black-journalist-you-probably-never-heard.

136n3 *rehired the staff:* Elaine Woo, "Marvel Cooke: Pioneering Black Journalist, Political Activist," *Los Angeles Times*, December 6, 2000.

137n1 *hiring halls had long been:* "Hiring Halls," National Labor Relations Board, accessed November 22, 2021, https://www.nlrb.gov/about-nlrb/rights-we-protect/the-law/employees/hiring-halls.

137n2 *"Our primary aim"*: Ella Baker and Marvel Cooke, "Bronx Slave Market," *The Crisis* 42, no. 11 (November 1935).

138 *first all-female labor union in the U.S.:* New York State Public Employees Federation, "Kate Mullany and the Collar Laundry Union," libcom.org, accessed November 22, 2021, https://libcom.org/history/kate-mullany-collar-laundry-union.

139 *chipped away:* Eileen Boris, and Premilla Nadasen, "Domestic Workers Organize!," *WorkingUSA* 11, no. 4 (2008): 413–37, https://doi.org/10.1111/j.1743-4580.2008.00217.x.

141n1 *"Efforts to improve conditions"*: Grace Chang, *Disposable Domestics* (Chicago: Haymarket Books, 2016), 73.

141n2 *an "ally"*: Robert L. Friedheim, "The Seattle General Strike of 1919," *The Pacific Northwest Quarterly* 52, no. 3 (1961): 81–98, http://www.jstor.org/stable/40487648.

142n1 *rocketed from $3 to $23:* Christy Garrison Harrison, "They Led and a Community Followed: The Community Activism of Ella Mae Wade Brayboy and Dorothy Bolden in Atlanta, Georgia, 1964–1994," 2007.

142n2 *1995 interview:* Chris Lutz, int., "Dorothy Bolden Oral History, 1995-08-31," Georgia State University Library, Special Collections and Archives, accessed November 22, 2021, http://webapps.library.gsu.edu/ohms-viewer/viewer.php?cachefile=BoldenD_L1995-12_03.xml.

142n3 *he told her:* Ibid.

142n4 *committed to a psychiatric institution:* Jacklyn Izsraael, "How Dorothy Bolden Inspired the National Domestic Workers Bill of Rights," *Medium*, ZORA, October 21, 2019, https://zora.medium.com/how-dorothy-bolden-inspired-the-national-domestic-workers-bill-of-rights-46ac8cdd0915.

143n1 *she later recalled:* Luntz, "Dorothy Bolden Oral History Interview."

143n2 *Eight women:* Harrison, "They Led and a Community Followed."

143n3 *told them in no uncertain terms:* Ibid.

143n4 *striking and organized labor:* Elizabeth Beck, "National Domestic Workers Union and the War on Poverty," *Journal of Sociology & Social Welfare* 28, no. 4 (2001), Article 11.

144n1 *eight original demands:* Harrison, "They Led and a Community Followed."

144n2 *told journalist Laura Bassett:* Laura Bassett, "Georgia Domestic Workers Mobilize for Stacey Abrams in the Birthplace of Their Movement," *HuffPost*, November 2, 2018, https://www.huffpost.com/entry/stacey-abrams-georgia-domestic-workers_n_5bd8a9cbe4b0da7bfc14a210.

145n1 *nearly a third:* Nina Banks, "Black Women's Labor Market History Reveals Deep-Seated Race and Gender Discrimination," *Economic Policy Institute*, February 19, 2019, https://www.epi.org/blog/black-womens-labor-market-history-reveals-deep-seated-race-and-gender-discrimination/.

145n2 *The Economic Policy Institute:* Julia Wolfe, Jori Kandra, Lora Engdahl, and Heidi Shierholz, "Domestic Workers Chartbook: A Comprehensive Look at the Demographics, Wages, Benefits, and Poverty Rates of the Professionals Who Care for Our Family Members and Clean Our Homes," Economic Policy Institute, May 14, 2020, https://www.epi.org/publication/domestic -workers-chartbook-a-comprehensive-look-at-the-demographics-wages-benefits-and-poverty-rates-of-the-professionals-who-care-for-our-family-members-and-clean-our-homes/.

146 *"Everyone said you can't win":* Randy Shaw, *Beyond the Fields: Cesar Chavez, the UFW, and the Struggle for Justice in the 21st Century* (Berkeley: University of California Press, 2011).

147 *June 15, 1990:* Gavin Musynske, "Los Angleles Justice for Janitors Campaign for Economic Justice at Century City, 1989–1990," April 12, 2009, Global Nonviolent Action Database, accessed November 22, 2021, https://nvdatabase.swarthmore.edu/content/los-angleles-justice-janitors-campaign-economic-justice-century-city-1989-1990.

148 *told Menendez:* Ana Menendez, "While Shalala Lives in Luxury, Janitors Struggle," News Leaders Association, March 1, 2006, https://members.newsleaders.org/article_content.asp?edition=2ion=6&article=24.

149n1 *2021 Cornell University report found:* Sanjay Pinto, Zoë West, and KC Wagner, *Sweeping Change: Building Survivor and Worker Leadership to Confront Sexual Harassment in the Janitorial Industry* (Ithaca, NY: Cornell University, ILR School, the Worker Institute).

149n2 *Bernice Yeung:* Bernice Yeung, *In a Day's Work: The Fight to End Sexual Violence Against America's Most Vulnerable Workers* (New York: The New Press, 2018).

150 New Labor Forum: Nadhia Rahman, "Healing into Power: An Approach for Confronting Workplace Sexual Violence," New Labor Forum, August 20, 2021, https://newlaborforum.cuny.edu/2021/05/05/healing-into-power-an-approach-for-confronting-workplace-sexual-violence/.

152n1 *65 percent of Americans:* "Working People Want a Voice at Work," Economic Policy Institute, April 21, 2021, https://www.epi.org/publication/working-people-want-a-voice/.

152n2 *48 percent of workers:* Ibid.

CHAPTER 8: THE FREEDOM FIGHTERS

153 *"The colored men":* Ida B. Wells-Barnett, "The Arkansas Race Riot," Northern Illinois University Digital Library, January 1, 1970, https://digital.lib.niu.edu/islandora/object/niu-gildedage%3A24320.

155 *Ulysses S. Bratton:* William H. Pruden, III, "Ulysses Simpson Bratton (1868–1947)," Encyclopedia of Arkansas, January 4, 2021, https://encyclopediaofarkansas.net/entries/ulysses-s-bratton-12933/.

156n1 *orders "to shoot to kill":* Francine Uenuma, "The Massacre of Black Sharecroppers That Led the Supreme Court to Curb the Racial Disparities of the Justice System," *Smithsonian*, August 2, 2018, https://www.smithsonianmag.com/history/death-hundreds-elaine-massacre-led-supreme-court-take-major-step-toward-equal-justice-african-americans-180969863/.

156n2 *fled to Kansas:* Grif Stockley, "Elaine Massacre of 1919," Encyclopedia of Arkansas, November 18, 2020, https://encyclopediaofarkansas.net/entries/elaine-massacre-of-1919-1102/.

157 *wrote one man: Wells-Barnett, "The Arkansas Race Riot."*

158n1 *Ed Ware:* Ibid.

158n2 *"It was a Declaration of Economic Independence":* Ida B. Wells-Barnett, "The Arkansas Race Riot," (Hume, OH: Hume Job Print, 1920).

158n3 *the* Guardian: Noa Yachot, "'We Want Our Land Back': For Descendants of the Elaine Massacre, History Is Far from Settled," *Guardian*, June 18, 2021, https://www.theguardian.com/us-news/2021/jun/18/elaine-massacre-red-summer-descendants-history.

159 *"If the Southern people":* Ida B. Wells-Barnett, *The Red Record* (Outlook Verlag, 2018).

161 *"We were in that world":* Malcolm X. and Alex Haley. *The Autobiography of Malcolm X: With the Assistance of Alex Haley* (New York: Ballantine Books, 1973).

164n1 *outspoken Pullman maids:* Melinda Chateauvert, "Marching Together: Women of the Brotherhood of Sleeping Car Porters," *NWSA Journal* 2, no. 4 (1990): 687–89, http://www.jstor.org/stable/4316092.

164n2 *became organizers in their own right:* Ibid.

164n3 *she once recalled:* David Pitts, "Rosina Tucker—A Century of Commitment," February 8, 1996, http://igmlnet.uohyd.ac.in:8000/InfoUSA/facts/history/rosina.htm.

165n1 *Elizabeth Gurley Flynn:* Philip S. Foner, "The IWW and the Black Worker," *The Journal of Negro History* 55, no. 1 (1970): 45–64, https://doi.org/10.2307/2716544.

165n2 *Lucille:* Misun *Bishop*, "Lucille Campbell Green Randolph (1883–1963)," Blackpast.org, June 11, 2017, https://www.blackpast.org/african-american-history/randolph-lucille-campbell-green-1883-1963/.

166n1 *"If we never have another":* Melinda Chateauvert, *Marching Together: Women of the Brotherhood of Sleeping Car Porters* (Urbana: University of Illinois Press, 1998).

166n2 *"Our responsibility":* Robert L. Allen, *The Brotherhood of Sleeping Car Porters: C.L. Dellums and the Fight for Fair Treatment and Civil Rights* (Boulder, CO: Paradigm Publishers, 2015).

167 *"Organization is not only necessary":* Ibid.

169 *"N-ggr, you're supposed to be scared":* "Nonviolence vs. Jim Crow," Civil Rights Teaching, accessed January 13, 2022, https://www.civilrightsteaching.org/traditional-narrative/nonviolence-vs-jim-crow.

170 *"This was going to be":* Bayard Rustin, *Time on Two Crosses: The Collected Writings of Bayard Rustin* (New York: Penguin Books, 2022).

171 *William P. Jones explained:* Michael Kazin, "The White Man Whose 'March on Washington' Speech You Should Remember Too," *New Republic*, November 22, 2021, https://newrepublic.com/article/114408/march-washington-50th-anniversary-walter-reuthers-speech.

172 *"The problems of the most":* Rustin, *Time on Two Crosses.*

173n1 *Rustin told a crowd of strikers:* "Strike Supporters Bring in Outside Help," Memphis Public Libraries, March 15, 1968, https://www.memphislibrary.org/diversity/sanitation-strike-exhibit/sanitation-strike-exhibit-march-10-to-16-edition/strike-supporters-bring-in-outside-help/.

173n2 *saluting the United Farm Workers:* Tim Ott, "Martin Luther King, Jr., Praised Cesar Chavez for His 'Indefatigable Work,'" Biography.com, October 15, 2020, https://www.biography.com/news/cesar-chavez-martin-luther-king-jr-telegram.

173n3 *writing to a group of striking laundry workers:* "Dr. Martin Luther King, Jr., on Labor," AFL–CIO Convention, 1961, accessed November 22, 2021, https://www.afscme.org/about/history/mlk/dr-martin-luther-king-jr-on-labor.

174n1 *"If I do not stop to help":* Martin Luther King, Jr., "I've Been to the Mountaintop," transcript of speech delivered in Memphis, TN, April 3, 1968, https://abcnews.go.com/Politics/martin-luther-kings-final-speech-ive-mountaintop-full/story?id=18872817.

174n2 *"It is up to us":* Rustin, *Time on Two Crosses.*

175n1 *fired them and brought in prison labor:* Danny Monteverde, "Sanitation Workers Say They Were Fired for Protests over Pay and Protective Equipment," wwltv.com, May 8, 2020, https://www.wwltv.com/article/news/health/coronavirus/sanitation-workers-say-they-were-fired-for-protests-over-pay-and-protective-equipment/289-1283daf0-9893-4bc1-b51b-f7fa89b7093e.

175n2 *"We, like many before us":* Kim Kelly, "New Orleans' Underpaid, Overexposed Sanitation Workers," *The New Republic*, January 14, 2022, https://newrepublic.com/article/158324/new-orleans-sanitation-workers-hoppers-union-underpaid-overexposed.

176 *"Nothing worthwhile is gained":* Martin Luther King and Clayborne Carson. *The Autobiography of Martin Luther King* (London, England: Abacus, 2006).

CHAPTER 9: THE MOVERS

177 *"Labor cannot stand still":* John Nichols, *Uprising: How Wisconsin Renewed the Politics of Protest from Madison to Wall Street* (New York: PublicAffairs, 2012), 119.

178n1 *the massive forty-five-day railroad strike:* Joseph Adamczyk, "Great Railroad Strike of 1877," *Britannica*, September 5, 2014, https://www.britannica.com/topic/Great-Railroad-Strike-of-1877.

178n2 *shut down the ports:* Peter Cole, "The Most Radical Union in the U.S. Is Shutting Down the Ports on Juneteenth," *In These Times*, June 16, 2020, https://inthesetimes.com/article/juneteenth-ilwu-dockworkers-strike-ports-black-lives-matter-george-floyd.

178n3 *The ILWU was born in blood* :Peter Cole, *Dockworker Power: Race and Activism in Durban and the San Francisco Bay Area* (Champaign: University of Illinois Press, 2018).

179 *"March Inland":* "The ILWU Story," International Longshore & Warehouse Union, accessed November 19, 2021, https://www.ilwu.org/history/the-ilwu-story/.

180n1 *ILWU lawyers secured an injunction:* Ibid.

180n2 *changed its name in 1997: Journal of Commerce* Staff, "What's in a Name? for ILWU, It's Not 'Men,'" *Journal of Commerce*, May 4, 1997, https://www.joc.com/whats-name-ilwu-its-not-men_19970504.html.

180n3 *the union made waves:* Peter Cole, "On May Day, Longshore Workers Stop Work to Protest Racist Police Brutality," *In These Times*, April 30, 2015, https://inthesetimes.com/article/may-day-police-brutality%20/.

181n1 *honorary members* Labor Video Project, "Angela Davis Becomes ILWU Local 10 Honorary Member on Juneteenth 2021," *IndyBay*, June 24, 2021, https://www.indybay.org/newsitems/2021/06/24/18843416.php.

181n2 *Oscar Grant* "Bay Area ILWU Members Endorse Rally Seeking Justice for Unarmed Civilian Killed by BART Police Officer," *International Longshore & Warehouse Union*, November 25, 2010.

181n3 *Walter Scott:* ilwu46, "Local 10 Leads Protest Against Police Brutality," International Longshore & Warehouse Union Local, June 2, 2015, https://ilwu46.com/local-10-leads-protest-against-police-brutality/.

181n4 *president Melvin Mackey said:* Ibid.

181n5 *The first rumblings* Allyson P. Brantley, *Brewing a Boycott: How a Grassroots Coalition Fought Coors and Remade American Consumer Activism* (Chapel Hill: University of North Carolina Press, 2021).

184 *the LGBTQ community:* Jerame Davis, "Op-ed: The Long, Powerful History Between Labor and LGBT Activists," *Advocate*, September 22, 2014, https://www.advocate.com/commentary/2014/09/22/op-ed-long-powerful-history-between-labor-and-lgbt-activists.

186n1 *"Union leadership was reactionary":* Scarlett C. Davis, "Queering Labour: The Marine Cooks and Stewards' Union," *New Socialist*, 1998.

186n2 *Allan Bérubé:* "Obituary: Allan Bérubé," *Guardian*, February 22, 2008, https://www.theguardian.com/theguardian/2008/feb/22/gayrights.

187n1 *New Socialist* magazine: Davis, "Queering Labour.

187n2 *drag shows:* Ibid.

187n3 *"Honolulu Queen":* Ibid.

187n4 *"It's anti-union to red-bait, race-bait, or queen-bait":* "Working-Class Pride in the Marine Cooks and Stewards Union," United Electrical, Radio & Machine Workers of America, June 18, 2021, https://www.ueunion.org/ue-news-feature/2021/working-class-pride-in-the-marine-cooks-and-stewards-union.

188n1 *served as the MCS's vice president: Davis, "Op-ed: The Long, Powerful History."*

188n2 *told him in the 1990s:* "Working-Class Pride in the Marine Cooks and Stewards Union."

188n3 *Frank McCormick:* Davis, "Op-ed: The Long, Powerful History."

188n4 *Howard Wallace:* Howard Wallace Papers, San Francisco Public Library, James C. Hormel LGBTQIA Center.

189 *"The fact that people hate me":* Anne Balay, *Semi Queer: Inside the World of Gay, Trans, and Black Truck Drivers* (Chapel Hill, NC: University of North Carolina Press, 2018), 8.

190n1 *conservative politics:* Leigh Ann Carey, "Inside the Growing World of Queer Truckers," *Rolling Stone*, October 4, 2019, https://www.rollingstone.com/culture/culture-features/queer-trucking-anne-balay-lgbtq-truck-driver-796994/.

190n2 Rolling Stone: Ibid.

191 *people participated:* Rachel Premack, "There's a Stark Reason Why America's 1.8 Million Long-Haul Truck Drivers Can't Strike," *Business Insider*, October 21, 2019, https://www.businessinsider.com/trucking-truck-driver-truckers-strike-reasons-2019-10.

192 *1955 law:* Anne M. Ross, "Public Employee Unions and the Right to Strike," *Monthly Labor Review* 92, no. 3 (1969): 14–18, http://www.jstor.org/stable/41837581.

194n1 *declining by nearly 90 percent:* Eric Dirnbach, "Strike Out: The Number of Large Strikes Continues to Decline," *Medium*, February 16, 2017, https://ericdirnbach.medium.com/strike-out-the-number-of-large-strikes-continues-to-decline-e9f505f79b60.

194n2 *dwindled into the single digits:* Ibid.

195n1 *due to the composition of its membership:* Planet Money, "When Reagan Broke the Unions," NPR, December 19, 2019, https://www.npr.org/transcripts/788002965.

195n2 *Boeing Air Transport Office:* Federal Aviation Administration, "Ellen Church and the Advent of the Sky Girls," https://web.archive.org/web/20210828214241/https://www.faa.gov/about/history/pioneers/media/Ellen_Church_and_the_Advent_of_the_Sky_Girls.pdf.

196n1 *"single, younger than 25":* Julia Cooke, *Come Fly the World* (New York: Mariner, 2021).

196n2 *2019 interview:* Svea Conrad, "On the Roads of Southside and Around the World: On Annie Watkins and Joan Dorsey," *Arizona Daily Sun*, March 2, 2020, https://azdailysun.com/entertainment/arts-and-theatre/on-the-roads-of-southside-and-around-the-world-on-annie-watkins-and-joan-dorsey/article_1f993b32-4ee7-5bbb-a40b-9754c5de74e9.html.

196n3 *"Equality was a big issue":* Svea Conrad, "Exhibit Tells Story of Flagstaff Women Past and Present," *Arizona Daily Sun*, August 22, 2019.

197n1 *William T. Simpson:* Phil Tiemeyer, "Male Stewardesses: Male Flight Attendants as a Queer Miscarriage of Justice," Genders 1998–2013, University of Colorado, Boulder, February 12, 2017, https://www.colorado.edu/gendersarchive1998-2013/2007/06/01/male-stewardesses-male-flight-attendants-queer-miscarriage-justice.

197n2 *"gay panic":* Graham Bunk, "1954 Miami Murder Leads to 'Homosexual Panic,'" *Erie Gay News*, accessed November 22, 2021, https://www.eriegaynews.com/news/article.php?recordid=201711williamtsimpson.

198n1 *Phil Tiemeyer:* Forrest Wickman, "How the Gay Airline Steward Became a Stereotype," *Slate*, July 3, 2013, https://slate.com/culture/2013/07/gay-male-flight-attendants-in-im-so-excited-the-history-of-the-gay-steward-stereotype.html.

198n2 *took the matter all the way to the Supreme Court*: *Diaz v. Pan Am. World Airways, Inc.*, 442 F.2d 385 (5th Cir. 1971).

199n1 *Tiemeyer:* Wickman, "How the Gay Airline Steward Became a Stereotype."

199n2 *"A large contingent":* Ibid.

199n3 *Ada Brown Greenfield, Frances Hall, Edith Lauterbach, Sally Thometz, and Sally Watt Keenan:* "Rafa Legacy," Retiree Association of Flight Attendants, accessed November 22, 2021, https://www.rafa-cwa.org/page-1820147.

200n1 *"I've literally had people"*: Wickman, "How the Gay Airline Steward Became a Stereotype."

200n2 *"Flight attendants, about 80 percent women"*: Post Opinions Staff, "The One Best Idea for Ending Sexual Harassment," The Washington Post, December 2, 2021, https://www.washingtonpost.com/blogs/post-partisan/wp/2017/12/08/the-one-best-idea-for-ending-sexual-harassment/.

200n3 *prim hemlines, sensible shoes, and modest caps:* Bryan Swopes, "Ellen Church Marshall Archives," This Day in Aviation, May 15, 2021, https://www.thisdayinaviation.com/tag/ellen-church-marshall/.

200n4 *Emirates:* Mateusz Maszczynski, "The Official Emirates Guidelines for How to Wear Afro Style Hair: Get the Official Approved Look," Paddle Your Own Kanoo, November 20, 2018, https://www.paddleyourownkanoo.com/2018/03/26/the-official-emirates-guidelines-for-how-to-wear-afro-style-hair-get-the-official-approved-look/.

201n1 *"fly me"*: "Pin on Union Strong," Pinterest, accessed November 22, 2021, https://www.pinterest.com/pin/289708188508625689/.

201n2 *pressure from the union:* Tamar Lewin, "USAir Agrees to Lift Rules on the Weight of Attendants," *New York Times*, April 8, 1994, https://www.nytimes.com/1994/04/08/us/usair-agrees-to-lift-rules-on-the-weight-of-attendants.html.

202n1 *"Patient Zero"*: Brian D. Johnson, "How a Typo Created a Scapegoat for the AIDS Epidemic," *Maclean's*, April 30, 2019, https://www.macleans.ca/culture/movies/how-a-typo-created-a-scapegoat-for-the-aids-epidemic/.

202n2 *"We actually fought for men"*: Wickman, "How the Gay Airline Steward Became a Stereotype."

203 *launching a public pressure campaign:* "Pride Month: AFA's Fight to Win Domestic Partner Benefits for Flight Attendants." Communications Workers of America, July 2, 2021, https://www.deltaafa.org/news/pride-month-afa-s-fight-win-domestic-partner-benefits-flight-attendants.

CHAPTER 10: THE METALWORKERS

205 *"You have made the decision"*: David Goldberg, "Detroit's Radical," *Jacobin*, May 2014, https://www.jacobinmag.com/2014/05/detroit-s-radical-general-baker.

206n1 *told* Smithsonian *magazine:* Lucie Levine, "Men of Steel: How Brooklyn's Native American Ironworkers Built New York," *6sqft*, July 25, 2018, https://www.6sqft.com/men-of-steel-how-brooklyns-native-american-ironworkers-built-new-york/.

206n2 *1928* Diabo vs. McCandless *case:* McCandless, Commissioner of Immigration. v. United States ex rel. Diabo, Circuit Court of Appeals, Third Circuit, March 9, 1928.

207 *"boom out"*: Jim Adams, "Nmai's 'Booming Out' Shows Towering Pres-

ence of Mohawks," *Indian Country Today*, May 5, 2002, https://indiancountrytoday.com/archive/nmais-booming-out-shows-towering-presence-of-mohawks.

209n1 *increased its output 39 percent:* Kate Aronoff, "African American Auto Workers Strike for Union Democracy and Better Working Conditions (DRUM), 1968–1970," Global Nonviolent Action Database, July 11, 2011, https://nvdatabase.swarthmore.edu/content/african-american-auto-workers-strike-union-democracy-and-better-working-conditions-drum-1968.

209n2 *"In this day and age":* David Goldberg, "Detroit's Radical," *Jacobin*, accessed January 14, 2022, https://www.jacobinmag.com/2014/05/detroit-s-radical-general-baker/.

211 *"People who recognize that":* Ronald Scott, "The Unedited StoryCorps Interview: Grace Lee Boggs, 1915–2015," StoryCorps, June 2007, https://storycorps.org/grace-lee-boggs-1915-2015/.

212n1 *assuming that a looming fear of deportation:* Omar Mansour, "Arab Detroit: The Arab Workers' Caucus and the Strike for Palestine," Arab America, June 2, 2021, https://www.arabamerica.com/arab-detroit-the-arab-workers-caucus-and-the-strike-for-palestine/.

212n2 *found common ground*: Ismael Ahmed, "Organizing an Arab Workers Caucus," *MERIP Reports*, no. 34 (1975): 17–22, https://doi.org/10.2307/3011472.

213n1 *read a flyer:* Dan Georgakas, "Arab Workers in Detroit," *MERIP Reports*, no. 34 (1975): 13–17, https://doi.org/10.2307/3011471.

213n2 *early 1900s* :Ahmed, "Organizing an Arab Workers Caucus."

213n3 *spend time at ACCESS:* "Rashida Tlaib for Congress Visiting Her Old Stomping Grounds and ACCESS Family," Facebook, August 10, 2018, https://www.facebook.com/ACCESScommunity/videos/1015566108 1587997.

214n1 *1999 interview:* Janice Frejj and Anan Ameri, Audio of Ismael Ahmed Oral History, https://aanm.contentdm.oclc.org/digital/collection/p16806coll15/id/44.

214n2 *noted that many of the Arab immigrants:* "Arabs Hold March in Dearborn," *Detroit Free Press*, August 27, 1973, 5.

214n3 *a two-thousand-person demonstration:* Ahmed, "Organizing an Arab Workers Caucus."

215 Jacobin: Jeff Schuhrke, "When Arab-American Detroit Auto Workers Struck for Palestinian Liberation," *Jacobin*, March 8, 2020, https://jacobinmag.com/2020/08/palestine-strike-wildcat-uaw.

218n1 *lawsuit ended with:* Stephen Ford Franklin, "Ford Pays Millions in Harassment Settlement," *Chicago Tribune*, September 8, 1999, https://www.chicagotribune.com/news/ct-xpm-1999-09-08-9909080151-story.html.

218n2 *from James J. Padilla:* Ibid.

219 *In 2014:* Shane McGlaun, "Judge Denies Female Ford Workers Class-

Action Status," Ford Authority, Motrolix, August 26, 2019, https://fordauthority.com/2019/08/judge-denies-female-ford-workers-class-action-status/.

221n1 *public support for LGBTQ rights* :Chelsea Engel, "USW Celebrates Pride Month and Recommits to Fighting for LGBTQ+ Community," United Steelworkers, June 3, 2019, https://www.usw.org/news/media-center/releases/2019/usw-celebrates-pride-month-and-recommits-to-fighting-for-lgbtq-community.

222n2 Pride at Work: "Historic Union Support for LGBTQ Equality Legislation," Pride at Work, April 24, 2021, https://www.prideatwork.org/historic-union-support-for-lgbtq-equality-legislation/.

222n3 Steel Pride: United Steelworkers, accessed November 19, 2021, https://www.usw.org/act/activism/civil-rights/resources/steel-pride.

221n4 *"You had to rely on":* Balay, Anne, *Steel Closets: Voices of Gay, Lesbian, and Transgender Steelworkers*, (Chapel Hill, NC: University of North Carolina Press, 2016).

CHAPTER 11: THE DISABLED WORKERS

223 *"When other people see you":* Judith E. Heumann, *Being Heumann: An Unrepentant Memoir of a Disability Rights Activist* (Boston: Beacon Press, 2020), 131.

224 *"sugar was made with blood":* Marcus Rediker, *The Fearless Benjamin Lay: The Quaker Dwarf Who Became the First Revolutionary Abolitionist* (Boston: Beacon Press, 2017), 35.

225n1 Kristin E. Holmes, "Cast out by the Quakers, Abington's Abolitionist Dwarf Finally Has His Day," *Philadelphia Inquirer*, April 19, 2018, https://www.inquirer.com/philly/news/quakers-benjamin-lay-dwarf-abolitionist-slavery-abington-friends-meeting-20180419.html.

225n2 *he had thundered:* Benjamin Lay, *All Slave-Keepers That Keep the Innocent in Bondage* (New York: Arno Press, 1969).

226 *224,000 of them came home injured:* Wendi A. Maloney, "World War I: Injured Veterans and the Disability Rights Movement," Library of Congress Blog, December 21, 2017, https://blogs.loc.gov/loc/2017/12/world-war-i-injured-veterans-and-the-disability-rights-movement/.

227 *2021 piece for* Wired: Britt H. Young, "My Body Is Used to Design Military Tech," *Wired*, October 26, 2021, https://www.wired.com/story/disability-justice-prosthetics-military-history/.

229n1 *Lavinia:* Jeff Nilsson and *Post* editors, "General Tom Thumb Gets Married," *Saturday Evening Post*, May 4, 2016, https://www.saturdayeveningpost.com/2013/02/general-tom-thumb-marries-lavinia-warren/.

229n2 *Joice Heth:* "The Joice Heth Exhibit: The Lost Museum Archive," accessed November 19, 2021, https://lostmuseum.cuny.edu/archive/exhibit/heth.

229n3 *I first wrote about this:* Kim Kelly, "The True Tale of a Bona Fide, One-of-a-Kind 'Lobster Girl.'" *Vox*, September 23, 2019, https://www.vox.com/the-highlight/2019/9/23/20870620/carnival-disability-coney-island-sideshow-ectrodactyly.

230n1 *Chang and Eng Bunker:* "Death Cast of Chang and Eng Bunker," The College of Physicians of Philadelphia Digital Library, accessed November 19, 2021, https://www.cppdigitallibrary.org/items/show/4377.

230n2 *Millie and Christine McKoy:* "The Two-Headed Nightingale," *Stanford*, May/June 2000, https://stanfordmag.org/contents/the-two-headed-nightingale.

230n3 *Sara Baartman:* Justin Parkinson, "The Significance of Sarah Baartman," BBC News, January 7, 2016, https://www.bbc.com/news/magazine-35240987.

232n1 *"It wasn't many years ago":* Kim Kelly, "The True Tale of a Bona Fide, One-of-a-Kind 'Lobster Girl,'" *Vox*, September 23, 2019, https://www.vox.com/the-highlight/2019/9/23/20870620/carnival-disability-coney-island-sideshow-ectrodactyly.

232n2 *According to the CDC:* "CDC: 1 in 4 US Adults Live with a Disability," Centers for Disease Control and Prevention, August 16, 2018, https://www.cdc.gov/media/releases/2018/p0816-disability.html.

232n3 *Bureau of Justice reporting:* Cynthia Stadel, "Disability and Criminal Justice Reform," Learning Disabilities Association of America, accessed November 19, 2021, https://ldaamerica.org/lda_today/disability-and-criminal-justice-reform/.

232n4 *The wage gap:* U.S. Census Bureau, B18140: Median Earnings in the Past 12 Months (In 2012 Inflation-Adjusted Dollars) by Disability Status by Sex for the Civilian Noninstitutionalized Population 16 Years and Over with Earnings—Universe: Civilian Noninstitutionalized Population 16 Years and Over with Earnings in the Past 12 Months, 2012 American Community Survey 1-Year Estimates. Retrieved May 20, 2014, from https://data.census.gov/cedsci/table?q=b18140&tid-ACSDT1Y2012.B18140.

233n1 *"50 percent of people":* Vilissa Thompson, "Understanding the Policing of Black, Disabled Bodies," Center for American Progress, March 21, 2017, https://www.americanprogress.org/article/understanding-policing-black-disabled-bodies/.

233n2 *left partially blind:* Charlie May, "'I'll Never See Again': Standing Rock Protester Suffers Permanent Injury After Police Attack with Tear Gas Canister," *Salon*, December 7, 2016, https://www.salon.com/2016/12/06/i-didn't-want-the-world-to-see-me-like-this-sioux-z-suffers-permanent-injury-after-police-attack-with-tear-gas-canister/.

234n1 *"We don't want charity":* Keith Rosenthal, "Pioneers in the Fight for Disability Rights," *International Socialist Review*, accessed January 24, 2022, https://isreview.org/issue/90/pioneers-fight-disability-rights/.

234n2 *Over the next year:* Keith Rosenthal, "Pioneers in the Fight for Disability

Rights," *International Socialist Review*, 2013, https://isreview.org/issue/90/pioneers-fight-disability-rights/.

234n3 *"You have to understand"*: Paul K. Longmore, *Why I Burned My Book and Other Essays on Disability* (Philadelphia, PA: Temple University Press, 2003).

236n1 *"The AFPH agenda"*: Audra Jennings, *Out of the Horrors of War: Disability Politics in World War II America* (Philadelphia, PA: University of Pennsylvania Press, 2016), 10.

236n2 *a 1944 hearing:* "New A.F.L. Program to Aid Disabled," *Organized Labor*, December 30, 1944.

236n3 *Henry Williams:* Robert F. Jefferson, "'Enabled Courage': Race, Disability, and Black World War II Veterans in Postwar America," *Historian* 65, no. 5 (2003): 1102–24, http://www.jstor.org/stable/24452485.

237n1 *Williams later reflected:* Ibid.

237n2 *Volunteers in Service to America (VISTA):* R. Wells, "Volunteers in Service to America," *Encyclopedia Britannica*, October 28, 2014, https://www.britannica.com/topic/Volunteers-in-Service-to-America.

238 *jailed for their trouble:* Richard A. Brisbin, *A Strike Like No Other Strike: Law and Resistance During the Pittston Coal Strike of 1989–1990* (United Kingdom: Johns Hopkins University Press, 2002), 82.

239n1 *told a roomful of senators* :Mollie Cecil, "The Widows of Farmington," March 7, 2020, https://molliececil.com/the-widows-of-farmington/.

239n2 *three thousand miners*: Jessie Wright-Mendoza, "The Militant Miners Who Exposed the Horrors of Black Lung . . . ," JSTOR *Daily*, September 26, 2018, https://daily.jstor.org/the-militant-miners-who-exposed-the-horrors-of-black-lung/.

239n3 *Westmoreland Coal's East Gulf Mine:* Paul Nyden, "Rank-and-File Rebellions in the Coalfields, 1964–80," *Monthly Review*, June 30, 2014, https://monthlyreview.org/2007/03/01/rank-and-file-rebellions-in-the-coalfields-1964-80/.

240n1 *one thousand miners:* Edward Peeks, "Coal Miners Sound Call of 'No Law, No Work,'" The Charleston Gazette, February 27, 1969, https://archive.wvculture.org/history/labor/blacklung02.html.

240n2 *carried a sign:* Ibid.

240n3 *March 12:* Immanuel Ness, Aaron Brenner, and Benjamin Day, *The Encyclopedia of Strikes in American History* (United Kingdom: Taylor & Francis, 2015).

240n4 *the first legislation:* "February 18, 1969: The Black Lung Strike," "Time Trail, West Virginia," February 1998 Programs, accessed November 19, 2021, https://archive.wvculture.org/history/timetrl/ttfeb.html#0218.

240n5 *1977 Federal Mine Safety and Health Act:* "Mine Disaster: 1968 Farmington Explosion Anniversary," Mine Safety and Health Administration, United States Department of Labor, accessed November 19, 2021, https://www.msha.gov/mine-disaster-1968-farmington-explosion-anniversary.

241n1 *1972 interview:* Nyden, "Rank-and-File Rebellions in the Coalfields, 1964-80."

241n2 *"If you believe in something":* Judith E. Heumann and Kristen Joiner, *Rolling Warrior: The Incredible, Sometimes Awkward, True Story of a Rebel Girl on Wheels Who Helped Spark a Revolution* (Boston: Beacon Press, 2021).

242 *Corbett O'Toole later wrote:* Eileen AJ Connelly, "Overlooked No More: Brad Lomax, a Bridge Between Civil Rights Movements," *New York Times*, August 8, 2020, sec. F.

243n1 *"allowed us to use":* Kitty Cone, "Short History of the 504 Sit In," Disability Rights Education & Defense Fund, July 6, 2021, https://dredf.org/504-sit-in-20th-anniversary/short-history-of-the-504-sit-in/.

243n2 *"A special congressional hearing":* "Short History of the 504 Sit In," Disability Rights Education & Defense Fund, July 6, 2021, https://dredf.org/504-sit-in-20th-anniversary/short-history-of-the-504-sit-in/.

243n3 *they sang:* Ibid.

243n4 *Cone wrote on its twentieth anniversary:* Cone, "Short History of the 504 Sit In."

244n1 *Jennifer Keelan:* Becky Little, "When the 'Capitol Crawl' Dramatized the Need for Americans with Disabilities Act," History.com, July 24, 2020, https://www.history.com/news/americans-with-disabilities-act-1990-capitol-crawl.

244n2 *in a 2020 interview:* Sunshine Mugrabi, "How an Eight-Year-Old Girl Made Disability History: A Conversation with Activist Jennifer Keelan-Chaffins and Children's Book Author Annette Bay Pimentel," Democratic Socialists of America (DSA), July 25, 2020, https://www.dsausa.org/democratic-left/how-an-eight-year-old-girl-made-disability-history-a-conversation-with-activist-jennifer-keelan-chaffins-and-childrens-book-author-annette-bay-pimentel/.

245n1 *"We looked beyond":* Heumann and Joiner, *Rolling Warrior.*

245n2 *"People with disabilities":* Cone, "Short History of the 504 Sit In."

246n1 *"The reason they get away with it":* Saru Jayaraman, *One Fair Wage: Ending Subminimum Pay in America* (New York, New Press, 2021), 162.

246n2 *this current inequitable reality:* Sara Luterman, "Why Businesses Can Still Get Away with Paying Pennies to Employees with Disabilities," *Vox*, March 16, 2020, https://www.vox.com/identities/2020/3/16/21178197/people-with-disabilities-minimum-wage.

246n3 *"who by reason of illness":* Ibid.

247n1 *In 2009, the* Des Moines Register*:* Erin Jordan, "What Atalissa, State Knew about the Bunkhouse," *Des Moines Register*, February 15, 2009, https://www.legis.iowa.gov.doc/publications/SD/9859.pdf.

247n2 *"People with disabilities"*: Saru Jayaraman, *One Fair Wage: Ending Subminimum Pay in America* (New York: New Press, 2021), 162.

CHAPTER 12: THE SEX WORKERS

251n1 *"Here's to the Ladies of the Night"*: Frédérique Delacoste and Priscilla Alexander, eds., *Sex Work: Writings by Women in the Sex Industry*, 2nd ed. (San Francisco: Cleis Press, 1998).

251n2 *periodically experienced homelessness and incarceration:* Jessica Stern, "This Is What Pride Looks Like: Miss Major and the Violence, Poverty, and Incarceration of Low-Income Transgender Women," S&F Online 10.1–10.2 (Fall 2011/Spring 2012), https://sfonline.barnard.edu/a-new-queer-agenda/this-is-what-pride-looks-like-miss-major-and-the-violence-poverty-and-incarceration-of-low-income-transgender-women/0/.

252n1 *"We fed people and clothed people"*: Ehn Nothing, "Introduction: Queens Against Society," in Street Transvestite Action Revolutionaries: Survival, Revolt, and Queer Antagonist Struggle, Untorelli Press, accessed November 22, 2021, https://archive.org/details/untorelli_2013_transvestite.

252n2 *proudly brandishing a can of Mace:* Ibid.

252n3 *STAR was more than a mutual aid project* :Tourmaline, "Honoring Sylvia Rivera and Marsha P. Johnson," *Vogue*, June 29, 2019, https://www.vogue.com/article/tourmaline-trans-day-of-action-op-ed.

252n4 *Rivera got onstage anyway:* Silvia Rivera, "Sylvia Rivera, Y'all Better Quiet Down, 1973," TBR Reading, April 9, 2019, https://www.tbr.fun/sylvia-rivera-yall-better-quiet-down-1973/.

252n5 *"I will not put up with this"*: Ibid.

253n1 *"I remember when someone threw"*: Ibid.

253n2 *"We're all part of one another."*: Raquel Willis, "How Miss Major Helped Spark the Modern Trans Movement," *them.*, March 8, 2018, https://www.them.us/story/transvisionaries-miss-major.

254 *brothel owner from Alabama named Laura Evans:* Arlene Shovald, "Learn the Inside Story of Laura Evans, Local Madam," *Herald Democrat*, June 24, 2015, https://www.leadvilleherald.com/leadville_life/arts_and_entertainment/article_0f3c0c0e-1abc-11e5-bd67-9344b7c37c1d.html.

255n1 *reformatory for female offenders*:"Bedford Hills Correctional Facility," New York State Archives, Cultural Education Center, August 18, 2016, https://snaccooperative.org/ark:/99166/w66b53xc.

255n2 *protecting newly arrived army recruits:* Kim Kelly, "A Forgotten War on Women," *New Republic*, November 22, 2021, https://newrepublic.com/article/148493/forgotten-war-women.

256 *the American Plan:* Scott W. Stern, "Behind the U.S. Government Plan to Jail 'Promiscuous' Women," *Time*, May 15, 2018, https://time.com/5276807/american-concentration-camps-promiscuous-women/.

257 *"corrupted on their way to and from church"*: Kaytlin Bailey, "The Vice-Loathing Reverend and the Sex Workers Who Took San Francisco by Storm in 1917," *Daily Beast*, February 3, 2021, https://www.thedailybeast.com/the-vice-loathing-reverend-and-the-sex-workers-who-took-san-francisco-by-storm-in-1917.

258n1 *she explained in her* writing: Devon Angus and Ivy Anderson, *Alice: Memoirs of a Barbary Coast Prostitute* (Berkeley, CA: Heyday, 2016).

258n2 *write out a speech for the next day's events:* Ibid.

259n1 "You want the city cleaned up": Ivy Anderson and Devon Angus, *Alice: Memoirs of a Barbary Coast Prostitute* (Berkeley, CA: Heyday, 2016).

259n2 *"One of the girls told me"*: Ibid.

259n3 *"one of the strangest gatherings that ever took place in San Francisco"*: Gary Kamiya, "Revolt of the Hookers: How Prostitutes Stared Down a Priest," *San Francisco Chronicle*, June 13, 2015, https://www.sfchronicle.com/bayarea/article/Revolt-of-the-hookers-How-prostitutes-stared-6324339.php.

259n4 *"the girls found themselves on the street"*: Ruth Rosen, *The Lost Sisterhood: Prostitution in America, 1900–1918* (Baltimore, MD: Johns Hopkins University Press, 1982), 67.

259n5 *Madam Reggie Gamble's place*: Jerry F. Schimmel, "A Day When Love No Longer Was for Sale," SFGATE, *San Francisco Chronicle*, February 8, 2012, https://www.sfgate.com/news/article/A-day-when-love-no-longer-was-for-sale-3135421.php.

260n1 *steps of San Francisco's Central Methodist Church:* Ivy Anderson, "International Day of Sex Workers' Rights: 100 Years of Struggle for Sex Workers' Rights," March 4, 2017, http://www.voicesfromtheunderworld.com/blog/2017/3/3/international-day-of-sex-workers-rights-100-years-of-struggle-for-sex-workers-rights.

260n2 *"will always be coming"*: Angus and Anderson, *Alice: Memoirs of a Barbary Coast Prostitute.*

260n3 *"You cannot help people by hunting them"*: Bailey, "The Vice-Loathing Reverend."

261n1 *majority of their labor was secured through kidnapping or outright enslavement*: Judy Yung, *Unbound Feet* (Berkeley: University of California Press), 1995.

261n2 *twenty-year-old named:* May Jeong, "Ah Toy, Pioneering Prostitute of Gold Rush California," *New York Review of Books*, June 24, 2020, https://www.nybooks.com/daily/2020/06/19/ah-toy-pioneering-prostitute-of-gold-rush-california/.

261n3 *stand in line and* pay an ounce of gold: Yen Le Espiritu, *Asian American Women and Men: Labor, Laws, and Love* (Lanham, MD: Rowman & Littlefield, 2008).

262n1 *Chinese immigrant sex workers were able to cash in:* Lucie Cheng Hirata, "Free, Indentured, Enslaved: Chinese Prostitutes in Nineteenth-

Century America," *Signs* 5, no. 1 (1979): 3–29, http://www.jstor.org/stable/3173531.

262n2 *"Men were not the only ones who exploited Chinese [sex workers] for profit"*: Yung, *Unbound Feet*.

263n1 *"crabgrass of prostitution"*: Sally Stanford, *The Lady of the House: the Autobiography of Sally Stanford* (New York: Putnam, 1966).

263n2 *"Race and class dynamics"*: Judy Yung, *Unbound feet* (Berkeley, CA: University of California Press, 1995), 29.

263n3 *"Although immigration provided some benefits for women"*: Espiritu, *Asian American Women and Men*.

263n4 *California politicians made numerous attempts:* Erika Lee, *America for Americans: A History of Xenophobia in the United States* (New York: Basic Books, 2019), 81–86.

264n1 *political gadfly with a checkered past:* G. S. Watkins, E. L. Warren, and Grace Heilman Stimson, *Rise of the Labor Movement in Los Angeles* (University of California Press, 1955), 62.

264n2 *San Francisco delegation to the Federation of Organized Trades and Labor Unions:* Ibid., 60

265n1 *remained in effect until 1943:* Office of the Historian, Foreign Service Institute, "Repeal of the Chinese Exclusion Act, 1943," U.S. Department of State, accessed November 22, 2021, https://history.state.gov/milestones/1937-1945/chinese-exclusion-act-repeal.

265n2 *largest strike wave since 1946:* Lane Windham, "Labor and the Long Seventies," *Jacobin*, February 25, 2018, https://www.jacobinmag.com/2018/02/lane-windham-interview-knocking-on-labors-door-unions.

266n1 *"never turned a trick"*: Katharine Q. Seelye, "Margo St. James, Advocate for Sex Workers, Dies at 83," The New York Times, January 20, 2021, https://www.nytimes.com/2021/01/20/us/margo-st-james-dead.html.

266n2 *criminal defense attorney* Vincent Hallinan: Caitlin Donahue, "The Lady Was a Champ: Remembering Margo St. James, Patron Saint of Sex Work," 48 hills, San Francisco Progressive Media Center, January 23, 2021, https://48hills.org/2021/01/the-lady-was-a-champ-remembering-margo-st-james-patron-saint-of-sex-work/.

266n3 *result, COYOTE, was formed:* Melinda Chateauvert, *Sex Workers Unite: A History of the Movement from Stonewall to SlutWalk* (Boston: Beacon Press, 2015).

267 *2007 interview with Dr. Siobhan Brooks:* Ibid.

268n1 *Task Force on Prostitution:* Dangerous Bedfellows, eds., *Policing Public Sex: Queer Politics and the Future of AIDS Activism* (United Kingdom: South End Press, 1996), 251–63.

268n2 *US PROStitutes Collective:* Sophie Body-Gendrot and Jacques Carré, A City of One's Own: Blurring the Boundaries Between Private and Public (Taylor & Francis, 2016).

268n3 *California Prostitutes Education Project:* Samantha Majic, "'I'm Just a

Woman. But I've Never Been a Victim': Re-Conceptualizing Prostitution Policy through Individual Narratives," *Journal of Women, Politics & Policy* 36, no. 4 (2015): 365–87, https://doi.org/10.1080/1554477x.2015.1082889.

268n4 *twenty thousand attendees from the back of an elephant:* Donahue, "The Lady Was a Champ."

270 *When she coined the term "sex worker":* Brooke Meredith Beloso, "Sex, Work, and the Feminist Erasure of Class," *Signs* 38, no. 1 (2012): 47–70, https://doi.org/10.1086/665808.

271n1 *favorite target of anti-porn crusader turned senator Dianne Feinstein* Jay Barmann, "RIP O'Farrell Theatre, the Mitchell Brothers' Infamous Tenderloin Strip Club," SFist, November 4, 2020, https://sfist.com/2020/11/04/rip-ofarrell-theatre-the-mitchell-brothers-infamous-tenderloin-strip-club/.

271n2 *interview with Dr. Siobhan Brooks:* Siobhan Brooks, "Interview with Dawn Passar," Bayswan.org, Exotic Dancers Alliance, accessed November 22, 2021, http://www.bayswan.org/siobIntvw.html.

271n3 *wage and hour claims with the State Labor Commission:* "Twenty Years of Giving Sex Workers a Voice," St. James Infirmary, December 9, 2013, https://www.stjamesinfirmary.org/wordpress/?p=2746.

272 *"she told me that the company lost money on Black women":* Siobhan Brooks, "Exotic Dancing and Unionizing: The Challenges of Feminist and Antiracist Organizing at the Lusty Lady Theater," *SIECUS Report* 33, no. 2 (2005): 12+, *Gale Academic OneFile* (accessed November 17, 2021).

273n1 *"Margo St. James and Carol Leigh":* Vicky Funari and Julia Query, *Live Nude Girls Unite!*, documentary film, United States: First Run Features, 2000.

273n2 *Dr. Brooks, who echoed generations:* Ibid.

274n1 *"We received four paid sick days":* Siobhan Brooks, "Exotic dancing and unionizing: the challenges of feminist and antiracist organizing at the Lusty Lady Theater," *SIECUS Report* 33, no. 2, 2005: *Gale Academic OneFile*, accessed January 24, 2022, https://link.gale.com/apps/doc/A136113226/AONE?u=nysl_oweb&sid=googleScholar&xid=cfb603d7.

274n2 *"Sex worker activists need to challenge racism and white supremacy":* Brooks, "Exotic Dancing and Unionizing."

275n1 *helped orchestrate a three-day strike:* "Burlesque Strike Ends," *New York Times*, March 31, 1935, 2.

275n2 Minsky Brothers' theater *locked out its stagehands:* Karen Abbott, *American Rose: A Nation Laid Bare: The Life and Times of Gypsy Rose Lee* (United Kingdom: Random House, 2012), 288.

276n1 *"burlesque striptease artist":* Rachel Shteir, *Gypsy: The Art of the Tease* (New Haven: Yale University Press, 2009), 53.

276n2 *The strike was settled that night* :Elaine LaPorte, "Ex-Broadway Showgirl

Marks 80 with Petaluma Bat Mitzvah," *J.*, December 28, 2016, https://live-jweekly.alleydev.com/1997/03/14/ex-broadway-showgirl-marks-80-with-petaluma-bat-mitzvah/.

277n1 *picketed outside Hollywood's Crazy Girls Club:* "Hollywood Strippers Seeking Fair Wages, End to Alleged Sexual Harassment and Assault," CBS Los Angeles, February 22, 2019, https://losangeles.cbslocal.com/2019/02/22/strippers-strike-hollywood/.

277n2 *SoP cofounder Crane:* Samuel Braslow, "L.A.'s Exotic Dancers Are Launching a Labor Movement," *Los Angeles*, March 4, 2019, https://www.lamag.com/citythinkblog/soldiers-of-pole-stripper-union/.

277n3 *"our goals of equality":* "CWA Takes on Stripper Union—Soldiers of Pole Update," Soldiers of Pole, March 11, 2020, https://soldiersofpole.com/cwa-takes-on-stripper-union/.

278n1 *$790,000 in rent, food, and medical assistanc:* Zoe Hollis, "Haymarket Pole," Haymarket Pole Collective, March 18, 2021, https://www.haymarketpole.com/past-services/winter-2020-COVID-19-equity-microgrants.

278n2 *"For the first time in history":* Alana Evans, "Lobbying for Porn," APAG, October 6, 2021, https://apagunion.com/2021/10/06/lobbying-for-porn/.

280n1 *PayPal, Venmo, Square, and Cash App:* Reina Sultan, "Inside Social Media's War on Sex Workers," Bitch Media, August 23, 2021, https://www.bitchmedia.org/article/inside-social-medias-war-on-sex-workers.

280n2 *post-SESTA/FOSTA, 99 percent of the sex workers:* Danielle Blunt and Ariel Wolf, "Erased: The Impact of FOSTA-SESTA and the Removal of Backpage on Sex Workers," *Anti-Trafficking Review*, no. 14 (April, 2020): 117–21, https://doi.org/10.14197/atr.201220148.

281n1 *"What do we do about prostitution?":* Melissa Grant, *Playing the Whore: The Work of Sex Work* (United Kingdom: Verso, 2014), 39.

281n2 *Black trans women:* National Center for Transgender Equality, *Prison and Detention Reform* (Washington, DC: National Center for Transgender Equality, 2012).

281n3 *Ninety percent of trans sex workers:* "To Protect Black Trans Lives, Decriminalize Sex Work," American Civil Liberties Union, November 20, 2020, https://www.aclu.org/news/lgbtq-rights/to-protect-black-trans-lives-decriminalize-sex-work/.

281n4 *"about profiling and policing people":* Melissa Grant, *Playing the Whore: The Work of Sex Work* (United Kingdom: Verso, 2014), 39.

281n5 *thirteen times more likely to experience sexual assault in prison:* Annamarie Forestiere, "America's War on Black Trans Women," *Harvard Civil Rights-Civil Liberties Law Review*, September 23, 2020, https://harvardcrcl.org/americas-war-on-black-trans-women/.

281n6 *11 percent of trans people have worked in the sex trade:* Erin Fitzgerald,

Sarah Elspeth, and Darby Hickey, *Meaningful Work: Transgender Experiences in the Sex Trade December 2015* (Brooklyn, NY: Red Umbrella Project, 2015), National Transgender Discrimination Survey.

282n1 *Cubilette-Polanco, who had a documented* history: Kate Sosin "New Video Reveals Layleen Polanco's Death at Rikers Was Preventable, Family Says," NBCNews.com, June 14, 2020, https://www.nbcnews.com/feature/nbc-out/new-video-reveals-layleen-polanco-s-death-rikers-was-preventable-n1230951.

282n2 *"They treated my sister like she was nothing":* Rosa Goldensohn and Savannah Jacobson, "Woman Who Died at Rikers Island Was in Solitary," *The City*, June 10, 2019, https://www.thecity.nyc/2019/6/10/21211014/woman-who-died-at-rikers-island-was-in-solitary.

282n3 *Red Canary Song:* "About," Red Canary Song, accessed November 17, 2021, https://www.redcanarysong.net/about-us.

283n1 *killing eight people; six of them were Asian women:* Ryan W. Miller, Trevor Hughes, Romina Ruiz-Goiriena, Jorge L. Ortiz, and Jordan Culver, "Hard Workers, Dedicated Mothers, Striving Immigrants: These Are the 8 People Killed in the Atlanta Area Spa Shootings," *USA Today*, March 22, 2021, https://www.usatoday.com/story/news/nation/2021/03/19/who-are-atlanta-shooting-spa-victims/4762802001/.

283n2 *"Whether or not":* Emily Lang, "NYC Virtual Vigil for Atlanta Shooting Victims Spotlights Vulnerabilities of Asian Women Massage Workers," Gothamist, New York Public Radio, March 20, 2021, https://gothamist.com/news/nyc-virtual-vigil-atlanta-shooting-victims-spotlights-vulnerabilities-asian-women-massage-workers.

283n3 *"Self-determination, bodily autonomy, workers' rights":* Red Canary Song, "The Massage Parlor Means Survival Here: Red Canary Song on Robert Kraft," *Tits and Sass*, April 12, 2019, https://titsandsass.com/the-massage-parlor-means-survival-here-red-canary-song-on-robert-kraft/.

284 *"The sex industry is the oldest industry for a reason,":* Reina Sultan, "Sex Workers Describe the Instability and Necessity of OnlyFans," *Vice*, August 25, 2021, https://www.vice.com/en/article/jg89mb/sex-workers-describe-the-instability-and-necessity-of-onlyfans.

CHAPTER 13: THE PRISONERS

285 *"It only takes one person":* "Details on the Founding of IWOC: Interview Selections." Wisconsin Prison Voices, September 30, 2020, https://wisconsinprisonvoices.org/organizing-inside/details-on-the-founding-of-iwoc-interview-selections/.

286 *First, by the millions of Indigenous people:* Rhaina Cohen, Maggie Penman, Tara Boyle, and Shankar Vedantam, "An American Secret: The Untold Story of Native American Enslavement," NPR, November 21, 2017, https://www.npr.org/2017/11/20/565410514/an-american-secret-the-untold-story-of-native-american-enslavement.

287 *at least 650 correctional institutions:* H. Claire Brown, "How Corporations Buy-and Sell-Food Made with Prison Labor," *Counter*, September 9, 2021, https://thecounter.org/how-corporations-buy-and-sell-food-made-with-prison-labor/.

288n1 *Wages for prison jobs:* Annie McGrew and Angela Hanks, "It's Time to Stop Using Inmates for Free Labor," Talk Poverty, October 20, 2017, https://talkpoverty.org/2017/10/20/want-prison-feel-less-like-slavery-pay-inmates-work/.

288n2 "*Once you've been convicted*": Shaka Senghor, *13th*, directed by Ava DuVernay (Netflix, 2016).

289 "*Oh, you want that job*": Maya Schenwar, Victoria Law, and Michelle Alexander. *Prison by Any Other Name: The Harmful Consequences of Popular Reforms* (New York: The New Press, 2021).

290n1 *Attica Liberation Faction, or Attica Brothers:* Marvin Mayfield, "A Half-Century After Attica, Prisoners' Demands Have Not Been Met," *Daily News* (New York), September 8, 2021, https://www.nydailynews.com/opinion/ny-oped-half-century-attica-20210908-drus54lc25h6ribz6szam2rhfa-story.html.

290n2 "*I said, 'we need to organize'* ": "WW Interviews Attica Survivor, Che Nieves, Part 2: 'I Carried the Legacy of Struggle in Prison,'" Mundo Obrero Workers World, August 25, 2021, https://www.workers.org/2021/08/58320/.

291n1 "*We started discussing*": Ibid.

291n2 *corrections officer Sergeant Jack English:* "The Attica Prison Uprising at 40," *Socialist Alternative*, accessed November 22, 2021, https://www.socialistalternative.org/sound-fury-oppressed/attica-prison-uprising-40/.

292 *Prisoners' Labor Union at Green Haven:* Edward Perlmutter, "Prisoners' Union Formed Upstate," *New York Times*, February 8, 1972, 1.

293n1 "*In virtually every prison*": Donald F. Tibbs, *From Black Power to Prison Power: The Making of Jones V. North Carolina Prisoners' Labor Union* (London: Palgrave Macmillan, 2012), 156.

293n2 *ran the prison themselves:* BBC World, "Witness History: When the Prisoners Ran the Prison," Apple Podcasts, March 30, 2021, https://podcasts.apple.com/au/podcast/when-the-prisoners-ran-the-prison/id339986758?i=1000514992858.

293n3 "*its workers, its employers*": Anjali Cadambi, "1973: Prisoners Take Control of Walpole Prison," Global Nonviolent Action Database, October 18, 2010, https://libcom.org/history/1973-prisoners-take-control-walpole-prison.

293n4 "*It's worth paying them*": Ibid.

294 *prisoners in Folsom, California:* Joël Charbit and Gwenola Ricordeau, "Prisoners on Strike in the United States," Books & Ideas, October 15, 2018, https://booksandideas.net/Prisoners-on-Strike-in-the-United-States-4202.html.

295n1 *"If free citizens"*: Donald F. Tibbs, *From Black Power to Prison Power: The Making of Jones V. North Carolina Prisoners' Labor Union*, (London: Palgrave Macmillan, 2012), 139.

295n2 *Robbie Purner:* Jonathan Michels, "Unions Are Needed Everywhere—Especially Prisons," *Scalawag*, June 23, 2021, https://scalawagmagazine.org/2018/07/if-free-people-are-not-allowed-to-have-unions-how-are-prisoners-to-have-unions-conversations-with-organizers-of-the-north-carolina-prisoners-labor-union/.

296n1 *Bedford Hills Correctional Facility in New York State:* JB Nicholas, "August Rebellion: New York's Forgotten Female Prison Riot," *Village Voice*, February 22, 2017, https://web.archive.org/web/20170516160529/https://www.villagevoice.com/news/august-rebellion-new-york-s-forgotten-female-prison-riot-9043794.

296n2 *On February 3, 1974:* Ibid.

296n3 *"like a roasted pig"*: Ibid.

296n4 *took control of the prison:* "Beyond Attica: The Untold Story of Women's Resistance Behind Bars," Alternet.org, February 10, 2021, https://www.alternet.org/2009/07/beyond_attica_the_untold_story_of_womens_resistance_behind_bars/.

297n1 *The* resulting lawsuit: Tessa Melvin, "Fund for Inmates Celebrated," *New York Times*, June 26, 1983, sec. 11.

297n2 *cacophonous* "noise strike": "Girls on 'Noise' Strike: Inmates of Bedford Reformatory Jangle Cell Doors and Scream," *New York Times*, January 25, 1920, 19.

297n3 *The Silvia Rivera Law Project:* "Transgender Incarcerated People in Crisis," Lambda Legal, accessed November 22, 2021, https://www.lambdalegal.org/know-your-rights/article/trans-incarcerated-people.

297n4 *According to Lambda Legal:* "Transgender Incarcerated People in Crisis," Lambda Legal, accessed January 24, 2022, https://www.lambdalegal.org/know-your-rights/article/trans-incarcerated-people.

297n5 *Alabama's Julia Tutwiler Prison for Women:* Chandra Bozelko, Amy Polacko, and Christina Lane, "Busting Four Myths About Incarcerated Women," *Ms.*, July 26, 2019, https://msmagazine.com/2019/07/26/busting-four-myths-about-incarcerated-women/.

298 *perpetrated by prison guards:* "Tutwiler Prison for Women," Equal Justice Initiative, November 15, 2019, https://eji.org/cases/tutwiler/.

299n1 *"there is no union, there has been no union, and there will not be so long as I am secretary"*: Gregory S. Taylor, *Central Prison: A History of North Carolina's State Penitentiary* (Baton Rouge, LA: LSU Press, 2021), 184.

299n2 *Justice Thurgood Marshall dissented:* Donald F. Tibbs, *From Black Power to Prison Power: The Making of* Jones v. North Carolina Prisoners' Labor Union (New York: Palgrave Macmillan, 2012).

299n3 *"It cemented this idea"*: Maya Schenwar, Victoria Law, and Michelle Alexander, *Prison by Any Other Name: The Harmful Consequences of Popular Reforms* (New York: The New Press, 2021).

300n1 *"it said the state gets to determine security issues"*: Jonathan Michels, "'Prisoners' Organizations Were Thought to Be Dangerous': Conversations with Organizers of the North Carolina Prisoners' Labor Union," *Scalawag*, September 16, 2020, https://scalawagmagazine.org/2018/06/prisoners-organizations-were-thought-to-be-dangerous-conversations-with-organizers-of-the-north-carolina-prisoners-labor-union/.

300n2 *"A lot of people have died to preserve freedom and human rights"*: Michels, "Unions Are Needed Everywhere—Especially Prisons."

300n3 *prisoners' rights movement began to take shape:* "Details on the Founding of the Incarcerated Workers Organizing Committee (IWOC)," September 2020, https://wisconsinprisonvoices.org/wp-content/uploads/2020/09/founding.iwoc_.interviews.pdf.

300n4 *weeklong work stoppage:* "Free Alabama Movement Strike," *Perilous Chronicle*, January 11, 2019, https://perilouschronicle.com/2014/01/01/free-alabama-movement-strike/.

302n1 *IWOC took full advantage of that* loophole: Arvind Dilawar, "How to Organize a Prison Strike," *Pacific Standard*, May 7, 2018, https://psmag.com/social-justice/how-to-organize-a-prison-strike.

302n2 *reflected on the horrors:* Hybachi LeMar, "Resistance Has Become My Ethical Obligation: Words of Reflection on the International Day in Support of Victims of Torture," Incarcerated Workers Organizing Committee, June 28, 2021, https://incarceratedworkers.org/campaigns/resistance-has-become-my-ethical-obligation-words-reflection-international-day-support.

304n1 *"A solid portion of the guys"*: Jessica Schulberg, "Rikers Island Worker Blows Whistle on Covid-19 Risk in Infamous New York Jail," HuffPost, July 31, 2020, https://www.huffpost.com/entry/rikers-island-coronavirus-whistleblower_n_5f207377c5b638cfec4b076e.

304n2 *forty-six facilities in twenty-four states:* "Nationwide Prison Strike Launches in 24 States and 40 Facilities over Conditions & Forced Labor," Democracy Now!, September 9, 2016, https://www.democracynow.org/2016/9/9/nationwide_prison_strike_launches_in_24.

305n1 *"To every prisoner in every state"*: Madison van Oort, "A Call to End Slavery in America: September 9 National Prisoner Work Stoppage," Verso, August 25, 2016, https://www.versobooks.com/blogs/2813-a-call-to-end-slavery-in-america-september-9-national-prisoner-work-stoppage.

305n2 *"If we really take seriously"*: Dan Berger, *Captive Nation: Black Prison Organizing in the Civil Rights Era* (Chapel Hill, NC: University of North Carolina Press, 2016).

306 *had been a child of the desert:* "Shawna L. Jones," National Fallen Firefighters Foundation, September 30, 2020, https://www.firehero.org/fallen-firefighter/shawna-l-jones/.

307 *Conservation Camp Program:* Paul D. Knothe, "AB 2147 Clears Career Paths for Formerly Incarcerated Persons Trained as Firefighters," California Public Agency Labor & Employment Blog, September 15, 2020, https://www.calpublicagencylaboremploymentblog.com/legislation/ab-2147-clears-career-paths-for-formerly-incarcerated-persons-trained-as-firefighters/.

308n1 *State legislators:* LA Times Editorial Board, "Editorial: Inmates Risking Their Lives to Fight California's Wildfires Deserve a Chance at Full-Time Jobs," *Los Angeles Times*, November 1, 2019, https://www.latimes.com/opinion/story/2019-11-01/california-inmate-firefighters.

308n2 *real pathway toward employment:* Eloise Reyes, "AB-1211 Firefighters," Bill Text—AB—211 Firefighters, February 22, 2019, https://leginfo.legislature.ca.gov/faces/billTextClient.xhtml?bill_id=201920200AB1211.

308n3 *craven factory owners, plantation overseers, and coal barons:* Philip Kennicott, "The American Worker: Exploited from the Beginning," *Washington Post*, November 20, 2017, https://www.washingtonpost.com/entertainment/museums/the-american-worker-exploited-from-the-beginning/2017/11/20/7ae8fe6a-c890-11e7-b0cf-7689a9f2d84e_story.html.

EPILOGUE

311 *eight hundred coal miners in rural Alabama are still out on a strike:* Nora De La Cour, "Alabama Miners Are Still on Strike After 8 Months," *Jacobin*, August 11, 2021, https://www.jacobinmag.com/2021/11/alabam-coal-miners-umwa-strike-blackrock-pickets-violence.

314 *Rep. Alexandria Ocasio-Cortez:* Alexandria Ocasio-Cortez, "#Striketober coming in hot after years of being underserved and taken for granted - & doubly so during the pandemic - workers are starting to authorize strikes across the country: from @IATSE production workers to @UAW John Deere & @BCTGM Kellogg workers,& many more.good," Twitter, October 14, 2021, https://twitter.com/AOC/status/1448664331344822272.

315n1 *"Here we go again":* Michael Foster "The Hearing officer of the Regional NLRB has recommended that it be a re election in Bessemer Alabama Amazon here we go again but this time with a Win Bigmikeunion1" Twitter, August 3, 2021, https://twitter.com/BigMikeUnion1/status/1422622496222765056.

315n2 *"fight back and organize your workplace":* Nivedita Balu and Jeffrey Dastin, "Amazon's Staten Island Warehouse Workers File Petition for Union Election," Reuters, October 26, 2021, https://www.reuters.com/business/amazons-staten-island-warehouse-workers-file-petition-union-election-nlrb-2021-10-25/.

315n3 *millions in debt relief:* Erum Salam, "New York City Taxi Drivers End Hunger Strike After Reaching Deal on Debt Relief," *Guardian*, November 4, 2021, https://www.theguardian.com/us-news/2021/nov/04/new-york-city-taxi-drivers-end-hunger-strike-debt-relief.

316n1 *striking nurse Marie Ritacco:* Ben Kesslen, "'This Is Not Where We Expected to Be': Massachusetts Nurses Strike Hits 7-Month Mark," NBC News.com, October 10, 2021, https://www.nbcnews.com/news/us-news/not-where-we-expected-be-massachusetts-nurses-strike-hits-7-n1281053.

316n2 *on January 3, 2022:* Aparna Gopalan, "Massachusetts Nurses Just Won an Epic 10-Month Strike," New Republic, January 7, 2022, https://newrepublic.com/article/164950/st-vincent-hospital-nurses-strike.

BIBLIOGRAPHY

CHAPTER 1: THE TRAILBLAZERS

AFL-CIO. "Atlanta's Washerwomen Strike." https://aflcio.org/about/history/labor-history-events/atlanta-washerwomen-strike.

Arnesen, Eric, ed. *The Human Tradition in American Labor History*. Human Tradition in America, no. 19. Wilmington, DE: SR Books, 2004.

"Balls and Strikes." *Code Switch*. NPR, September 2, 2020. https://www.npr.org/2020/09/01/908305393/balls-and-strikes.

Bentley, Rosalind. "Black Woman Magic: The Atlanta Laundry Workers' Strike of 1881." *The Atlanta Journal-Constitution*, February 11, 2019.

Cruea, Susan M. "Changing Ideals of Womanhood During the Nineteenth-Century Woman Movement." *American Transcendental Quarterly* 19, no. 3 (September 2005): 187–204, 237.

DeFrancesco, Joey La Neve. "Pawtucket, America's First Factory Strike." *Jacobin*, June 6, 2018. https://jacobinmag.com/2018/06/factory-workers-strike-textile-mill-women.

"Factory Girls' Association." In *St. James Encyclopedia of Labor History Worldwide: Major Events in Labor History and Their Impact*. Detroit: Gale Group, 2003.

Foner, Philip S., ed. *The Factory Girls: A Collection of Writings on Life and Struggles in the New England Factories of the 1840s*. Urbana: University of Illinois Press, 1977.

———, and Ronald L. Lewis, eds. *The Black Worker, Volume 2: The Black Worker During the Era of the National Labor Union*. Philadelphia: Temple University Press, 2019. https://doi.org/10.2307/j.ctvn5tvwc.

Greenlees, Janet. "Workplace Health and Gender among Cotton Workers in America and Britain, c.1880s–1940s." *International Review of Social History* 61, no. 3 (December 2016): 459–85. https://doi.org/10.1017/S0020859016000493.

Hunter, Tera W. *To 'Joy My Freedom: Southern Black Women's Lives and Labors after the Civil War*. Cambridge: Harvard University Press, 1999.

Keenan, Sean Richard. "GSU Researcher Takes Deep Dive into Summerhill's

Fascinating, Turbulent History." *Curbed Atlanta* (blog), June 27, 2019. https://atlanta.curbed.com/2019/6/27/18761209/gsu-historian-deep-dive-georgia-avenue-summerhill.

Larcom, Lucy. *Idyl of Work*. Ann Arbor: University of Michigan Humanities Text Initiative, 1996. http://name.umdl.umich.edu/BAD5902.0001.001.

Larrabee, John. "Slater Mill Exhibit Recalls the 'Mother of All Strikes.'" *The Sun Chronicle*, May 22, 2014. https://www.thesunchronicle.com/devices/features/stories/slater-mill-exhibit-recalls-the-mother-of-all-strikes/article_68f6d792-bc36-5faf-bcfe-b4f0022c81cf.html.

Lawrence, Ken. "Mississippi's First Labour Union." *Libcom.org* (blog), September 10, 2016. http://libcom.org/history/mississippis-first-labour-union-ken-lawrence.

Lowell National Historical Park. "Sarah Bagley," April 27, 2021. https://www.nps.gov/lowe/learn/historyculture/sarah-bagley.htm.

Moran, William. *The Belles of New England: The Women of the Textile Mills and the Families Whose Wealth They Wove*. New York: Thomas Dunne Books, 2004.

Morris, Richard Brandon. "The Emergence of American Labor." In *The U.S. Department of Labor Bicentennial History of the American Worker*. Washington, DC: U.S. Government Printing Office, 1976. https://www.dol.gov/general/aboutdol/history/chapter1.

New England Historical Society. "Girl Power in 1824: The First Factory Strike in America." August 3, 2018. https://www.newenglandhistoricalsociety.com/1824-factory-strike-1824/.

———. "Sarah Bagley Avenges the New England Mill Girls," April 19, 2014. https://www.newenglandhistoricalsociety.com/sarah-bagley-avenges-new-england-mill-girls/.

New York Historical Society Museum & Library. "Laundry Workers' Strike." https://wams.nyhistory.org/a-nation-divided/reconstruction/laundry-workers-strike/.

"Notes & Queries: What Were William Blake's Dark Satanic Mills?" Life and Style. *The Guardian*, September 12, 2012. https://www.theguardian.com/lifeandstyle/2012/sep/12/william-blakes-dark-satanic-mills.

Obadele-Starks, Ernest. *Black Unionism in the Industrial South*. College Station: Texas A & M University Press, 2001.

Patmore, Coventry. *The Angel in the House*. Boston: Ticknor & Fields, 1864.

Shelton, Robert S. "'Built by the Irishman, the Negro and the Mule:' Labor Militancy across the Color Line in Post-Reconstruction Texas." *East Texas Historical Journal* 46, no. 2 (October 2008): 15–26. https://scholarworks.sfasu.edu/ethj/vol46/iss2/7.

Taylor, Barilla. "The Role of Women in the Industrial Revolution." Tsongas Industrial History Center. https://www.uml.edu/Tsongas/barilla-taylor/women-industrial-revolution.aspx.

"The Doughty Washwomen: Holding Out for an Advance in Wages." *Atlanta Constitution*, July 26, 1881. https://shec.ashp.cuny.edu/items/show/897.

University of Texas at San Antonio Libraries. "Emigration, Immigration, and Migration Collection." https://libguides.utsa.edu/c.php?g=515536&p=5730362.

Ward, Donna Patricia. "Former Slaves Went on Strike in 1881 Weeks before a World's Fair in Atlanta." *History Collection* (blog), November 19, 2018. https://historycollection.com/former-slaves-went-on-strike-in-1881-weeks-before-a-worlds-fair-in-atlanta/.

CHAPTER 2: THE GARMENT WORKERS

Breitman, Jessica. "Frances Perkins." FDR Presidential Library & Museum. https://www.fdrlibrary.org/perkins.

Castaneda, Manuel, dir. "The People vs. Willie Farah." 1973. Texas Archive of the Moving Image. Television program, 21:43. https://texasarchive.org/2011_02871.

Coyle, Laurie, Gail Hershatter, and Emily Honig. "Women at Farah: An Unfinished Story." In *A Needle, A Bobbin, A Strike: Women Needleworkers in America*, edited by Susan Davidson and Joan Jensen, 227–277. Philadelphia: Temple University Press, 1984.

Foner, Philip S. *Women and the American Labor Movement*. Chicago: Haymarket Books, 2018.

Jensen, Joan M., and Sue Davidson, eds. *A Needle, a Bobbin, a Strike: Women Needleworkers in America*. Philadelphia: Temple University Press, 2018. https://doi.org/10.2307/j.ctv941x68.

Kelly, Kim. "Unsung Heroes of Latinx Farmworkers' Labor Movement, from Maria Moreno to Fast Food Boycotters." *Teen Vogue*, October 15, 2018. https://www.teenvogue.com/story/unsung-heroes-latinx-farmworkers-labor-movement-maria-moreno-to-fast-food-boycotters.

King, Loren. "Maine's Frances Perkins Center Gives FDR's New Deal Architect Her Due." *Boston Spirit Magazine*, May 11, 2021. https://bostonspiritmagazine.com/2021/05/maines-frances-perkins-center-gives-fdrs-new-deal-architect-her-due/.

Martin, Douglas. "Rose Freedman, Last Survivor of Triangle Fire, Dies at 107." *The New York Times*, February 17, 2001. https://www.nytimes.com/2001/02/17/nyregion/rose-freedman-last-survivor-of-triangle-fire-dies-at-107.html.

Michels, Tony. "Uprising of 20,000 (1909)." In *The Shalvi/Hyman Encyclopedia of Jewish Women*. Jewish Women's Archive, December 31, 1999. https://jwa.org/encyclopedia/article/uprising-of-20000-1909.

Morales, Marko. "Farah Company Veterans Relive the Garment Maker's Rise and Fall." *Borderzine*, October 28, 2010. https://borderzine.com/2010/10/farah-company-veterans-relive-the-garment-maker%e2%80%99s-rise-and-fall/.

PBS American Experience. "Clara Lemlich and the Uprising of the 20," August 10, 2017. https://www.pbs.org/wgbh/americanexperience/features/biography-clara-lemlich/.

Shabecoff, Philip. "Farah Strike Has Become War of Attrition." *The New York Times*, June 16, 1973. https://www.nytimes.com/1973/06/16/archives/farah-strike-has-become-war-of-attriton-the-worst-part.html.

Shepherd, William. "Eyewitness at the Triangle." *Milwaukee Journal*, March 27, 1911. https://trianglefire.ilr.cornell.edu/primary/testimonials/ootss_William Shepherd.html.

Sprague, Leah W. "Her Life: The Woman Behind the New Deal." *Frances Perkins Center* (blog), June 1, 2014. https://francesperkinscenter.org/life-new/.

Stein, Leon. *The Triangle Fire*. Ithaca, NY: ILR Press, 2011. http://site.ebrary.com/id/10588003.

"Sylvia M. Trevino (1947–2020)." *San Antonio Express-News*, January 15, 2020.

University of Iowa Labor Center. "Child Labor in U.S. History." https://laborcenter.uiowa.edu/special-projects/child-labor-public-education-project/about-child-labor/child-labor-us-history.

U.S. Department of Labor. "Hall of Honor Inductee: Frances M. Perkins." https://www.dol.gov/general/aboutdol/hallofhonor/1989_perkins.

U.S. National Park Service. "Frances Perkins," March 22, 2021. https://www.nps.gov/people/frances-perkins.htm.

Vargas, Zaragosa. "Empleo." U.S. National Park Service, July 9, 2020. https://www.nps.gov/articles/000/themestudyempleo.htm.

Yung, Judy. *Unbound Feet: A Social History of Chinese Women in San Francisco*. Berkeley: University of California Press, 1995.

CHAPTER 3: THE MILL WORKERS

Brecher, Jeremy. *Strike!* Revised, Expanded, and Updated edition. Oakland: PM Press, 2014.

Editors of Encyclopaedia Britannica. "National Recovery Administration." In *Encyclopaedia Britannica*, December 10, 2019.

Fink, Gary M. *The Fulton Bag and Cotton Mills Strike of 1914–1915: Espionage, Labor Conflict, and New South Industrial Relations*. Cornell Studies in Industrial and Labor Relations, no. 28. Ithaca, N.Y: ILR Press, 1993.

Flanagan, Alice K. *The Lowell Mill Girls*. We the People. Minneapolis: Compass Point Books, 2006.

Georgia State University Library Digital Collections. "The Uprising of '34 Collection," 1995. https://digitalcollections.library.gsu.edu/digital/collection/uprising.

Glass, Brent D., and Michael Hill. "Gastonia Strike." In *Encyclopedia of North Carolina*, edited by William S. Powell. Chapel Hill: University of North Carolina Press, 2006. https://www.ncpedia.org/gastonia-strike.

Graham, Nicholas. "This Month in North Carolina History: Strike at Loray Mill." *UNC University Libraries* (blog), June 2004. https://web.archive.org/web/20090531012624/http:/www.lib.unc.edu/ncc/ref/nchistory/jun2004/.

Hall, Jacquelyn Dowd. "Disorderly Women: Gender and Labor Militancy in the Appalachian South." *The Journal of American History* 73, no. 2 (September 1986): 354. https://doi.org/10.2307/1908226.

———. "O. Delight Smith: A Labor Organizer's Odyssey." In *Forgotten Heroes: Inspiring American Portraits from Our Leading Historians*, edited by Susan Ware. Collingdale, PA: Diane Publishing, 1998.

———. "O. Delight Smith's Progressive Era: Labor, Feminism and Reform in the Urban South." In *Visible Women: New Essays on American Activism*, edited by Nancy A. Hewitt and Suzanne Lebsock, 166–98. Women in American History. Urbana: University of Illinois Press, 1993.

Hall, Jacquelyn Dowd, James L. Leloudis, Robert Rodgers Korstad, Mary Murphy, Lu Ann Jones, Michael H. Frisch, and Christopher B. Daly. *Like a Family: The Making of a Southern Cotton Mill World*. Chapel Hill: University of North Carolina Press, 2012.

Kuhn, Cliff. *Contesting the New South Order: The 1914–1915 Strike at Atlanta's Fulton Mills*. Chapel Hill: University of North Carolina Press, 2001.

Murray, Jonathan. "Textile Strike of 1934." North Carolina History Project, March 7, 2016. https://northcarolinahistory.org/encyclopedia/textile-strike-of-1934/.

"Negro Help Causes a Strike; Six Hundred White Operatives Leave Work in Atlanta Cotton Mills, Factory Forced to Shut Down." *The New York Times*, August 5, 1897. https://www.nytimes.com/1897/08/05/archives/negro-help-causes-a-strike-six-hundred-white-operatives-leave-work.html.

Obadele-Starks, Ernest. *Black Unionism in the Industrial South*. College Station: Texas A & M University Press, 2001.

Salmond, John A. "'The Burlington Dynamite Plot': The 1934 Textile Strike and Its Aftermath in Burlington, North Carolina." *The North Carolina Historical Review* 75, no. 4 (October 1998): 398–434.

———. *Gastonia 1929: The Story of the Loray Mill Strike*. Chapel Hill: University of North Carolina Press, 2009.

"Strike Wages in Georgia Factor." *The Atlanta Evening Herald*. August 15, 1914.

Talmadge, Eugene. "Martial Law in Georgia." Georgia Journeys. https://georgiajourneys.kennesaw.edu/items/show/419.

Troxler, George W. "Flying Squadrons." In *Encyclopedia of North Carolina*, edited by William S. Powell. Chapel Hill: University of North Carolina Press, 2006.

Whittelse, Sarah Scovill. *Massachusetts Labor Legislation, An Historical and Critical Study*. New York: Kraus Reprint Co., 1970. https://www.jstor.org/stable/pdf/1010335.pdf.

CHAPTER 4: THE REVOLUTIONARIES

AFL-CIO. "The Battle of Cripple Creek." https://aflcio.org/about/history/labor-history-events/battle-cripple-creek.

———. "Our Labor History Timeline." https://aflcio.org/about-us/history.

Alperovitz, D. J. "IWW Members Killed Year by Year 1907–1974." IWW History Project, University of Washington, 2013. https://depts.washington.edu/iww/map_killed.shtml.

"Arrests, Prosecutions, Beatings, and Other Violence 1906–1920." IWW History Project, University of Washington, n.d. https://depts.washington.edu/iww/persecution.shtml.

Botkin, Jane Little. *Frank Little and the IWW: The Blood That Stained an American Family*. Norman: University of Oklahoma Press, 2017.

Buhle, Paul. "The IWW Saga in New Light." *MR Online* (blog), October 29, 2017. https://mronline.org/2017/10/28/the-iww-saga-in-new-light/.

Cole, Peter. "The Great Black Radical You've Never Heard Of." *In These Times*, December 1, 2020. https://inthesetimes.com/article/ben-fletcher-iww-wobblies-worker-organizing.

———. "IWW Local 8: Philadelphia's Interracial Longshore Union." IWW History Project, University of Washington, 2015. https://depts.washington.edu/iww/local8iww.shtml.

———. "Philadelphia's Lords of the Docks: Interracial Unionism Wobbly-Style." *The Journal of the Gilded Age and Progressive Era* 6, no. 3 (July 2007): 310–38.

Cole, Peter, and Ben Fletcher. *Ben Fletcher: The Life and Times of a Black Wobbly*. 2nd ed. Oakland: PM Press, 2021.

"Constitution and By-Laws of Industrial Workers of the World." Chicago: Industrial Workers of the World, 1905.

Dolgoff, Sam. "Revolutionary Tendencies in American Labor, Part 2." In *The American Labor Movement: A New Beginning*. Chicago: Industrial Workers of the World. https://archive.iww.org/history/library/Dolgoff/newbeginning/5/.

Editors of Encyclopaedia Britannica. "Knights of Labor." In *Encyclopaedia Britannica*, May 25, 2001.

Encyclopedia Staff. "Western Federation of Miners." Colorado Encyclopedia, June 17, 2021. https://coloradoencyclopedia.org/article/western-federation-miners.

Frank, Miriam. *Out in the Union: A Labor History of Queer America*. Philadelphia: Temple University Press, 2015.

Garlock, Jonathan. "Knights of Labor History and Geography 1869–1899." Mapping American Social Movements Project, University of Washington. https://depts.washington.edu/moves/knights_labor_map.shtml.

Gauvreau, Christine. "The Joan of Arc of Shelton, the Efficiency Man, the O'Brien's, and Sidney Blumenthal." Connecticut Digital Newspaper Project, December 30, 2015. https://ctdigitalnewspaperproject.org/2015/12/the-joan-of-arc-of-shelton-the-efficiency-man-the-obriens-and-sidney-blumenthal/.

Helquist, Michael. *Marie Equi: Radical Politics and Outlaw Passions*. Corvallis: Oregon State University Press, 2015.

Hyde, Liss Waters, and Jaime Caro. "Industrial Unions and the IWW Explained." *Industrial Worker*, August 5, 2020. https://industrialworker.org/industrial-unions-and-the-iww-explained/.

Industrial Workers of the World. "Fellow Worker Eugene V Debs." https://archive.iww.org/history/biography/EugeneDebs/1/.

———. "Fellow Worker Hubert Harrison." https://archive.iww.org/history/biography/HubertHarrison/1/.

———. "How the IWW Differs from Business Unions." https://archive.iww.org/about/how-iww-differs-business-unions/.

———. "IWW Campaigns." https://archive.iww.org/history/campaigns/.

———. "Lucy Parsons: Woman of Will." https://archive.iww.org/history/biography/LucyParsons/1/.

"IWW Copper Strike." In *St. James Encyclopedia of Labor History Worldwide: Major Events in Labor History and Their Impact*. Detroit: Gale Group, 2003.

Jones, Jacqueline. *Goddess of Anarchy: The Life and Times of Lucy Parsons, American Radical*. New York: Basic Books, 2017.

Lawrence History Center. "1912 Strike Victim." September 1, 2008. http://www.lawrencehistory.org/node/206.

Mayer, Heather. *Beyond the Rebel Girl: Women and the Industrial Workers of the World in the Pacific Northwest, 1905–1924*. Corvallis: Oregon State University Press, 2018.

Moran, William. *The Belles of New England: The Women of the Textile Mills and the Families Whose Wealth They Wove*. New York: Thomas Dunne Books, 2004.

O'Donnell, L. A. "Irish Yeast in the Trade Unions." *Talkin' Union*, September, 1987.

Parfitt, Steven. "Justice Department Campaign Against the IWW, 1917–1920." IWW History Project, University of Washington, 2015. https://depts.washington.edu/iww/justice_dept.shtml#_edn2.

Parsons, Lucy E. "To Tramps." *Alarm*, October 4, 1884. https://theanarchistlibrary.org/library/lucy-e-parsons-to-tramps

Perry, Jeffrey B. "Hubert Harrison." Zinn Education Project, December 17, 2013. https://www.zinnedproject.org/materials/harrison-hubert/.

Rabinowitz, Matilda, Robbin Henderson, and Ileen A. DeVault. *Immigrant Girl, Radical Woman: A Memoir from the Early Twentieth Century*. Ithaca: ILR Press, 2017.

Rosenthal, Keith. "More Dangerous than a Thousand Rioters." *Socialist Worker*, September 22, 2011. http://socialistworker.org/2011/09/22/lucy-parsons.

Seraile, William. "Ben Fletcher, I.W.W. Organizer." *Pennsylvania History: A Journal of Mid-Atlantic Studies* 46, no. 3 (July 1979): 212–32.

Spicuzza, Mary. "Consiglia Rocco Teutonica." *Metroactive*, March 10, 1999. https://www.metroactive.com/papers/cruz/03.10.99/women3-9910.html.

Thornton, Steve. "Jewish Women Who Were Local Labor Organizers." *The Shoeleather History Project* (blog), September 23, 2019. https://shoeleatherhistoryproject.com/2019/09/23/local-jewish-women-who-were-labor-organizers/.

Trickey, Erick. "When America's Most Prominent Socialist Was Jailed for Speaking Out Against World War I." *Smithsonian Magazine*, June 15, 2018.

https://www.smithsonianmag.com/history/fiery-socialist-challenged-nations-role-wwi-180969386/.

University of Washington University Libraries. "WWI Exhibit: Spruce Production and Northwest Labor Unrest." https://content.lib.washington.edu/exhibits/WWI/spruce.html.

VCU Libraries Social Welfare History Project. "Labor History Timeline: 1607–1999," October 21, 2015. https://socialwelfare.library.vcu.edu/organizations/labor/labor-history-timeline-1607-1999/.

CHAPTER 5: THE MINERS

Absolute Michigan. "Calumet's Big Annie." April 6, 2006. http://absolutemichigan.com/michigan/calumets-big-annie/.

AFL-CIO. "Mother Jones." https://aflcio.org/about/history/labor-history-people/mother-jones.

"Alabama Judge Issues Unconstitutional Order at Warrior Met Strike." United Mine Workers of America, October 28, 2021. https://umwa.org/news-media/press/alabama-judge-issues-unconstitutional-order-at-warrior-met-strike/.

Alabama NewsCenter Staff. "On This Day in Alabama History: Mine Workers Went on Strike." *Alabama NewsCenter* (blog), July 8, 2018. https://www.alabamanewscenter.com/2018/07/08/day-alabama-history-july-8/.

Allen, Reniqua. "In W.Va., Fortunes of Black Minority Fall along with Coal." Al Jazeera America, February 14, 2016. http://america.aljazeera.com/articles/2016/2/14/fortunes-of-black-miners-in-wva-are-a-casualty-of-coal.html.

Ascarza, William. "Native Americans Mined Variety of Minerals Early On." *Arizona Daily Star*, May 20, 2013. https://tucson.com/news/local/native-americans-mined-variety-of-minerals-early-on/article_8d64025e-b0a7-5c5a-920d-b67f53073ef5.html.

Associated Press. "Coal Company Will Pay 78 Women Denied Jobs." *The New York Times*, November 26, 1978. https://www.nytimes.com/1978/11/26/archives/coal-company-will-pay-78-women-denied-jobs.html.

———. "Woman Miners Seek Damages in Harassment Suit." *The New York Times*, April 29, 1982. https://www.nytimes.com/1982/04/29/us/woman-miners-seek-damages-in-harassment-suit.html.

———. "Women Coal Miners' Suit Breaks New Ground." *The Nevada Daily Mail*, April 26, 1982.

Baker, Carrie N. *The Women's Movement against Sexual Harassment*. New York: Cambridge University Press, 2008.

Bakken, Gordon, and Brenda Farrington. *Encyclopedia of Women in the American West*. Thousand Oaks, CA: SAGE Publications, 2003. https://doi.org/10.4135/9781412950626.

Blasi, Brigida R. "How Wyoming's Black Coal Miners Shaped Their Own History." *High Country News*, January 28, 2021. https://www.hcn.org/issues/53

.2/north-people-places-how-wyomings-black-coal-miners-shaped-their-own-history.

———. "The Forgotten History of Wyoming's Black Miners." *Mother Jones*, February 1, 2021. https://www.motherjones.com/environment/2021/02/the-forgotten-history-of-wyomings-black-miners/.

Curtin, Mary Ellen. "Convict-Lease System." Encyclopedia of Alabama, Alabama Humanities Alliance, September 12, 2007. http://encyclopediaofalabama.org/article/h-1346.

Daniel, Leon. "Women Coal Miners Fight Sexual Harassment." *United Press International*, June 17, 1985. https://www.upi.com/Archives/1985/06/17/Women-coal-miners-fight-sexual-harassment/8607487828800/.

Davidson, John Nelson. *Negro Slavery in Wisconsin*. Milwaukee, MN: Parkman Club, 1896.

Easter, Makeda. "Slavery Documents from Southern Saltmakers Bring Light to Dark History." *Los Angeles Times*, April 16, 2020. https://www.latimes.com/entertainment-arts/story/2020-04-16/huntington-slavery-collection-west-virginia-salt-works.

Errick, Jennifer. "Exploring 70 Centuries of Mining History." *National Parks Conservation Association* (blog), September 26, 2019. https://www.npca.org/articles/2309-exploring-70-centuries-of-mining-history.

Fallows, James. "The Past Is Never Past: Slave Labor in the West Virginia Salt Works." *The Atlantic*, December 8, 2014. https://www.theatlantic.com/business/archive/2014/12/the-past-is-never-past-west-virginia-salt-works-edition/383493/.

Fisher, Allen. "Women's Rights and the Civil Rights Act of 1964." National Archives, July 3, 2019. https://www.archives.gov/women/1964-civil-rights-act.

Foner, Philip S. *Women and the American Labor Movement*. Chicago: Haymarket Books, 2018.

Forman, Cyrus. "A Briny Crossroads: Salt, Slavery, and Sectionalism in The Kanawha Salines." MA thesis, CUNY City College, 2014. https://academicworks.cuny.edu/cc_etds_theses/275.

Franklin, Ben A. "Women Who Work in Mines Assail Harassment and Unsafe Conditions." *The New York Times*, November 11, 1979. https://www.nytimes.com/1979/11/11/archives/women-who-work-in-mines-assail-harassment-and-unsafe-conditions.html.

Franklin, Stephen. "Women Last In, First Out of the Mines." *Chicago Tribune*, October 4, 1987. https://www.chicagotribune.com/news/ct-xpm-1987-10-04-8703150093-story.html.

Friedman, Gail. "March of the Mill Children." The Encyclopedia of Greater Philadelphia, Rutgers University, 2014. https://philadelphiaencyclopedia.org/archive/march-of-the-mill-children/.

Gearhart, Dona G. "'Surely, a Wench Can Choose Her Own Work!' Women Coal Miners in Paonia, Colorado, 1976–1987." PhD diss., University of Nevada, Las Vegas, 1996.

Giesen, Carol A. B. *Coal Miners' Wives: Portraits of Endurance*. Lexington: University Press of Kentucky, 1995.

Gorn, Elliott J. "The History of Mother Jones." *Mother Jones*, May 2001. https://www.motherjones.com/about/history/.

———. *Mother Jones: The Most Dangerous Woman in America*. New York: Hill and Wang, 2002.

Gray, Jeremy. "The Week in Birmingham History: Coal Mine Strike of 1908; Birmingham's Deadliest Plane Crash." Birmingham Real-Time News, July 6, 2014. https://www.al.com/news/birmingham/2014/07/the_week_in_birmingham_history_4.html.

Hammond, Adam. "Ludlow Massacre Survivor Turns 104." KMGH, January 13, 2018. https://www.thedenverchannel.com/thenow/ludlow-massacre-survivor-turns-104.

Harrison Coal & Reclamation Historical Park. "Ida Mae Stull: First Woman Coal Miner." Facebook, April 10, 2020. https://www.facebook.com/HCRHP/posts/ida-mae-stull-first-woman-coal-miner-born-feb-4-1896-one-of-18-children-to-samue/2989879984404097/.

Horne, Madison. "These Appalling Images Exposed Child Labor in America." History.com, April 26, 2018. https://www.history.com/news/child-labor-lewis-hine-photos.

"Ida Mae Stull." n.d. https://www.findagrave.com/memorial/131896794/ida-mae-stull.

Jones, James B., Jr. "Convict Lease Wars." Tennessee Encyclopedia, Tennessee Historical Society, October 8, 2017. https://tennesseeencyclopedia.net/entries/convict-lease-wars/.

Jones, Mary Harris. "Mother." *Autobiography of Mother Jones*. Industrial Workers of the World, 1925.

J. Q. Dickinson Salt-Works. "Our History." https://www.jqdsalt.com/timeline/.

Kahle, Trish. "'A Woman's Place Is in the UMWA': Women Miners and the Struggle for a Democratic Union in Western Pennsylvania, 1973–1979." *Labor* 13, no. 1 (February 2016): 41–63. https://doi.org/10.1215/15476715-3341058.

Keegan, Anne. "Ida Mae: She Preferred Coal Dust to a Powder Puff." *Chicago Tribune*, May 7, 1980.

Kelly, Kim. "Alabama's Coal Miners Are Striking for Their Lives." June 11, 2021. https://www.thenation.com/article/economy/alabama-warrior-met-coal/.

———. "The Miners Take Manhattan." *The Real News Network*, November 10, 2021. http://therealnews.com/the-miners-take-manhattan.

Keweenaw National Historical Park. "Anna Klobuchar Clemenc." March 13, 2019. https://www.nps.gov/kewe/anna-klobuchar-clemenc.htm.

Kingsolver, Barbara. *Holding the Line: Women in the Great Arizona Mine Strike of 1983*. New York: ILR Press, 1996.

Klemesrud, Judy. "In Coal Mine No. 29, Two Women Work Alongside the

Men." *The New York Times*, May 18, 1974. https://www.nytimes.com/1974/05/18/archives/in-coal-mine-no-29-two-women-work-alongside-the-men-kin-tried-to.html.

Knoche, Sterling. "Lead Mining: Wisconsin, United States (19th c)." *Anthropocene in Objects* (blog), February 26, 2021. https://web.archive.org/web/20210226131313/https://anthropoceneobjects.net/portfolio/lead-mining-wisconsin-united-states-19th-c/.

Kuykendall, Taylor, and Ellie Potter. "Coal Mining Conditions, Culture Create Unique Challenges in Gender-Parity Push." *S&P Global* (blog), March 6, 2019. https://www.spglobal.com/marketintelligence/en/news-insights/latest-news-headlines/coal-mining-conditions-culture-create-unique-challenges-in-gender-parity-push-50282862.

"Law Takes Her Out of the Mines." *St. Louis Post-Dispatch*, February 2, 1934.

Lawrence, Anne T., and Catherine Venable Moore. *On Dark and Bloody Ground: An Oral History of the West Virginia Mine Wars*. Morgantown: West Virginia University Press, 2021.

Lewis, Ronald L. "'The Darkest Abode of Man': Black Miners in the First Southern Coal Field, 1780–1865." *The Virginia Magazine of History and Biography* 87, no. 2 (1979): 190–202. http://www.jstor.org/stable/4248298.

Little Cities of Black Diamonds. "THANK YOU to all of you, our followers and supporters, for making Little Cities Fest last week a success!" Facebook, October 12, 2020. https://www.facebook.com/thelittlecitiesofblackdiamonds/posts/10157200440345443.

McKiven, Henry M., Jr. "United Mine Workers in Alabama." Encyclopedia of Alabama, Alabama Humanities Alliance, October 12, 2010.

Moore, Marat. "Hard Labor: Voices of Women from the Appalachian Coalfields." *Yale Journal of Law & Feminism* 2, no. 2 (1989): 199–238. https://digitalcommons.law.yale.edu/yjlf/vol2/iss2/2/.

Mountain Eagle Staff. "Nation's First Female Miner Remembered." *The Mountain Eagle*, June 1, 2016. https://www.themountaineagle.com/articles/nations-first-female-miner-remembered/.

Oakland Museum of California. "Silver and Gold: Native Californian," 1998. http://explore.museumca.org/goldrush/silver-native.html.

"Only Woman Coal Miner Loses Job." *The Cushing Daily Citizen*, January 29, 1934.

PBS. "Slavery By Another Name: Convict Leasing." https://www.pbs.org/tpt/slavery-by-another-name/themes/convict-leasing/.

Portelli, Alessandro. *They Say in Harlan County: An Oral History*. New York: Oxford University Press, 2012.

Pyle, Kai Minosh. "The Indigenous Women Miners of the Driftless Area." *An Indigenous History of North America* (blog), February 18, 2015. https://indigenoushistory.wordpress.com/2015/02/18/the-indigenous-women-miners-of-the-driftless-area/.

Raye, Janet. "Hellraisers Journal: Whereabouts & Doings of Mother Jones for November 1900, Part IV: Found with Silk Strikers of Wilkes-Barre & Carbondale, Pennsylvania." *We Never Forget* (blog), December 20, 2020. https://weneverforget.org/hellraisers-journal-whereabouts-doings-of-mother-jones-for-november-1900-part-iv-found-with-silk-strikers-of-wilkes-barre-carbondale-pennsylvania/.

Riley, Glenda. "Feminizing the History of the Gold Rush." *The Western Historical Quarterly* 30, no. 4 (1999): 445–48. https://doi.org/10.2307/971421.

Rosenblum, Jonathan D. *Copper Crucible: How the Arizona Miners' Strike of 1983 Recast Labor Management Relations in America*. 2nd ed. Ithaca, NY: ILR Press, 1998.

Satterfield, Emma. "Historic Malden, West Virginia Tour." Clio, February 22, 2020. https://theclio.com/tour/1102.

Savage, Carletta. "Re-Gendering Coal: Female Miners and Male Supervisors." *Appalachian Journal* 27, no. 3 (2000): 232–48. http://www.jstor.org/stable/41057390.

Simmons, Alexy. "Red Light Ladies in the American West: Entrepreneurs and Companions." *Australian Journal of Historical Archaeology* 7 (1989): 63–69. http://www.jstor.org/stable/29543241.

Stepenoff, Bonnie. "Child Labor in Pennsylvania's Silk Mills: Protest and Change, 1900–1910." *Pennsylvania History: A Journal of Mid-Atlantic Studies* 59, no. 2 (1992): 101–21. http://www.jstor.org/stable/27773524.

———. "Keeping It in the Family: Mother Jones and the Pennsylvania Silk Strike of 1900–1901." *Labor History* 38, no. 4 (September 1997): 432–49. https://doi.org/10.1080/00236649712331387214.

Tallichet, Suzanne E. *Daughters of the Mountain: Women Coal Miners in Central Appalachia*. Rural Studies. University Park: Pennsylvania State University Press, 2006.

University of Georgia Libraries. "New Exhibit Examines the History of Convict Labor in Georgia," September 11, 2019. https://www.libs.uga.edu/news/exhibit-examines-convict-labor-in-georgia.

Washington, Booker T. *Up from Slavery: An Autobiography*. Cambridge: Cambridge University Press, 2014.

Wilkerson, Jessica. *To Live Here, You Have to Fight: How Women Led Appalachian Movements for Social Justice*. Champaign: University of Illinois Press, 2019.

Williams, Carol, ed. *Indigenous Women and Work: From Labor to Activism*. Urbana: University of Illinois Press, 2012.

Wisconsin Historical Society. "Lead Mining in Southwestern Wisconsin," August 3, 2012. https://www.wisconsinhistory.org/Records/Article/CS408.

Wool, Harold. "Coal Industry Resurgence Attracts Variety of New Workers." *Monthly Labor Review* 104, no. 1 (1981): 3–8. http://www.jstor.org/stable/41841342.

CHAPTER 6: THE HARVESTERS

"1946 Sakada Filipinos and the ILWU." ILWU Local I 142, April 1996. http://thesakadaseries.com/images/1946_Sakadas.pdf.

"Agricultural Worker Demographics." Fact Sheet. Buda, TX: National Center for Farmworker Health, April 2018.

"Agricultural Workers' Rights under the Agricultural Labor Relations Act." Dolores Huerta Foundation, November 2006. http://doloreshuerta.org/wp-content/uploads/2020/04/Handout-CA-Agricultural-Labor-Relations-Act-1.pdf.

Alameri, Rua'a. "Brutal Killing that Made a Yemeni Immigrant Hero of US Labor Movement." Al Arabiya English, February 17, 2017. https://english.alarabiya.net/features/2017/02/15/Rediscovering-brave-but-tragic-legacy-of-Yemeni-immigrant-labor-leader-in-US-history.

Asbed, Greg. "What Happens If America's 2.5 Million Farmworkers Get Sick?" *The New York Times*, April 3, 2020. https://www.nytimes.com/2020/04/03/opinion/coronavirus-farm-workers.html.

Bernard, Diane. "The Time a President Deported 1 Million Mexican Americans for Supposedly Stealing U.S. Jobs." *Washington Post*, August 13, 2018. https://www.washingtonpost.com/news/retropolis/wp/2018/08/13/the-time-a-president-deported-1-million-mexican-americans-for-stealing-u-s-jobs/.

Bloch, Sam. "You Already Know Cesar Chavez. What about Maria Moreno?" *The Counter*, September 23, 2019. https://thecounter.org/cesar-chavez-maria-moreno-ufw-awoc-farm-labor/.

Brown, Patricia Leigh. "Forgotten Hero of Labor Fight; His Son's Lonely Quest." *The New York Times*, October 19, 2012. https://www.nytimes.com/2012/10/19/us/larry-itliong-forgotten-filipino-labor-leader.html.

Cardoso, Lawrence A. "Labor Emigration to the Southwest, 1916 to 1920: Mexican Attitudes and Policy." *The Southwestern Historical Quarterly* 79, no. 4 (1976): 400–16. http://www.jstor.org/stable/30238403.

Chacón, Justin Akers. *Radicals in the Barrio: Magonistas, Socialists, Wobblies, and Communists in the Mexican American Working Class*. Durham, NC: Duke University Press, 2018.

Chew, Ron. *Remembering Silme Domingo and Gene Viernes: The Legacy of Filipino American Labor Activism*. Seattle: Alaskero Foundation: University of Washington Press, 2012.

Coalition of Immokalee Workers. "Announcing: Farmworker Women Launch 'Harvest without Violence' Campaign to End Sexual Violence in Wendy's Supply Chain!," *CIW Online* (blog), September 27, 2017. https://ciw-online.org/blog/2017/09/harvest-without-violence/.

———. "Part Two: 'We Are Not Victims—We Are Not Asking for Charity, We Are Calling for Justice!,'" *CIW Online* (blog), October 27, 2017. https://ciw-online.org/blog/2017/10/part-two-we-are-not-victims-we-are-not-asking-for-charity-we-are-calling-for-justice/.

Coyle, Laurie, dir. *VOCES*. Season 3, Episode 2, "Adios Amor: The Search for Maria Moreno." Aired September 27, 2019 on PBS. https://www.pbs.org/video/adios-amor-the-search-for-maria-moreno-szv268/.

Evich, Helena Bottemiller, Ximena Bustillo, and Liz Crampton. "Harvest of

Shame: Farmworkers Face Coronavirus Disaster." Politico, September 8, 2020. https://www.politico.com/news/2020/09/08/farmworkers-coronavirus-disaster-409339.

Food Empowerment Project. "Slavery in the U.S." November 18, 2021. https://foodispower.org/human-labor-slavery/slavery-in-the-us/.

Gaber, Suzanne, Will Thomson, Alex Atack, Nadeen Shaker, Zeina Dowidar, Shraddha Joshi, and Abde Amr. "Viva Brother Nagi." Podcast. Kerning Cultures, aired April 2, 2021. https://kerningcultures.com/viva-brother-nagi/.

García, Juan Ramon. *Operations Wetback: The Mass Deportation of Mexican Undocumented Workers in 1954.* Westport, CT: Greenwood Press, 1980.

Garcia, Matthew. *From the Jaws of Victory: The Triumph and Tragedy of Cesar Chavez and the Farm Worker Movement*. Berkeley: University of California Press, 2014.

Glick, Clarence Elmer. *Sojourners and Settlers: Chinese Migrants in Hawaii*. Honolulu: University Press of Hawaii, 1980.

Greenhouse, Steven. "In Florida Tomato Fields, a Penny Buys Progress." *The New York Times*, April 25, 2014. https://www.nytimes.com/2014/04/25/business/in-florida-tomato-fields-a-penny-buys-progress.html.

"Hawaii: Life in a Plantation Society." Library of Congress. https://www.loc.gov/classroom-materials/immigration/japanese/hawaii-life-in-a-plantation-society/.

Hilo Sugar Company v. Mioshi, No. 201 (8 Haw. March 5, 1891).

Huerta, Dolores. "Speech at the NFWA March and Rally," April 10, 1966, Sacramento, CA. Iowa State University Archives of Women's Political Communication. Partial transcript from radio broadcast. https://awpc.cattcenter.iastate.edu/2017/03/09/nfwa-march-and-rally-april-10–1966/.

Janos, Adam. "How Cesar Chavez Joined Larry Itliong to Demand Farm Workers' Rights." History.com, January 22, 2021. https://www.history.com/news/chavez-itliong-delano-grape-strike.

Kelly, Kim. "Dolores Huerta Wants You to Fight for Your Rights." *Teen Vogue*, March 31, 2020. https://www.teenvogue.com/story/dolores-huerta-cesar-chavez-day.

———. "Unsung Heroes of Latinx Farmworkers' Labor Movement, from Maria Moreno to Fast Food Boycotters." *Teen Vogue*, October 15, 2018. https://www.teenvogue.com/story/unsung-heroes-latinx-farmworkers-labor-movement-maria-moreno-to-fast-food-boycotters.

Kubota, Gaylord C. "The Lynching of Katsu Goto." In *Hawai'i Chronicles: Island History from the Pages of Honolulu Magazine*, edited by Bob Dye, 197–214. University of Hawai'i Press, 1996. https://www.hawaii.edu/uhwo/clear/home/KatsuGoto.html.

"Labor Organizing Changed the Hawaiian Islands Forever." *The American Postal Worker*, April 30, 2003. https://www.apwu.org/news/labor-organizing-changed-hawaiian-islands-forever.

Lazo, Robert. "Latinos and the AFL-CIO: The California Immigrant Workers

Association as an Important New Development." *Berkeley La Raza Law Journal* 4, no. 1 (November 26, 2019): 22. https://doi.org/10.15779/Z38Q661.

Lee, Erika. *America for Americans: A History of Xenophobia in the United States.* New York: Basic Books, 2019.

Lopez, Angelo. "Filipino Americans and the Farm Labor Movement." *Portside* (blog), May 12, 2014. https://portside.org/2014-05-12/filipino-americans-and-farm-labor-movement.

Magagnini, Stephen. "New Light Shed on Pioneering Filipino American." *The Sacramento Bee*, December 28, 1996.

Mansour, Omar. "Nagi Mohsin Daifullah and the Yemeni Farm Workers of California." Arab America, May 19, 2021. https://www.arabamerica.com/nagi-mohsin-daifullah-and-the-forgotten-yemeni-farmworkers-of-california/.

Marquis, Susan L. *I Am Not a Tractor! How Florida Farmworkers Took On the Fast Food Giants and Won.* Ithaca: ILR Press, 2017.

Martin, Philip. "Mexican Braceros and US Farm Workers." *Wilson Center Mexico Institute* (blog), July 10, 2020. https://www.wilsoncenter.org/article/mexican-braceros-and-us-farm-workers.

Martinez, Valentina. "Katsu Goto: Murder in Honoka'a." *Ke Kalahea*, October 10, 2016. https://hilo.hawaii.edu/news/kekalahea/KG-Murder.

McElrath, Ah Quon. "Hawaiian Strikes, esp. 1946." Interview by Robynn Takayama. March 26, 2017. Crossing East Archive. Transcript. http://www.crossingeast.org/crossingeastarchive/2017/03/26/ah-quon-mcelrath-hawaiian-strikes-esp-1946/.

Misra-Bhambri, Nikhil. "Yemenis in the San Joaquin Valley: The Embodiment of Pride, Duty and Loyalty." *The Arab American News*, February 22, 2021. https://www.arabamericannews.com/2021/02/22/yemenis-in-the-san-joaquin-valley-the-embodiment-of-pride-duty-and-loyalty/.

National Farm Worker Ministry. "Women in Agriculture." July 2018. http://nfwm.org/farm-workers/farm-worker-issues/womens-issues/.

Parks, Shoshi. "The Not-so-Sweet Story of How Filipino Workers Tried to Take on Big Sugar in Hawaii." *Timeline* (blog), June 1, 2018. https://timeline.com/filipino-workers-sugar-strike-fa58953e78e.

Partida, Maria Guadalupe. "1938: Pecan Shellers Strike." Research guide. Library of Congress. https://guides.loc.gov/latinx-civil-rights/pecan-shellers-strike.

Pawel, Miriam. *The Crusades of Cesar Chavez: A Biography.* Berkeley: University of California Press, 2015.

People's World. "Today in Labor History: United Farm Workers Launch the Lettuce Boycott." August 24, 2015. https://www.peoplesworld.org/article/today-in-labor-history-united-farm-workers-launch-the-lettuce-boycott/.

"Pineapple Workers End Hawaii Strike." *The New York Times*, July 17, 1947. https://www.nytimes.com/1947/07/17/archives/pineapple-workers-end-hawaii-strike.html.

Puette, William. *The Hilo Massacre: Hawaii's Bloody Monday, August 1st, 1938.*

Honolulu: University of Hawaii, Center for Labor Education & Research, 1988.

Quintana, Maria, and Oscar Rosales Castañeda. "Asians and Latinos Enter the Fields." Seattle Civil Rights and Labor History Project, University of Washington. https://depts.washington.edu/civilr/farmwk_ch4.htm#_edn22.

Ramchandani, Ariel. "There's a Sexual-Harassment Epidemic on America's Farms." *The Atlantic*, January 29, 2018. https://www.theatlantic.com/business/archive/2018/01/agriculture-sexual-harassment/550109/.

Rayson, Ann. *Modern Hawaiian History*. Honolulu: Bess Press, 1984.

Rice & Roses, prods. *1946: The Great Hawai'i Sugar Strike*. Documentary. Center for Labor Education and Research, University of Hawai'i West O'ahu, 1996.

Rodriguez-Cayro, Kyli. "6 Latina Women Leading the Labor Movement You Probably Never Learned about in School." *Bustle*, November 2, 2017. https://www.bustle.com/p/6-latina-women-leading-the-labor-movement-you-probably-never-learned-about-in-school-3209474.

Romasanta, Gayle. "Why It Is Important to Know the Story of Filipino-American Larry Itliong." *Folklife Smithsonian Magazine*, July 24, 2019. https://www.smithsonianmag.com/smithsonian-institution/why-it-is-important-know-story-filipino-american-larry-itliong-180972696/.

Schwartz, Harvey. "Frank Thompson: Islands Organizer, 1944–1946." *International Longshore & Warehouse Union* (blog), https://www.ilwu.org/frank-thompson-islands-organizer-1944-1946/.

"Slavery in the Fields and the Food We Eat." Coalition of Immokalee Workers, August 6, 2012. https://ciw-online.org/wp-content/uploads/12SlaveryintheFields.pdf.

Soriano, Scott. "The Rape Crisis among California's Farm Workers." Capitol Weekly, January 9, 2020. https://capitolweekly.net/the-rape-crisis-among-californias-farm-workers/.

Students for a Democratic Society. "Farm Workers and Organized Labor." In *Wind in the Fields: A Report on Farm Labor*. 1965.

Takaki, Ronald T. *Pau Hana: Plantation Life and Labor in Hawaii, 1835–1920*. Honolulu: University of Hawaii Press, 1984.

"Tydings-McDuffie Act of 1934," Immigration History. May 4, 2018. https://immigrationhistory.org/item/tydings-mcduffie-act/.

United Food & Commercial Workers International Union. "New York Agricultural Workers Make History by Joining RWDSU/UFCW," October 19, 2021. https://www.ufcw.org/actions/victories/new-york-agricultural-workers-make-history-by-joining-rwdsu-ufcw/.

U.S. Department of State Office of the Historian. "Milestones: 1866–1898." https://history.state.gov/milestones/1866-1898/chinese-immigration.

U.S. National Park Service. "Emma Tenayuca." https://www.nps.gov/people/emma-tenayuca.htm.

CHAPTER 7: THE CLEANERS

Baker, Ella, and Marvel Cooke. "Bronx Slave Market." *The Crisis*, November 1, 1935.

Banks, Nina. "Black Women's Labor Market History Reveals Deep-Seated Race and Gender Discrimination." *Economic Policy Institute* (blog), February 19, 2019. https://www.epi.org/blog/black-womens-labor-market-history-reveals-deep-seated-race-and-gender-discrimination/.

Bassett, Laura. "Georgia Domestic Workers Mobilize for Stacey Abrams in the Birthplace of Their Movement." *HuffPost*, October 31, 2018. https://www.huffpost.com/entry/stacey-abrams-georgia-domestic-workers_n_5bd8a9cbe4b0da7bfc14a210.

Beck, Elizabeth. "The National Domestic Workers Union and the War on Poverty." *The Journal of Sociology & Social Welfare* 28, no. 4 (December 1, 2001). https://scholarworks.wmich.edu/jssw/vol28/iss4/11.

Blumgart, Jake. "The Historical Roots of American Domestic Worker Organizing Run Deep." *In These Times*, September 21, 2015. https://inthesetimes.com/article/domestic-workers-premilla-nadasen-interview.

Bolden, Dorothy. "A Talk with Dorothy Bolden." Interview by Chris Lutz. Atlanta, GA, August 31, 1995. Special Collections and Archives, Georgia State University Library. Transcript and audio. http://webapps.library.gsu.edu/ohms-viewer/viewer.php?cachefile=BoldenD_L1995-12_03.xml.

Boris, Eileen, and Premilla Nadasen. "Domestic Workers Organize!" *Working USA* 11, no. 4 (December 2008): 413–37. https://doi.org/10.1111/j.1743-4580.2008.00217.x.

Campbell, Alexia Fernández. "How a Button Became One of the Greatest #MeToo Victories." *Vox*, October 1, 2019. https://www.vox.com/identities/2019/10/1/20876119/panic-buttons-me-too-sexual-harassment.

Carson, Jenny. *A Matter of Moral Justice: Black Women Laundry Workers and the Fight for Justice*. The Working Class in American History. Urbana: University of Illinois Press, 2021.

Chang, Grace, Ai-Jen Poo, Mimi Abramovitz, and Alicia Garza. *Disposable Domestics: Immigrant Women Workers in the Global Economy*. Chicago: Haymarket Books, 2016.

Cooke, Marvel. "The Bronx Slave Market (1950)." *Viewpoint Magazine*, October 31, 2015. https://viewpointmag.com/2015/10/31/the-bronx-slave-market-1950/.

Economic Policy Institute. "Working People Want a Voice at Work." Fact sheet. April 21, 2021. https://www.epi.org/publication/working-people-want-a-voice/.

Felber, Garrett. "The Mysterious Thelma X and the Struggle of Black Domestic Workers." *Black Perspectives* (blog), April 3, 2016. https://www.aaihs.org/the-mysterious-thelma-x/.

Goldberg, Harmony. "Our Day Has Finally Come: Domestic Worker Organizing in New York City." PhD diss., City University of New York, 2014.

https://academicworks.cuny.edu/cgi/viewcontent.cgi?article=1421&context=gc_etds.

Harrison, Christy Garrison. "They Led and a Community Followed: The Community Activism of Ella Mae Wade Brayboy and Dorothy Bolden in Atlanta, Georgia 1964–1994." MA thesis, Clark Atlanta University, 2007. https://radar.auctr.edu/islandora/object/cau.td:2007_harrison_christy_g.

Hogan, Gwynne. "Williamsburg Day Laborers Command Top Dollar on 'Day Without Immigrants.'" *DNAinfo New York* (blog), February 17, 2017. https://www.dnainfo.com/new-york/20170217/williamsburg/hasidic-williamsburg-immigrant-day-labor-work-undocumented.

Izsraael, Jacklyn. "How Dorothy Bolden Inspired the National Domestic Workers Bill of Rights." *ZORA* (blog), October 21, 2019. https://zora.medium.com/how-dorothy-bolden-inspired-the-national-domestic-workers-bill-of-rights-46ac8cdd0915.

James, Joy. "Ella Baker, 'Black Women's Work' and Activist Intellectuals." *The Black Scholar* 24, no. 4 (1994): 8–15. http://www.jstor.org/stable/41069719.

Kelly, Kim. "This Holiday Season, Thank a Janitor." *The Baffler*, December 30, 2019. https://thebaffler.com/working-stiff/thank-a-janitor-kim-kelly.

———. "What It Means to Go on Strike." *Teen Vogue*, November 4, 2018. https://www.teenvogue.com/story/strikes-and-picket-lines-explained.

Klein, Christopher. "Last Hired, First Fired: How the Great Depression Affected African Americans." History.com, August 31, 2018. https://www.history.com/news/last-hired-first-fired-how-the-great-depression-affected-african-americans.

Lerner, Stephen, and Jono Shaffer. "25 Years Later: Lessons From the Organizers of Justice for Janitors." *The Nation*, June 16, 2015. https://www.thenation.com/article/archive/25-years-later-lessons-from-the-organizers-of-justice-for-janitors/.

McIntyre, Julie. "Care Work and the Power of Women: An Interview with Selma James." *Viewpoint Magazine*, March 19, 2012. https://viewpointmag.com/2012/03/19/care-work-and-the-power-of-women-an-interview-with-selma-james/.

Menendez, Ana. "While Shalala Lives in Luxury, Janitors Struggle." *The Miami Herald*, March 1, 2006.

Musynske, Gavin. "Los Angleles Justice for Janitors Campaign for Economic Justice at Century City, 1989–1990." Database. Global Nonviolent Action Database, April 12, 2009. https://nvdatabase.swarthmore.edu/content/los-angleles-justice-janitors-campaign-economic-justice-century-city-1989-1990.

Nadasen, Premilla. *Household Workers Unite: The Untold Story of African American Women Who Built a Movement*. Boston: Beacon Press, 2015.

National Labor Relations Board. "Hiring Halls," n.d. https://www.nlrb.gov/about-nlrb/rights-we-protect/the-law/employees/hiring-halls.

New York State Public Employees Federation. "Kate Mullany and the Collar

Laundry Union." libcom.org, February 1, 2018. http://libcom.org/history/kate-mullany-collar-laundry-union.

Pinto, Sanjay, Zoë West, and K. C. Wagner. "Healing into Power: An Approach for Confronting Workplace Sexual Violence." *New Labor Forum*, May 5, 2021. https://newlaborforum.cuny.edu/2021/05/05/healing-into-power-an-approach-for-confronting-workplace-sexual-violence/.

Bergman, Lowell, dir. *Frontline.* Season 2018, episode 11, "Rape on the Night Shift." Aired January 16, 2018, on PBS. https://www.pbs.org/wgbh/frontline/film/rape-on-the-night-shift/.

Rotondi, Jessica Pearce. "Underpaid, But Employed: How the Great Depression Affected Working Women." History.com, March 11, 2019. https://www.history.com/news/working-women-great-depression.

Sainato, Michael. "Overworked, Underpaid: Workers Rail against Hotel Chains' Cost-Cutting." *The Guardian*, July 5, 2021. https://www.theguardian.com/us-news/2021/jul/05/overworked-underpaid-hotel-workers-employees.

Shaw, Randy. *Beyond the Fields: Cesar Chavez, the UFW, and the Struggle for Justice in the 21st Century.* Berkeley: University of California Press, 2011.

Slotnik, Daniel E. "Overlooked No More: Dorothy Bolden, Who Started a Movement for Domestic Workers." *The New York Times*, February 20, 2019. https://www.nytimes.com/2019/02/20/obituaries/dorothy-bolden-overlooked.html.

Small, Raia. "Silvia Federici Reflects on Wages for Housework." *New Frame*, October 18, 2018. https://www.newframe.com/silvia-federici-reflects-wages-housework/.

Stangler, Cole. "Organizing the Corner: How Williamsburg's Female Housecleaners Are Fighting for Higher Wages." *The Village Voice*, August 8, 2016. https://www.villagevoice.com/2016/08/08/organizing-the-corner-how-williamsburgs-female-housecleaners-are-fighting-for-higher-wages/.

Trotter, Joe William. *Workers on Arrival: Black Labor in the Making of America.* Oakland: University of California Press, 2019.

Vives, Ruben. "Amid Shades of Great Recession, Day Laborers Struggle to Find Work during Coronavirus." *Los Angeles Times*, March 30, 2020. https://www.latimes.com/california/story/2020-03-30/coronavirus-day-laborer-struggle-employment.

Wallace, Lewis. "One of the Most Influential Black Journalists You Probably Never Heard Of." Podcast. *On the Media*, aired June 9, 2021. https://www.wnycstudios.org/podcasts/otm/episodes/most-influential-black-journalist-you-probably-never-heard.

West, Zoë, Sanjay Pinto, and K. C. Wagner. *Sweeping Change: Building Survivor and Worker Leadership to Confront Sexual Harassment in the Janitorial Industry.* (Ithaca, NY: The Worker Institute, January 1, 2020). https://hdl.handle.net/1813/74351.

Wolfe, Julia, Jori Kandra, Lora Engdahl, and Heidi Shierholz. *Domestic Workers Chartbook: A Comprehensive Look at the Demographics, Wages, Benefits, and*

Poverty Rates of the Professionals Who Care for Our Family Members and Clean Our Homes. (Washington, D.C.: Economic Policy Institute, May 14, 2020). https://www.epi.org/publication/domestic-workers-chartbook-a-comprehensive-look-at-the-demographics-wages-benefits-and-poverty-rates-of-the-professionals-who-care-for-our-family-members-and-clean-our-homes/.

Woo, Elaine. "Marvel Cooke; Pioneering Black Journalist, Political Activist." *Los Angeles Times*, December 6, 2000. https://www.latimes.com/archives/la-xpm-2000-dec-06-me-61800-story.html.

Yeung, Bernice. *In a Day's Work: The Fight to End Sexual Violence against America's Most Vulnerable Workers.* New York: The New Press, 2018.

CHAPTER 8: THE FREEDOM FIGHTERS

Berman, Edward. "The Pullman Porters Win." *The Nation*, August 21, 1935.

Bishop, Misun. "Lucille Campbell Green Randolph (1883–1963)." *Black Past* (blog), June 11, 2017. https://www.blackpast.org/african-american-history/randolph-lucille-campbell-green-1883-1963/.

Chateauvert, Melinda. *Marching Together: Women of the Brotherhood of Sleeping Car Porters.* Women in American History. Urbana: University of Illinois Press, 1998.

Cobb, William H. "Southern Tenant Farmers' Union." Encyclopedia of Arkansas. Central Arkansas Library System, August 24, 2021. https://encyclopediaofarkansas.net/entries/southern-tenant-farmers-union-35/.

Cochran, David. "The Lessons of A. Philip Randolph's Life for Racial Justice and Labor Activists Today." *In These Times*, March 1, 2016. https://inthesetimes.com/article/a-philip-randolph-march-on-washington.

Day, Meagan. "The First Black-Led Union Wouldn't Have Existed without This Woman." *Timeline* (blog), June 18, 2018. https://timeline.com/rosina-tucker-pullman-porters-37ba63c2b9eb.

D'Emilio, John. *Lost Prophet: The Life and Times of Bayard Rustin.* Chicago: University of Chicago Press, 2004.

Foner, Philip S. "The IWW and the Black Worker." *The Journal of Negro History* 55, no. 1 (1970): 45–64. https://doi.org/10.2307/2716544.

Foner, Philip S., and Ronald L. Lewis, eds. *The Black Worker, Volume 6: The Era of Post-War Prosperity and the Great Depression, 1920–1936.* Temple University Press, 2019. https://doi.org/10.2307/j.ctvn5tvxv.

Gude, Shawn. "The Tragedy of Bayard Rustin." *Jacobin*, May 23, 2018. https://jacobinmag.com/2018/05/the-tragedy-of-bayard-rustin.

History.com Editors. "President Truman Ends Discrimination in the Military." History.com, July 23, 2021. https://www.history.com/this-day-in-history/president-truman-ends-discrimination-in-military.

Jones, Adrienne. "Black Labor Organizing: The Progressive Farmers and Household Union of America." *Elaine Race Massacre* (blog), June 20, 2019. https://ualrexhibits.org/elaine/100-years-ago/organizing-labor/.

Jones, William Powell. *The March on Washington: Jobs, Freedom, and the Forgotten History of Civil Rights*. New York: W. W. Norton, 2014.

Kelly, Kim. "New Orleans' Underpaid, Overexposed Sanitation Workers." *The New Republic*, June 29, 2020. https://newrepublic.com/article/158324/new-orleans-sanitation-workers-hoppers-union-underpaid-overexposed.

King, Martin Luther, Jr. "I've Been to the Mountaintop." Memphis, TN, 1968. American Federation of State, County & Municipal Employees. Transcript. https://www.afscme.org/about/history/mlk/mountaintop.

McCollom, Jason. "Progressive Farmers and Household Union of America (PFHUA)." Encyclopedia of Arkansas. Central Arkansas Library System, November 18, 2020. https://encyclopediaofarkansas.net/entries/progressive-farmers-and-household-union-of-america-3027/.

Memphis Public Libraries. "Strike Supporters Bring in Outside Help," July 6, 2018. https://www.memphislibrary.org/diversity/sanitation-strike-exhibit/sanitation-strike-exhibit-march-10-to-16-edition/strike-supporters-bring-in-outside-help/.

"Memphis Sanitation Workers' Strike." In *King Encyclopedia*. Stanford, CA: Martin Luther King Jr. Research and Education Institute, June 4, 2018.

Monteverde, Danny. "Sanitation Workers Say They Were Fired for Protests over Pay and Protective Equipment." 4WWL Eyewitness News, May 6, 2020. https://www.wwltv.com/article/news/health/coronavirus/sanitation-workers-say-they-were-fired-for-protests-over-pay-and-protective-equipment/289-1283daf0-9893-4bc1-b51b-f7fa89b7093e.

Ott, Tim. "Martin Luther King Jr. Praised Cesar Chavez for His 'Indefatigable Work.'" Biography, October 15, 2020. https://www.biography.com/news/cesar-chavez-martin-luther-king-jr-telegram.

PBS. "Slavery by Another Name: Sharecropping." February 12, 2012. https://www.pbs.org/tpt/slavery-by-another-name/themes/sharecropping/.

Pitts, David. "Rosina Tucker: A Century of Commitment." United States Information Agency, February 8, 1996.

Randolph, A. Philip, and Bayard Rustin. "The Civil-Rights Movement's Plan to End Poverty, Annotated." *The Atlantic*, April 2, 2018. https://www.theatlantic.com/magazine/archive/2018/02/a-freedom-budget-for-all-americans-annotated/557024/.

Raye, Janet. "Hellraisers Journal: 'White Landlords, Robbing Negro Tenants, Let Loose Arkansas Reign of Terror,' Part II." *We Never Forget* (blog), February 20, 2020. https://weneverforget.org/hellraisers-journal-white-landlords-robbing-negro-tenants-let-loose-arkansas-reign-of-terror-part-ii/.

"Rustin, Bayard." In *King Encyclopedia*. Stanford, CA: Martin Luther King Jr. Research and Education Institute, April 5, 2018.

Rustin, Bayard, Devon W. Carbado, and Donald Weise. *Time on Two Crosses: The Collected Writings of Bayard Rustin*. San Francisco: Cleis Press, 2003.

Stockley, Grif. "Elaine Massacre of 1919." Encyclopedia of Arkansas. Central Arkansas Library System, November 18, 2020.

Taylor, Cynthia. "The Men behind the March: Randolph and Rustin Together Again." *NYU Press Blog* (blog), August 27, 2013. https://www.fromthesquare.org/the-men-behind-the-march-randolph-and-rustin-together-again/.

Trotter, Joe William. *Workers on Arrival: Black Labor in the Making of America.* Oakland: University of California Press, 2019.

Tye, Larry. *Rising from the Rails: Pullman Porters and the Making of the Black Middle Class.* New York: Owl Books, 2005.

Uenuma, Francine. "The Massacre of Black Sharecroppers that Led the Supreme Court to Curb the Racial Disparities of the Justice System." *Smithsonian Magazine*, August 2, 2018. https://www.smithsonianmag.com/history/death-hundreds-elaine-massacre-led-supreme-court-take-major-step-toward-equal-justice-african-americans-180969863/.

Wells-Barnett, Ida B. *The Arkansas Race Riot.* Chicago: Northern Illinois University Library, 1920. https://digital.lib.niu.edu/islandora/object/niu-gildedage%3A24320.

———. *The East St. Louis Massacre: The Greatest Outrage of the Century.* Chicago: The Negro Fellowship Herald Press, 1917.

Wells-Barnett, Ida B., and Frederick Douglass. *A Red Record: Tabulated Statistics and Alleged Causes of Lynching in the United States.* Chicago: Donohue and Henneberry, 1895.

Woodruff, Nan Elizabeth. *American Congo: The African American Freedom Struggle in the Delta.* Cambridge, MA: Harvard University Press, 2003.

Yachot, Noa. "'We Want Our Land Back': For Descendants of the Elaine Massacre, History Is Far from Settled." *The Guardian*, June 18, 2021. https://www.theguardian.com/us-news/2021/jun/18/elaine-massacre-red-summer-descendants-history.

CHAPTER 9: THE MOVERS

AFA Admin. "PRIDE Month: AFA's Fight to Win Domestic Partner Benefits for Flight Attendants." Delta AFA, July 2, 2021. https://www.deltaafa.org/news/pride-month-afa-s-fight-win-domestic-partner-benefits-flight-attendants.

Balay, Anne. *Semi Queer: Inside the World of Gay, Trans, and Black Truck Drivers.* Chapel Hill: University of North Carolina Press, 2018.

Bérubé, Allan. *The Story of the Marine Cooks and Stewards Union*, 2016.

Bérubé, Allan, John D'Emilio, and Estelle B. Freedman. *My Desire for History: Essays in Gay, Community, and Labor History.* Chapel Hill: University of North Carolina Press, 2011.

Brantley, Allyson, and B. Erin Cole. "The Coors Boycott: When a Beer Can Signaled Your Politics." Colorado Public Radio, October 3, 2014. https://www.cpr.org/2014/10/03/the-coors-boycott-when-a-beer-can-signaled-your-politics/.

Brantley, Allyson P. *Brewing a Boycott: How a Grassroots Coalition Fought Coors and Remade American Consumer Activism*. Justice, Power, and Politics. Chapel Hill: University of North Carolina Press, 2021.

Brunk, Graham. "1954 Miami Murder Leads to 'Homosexual Panic.'" *Erie Gay News*, October 18, 2017. https://www.eriegaynews.com/news/article.php?recordid=201711williamtsimpson.

Burns, Joe. *Strike Back: Rediscovering Militant Tactics to Confront the Attack on Public Employee Unions*. New York: Ig Publishing, 2019.

———. "The PATCO Strike, Reagan and the Roots of Labor's Decline." *In These Times*, November 1, 2011. https://inthesetimes.com/article/the-patco-strike-reagan-and-the-roots-of-labors-decline.

Carey, Leigh Ann. "Inside the Growing World of Queer Truckers." *Rolling Stone*, February 24, 2019. https://www.rollingstone.com/culture/culture-features/queer-trucking-anne-balay-lgbtq-truck-driver-796994/.

Chacón, Justin Akers. *Radicals in the Barrio: Magonistas, Socialists, Wobblies, and Communists in the Mexican American Working Class*. Durham, NC: Duke University Press, 2018.

Cole, Peter. *Dockworker Power: Race and Activism in Durban and the San Francisco Bay Area*. The Working Class in American History. Urbana: University of Illinois Press, 2018.

———. "On May Day, Longshore Workers Stop Work to Protest Racist Police Brutality." *In These Times*, April 30, 2015. https://inthesetimes.com/article/may-day-police-brutality.

———. "The Most Radical Union in the U.S. Is Shutting Down the Ports on Juneteenth." *In These Times*, June 16, 2020. https://inthesetimes.com/article/juneteenth-ilwu-dockworkers-strike-ports-black-lives-matter-george-floyd.

Coles, Joe. "Plane Queer: How Flight Attendants Became Sexy & the Truth behind the Male 'Trolley Dolly.'" *Hush-Kit* (blog), September 10, 2020. https://hushkit.net/2020/09/10/plane-queer-how-flight-attendants-became-sexy-the-truth-behind-the-male-trolley-dolly/.

Conrad, Svea. "On the Roads of Southside and around the World: On Annie Watkins and Joan Dorsey." *Arizona Daily Sun*, September 1, 2019. https://azdailysun.com/entertainment/arts-and-theatre/on-the-roads-of-southside-and-around-the-world-on-annie-watkins-and-joan-dorsey/article_1f993b32-4ee7-5bbb-a40b-9754c5de74e9.html.

Davis, Jerame. "The Long, Powerful History between Labor and LGBT Activists." *The Advocate*, September 22, 2014. http://www.advocate.com/commentary/2014/09/22/op-ed-long-powerful-history-between-labor-and-lgbt-activists.

Davis, Scarlett C. "Queering Labour: The Marine Cooks and Stewards' Union." *New Socialist Magazine*, June 1998. http://newsocialist.org/old_mag/magazine/14/article04.html.

Diaz v. Pan Am. World Airways, Inc., No. 442 F.2d 385 (5th Cir. May 10, 1971).

Dirnbach, Eric. "The PATCO Syndrome." *Labor Notes* (blog), December 29, 2011. https://labornotes.org/blogs/2011/12/patco-syndrome.

———. "Strike Out: The Number of Large Strikes Continues to Decline." *Medium* (blog), February 16, 2017. https://ericdirnbach.medium.com/strike-out-the-number-of-large-strikes-continues-to-decline-e9f505f79b60.

Dodge, Mark. "Organized Labor at the Coors Brewery in 1977, Golden, Colorado." *Golden History Museum & Park* (blog), March 4, 2021. https://www.goldenhistory.org/organized-labor-at-the-coors-brewery/.

Epstein, Edward. "United Airlines Capitulates on Partners Issue: Full Benefits Worldwide for Gay, Lesbian Couples." SFGate, July 31, 1999. https://www.sfgate.com/news/article/United-Airlines-Capitulates-on-Partners-Issue-2917303.php.

History.com Editors. "Ronald Reagan Fires 11,359 Air-Traffic Controllers." History.com, February 9, 2010. https://www.history.com/this-day-in-history/reagan-fires-11359-air-traffic-controllers.

International Brotherhood of Teamsters. "Teamsters Pride at Work: A Look Back at the Coors Boycott," June 2, 2017. https://teamster.org/2017/06/teamsters-pride-work-look-back-coors-boycott/.

International Longshore & Warehouse Union. "Bay Area ILWU Members Endorse Rally Seeking Justice for Unarmed Civilian Killed by BART Police Officer," November 25, 2010. https://www.ilwu.org/bay-area-ilwu-members-endorse-rally-seeking-justice-for-unarmed-civilian-killed-by-bart-police-officer/.

———. "The ILWU Story." https://www.ilwu.org/history/the-ilwu-story/.

———. "Local 10 Leads Protest against Police Brutality," May 20, 2015. https://www.ilwu.org/local-10-leads-protest-against-police-brutality/.

Johnson, Brian D. "How a Typo Created a Scapegoat for the AIDS Epidemic." *Macleans*, April 17, 2019. https://www.macleans.ca/culture/movies/how-a-typo-created-a-scapegoat-for-the-aids-epidemic/.

Johnson, Kate, and Albert Garcia. "'Male Stewardess' Just Didn't Fly." *Los Angeles Times*, September 27, 2007. https://www.latimes.com/archives/la-xpm-2007-sep-27-oe-johnson27-story.html.

Journal of Commerce Staff. "What's in a Name? For ILWU, It's Not 'Men.'" *The Journal of Commerce*, May 4, 1997. https://www.joc.com/whats-name-ilwu-its-not-men_19970504.html.

Kelly, Kim. "Sara Nelson's Art of War." *The New Republic*, May 13, 2019. https://newrepublic.com/article/153797/sara-nelsons-art-war.

Kraus, Terry. "Ellen Church and the Advent of the Sky Girls." Federal Aviation Administration, March 14, 2019. Wayback Machine. http://web.archive.org/web/20210325134107/https://www.faa.gov/about/history/pioneers/media/Ellen_Church_and_the_Advent_of_the_Sky_Girls.pdf.

Labor Video Project. "Angela Davis Becomes ILWU Local 10 Honorary Member on Juneteenth 2021." Indybay, June 24, 2021. https://www.indybay.org/newsitems/2021/06/24/18843416.php.

Lecklider, Aaron S. *Love's Next Meeting: The Forgotten History of Homosexuality and the Left in American Culture*. Oakland: University of California Press, 2021.

———. "On Board with Queer Labor and Racial Solidarity." *YES! Magazine*, June 17, 2021. https://www.yesmagazine.org/social-justice/2021/06/17/queer-labor-racial-solidarity-marine-cooks-stewards.

Lewin, Tamar. "USAir Agrees to Lift Rules on the Weight of Attendants." *The New York Times*, April 8, 1994. https://www.nytimes.com/1994/04/08/us/usair-agrees-to-lift-rules-on-the-weight-of-attendants.html.

"Liner Sails After 2-Hour Walkout of Stewards." *Hanford Morning Journal*, May 5, 1950.

Malone, Kenny, and Julia Simon. "When Reagan Broke the Unions." *Planet Money*. Aired December 18, 2019, on NPR. Radio broadcast, transcript.

Maszczynski, Mateusz. "The Official Emirates Guidelines for how to Wear Afro Style Hair: Get the Official Approved Look." *Paddle Your Own Kanoo* (blog), March 26, 2018. https://www.paddleyourownkanoo.com/2018/03/26/the-official-emirates-guidelines-for-how-to-wear-afro-style-hair-get-the-official-approved-look/.

Murphy, Ryan. "Flight Attendant Unions Make the Economy Work for Queer Families." *Notches* (blog), January 31, 2017. https://notchesblog.com/2017/01/31/flight-attendant-unions-make-the-economy-work-for-queer-families/.

Murphy, Ryan Patrick. *Deregulating Desire: Flight Attendant Activism, Family Politics, and Workplace Justice*. Sexuality Studies. Philadelphia: Temple University Press, 2016.

Nelson, Sara. "Beyond the Headlines: Combatting Service Sector Sexual Harassment in the Age of #MeToo." Testimony presented at the Congressional Caucus for Women's Issues, United States House of Representatives, March 19, 2018.

Olson, Carly, and Johana Bhuiyan. "Uber and Lyft Drivers Strike over Pay, Gig-Work Conditions." *Los Angeles Times*, July 21, 2021. https://www.latimes.com/business/story/2021-07-21/uber-and-lyft-rideshare-drivers-strike-rally-for-pro-act-union.

Premack, Rachel. "There's a Stark Reason Why America's 1.8 Million Long-Haul Truck Drivers Can't Strike." *Business Insider*, October 21, 2019. https://www.businessinsider.com/trucking-truck-driver-truckers-strike-reasons-2019-10.

Ross, Anne M. "Public Employee Unions and the Right to Strike." *Monthly Labor Review* 92, no. 3 (1969): 14–18. http://www.jstor.org/stable/41837581.

Schembs, Stephen R. "AFA-CWA LGBT Fact Sheet." Association of Flight Attendants-CWA, June 2, 2011. http://legislative.afacwa.org/lgbt.pdf.

Smith, Richard. "Allan Bérubé." *The Guardian*, February 22, 2008. https://www.theguardian.com/theguardian/2008/feb/22/gayrights.

———. "The Not So Friendly Skies for Women." Podcast. *Labor History in 2:00*, aired October 8, 2015. https://www.podbean.com/media/share/pb-6vkc3-593934#.VhZLW36fGLc.facebook.

Swopes, Bryan. "15 May 1930: Ellen Church Marshall." *This Day in Aviation* (blog), May 15, 2021. https://www.thisdayinaviation.com/tag/ellen-church-marshall/.

Tiemeyer, Philip James. "Male Stewardesses: Male Flight Attendants as a Queer Miscarriage of Justice." *University of Colorado Boulder Genders* 6, no. 1 (June 1, 2007). https://www.colorado.edu/gendersarchive1998-2013/2007/06/01/male-stewardesses-male-flight-attendants-queer-miscarriage-justice.

———. "Manhood up in the Air: Gender, Sexuality, Corporate Culture, and the Law in Twentieth Century America." PhD diss., University of Texas at Austin, 2007.

———. *Plane Queer: Labor, Sexuality, and AIDS in the History of Male Flight Attendants.* Berkeley: University of California Press, 2013.

"Timeline: America's Air-Traffic Controllers Strike." *NPR*, August 3, 2006. https://www.npr.org/templates/story/story.php?storyId=5599271.

"Unionists Demand Expulsion of Hoover Men if Guilty." *Honolulu Star-Bulletin*, December 17, 1937.

United Electrical, Radio & Machine Workers of America. "Working-Class Pride in the Marine Cooks and Stewards Union." June 18, 2021. https://www.ueunion.org/ue-news-feature/2021/working-class-pride-in-the-marine-cooks-and-stewards-union.

Howard Wallace Papers. San Francisco Public Library, James C. Hormel LGBTQIA Center. https://oac.cdlib.org/findaid/ark:/13030/c8r49w8g/.

Wickman, Forrest. "How the Gay Airline Steward Became a Stereotype." *Slate*, July 3, 2013. https://slate.com/culture/2013/07/gay-male-flight-attendants-in-im-so-excited-the-history-of-the-gay-steward-stereotype.html.

CHAPTER 10: THE METALWORKERS

ACCESS. "Rashida Tlaib Visiting Her Old Stomping Grounds and ACCESS Family!" Facebook Live video, August 10, 2018. https://www.facebook.com/ACCESScommunity/videos/10155661081587997/.

Adams, Jim. "NMAI's 'Booming Out' Shows Towering Presence of Mohawks." *Indian Country Today*, May 5, 2002. https://indiancountrytoday.com/archive/nmais-booming-out-shows-towering-presence-of-mohawks.

Ahmed, Ismael. "Arab Americans and the Automobile. Interview by Janice Freij and Anan Ameri." September 1, 1999. Arab American National Museum. Audio, 54:46. https://aanm.contentdm.oclc.org/digital/collection/p16806coll15/id/44.

———. "Organizing an Arab Workers Caucus." *MERIP Reports*, no. 34 (1975): 17–22. https://doi.org/10.2307/3011472.

"Arabs Hold March in Dearborn." *Detroit Free Press*, August 27, 1973.

Aronoff, Kate. "African American Auto Workers Strike for Union Democracy and Better Working Conditions (DRUM), 1968–1970." Database. Global Nonviolent Action Database, July 11, 2011. https://nvdatabase.swarthmore

.edu/content/african-american-auto-workers-strike-union-democracy-and-better-working-conditions-drum-1968.

Balay, Anne. *Steel Closets: Voices of Gay, Lesbian, and Transgender Steelworkers*. Chapel Hill: University of North Carolina Press, 2016. http://www.vlebooks.com/vleweb/product/openreader?id=none&isbn=9781469614014.

Booming Out: Mohawk Ironworkers Build New York. Photographs. Smithsonian Institution, April 25, 2002. https://www.si.edu/exhibitions/booming-out-mohawk-ironworkers-build-new-york-event-exhib-2840.

Chira, Susan, and Catrin Einhorn. "How Tough Is It to Change a Culture of Harassment? Ask Women at Ford." *The New York Times*, December 19, 2017. https://www.nytimes.com/interactive/2017/12/19/us/ford-chicago-sexual-harassment.html.

Engel, Chelsey. "USW Celebrates Pride Month and Recommits to Fighting for LGBTQ+ Community." United Steelworkers, June 3, 2019. https://www.usw.org/news/media-center/releases/2019/usw-celebrates-pride-month-and-recommits-to-fighting-for-lgbtq-community.

"Female Ford Workers Describe Decades of Harassment at Chicago Plants." CBS Chicago, February 20, 2018. https://chicago.cbslocal.com/2018/02/20/ford-workers-sexual-harassment/.

Frank, Miriam. *Out in the Union: A Labor History of Queer America*. Philadelphia: Temple University Press, 2015.

Franklin, Stephen. "Ford Pays Millions in Harassment Settlement." *Chicago Tribune*, September 8, 1999. https://www.chicagotribune.com/news/ct-xpm-1999-09-08-9909080151-story.html.

Georgakas, Dan, and Marvin Surkin. *Detroit: I Do Mind Dying: A Study in Urban Revolution*. 3rd ed. Chicago: Haymarket Books, 2012.

Hamlin, Michael, and Michele Gibbs. *A Black Revolutionary's Life in Labor: Black Workers Power in Detroit*. Detroit: Against the Tide Books, 2013.

Howard, Phoebe Wall. "Ford Worker's Suit Alleges Sex Assault." *USA Today*, June 29, 2021.

Levine, Lucie. "Men of Steel: How Brooklyn's Native American Ironworkers Built New York." *6sqft* (blog), July 25, 2018. https://www.6sqft.com/men-of-steel-how-brooklyns-native-american-ironworkers-built-new-york/.

Mansour, Omar. "Arab Detroit: The Arab Workers' Caucus and the Strike for Palestine." *Arab America*, June 2, 2021. https://www.arabamerica.com/arab-detroit-the-arab-workers-caucus-and-the-strike-for-palestine/.

McCandless, Commissioner of Immigration v. United States ex rel. Diabo. No. 25 F.2d 71 (3rd Cir. March 9, 1928).

McGlaun, Shane. "Judge Denies Female Ford Workers Class-Action Status." *Ford Authority* (blog), August 26, 2019. https://fordauthority.com/2019/08/judge-denies-female-ford-workers-class-action-status/.

Pride at Work. "Model Contract Language." November 8, 2014. https://www.prideatwork.org/resources/model-contract-language/.

P@WAdmin. "Historic Union Support for LGBTQ Equality Legislation." *Pride at Work* (blog), February 22, 2021. https://www.prideatwork.org/historic-union-support-for-lgbtq-equality-legislation/.

Schuhrke, Jeff. "When Arab-American Detroit Auto Workers Struck for Palestinian Liberation." *Jacobin*, August 3, 2020. https://jacobinmag.com/2020/08/palestine-strike-wildcat-uaw.

Shindel, Len. "They Acted Like Men and Were Treated Like Men." *The Baltimore Sun*, February 17, 1992. https://www.baltimoresun.com/news/bs-xpm-1992-02-17-1992048100-story.html.

Trotter, Joe William. *Workers on Arrival: Black Labor in the Making of America*. Oakland: University of California Press, 2019.

United Steelworkers. "Steel Pride." https://www.usw.org/act/activism/civil-rights/resources/steel-pride.

CHAPTER 11: THE DISABLED WORKERS

Barbarin, Imani. "How to Properly Celebrate a Civil Rights Law during a Pandemic in which Its Subjects Were Left to Die: The Americans with Disabilities Act." *Crutches and Spice* (blog), July 26, 2020. https://crutchesandspice.com/2020/07/26/how-to-properly-celebrate-a-civil-rights-law-during-a-pandemic-in-which-its-subjects-were-left-to-die-the-americans-with-disabilities-act/.

Barry, Dan. *The Boys in the Bunkhouse: Servitude and Salvation in the Heartland*. New York: Harper, 2016.

Baylor College of Medicine Center for Research on Women with Disabilities. "Demographics." https://www.bcm.edu/research/research-centers/center-for-research-on-women-with-disabilities/demographics.

Brenner, Aaron, Benjamin Day, and Immanuel Ness, eds. *The Encyclopedia of Strikes in American History*. Armonk, NY: M.E. Sharpe, 2009.

Brisbin, Richard A. *A Strike like No Other Strike: Law & Resistance during the Pittston Coal Strike of 1989–1990*. Morgantown: West Virginia University Press, 2010.

Brown, Keah. *The Pretty One: On Life, Pop Culture, Disability, and Other Reasons to Fall in Love with Me*. New York: Atria Paperback, 2019.

Burch, Susan, ed. *Encyclopedia of American Disability History*. Facts on File Library of American History. New York: Facts on File, 2009.

Carmel, Julia. "Before the A.D.A., There Was Section 504." *The New York Times*, July 22, 2020. https://www.nytimes.com/2020/07/22/us/504-sit-in-disability-rights.html.

———. "'Nothing About Us without Us': 16 Moments in the Fight for Disability Rights." *The New York Times*, July 22, 2020. https://www.nytimes.com/2020/07/22/us/ada-disabilities-act-history.html.

"CDC: 1 in 4 US Adults Live with a Disability." CDC Online Newsroom. Centers for Disease Control and Prevention, April 10, 2019. https://www.cdc.gov/media/releases/2018/p0816-disability.html.

Cecil, Mollie. "The Widows of Farmington." *Mollie Cecil* (blog), March 7, 2020. https://molliececil.com/the-widows-of-farmington/.

Clinton, Catherine. *Harriet Tubman: The Road to Freedom*. New York: Little, Brown, 2005.

Cohen, Adam. *Imbeciles: The Supreme Court, American Eugenics, and the Sterilization of Carrie Buck*. New York: Penguin Books, 2017.

Cone, Kitty. "Political Organizer for Disability Rights, 1970s–1990s, and Strategist for Section 504 Demonstrations, 1977." Interview by David Landes. Online Archive of California, 2000. Transcript. https://oac.cdlib.org/view?docId=kt1w1001mt&brand=oac4&doc.view=entire_text.

———. "Short History of the 504 Sit In." Disability Rights Education & Defense Fund, April 4, 2013. https://dredf.org/504-sit-in-20th-anniversary/short-history-of-the-504-sit-in/.

Connelly, Eileen A. J. "Overlooked No More: Brad Lomax, a Bridge Between Civil Rights Movements." *The New York Times*, July 8, 2020. https://www.nytimes.com/2020/07/08/obituaries/brad-lomax-overlooked.html.

Cowie, Jefferson. *Stayin' Alive: The 1970s and the Last Days of the Working Class*. New York: The New Press, 2012.

Death Cast of Chang & Eng Bunker. 1874. Plaster. The Mütter Museum at The College of Physicians of Philadelphia. http://memento.muttermuseum.org/detail/death-cast-of-chang-eng-bunker.

"Fact Sheet #39: The Employment of Workers with Disabilities at Subminimum Wages." U.S. Department of Labor, July 2008. https://www.dol.gov/agencies/whd/fact-sheets/39-14c-subminimum-wage.

Fry, Richard. "Fighting for Survival: Coal Miner and the Struggle Over Health and Safety in the United States, 1968–1988." PhD diss., Wayne State University, 2010. https://core.ac.uk/download/pdf/56687365.pdf.

Gitter, Elisabeth. *The Imprisoned Guest: Samuel Howe and Laura Bridgman, the Original Deaf-Blind Girl*. New York: Farrar, Straus and Giroux, 2001.

Gupta, Shalene. "'You Have to Scream Out.'" *The Atlantic*, September 21, 2021. https://www.theatlantic.com/ideas/archive/2021/09/what-its-like-to-be-black-and-disabled-in-america/620070/.

Hamby, Chris. *Soul Full of Coal Dust: A Fight for Breath and Justice in Appalachia*. New York: Little, Brown, 2020.

Harden, Olivia. "Why Don't More People Know Harriet Tubman Was Disabled?" *Rooted in Rights* (blog), July 14, 2021. https://rootedinrights.org/why-dont-more-people-know-harriet-tubman-was-disabled/.

Heumann, Judith E. *Being Heumann: An Unrepentant Memoir of a Disability Rights Activist*. Boston: Beacon Press, 2020.

Jayaraman, Sarumathi. *One Fair Wage: Ending Subminimum Pay in America*. New York: The New Press, 2021.

Jefferson, Robert F. "'Enabled Courage': Race, Disability, and Black World War II Veterans in Postwar America." *The Historian* 65, no. 5 (2003): 1102–24. http://www.jstor.org/stable/24452485.

Jennings, Audra. *Out of the Horrors of War: Disability Politics in World War II America*. Politics and Culture in Modern America. Philadelphia: University of Pennsylvania Press, 2016.

Jensen, Dean. *The Lives and Loves of Daisy and Violet Hilton: A True Story of Conjoined Twins*. Berkeley: Ten Speed Press, 2006.

Kelly, Kim. "Before the ADA, There Was the Freak Show." *Strikewave* (blog), July 31, 2020. https://www.thestrikewave.com/original-content/before-the-ada-was-the-freak-show.

———. "The True Tale of a Bona Fide, One-of-a-Kind 'Lobster Girl.'" *Vox*, September 23, 2019. https://www.vox.com/the-highlight/2019/9/23/20870620/carnival-disability-coney-island-sideshow-ectrodactyly.

Kinder, John M. *Paying with Their Bodies: American War and the Problem of the Disabled Veteran*. Chicago: University of Chicago Press, 2016.

Lange, Gill. "11 Things You Didn't Know about the Fascinating Life of Sarah Baartman." *Culture Trip* (blog), November 13, 2017. https://theculturetrip.com/africa/south-africa/articles/11-things-you-didnt-know-about-the-fascinating-life-of-sarah-baartman/.

Larson, Kate Clifford. *Rosemary: The Hidden Kennedy Daughter*. Boston: Mariner Books, 2016.

LaSpina, Nadina. *Such a Pretty Girl: A Story of Struggle, Empowerment, and Disability Pride*. New York: New Village Press, 2019.

Lay, Benjamin. *All Slave-Keepers That Keep the Innocent in Bondage, Apostates*. Philadelphia: Printed for the author, 1737.

Little, Becky. "When the 'Capitol Crawl' Dramatized the Need for Americans with Disabilities Act." History.com. https://www.history.com/news/americans-with-disabilities-act-1990-capitol-crawl.

Lost Museum Archive. "Joice Heth Exhibit." https://lostmuseum.cuny.edu/archive/exhibit/heth.

Lu, Wendy. "Overlooked No More: Kitty Cone, Trailblazer of the Disability Rights Movement." *The New York Times*, March 26, 2021. https://www.nytimes.com/2021/03/26/obituaries/kitty-cone-overlooked.html.

Luterman, Sara. "Why Businesses Can Still Get Away with Paying Pennies to Employees with Disabilities." *Vox*, March 16, 2020. https://www .vox.com/identities/2020/3/16/21178197/people-with-disabilities-minimum-wage.

Maloney, Wendi A. "World War I: Injured Veterans and the Disability Rights Movement." *Library of Congress Blog* (blog), December 21, 2017. //blogs.loc.gov/loc/2017/12/world-war-i-injured-veterans-and-the-disability-rights-movement/.

May, Charlie. "'I'll Never See Again': Standing Rock Protester Suffers Permanent Injury after Police Attack with Tear Gas Canister." *Salon*, December 7, 2016. https://www.salon.com/2016/12/06/i-didnt-want-the-world-to-see-me-like-this-sioux-z-suffers-permanent-injury-after-police-attack-with-tear-gas-canister/.

McCormick, Ginny. "The Two-Headed Nightingale." *Stanford Magazine*, May 2000. https://stanfordmag.org/contents/the-two-headed-nightingale.

Moores, Alan. "The Long-Simmering Scandal of 'The Boys in the Bunkhouse.'" *The Seattle Times*, May 29, 2016. https://www.seattletimes.com/entertainment/books/the-long-simmering-scandal-of-the-boys-in-the-bunkhouse/.

Mugrabi, Sunshine. "How an Eight-Year-Old Girl Made Disability History: A Conversation with Activist Jennifer Keelan-Chaffins and Children's Book Author Annette Bay Pimentel." *Democratic Left*, July 23, 2020. https://www.dsausa.org/democratic-left/how-an-eight-year-old-girl-made-disability-history-a-conversation-with-activist-jennifer-keelan-chaffins-and-childrens-book-author-annette-bay-pimentel/.

National Disability Rights Network. "Harriet Tubman: Disability Rights in Black 2020." February 1, 2020. https://www.ndrn.org/resource/drib2020-harriet-tubman/.

"New AFL Program to Aid Disabled." *Organized Labor* 45, no. 52 (December 30, 1944).

Nielsen, Kim E. *A Disability History of the United States*. Paperback ed. Revisioning American History. Boston: Beacon Press, 2012.

Nilsson, Jeff. "General Tom Thumb Gets Married." *The Saturday Evening Post*, February 9, 2013. https://www.saturdayeveningpost.com/2013/02/general-tom-thumb-marries-lavinia-warren/.

Nishar, Shivani. "The Legacy of 'Deinstitutionalization.'" *Mental Health America* (blog), July 29, 2020. https://mhanational.org/blog/legacy-deinstitutionalization.

Nyden, Paul J. "Rank-and-File Rebellions in the Coalfields, 1964–80." *Monthly Review* 58, no. 10 (March 1, 2007). https://monthlyreview.org/2007/03/01/rank-and-file-rebellions-in-the-coalfields-1964–80/.

O'Brien, Ruth. *Crippled Justice: The History of Modern Disability Policy in the Workplace*. Chicago: The University of Chicago Press, 2002.

Parkinson, Justin. "The Significance of Sarah Baartman." *BBC News Magazine*, January 7, 2016. https://www.bbc.com/news/magazine-35240987.

Peeks, Edward. "Coal Miners Sound Call of 'No Law, No Work.'" *Charleston Gazette*, February 27, 1969. West Virginia Archives & History. https://archive.wvculture.org/history/labor/blacklung02.html.

Rediker, Marcus. *The Fearless Benjamin Lay: The Quaker Dwarf Who Became the First Revolutionary Abolitionist*. Boston: Beacon Press, 2017.

Stadel, Cynthia. "Disability and Criminal Justice Reform." *Learning Disabilities Association of America Today* 3, no. 4 (August 2016). https://ldaamerica.org/lda_today/disability-and-criminal-justice-reform/.

Thompson, Vilissa. "Understanding the Policing of Black, Disabled Bodies." *Center for American Progress* (blog), February 10, 2021. https://www.americanprogress.org/article/understanding-policing-black-disabled-bodies/.

U.S. Department of Labor. "Mine Disaster: 1968 Farmington Explosion

Anniversary." https://www.msha.gov/mine-disaster-1968-farmington-explosion-anniversary.

Vecsey, George. "Work Call Defied by 16,000 Miners." *The New York Times*, November 23, 1971. https://www.nytimes.com/1971/11/23/archives/work-call-defied-by-16000-miners-but-union-officials-estimate-90.html.

Weill-Greenberg, Elizabeth. "Disabled and Abandoned in New York State Prisons." *The Nation*, October 25, 2021. https://www.thenation.com/article/society/prisons-disability-new-york/.

Wells, Ryan. "Volunteers in Service to America." In *Encyclopaedia Britannica*. Britannica.com, February 10, 2014. https://www.britannica.com/topic/Volunteers-in-Service-to-America.

West Virginia Archives & History. "Time Trail, West Virginia." February 1998. https://archive.wvculture.org/history/timetrl/ttfeb.html#0218.

Wilson, Robert. *Barnum: An American Life*. New York: Simon & Schuster, 2019.

Wong, Alice. "Indigenous Lives and Disability Justice." *Disability Visibility Project* (blog), March 18, 2019. https://disabilityvisibilityproject.com/2019/03/17/indigenous-lives-and-disability-justice/.

Woolf, John. *The Wonders: The Extraordinary Performers Who Transformed the Victorian Age*. W. W. Norton, 2019.

Wright-Mendoza, Jessie. "The Militant Miners Who Exposed the Horrors of Black Lung." *JSTOR Daily* (blog), September 25, 2018. https://daily.jstor.org/the-militant-miners-who-exposed-the-horrors-of-black-lung/.

Young, Britt H. "'My Body Is Used to Design Military Tech.'" *Wired*, October 26, 2021. https://www.wired.com/story/disability-justice-prosthetics-military-history/.

CHAPTER 12: THE SEX WORKERS

Alexandra, Rae. "The Tenderloin Brothel Madam Who Became Mayor of Sausalito." *KQED* (blog), July 2, 2018. https://www.kqed.org/pop/103907/rebel-girls-from-bay-area-history-sally-stanford-brothel-madam-turned-mayor.

Anderson, Ivy, and Devon Angus. "International Day of Sex Workers' Rights: 100 Years of Struggle for Sex Workers' Rights." *Alice: Memoirs of a Barbary Coast Prostitute* (blog), March 3, 2017. http://www.voicesfromtheunderworld.com/blog/2017/3/3/international-day-of-sex-workers-rights-100-years-of-struggle-for-sex-workers-rights.

Avery, Dan. "Trans Advocates Breathe Sigh of Relief as Manhattan Stops Prosecuting Sex Work." NBC News, April 23, 2021. https://www.nbcnews.com/feature/nbc-out/trans-advocates-breathe-sigh-relief-manhattan-stops-prosecuting-sex-work-n1265070.

Bailey, Kaytlin. "The Vice-Loathing Reverend and the Sex Workers Who Took San Francisco by Storm in 1917." *The Daily Beast*, January 24, 2021. https://www.thedailybeast.com/the-vice-loathing-reverend-and-the-sex-workers-who-took-san-francisco-by-storm-in-1917.

Barmann, Jay. "RIP O'Farrell Theatre, the Mitchell Brothers' Infamous Tenderloin Strip Club." *SFist* (blog), November 4, 2020. https://sfist.com/2020/11/04/rip-ofarrell-theatre-the-mitchell-brothers-infamous-tenderloin-strip-club/.

Barry, Dan, and Jeffrey E. Singer. "The Case of Jane Doe Ponytail." *The New York Times*, October 11, 2018. https://www.nytimes.com/interactive/2018/10/11/nyregion/sex-workers-massage-parlor.

Beach, Tracy. *My Life as a Whore: The Biography of Madam Laura Evens, 1871–1953*. Boulder, CO: Johnson Books, 2015.

Blunt, Danielle, and Ariel Wolf. "Erased: The Impact of FOSTA-SESTA." Hacking//Hustling, January 20, 2020. https://hackinghustling.org/wp-content/uploads/2020/01/HackingHustling-Erased.pdf.

Brooks, Siobhan. "An Interview with Gloria Lockett." In *Working Sex: Sex Workers Write About a Changing Industry*, edited by Annie Oakley, 138–59. New York: Basic Books, 2007.

———. "Exotic Dancing and Unionizing: The Challenges of Feminist and Antiracist Organizing at the Lusty Lady Theater." *SIECUS Report* 33, no. 2 (Spring 2005): 12+. https://link.gale.com/apps/doc/A136113226/AONE.

———. *Unequal Desires: Race and Erotic Capital in the Stripping Industry*. Albany: State University of New York Press, 2010.

"Burlesque Strike Ends.; Minsky Brothers Agree Not to Cut Number in Orchestras." *The New York Times*, March 31, 1935. https://www.nytimes.com/1935/03/31/archives/burlesque-strike-ends-minsky-brothers-agree-not-to-cut-number-in.html.

Burns, Katelyn. "Why Police Often Single Out Trans People for Violence." *Vox*, June 23, 2020. https://www.vox.com/identities/2020/6/23/21295432/police-black-trans-people-violence.

Butler, Anne M. *Daughters of Joy, Sisters of Misery: Prostitutes in the American West, 1865–90*. Urbana: University of Illinois Press, 1987.

California Prostitutes Education Project. "About." June 21, 2016. https://www.calpep.org/about/.

Chateauvert, Melinda. *Sex Workers Unite: A History of the Movement from Stonewall to SlutWalk*. Boston: Beacon Press, 2013.

Culver, Jordan, Ryan W. Miller, Trevor Hughes, Romina Ruiz-Goiriena, and Jorge L. Ortiz. "Hard Workers, Dedicated Mothers, Striving Immigrants: These Are the 8 People Killed in the Atlanta Area Spa Shootings." *USA Today*, March 22, 2021. https://www.usatoday.com/story/news/nation/2021/03/19/who-are-atlanta-shooting-spa-victims/4762802001/.

Decriminalize Sex Work. "Hero(es) of the Month: Honoring the Dancers of the Lusty Lady," September 1, 2020. https://decriminalizesex.work/sept-hero-of-month/.

Delacoste, Frédérique, and Priscilla Alexander, eds. *Sex Work: Writings by Women in the Sex Industry*. 2nd ed. San Francisco: Cleis Press, 1998.

Donohue, Caitlin. "Remembering Margo St. James, Patron Saint of Sex Work."

FoundSF (blog), January 22, 2021. https://www.foundsf.org/index.php?title=Remembering_Margo_St._James,_Patron_Saint_of_Sex_Work.

Espiritu, Yen Le. *Asian American Women and Men: Labor, Laws and Love.* Gender Lens, vol. 1. Thousand Oaks, CA: Sage Publications, 1997.

———. "Lobbying For Porn." *Adult Performance Artists Guild* (blog), October 6, 2021. https://apagunion.com/2021/10/06/lobbying-for-porn/.

Fisher, Harry. *Comrades: Tales of a Brigadista in the Spanish Civil War.* Lincoln: University of Nebraska Press, 1999.

Forestiere, Annamarie. "America's War on Black Trans Women." *Harvard Civil Rights-Civil Liberties Law Review* (blog), September 23, 2020. https://harvardcrcl.org/americas-war-on-black-trans-women/.

Friedman, Andrea. *Prurient Interests: Gender, Democracy, and Obscenity in New York City, 1909–1945.* Columbia Studies in Contemporary American History. New York: Columbia University Press, 2000.

Goldensohn, Rosa. *Playing the Whore: The Work of Sex Work.* New York: Verso, 2014.

———. "Woman Who Died at Rikers Island Was in Solitary." *The City*, June 10, 2019. https://www.thecity.nyc/2019/6/10/21211014/woman-who-died-at-rikers-island-was-in-solitary.

Hancock, Alice, and Patricia Nilsson. "OnlyFans Feels the Lockdown Love as Transactions Hit £1.7bn." *Financial Times*, April 26, 2021. https://www.ft.com/content/6d4562f8–166f-4a89-a3cb-db97123a6cf0.

Himmel, Jerry F. "A Day When Love No Longer Was for Sale." *SFGate* (blog), February 14, 1997. https://www.sfgate.com/news/article/A-day-when-love-no-longer-was-for-sale-3135421.php.

International Entertainment Adult Union. "About I.E.A.U." https://www.entertainmentadultunion.com/?zone=/unionactive/view_page.cfm&page=WHY20THE2020IEAU.

Kamiya, Gary. "Revolt of the Hookers: How Prostitutes Stared Down a Priest." *San Francisco Chronicle*, June 12, 2015. https://www.sfchronicle.com/bayarea/article/Revolt-of-the-hookers-How-prostitutes-stared-6324339.php.

Kelly, Kim. "A Forgotten War on Women." *The New Republic*, May 22, 2018. https://newrepublic.com/article/148493/forgotten-war-women.

Laporte, Elaine. "Ex-Broadway Showgirl Marks 80 with Petaluma Bat Mitzvah." *The Jewish News of Northern California*, March 14, 1997. https://live-jweekly.alleydev.com/1997/03/14/ex-broadway-showgirl-marks-80-with-petaluma-bat-mitzvah/.

Lee, Erika. *America for Americans: A History of Xenophobia in the United States.* New York: Basic Books, 2019.

———. "P.I.M.P. (Prostitutes in Municipal Politics)." In *Policing Public Sex: Queer Politics and the Future of AIDS Activism*, edited by Ephen Glenn Colter and Dangerous Bedfellows, 250–62. Boston: South End Press, 1996.

Passar, Dawn. "Interview with Dawn Passar." Interview by Siobhan Brooks. 1998. Transcript. http://www.bayswan.org/siobIntvw.html.

"Prison Detention and Reform." National Center for Transgender Equality, March 13, 2012. https://transequality.org/sites/default/files/docs/resources/NCTE_Blueprint_for_Equality2012_Prison_Reform.pdf.

Query, Julia, and Vicky Funari. *Live Nude Girls UNITE!* Documentary. First Run Features, 2000.

Red Canary Song. "About." https://www.redcanarysong.net/about-us.

———. "The Massage Parlor Means Survival Here: Red Canary Song on Robert Kraft." *Tits and Sass* (blog), April 11, 2019. https://titsandsass.com/the-massage-parlor-means-survival-here-red-canary-song-on-robert-kraft/.

"Red Canary Song Response to the Shootings at Gold Massage Spa, Young's Asian Massage, & Aroma Therapy Spa." Red Canary Song, March 28, 2021. https://docs.google.com/document/d/1_Q0mFJnivTZL5fcCS7eUZn9EhOJ1XHtFBGOGqVaUY_8/edit.

Rivera, Sylvia. "Y'all Better Quiet Down." New York, NY, 1973. TBR Reading. Transcript. https://www.tbr.fun/sylvia-rivera-yall-better-quiet-down-1973/.

Rosen, David. *Sin, Sex & Subversion: How What Was Taboo in 1950s New York Became America's New Normal*. New York: Carrel Books, 2016.

Rosen, Ruth. *The Lost Sisterhood: Prostitution in America, 1900–1918*. Baltimore: Johns Hopkins University Press, 1994.

Russell, Thaddeus. *A Renegade History of the United States*. New York: Free Press, 2014.

Shteir, Rachel. *Gypsy: The Art of the Tease*. Icons of America. New Haven: Yale University Press, 2009.

Siler, Julia Flynn. *The White Devil's Daughters: The Women Who Fought Slavery in San Francisco's Chinatown*. New York: Alfred A. Knopf, 2019.

sjidirector. "San Francisco's Own Legendary Margo St. James Dies." *St. James Infirmary* (blog), January 14, 2021. https://www.stjamesinfirmary.org/wordpress/?p=5403.

Smith, Alice, Ivy Anderson, and Devon Angus. *Alice: Memoirs of a Barbary Coast Prostitute*. Berkeley: Heyday, 2016.

Smith, Molly, and Juno Mac. *Revolting Prostitutes: The Fight for Sex Workers' Rights*. New York: Verso, 2018.

Social Networks and Archival Context. "Bedford Hills Correctional Facility." August 18, 2016. http://n2t.net/ark:/99166/w66b53xc.

Soldiers of Pole. "Stripper Community Building." June 10, 2020. https://soldiersofpole.com/stripper-union-work/.

Song, Sandra. "How Red Canary Song Is Advocating for Migrant Sex Workers." *PAPER Magazine*, October 30, 2019. https://www.papermag.com/red-canary-song-interview-2641163041.html.

Sosin, Kate. "New Video Reveals Trans Woman's Death at Rikers Was Preventable, Family Says." NBC News, June 13, 2020. https://www.nbcnews.com/feature/nbc-out/new-video-reveals-layleen-polanco-s-death-rikers-was-preventable-n1230951.

Stanford, Sally. *The Lady of the House: The Autobiography of Sally Stanford*. New York: Putnam, 1966.

Stern, Jessica. "This Is What Pride Looks Like: Miss Major and the Violence, Poverty, and Incarceration of Low-Income Transgender Women." *Scholar & Feminist Online*, no. 10.1–10.2 (2011). https://sfonline.barnard.edu/a-new-queer-agenda/this-is-what-pride-looks-like-miss-major-and-the-violence-poverty-and-incarceration-of-low-income-transgender-women/.

Stern, Scott W. "The U.S. Detained 'Promiscuous' Women in What One Called a 'Concentration Camp.' That Word Choice Matters." *Time*, May 15, 2018. https://time.com/5276807/american-concentration-camps-promiscuous-women/.

Stimson, Grace Heilman. *Rise of the Labor Movement in Los Angeles*. Berkeley: University of California Press, 1955.

St. James Infirmary. "Twenty Years of Giving Sex Workers a Voice." May 16, 2013. https://www.stjamesinfirmary.org/wordpress/?p=2746.

Street Transvestite Action Revolutionaries: Survival, Revolt, and Queer Antagonist Struggle. Zine. Untorelli Press, 2013.

Sultan, Reina. "Inside Social Media's War on Sex Workers." *Bitch Media* (blog), August 23, 2021. https://www.bitchmedia.org/article/inside-social-medias-war-on-sex-workers.

———. "Sex Workers Describe the Instability—and Necessity—of OnlyFans." *Vice News*, August 25, 2021. https://www.vice.com/en/article/jg89mb/sex-workers-describe-the-instability-and-necessity-of-onlyfans.

Tourmaline. "Sylvia Rivera and Marsha P. Johnson's Fight to Free Incarcerated Trans Women of Color Is Far from Over." *Vogue*, June 29, 2019. https://www.vogue.com/article/tourmaline-trans-day-of-action-op-ed.

US PROStitutes Collective. "About." May 10, 2012. https://uspros.net/about/.

Walker, Kaniya. "To Protect Black Trans Lives, Decriminalize Sex Work." *American Civil Liberties Union* (blog), November 20, 2020. https://www.aclu.org/news/lgbtq-rights/to-protect-black-trans-lives-decriminalize-sex-work/.

Willis, Raquel. "How Miss Major Helped Spark the Modern Trans Movement." *Them.* (blog), March 8, 2018. https://www.them.us/story/transvisionaries-miss-major.

Windham, Lane. "Labor and the Long Seventies." Interview by Chris Brooks. *Jacobin*, February 25, 2018. Transcript. https://www.jacobinmag.com/2018/02/lane-windham-interview-knocking-on-labors-door-unions.

Yung, Judy. *Unbound Feet: A Social History of Chinese Women in San Francisco*. Berkeley: University of California Press, 1995.

CHAPTER 13: THE PRISONERS

"26 Transferred, 50 Penalized for Stoppage at Attica Prison." *The New York Times*, August 19, 1970. https://www.nytimes.com/1970/08/19/archives/26-transferred-50-penalized-for-stoppage-at-attica-prison.html.

Armstrong, Keith. "'You May Be Down and Out, But You Ain't Beaten': Collective Bargaining for Incarcerated Workers." *Journal of Criminal Law and Criminology* 110, no. 3 (January 1, 2020): 593. https://scholarlycommons.law.northwestern.edu/jclc/vol110/iss3/5.

"Attica Prisoners Demands." Attica Liberation Faction, September 9, 1971.

"The Attica Prison Uprising at 40." *Socialist Alternative*, n.d. https://www.socialistalternative.org/sound-fury-oppressed/attica-prison-uprising-40/.

Badillo, Herman, and Milton Haynes. *A Bill of No Rights: Attica and the American Prison System*. New York: Outerbridge & Lazard, 1972.

Berger, Dan. *Captive Nation: Black Prison Organizing in the Civil Rights Era*. Chapel Hill: University of North Carolina Press, 2016. http://www.vlebooks.com/vleweb/product/openreader?id=none&isbn=9781469618258.

———. *Struggle within: Prisons, Political Prisoners, and Mass Movements in the United States*. Oakland: PM Press, 2014.

Berger, Dan, and Toussaint Losier. *American Social and Political Movements of the 20th Century: Rethinking the American Prison Movement*. New York: Routledge. http://search.ebscohost.com/login.aspx?direct=true&site=edspub-live&scope=site&type=44&db=edspub&authtype=ip,guest&custid=ns011247&groupid=main&profile=eds&bquery=AN%2014991087.

"Beyond Attica: The Untold Story of Women's Resistance Behind Bars." *AlterNet*, July 21, 2009. https://www.alternet.org/2009/07/beyond_attica_the_untold_story_of_womens_resistance_behind_bars/.

Bozelko, Chandra. "Busting Four Myths about Incarcerated Women." *Ms. Magazine*, July 26, 2019. https://msmagazine.com/2019/07/26/busting-four-myths-about-incarcerated-women/.

Brianna, and Lemar Hybachi. "Details on the Founding of the Incarcerated Workers Organizing Committee (IWOC)." From *These Conditions Can Be Changed: IWW Oral History Project*, n.d. Transcript. https://wisconsinprisonvoices.org/wp-content/uploads/2020/09/founding.iwoc_.interviews.pdf.

Brown, H. Claire. "How Corporations Buy—and Sell—Food Made with Prison Labor." *The Counter*, May 18, 2021. https://thecounter.org/how-corporations-buy-and-sell-food-made-with-prison-labor/.

Cadambi, Anjali. "Outside Observers Campaign for Prison Reform at Walpole Prison, U.S., 1973." Database. Global Nonviolent Action Database, November 29, 2010. https://nvdatabase.swarthmore.edu/content/outside-observers-campaign-prison-reform-walpole-prison-us-1973.

Campbell, Alexia Fernández. "The Federal Government Markets Prison Labor to Businesses as the 'Best-Kept Secret.'" *Vox*, August 24, 2018. https://www.vox.com/2018/8/24/17768438/national-prison-strike-factory-labor.

Cohen, Rhaina, Maggie Penman, Tara Boyle, and Shankar Vedantam. "An American Secret: The Untold Story of Native American Enslavement." NPR, November 20, 2017. https://www.npr.org/2017/11/20/565410514/an-american-secret-the-untold-story-of-native-american-enslavement.

Dilawar, Arvind. "How to Organize a Prison Strike." *Pacific Standard*, May 7, 2018. https://psmag.com/social-justice/how-to-organize-a-prison-strike.

Du Bois, W. E. B. *Black Reconstruction: An Essay Toward a History of the Part which Black Folk Played in the Attempt to Reconstruct Democracy in America, 1860–1880*. New York: Harcourt, Brace, 1935.

Dwinell, Alexander, and Sanya Hyland. *National Prisoners Reform Association*. December 2010. Offset Print. Boston: Just Seeds Collective.

Equal Justice Initiative. "Tutwiler Prison for Women." September 30, 2019. https://eji.org/cases/tutwiler/.

Falkof, Bradley B. "Prisoner Representative Organizations, Prison Reform, and Jones v. North Carolina Prisoners' Labor Union: An Argument for Increased Court Intervention in Prison Administration." *Journal of Criminal Law and Criminology* 70, no. 1 (Spring 1979): 42–56.

"Free Alabama Movement Strike." Perilous Chronicle, January 1, 2014. https://perilouschronicle.com/2014/01/01/free-alabama-movement-strike/.

"Girls on 'Noise' Strike: Inmates of Bedford Reformatory Jangle Cell Doors and Scream." *The New York Times*, January 25, 1920. https://www.nytimes.com/1920/01/25/archives/girls-on-noise-strike-inmates-of-bedford-reformatory-jangle-cell.html.

Griffin, W. B. "Case Notes—The 'Hands-Off Doctrine' Revisited Jones V North Carolina Prisoners' Labor Union, Inc. 97 S Ct 2532 (1977)." *Wake Forest Law Review* 14, no. 3 (June 1978): 647–61. https://www.ojp.gov/ncjrs/virtual-library/abstracts/case-notes-hands-doctrine-revisited-jones-v-north-carolina.

"Guide to the United Automobile Workers of America, District 65 Records." July 1, 2019. The Tamiment Library & Robert F. Wagner Labor Archives. http://dlib.nyu.edu/findingaids/html/tamwag/wag_006/bioghist.html.

Hudson Jr., David L. "Jones v. North Carolina Prisoners' Union (1977)." In *The First Amendment Encyclopedia*. Murfreesboro: Free Speech Center at Middle Tennessee State University, 2009. https://www.mtsu.edu/first-amendment/article/535/jones-v-north-carolina-prisoners-union.

Incarcerated Workers Organizing Committee. "2016 Prison Strike Call to Action." January 11, 2017. https://incarceratedworkers.org/resources/2016-prison-strike-call-action.

"Inmates Risking Their Lives to Fight California's Wildfires Deserve a Chance at Full-Time Jobs." *Los Angeles Times*, November 1, 2019. https://www.latimes.com/opinion/story/2019-11-01/california-inmate-firefighters.

Jackson, George. *Soledad Brother: The Prison Letters of George Jackson*. Chicago: Lawrence Hill Books, 1994.

Jones v. North Carolina Prisoners' Labor Union, Inc. 433 U.S. 119 (1977).

Kelly, Kim. "The Fight to Secure Labor Rights for Exploited Prisoners." *Teen Vogue*, December 9, 2019. https://www.teenvogue.com/story/prison-labor-us-conditions.

———. "How Prison Labor Exploits Incarcerated People." *Teen Vogue*, September 3, 2018. https://www.teenvogue.com/story/labor-day-2018-how-the-ongoing-prison-strike-is-connected-to-the-labor-movement

Kennicott, Philip. "The American Worker: Exploited from the Beginning." *The Washington Post*, November 20, 2017. https://www.washingtonpost.com/entertainment/museums/the-american-worker-exploited-from-the-beginning/2017/11/20/7ae8fe6a-c890-11e7-b0cf-7689a9f2d84e_story.html.

Kim, E. Tommy. "A National Strike Against 'Prison Slavery.'" *The New Yorker*, October 3, 2016. https://www.newyorker.com/news/news-desk/a-national-strike-against-prison-slavery.

Knothe, Paul D. "AB 2147 Clears Career Paths for Formerly Incarcerated Persons Trained as Firefighters." *California Public Agency Labor & Employment Blog* (blog), September 15, 2020. https://www.calpublicagencylaboremploymentblog.com/legislation/ab-2147-clears-career-paths-for-formerly-incarcerated-persons-trained-as-firefighters/.

Lambda Legal. "Transgender Incarcerated People in Crisis." Know Your Rights, n.d. https://www.lambdalegal.org/know-your-rights/article/trans-incarcerated-people.

Lanchin, Mike. "When the Prisoners Ran the Prison." BBC Witness History, March 30, 2021. https://www.bbc.co.uk/sounds/play/w3ct1x52.

Law, Victoria. *"Prisons Make Us Safer": And 20 Other Myths about Mass Incarceration*. Boston: Beacon Press, 2021.

———. *Resistance behind Bars: The Struggles of Incarcerated Women*. Oakland: PM Press, 2009.

———. "Why Do People in Prison Go on Hunger Strike?" *Bitch Media* (blog), February 24, 2014. https://www.bitchmedia.org/post/why-would-people-in-prison-launch-a-hunger-strike-hint-its-not-just-one-minor-issue.

Lawrence, Shammara. "The Attica Riot of 1971 Sparked the Prison Reform Movement." *Teen Vogue*, September 13, 2018. https://www.teenvogue.com/story/attica-prison-riot-reminder-failing-prison-system-reform-og-history.

LeMar, Hybachi. *The Deprived and Depraved*. Detroit: P&L, 2015.

———. "Resistance Has become My Ethical Obligation: Words of Reflection on the International Day in Support of Victims of Torture." Incarcerated Workers Organizing Committee, June 26, 2021. https://incarceratedworkers.org/campaigns/resistance-has-become-my-ethical-obligation-words-reflection-international-day-support.

———. *Writings of a Ghetto-Bred Anarchist*. Zine. Detroit, MI, n.d.

Lowe, Jaime. *Breathing Fire: Female Inmate Firefighters on the Front Lines of California's Wildfires*. New York: MCD, 2021.

Mayfield, Marvin. "A Half-Century after Attica, Prisoners' Demands Have Not Been Met." *Daily News* (New York), September 8, 2021. https://www.nydailynews.com/opinion/ny-oped-half-century-attica-20210908-drus54lc25h6ribz6szam2rhfa-story.html.

McCray, Rebecca. "Prison Work Is Work." *Popula*, August 28, 2018. https://popula.com/2018/08/28/prison-work-is-work/.

McGrew, Annie. "It's Time to Stop Using Inmates for Free Labor." *Talk Poverty* (blog), October 20, 2017. https://talkpoverty.org/2017/10/20/want-prison-feel-less-like-slavery-pay-inmates-work/.

Michels, Jonathan. "'Prisoners' Organizations Were Thought to Be Dangerous.': Conversations with Organizers of the North Carolina Prisoners' Labor Union." *Scalawag*, June 26, 2018. https://scalawagmagazine.org/2018/06/prisoners-organizations-were-thought-to-be-dangerous-conversations-with-organizers-of-the-north-carolina-prisoners-labor-union/.

———. "Unions Are Needed Everywhere—Especially Prisons." *Scalawag*, July 5, 2018. http://scalawagmagazine.org/2018/07/if-free-people-are-not-allowed-to-have-unions-how-are-prisoners-to-have-unions-conversations-with-organizers-of-the-north-carolina-prisoners-labor-union/.

Moon, Emily. "'Modern Slavery': The Labor History behind the New Nationwide Prison Strike." *Pacific Standard*, August 22, 2018. https://psmag.com/social-justice/modern-slavery-the-labor-history-behind-the-new-nationwide-prison-strike.

Moorehead, Monica. "WW Interviews Attica Survivor, Che Nieves, Part 2: 'I Carried the Legacy of Struggle in Prison.'" *Workers World* (blog), August 11, 2021. https://www.workers.org/2021/08/58320/.

Mount, Guy Emerson. "When Slaves Go on Strike: W. E. B. Du Bois's Black Reconstruction 80 Years Later." *Black Perspectives* (blog), December 28, 2015. https://www.aaihs.org/when-slaves-go-on-strike/.

Nam-Sonenstein, Brian. "Why Women Joined—And Didn't Join—A National Prison Strike." *Shadowproof* (blog), September 29, 2016. https://shadowproof.com/2016/09/29/incarcerated-women-speak-out-about-prison-strike/.

National Fallen Firefighters Foundation. "Shawna L. Jones." July 5, 2017. https://www.firehero.org/fallen-firefighter/shawna-l-jones/.

National Prisoners Reform Association v. John Sharkey. F. Supp. 1234 347 (D. Rhode Island 1972).

Nicholas, J. B. "August Rebellion: New York's Forgotten Female Prison Riot." *The Village Voice*, August 30, 2016. https://www.villagevoice.com/2016/08/30/august-rebellion-new-yorks-forgotten-female-prison-riot/.

Perlmutter, Emanuel. "Prisoners' Union Formed Upstate." *The New York Times*, February 8, 1972. https://www.nytimes.com/1972/02/08/archives/prisoners-union-formed-upstate-green-haven-inmates-seek-to.html.

Phillips, Lisa. "The Forgotten Union." *Jacobin*, August 10, 2016. https://jacobinmag.com/2016/08/unions-low-wage-service-sector-new-york-labor.

Political Women Prisoners in the U.S. Zine. Rev. ed. Bay Area, CA: Revolting Lesbians, 1988.

"Prisoners Union: Convicts, Ex-Convicts, and Individuals Fighting to Promote and Uphold the Rights and Welfare of California Prisoners." The Prisoners Union, n.d. Freedom Archives. https://freedomarchives.org/Documents/Finder/DOC510_scans/Prisoners_Union/510.pamphlet.prisoners.union.pdf.

"Puerto Ricans and the Attica Prison Uprising of 1971." *Centro Voices*, June 21,

2017. https://centropr.hunter.cuny.edu/centrovoices/chronicles/puerto-ricans-and-attica-prison-uprising-1971.

Reyes, Eloise. Firefighters. Pub. L. No. AB-1211 (2019).

Ricordeau, Gwenola, and Joël Charbit. "Prisoners on Strike in the United States." Translated by Sarah M. Smith. *Books & Ideas*, October 15, 2018. https://booksandideas.net/Prisoners-on-Strike-in-the-United-States-4202.html.

Schenwar, Maya. *Locked Down, Locked Out: Why Prison Doesn't Work and How We Can Do Better.* San Francisco: BK Currents, 2014.

Steel, Lewis M. "Understanding the Legacy of the Attica Prison Uprising." *The Nation*, September 26, 2016. https://www.thenation.com/article/archive/understanding-the-legacy-of-the-attica-prison-uprising/.

Thompson, Christie. "Do Prison Strikes Work?" *The Marshall Project*, September 21, 2016. https://www.themarshallproject.org/2016/09/21/do-prison-strikes-work.

Thompson, Heather Ann. *Blood in the Water: The Attica Prison Uprising of 1971 and Its Legacy.* New York: Pantheon Books, 2016.

———. "Rethinking Working-Class Struggle through the Lens of the Carceral State: Toward a Labor History of Inmates and Guards." *Labor* 8, no. 3 (September 1, 2011): 15–45. https://doi.org/10.1215/15476715-1275226.

Tibbs, Donald F. *From Black Power to Prison Power: The Making of* Jones v. North Carolina Prisoners' Labor Union. Contemporary Black History. New York: Palgrave Macmillan, 2012.

Trotter, Joe William. *Workers on Arrival: Black Labor in the Making of America.* Oakland: University of California Press, 2019.

Vongkiatkajorn, Kanyakrit. "Prison Labor: Virtually Unseen and 'Utterly Exploitative.'" *Mother Jones*, October 6, 2016. https://www.motherjones.com/politics/2016/10/prison-labor-strike-history-heather-ann-thompson/.

Washington, Keith. "Malik: Reflections of an Incarcerated Worker." *The Brooklyn Rail*, June 5, 2019. https://brooklynrail.org/2019/06/field-notes/Reflections-of-an-Incarcerated-Worker.

Women Against Prison. "Dykes Behind Bars." *DYKE, a Quarterly*, 1975.

ACKNOWLEDGMENTS

This book would not exist without the labor and expertise of a whole team of people who believed in its message, and I can't thank them all enough for bringing this dream of mine to life.

My incredible agent, Chad Luibl at Janklow & Nesbit, for all these years of encouragement, wise counsel, and kindness; for always answering my panicky text messages, hyping me up, and giving me room to grow. You're the best book dad a heavy metal Jersey girl could ever hope for, and I can't wait for our next adventure.

My phenomenal editor, Nick Ciani, whom I cannot thank enough for fighting for this book and pouring so much dedication, thoughtfulness, and care into helping shape it (and especially for putting in all those extra hours to make sure it got done on time!). Lots of love to everyone at One Signal, Atria, and Simon & Schuster who had a hand in *Fight Like Hell*, especially Julia Cheiffetz, Amara Balan, Joanna Pinsker, Karlyn Hixson, and Raaga Rajagopala.

My dear union sister Sara Nelson, thank you so much for writing the foreword to the book and sharing your boundless passion and fierce wisdom with me; you're a true inspiration, and a true friend. Thank you to Joy Crane for her invaluable and thorough work in fact-checking this beast, and to Mona Marbelle and David Campbell for their sensitivity reads; it was so important to me to get this book right, and all of your work here is so very appreciated. (Special thanks to Professor Joe McCartin for an especially eagle-eyed early read!)

A thousand thanks to every person who allowed me to interview them for this book, both on record and on background, and to those who helped facilitate some of those interviews (shout-out to the comms folk and translators!). I am thankful to the authors, journalists, academics, historians, and archivists who preserved so much about the lives of the working-class heroes who feature in this book, and to those who are continuing to do that work today. I am constantly in awe of my colleagues in that space—as well as all the workers and organizers who give us a reason to exist!

The first half of this book was written in the early days of the pandemic in a tiny South Philly trinity house. Once it became possible, escape was crucial, and the Free Library of Philadelphia was an extraordinarily useful resource that also gave me a quiet place to write, research, and lose myself in the past. I also want to thank the Economic Hardship Reporting Project, the Sidney Hillman Foundation, The Leonard C. Goodman Institute for Investigative Reporting, and the Omidyar Network Reporters in Residence program for all their support.

For independent journalists, there's no such thing as book leave, so I'm very grateful to my editors for giving me the space to dive headlong into this project; freelancing is a dicey business at best, but working with people like Alli Maloney, Allegra Kirkland, Evette Dionne, Jess Berger, Michelle Legro, Katherine Kreuger, Christopher Shay, Shanté Cosme, Meredith Bennet-Smith, Erica Palan, Lavanya Ramanthan, and everyone at Strikewave and *Protean Magazine* has made it a pleasure. To Brandon Stosuy—Chatsworth forever.

To everyone who's supported my work over the years, from my

earlier days as a metal blogger to my time wreaking anarchist black metal havoc at Noisey to my ongoing foray into labor, I appreciate you so much and will keep doing my best not to let you down. To the Black Tusk boys and every other band I've toured with, slung merch for, or generally gotten wild with—thanks for the memories and the hangovers. To everyone who came out to Black Flags Over Brooklyn in 2019, thank you for proving that metal is too good for Nazis. And as always, thank you to Bolt Thrower for being Bolt Thrower.

To my beloved friends and comrades in the struggle, from Iceland to Alabama and so many points in between; I love you all, and our ever-expanding constellation of Signal threads, group chats, and Twitter DMs made a lonesome year so much brighter (as did actually getting to see some of your beautiful faces in person as the months went on). Rupa, whose endless wisdom, encouragement, and lovingly brutal honesty kept me going even when it felt like my brain was melting; I may call you "mom," but you know you're really my big sister.

And to my best friend, Kelly: We've spent more than half our lives now going on adventures, getting weird, and indulging in a remarkably wholesome amount of mischief. I'd be lost without you. Free pizza for life.

Speaking of family, I promised my granddad I'd publish my first book by the time I hit thirty. I was a little behind schedule, but he's not here to rib me about it—he died in early 2020, two months before I signed my book contract. He had never finished high school and wasn't much of a reader, but he was still my biggest fan (and I noticed a distinct uptick in interest when I told him I'd started writing about unions instead of heavy metal). As much as it pains me knowing that he won't be able to see his name in the dedication or hold this book in his huge, work-hardened steelworker hands, I do know that he had total faith in me (and he did always love giving me shit about being late). This one's for you, Poppy—and for you, too, Nanny, for teaching me how to read when I was three and instilling in me a lifelong love of words, writing, and books. I know you wanted me to be a librarian, but hey, "author" ain't that far off, right? Mom, thanks for making me tough, and Dad—thanks for teaching me the value of hard work, standing your ground, joining the union, and disrespecting authority. It's definitely come in handy.

And finally, to my partner in crime, Shawn: you've been there for me every step of the way. I truly couldn't have pulled this off without all your patience, devotion, and understanding. You're the Lucy to my Albert. I love you so much.

INDEX